WHAT CRITICS AND PROFESSIONALS SAY ABOUT THE IMPACT GUIDES

"THE DEFINITIVE GUIDE to shopping in Asia."—**Arthur Frommer**, The Arthur From...

"THE BEST travel book I've c... West

"AN EXCELLENT, EXHA... at shopping in the East . . . it's ... without this pocket-size book in hand. —Travel & Leisure

"BOOKS IN THE SERIES help travelers recognize quality and gain insight to local customs."—**Travel-Holiday**

"THE BEST GUIDE I've seen on shopping in Asia. If you enjoy the sport, you'll find it hard to put down . . . They tell you not only the where and what of shopping but the important how, and all in enormous but easy-to-read detail."—**Seattle Post-Intelligencer**

"ONE OF THE BEST GUIDEBOOKS of the season—not just shopping strategies, but a Baedeker to getting around . . . definitely a quality work. Highly recommended."—**Arkansas Democrat**

"WILL WANT TO LOOK INTO . . . has shopping strategies and travel tips about making the most of a visit to those areas. The book covers Asia's shopping centers, department stores, emporiums, factory outlets, markets and hotel shopping arcades where visitors can find jewelry, leather goods, woodcarvings, textiles, antiques, cameras, and primitive artifacts."—**Chicago Tribune**

"FULL OF SUGGESTIONS. The art of bartering, including everyday shopping basics are clearly defined, along with places to hang your hat or lift a fork."—**The Washington Post**

"A WONDERFUL GUIDE . . . filled with essential tips as well as a lot of background information . . . a welcome addition on your trip."— **Travel Book Tips**

"WELL ORGANIZED AND COMPREHENSIVE BOOK. A useful companion for anyone planning a shopping spree in Asia."— **International Living**

"OFFERS SOME EXTREMELY VALUABLE INFORMATION and advice about what is all too often a spur-of-the-moment aspect of your overseas travel."—**Trip & Tour**

"A MORE UNUSUAL, PRACTICAL GUIDE than most and is no mere listing of convenience stores abroad . . . contains unusual tips on bargaining in Asia . . . country-specific tips are some of the most valuable chapters of the guidebook, setting it apart from others which may generalized upon Asia as a whole, or focus upon the well-known Hong Kong shopping pleasures."—**The Midwest Book Review**

"I LOVED THE BOOK! Why didn't I have this book two months ago! . . . a valuable guide . . . very helpful for the first time traveler in Asia . . . worth packing in the suitcase for a return visit."—Editor, **Unique & Exotic Travel Reporter**

"VERY USEFUL, PERFECTLY ORGANIZED. Finally a guide that combines Asian shopping opportunities with the tips and know-how to really get the best buys."—**National Motorist**

"INFORMATION-PACKED PAGES point out where the best shops are located, how to save time when shopping, and where and when to deal . . . You'll be a smarter travel shopper if you follow the advice of this new book."—**AAA World**

"DETAILED, AND RELEVANT, EVEN ABSORBING in places . . . The authors know their subject thoroughly, and the reader can benefit greatly from their advice and tips. They go a long way to removing any mystery or uneasiness about shopping in Asia by the neophyte."—**The Small Press Book Review**

WHAT SEASONED TRAVELERS SAY

"IMMENSELY USEFUL . . . thanks for sharing the fruits of your incredibly thorough research. You saved me hours of time and put me in touch with the best."—**C.N.**, DeKalb, Illinois

"FABULOUS! I've just returned from my third shopping trip to Southeast Asia in three years. This book, which is now wrinkled, torn, and looking much abused, has been my bible for the past three years. All your suggestions (pre-trip) and information was so great. When I get ready to go again, my 'bible,' even though tattered and torn, will accompany me again! Thanks again for all your wonderful knowledge, and for sharing it!"—**D.P.**, Havertown, Pennsylvania

"I LOVE IT. I've read a lot of travel books, and of all the books of this nature, this is the best I've ever read. Especially for first timers, the how-to information is invaluable."—**A.K.**, Portland, Oregon

"THE BEST TRAVEL BOOK I'VE EVER READ. Believe me, I know my travel books!"—**S.T.**, Washington, DC

"MANY MANY THANKS for your wonderful, useful travel guide! You have done a tremendous job. It is so complete and precise and full of neat info."—**K.H.**, Seattle, Washington

"FABULOUS BOOK! I just came back from Hong Kong, Thailand, and Singapore and found your book invaluable. Every place you recommended I found wonderful quality shopping. Send me another copy for my friend in Singapore who was fascinated with it."—**M.G.**, Escondido, California

"THIS IS MY FIRST FAN LETTER...you made our trip more special than I can ever say."—**N.H.**, New York, New York

THE TREASURES AND PLEASURES OF THAILAND

By Drs. Ron and Caryl Krannich

TRAVEL AND INTERNATIONAL BOOKS

International Jobs Directory
Jobs For People Who Love to Travel
Mayors and Managers in Thailand
Politics of Family Planning Policy in Thailand
Shopping and Traveling in Exotic Asia
Shopping in Exotic Places
Shopping the Exotic South Pacific
Travel Planning on the Internet
Treasures and Pleasures of Australia
Treasures and Pleasures of China
Treasures and Pleasures of Egypt
Treasures and Pleasures of Hong Kong
Treasures and Pleasures of India
Treasures and Pleasures of Indonesia
Treasures and Pleasures of Israel and Jordan
Treasures and Pleasures of Italy
Treasures and Pleasures of Paris and the French Riviera
Treasures and Pleasures of Rio and São Paulo
Treasures and Pleasures of Singapore and Bali
Treasures and Pleasures of Singapore and Malaysia
Treasures and Pleasures of Thailand

BUSINESS AND CAREER BOOKS AND SOFTWARE

101 Dynamite Answers to Interview Questions
101 Secrets of Highly Effective Speakers
201 Dynamite Job Search Letters
Best Jobs For the 21st Century
Change Your Job, Change Your Life
The Complete Guide to International Jobs and Careers
The Complete Guide to Public Employment
The Directory of Federal Jobs and Employers
Discover the Best Jobs For You!
Dynamite Cover Letters
Dynamite Networking For Dynamite Jobs
Dynamite Resumes
Dynamite Salary Negotiations
Dynamite Tele-Search
The Educator's Guide to Alternative Jobs and Careers
Find a Federal Job Fast!
From Air Force Blue to Corporate Gray
From Army Green to Corporate Gray
From Navy Blue to Corporate Gray
Get a Raise in Seven Days
High Impact Resumes and Letters
Interview For Success
Job-Power Source CD-ROM
Jobs and Careers With Nonprofit Organizations
Moving Out of Education
Moving Out of Government
Re-Careering in Turbulent Times
Resumes & Job Search Letters For Transitioning Military Personnel
Savvy Interviewing
Savvy Networker
Savvy Resume Writer
Ultimate Job Source CD-ROM

IMPACT GUIDES

THE TREASURES AND PLEASURES OF

Thailand

BEST OF THE BEST

RON AND CARYL KRANNICH, PH.DS

IMPACT PUBLICATIONS
MANASSAS PARK, VA

Copyright © 2000, 1996, 1992, 1989 by Ronald L. Krannich and Caryl Rae Krannich

Cover art courtesy of the Tourism Authority of Thailand.

All rights reserved. Printed in the United States of America. No part of this book may be used or reproduced in any manner whatsoever without written permission of the publisher: Impact Publications, 9104 Manassas Drive, Suite N, Manassas Park, VA 20111-5211, Tel. 703-361-7300 or Fax 703-335-9486. E-mail: *thailand@impactpublications.com*

Library of Congress Cataloging-in-Publication Data

Krannich, Ronald L.
    The treasures and pleasures of Thailand: best of the best/ Ronald L. Krannich, Caryl Rae Krannich.—4th ed.
        p. cm.—(Impact guides)
    Includes bibliographical references and index.
    ISBN 1-57023-076-5 (alk. paper)
        1. Shopping—Thailand—Guidebooks. 2. Thailand—Guidebooks. I. Title: Thailand. II. Krannich, Caryl Rae. III. Title. IV. Series

    TX337.T5 K74   2000
    380.1'45'00025593—dc21   00-036943

Publisher: For information, including current and forthcoming publications, authors, press kits, and submission guidelines, visit Impact's Web site: *www.impactpublications.com*

Publicity/Rights: For information on publicity, author interviews, and subsidiary rights, contact Media Relations: Tel. 703-361-7300 or Fax 703-335-9486.

Sales/Distribution: For information on distribution or quantity discount rates, call (703-361-7300), fax (703-335-9486), e-mail (*thailand@impactpublications.com*) or write: Sales Department, Impact Publications, 9104 Manassas Drive, Suite N, Manassas Park, VA 20111. Bookstore orders should be directed to our trade distributor: National Book Network, 15200 NBN Way, Blue Ridge Summit, PA 17214, Tel. 1-800-462-6420.

Contents

PART II
Acquiring Unique Treasures

Preface

WELCOME TO ANOTHER IMPACT GUIDE THAT explores the many unique treasures and pleasures of shopping and traveling in one of the world's most fascinating places—Thailand. Join us as we explore this country from a very different perspective than found in other travel books. We'll take you on an unforgettable journey that will put you in touch with some of the best quality shops, hotels, and restaurants in the world. If you follow us to the end, you'll discover a whole new dimension to both Thailand and travel. Indeed, as the following pages unfold, you'll learn there is a lot more to Thailand, and travel in general, than taking tours, visiting popular tourist sites, and acquiring an unwelcome weight gain attendant with new on-the-road dining habits.

Exotic Thailand offers wonderful treasures and pleasures for those who know what to look for, where to go, and how to properly travel and shop its many cities, towns, villages, and islands. We discovered this years ago. For more than three decades we have repeatedly returned as students, scholars, development workers, businesspeople, advisors, tourists, and curious travelers to further discover this ever-changing and delightful country as well as explore its many hotels, restaurants, shopping centers, arcades, department stores, shophouses, factories, markets, villages, and islands. Thailand remains one of our favorite destinations. Its people and products continue to enrich our lives.

If you are familiar with our other Impact Guides, you know this will not be another standard travel guide to Thailand. Our approach to travel is very different from most guidebooks. We operate from a particular perspective, and we frequently show our attitude rather than just present you with the sterile "travel facts." While we seek good travel value, we're not budget travelers who are interested in taking you along the low road to Thailand; we don't find that to be an attractive road nor particularly enlightening. We've been there, done that at one stage in our lives. If that's the way you want to go, you'll find lots of guidebooks on budget travel to Thailand. What you will quickly discover is the cost of going first-class is very reasonable in Thailand these days, especially since the post-1997 economic downturn. Regardless of your budget, Thailand is a bargain destination these days—one of the best travel buys in the world. At the same time, we're not obsessed with local history and sightseeing. We get just enough history and sightseeing to make our travels interesting rather than obsessive. Accordingly, we include very little on history and sightseeing because they are not our main focus; we also assume you have that information covered from other resources. We're very focused—we're in search of quality shopping and travel. As such, we're very people-oriented. Through shopping, we meet many interesting people and learn a great deal about the country.

What we really enjoy doing, and think we do it well, is shop. Indeed, we're street people who love "the chase" and the serendipity that comes with our style of travel. We especially enjoy discovering quality products; meeting local artists and craftspeople; unraveling new travel and shopping rules; making new friendships with local business people; staying in fine places; and dining in the best restaurants where we often meet the talented chefs and visit their fascinating kitchens.

Like Winston Churchill and many other travelers, our travel philosophy is very simple and focused: *"My needs are very simple—I simply want the best of everything."* When we travel, we seek out the best of the best—just like we often do back home. In the case of Thailand, we want to find the best quality antiques, furniture, clothes, and jewelry as well as discover the works of the best artists and craftspeople. In so doing, we learn a great deal about Thailand and its talented population. For us, shopping makes for great travel adventure. It especially becomes an adventure when we explore the neighboring countries of Laos, Cambodia, Vietnam, and Myanmar (Burma), which we explore in Chapters 13 and 14.

The chapters that follow represent a particular perspective on Thailand. We purposefully decided to write more than just another travel guide with a few pages on shopping. While some travel guides include a brief and usually dated section on the "whats" and "wheres" of shopping, we saw a need to also explain the "how-tos" of shopping in Thailand. Such a book would both educate and guide you through Thailand's shopping maze as well as put you in contact with the best of the best in accommodations, restaurants, and sightseeing. Accordingly, this book focuses primarily on the shopping **process**; it provides the necessary details for making excellent shopping **choices** in specific shopping areas, arcades, centers, department stores, markets, and shops.

Rather than just describe the "what" and "where" of travel and shopping, we include the critical "how"—what to do before you depart on your trip and when you are in Thailand. We believe you are best served with a book which leads to both **understanding and action**. Therefore, you'll find little in these pages about the history, culture, economics, and politics of Thailand; these topics are covered well in other types of books. Instead, we focus on the whole shopping process in reference to Thailand's major shopping strengths.

The perspective we develop throughout this book is based on our belief that traveling should be more than just another adventure in eating, sleeping, sightseeing, and taking pictures of unfamiliar places. Whenever possible, we attempt to bring to life the fact that Thailand has real people and interesting products that you, the visitor, will find exciting. This is a country of very talented designers, craftspeople, traders, and entrepreneurs who offer you some wonderful opportunities to participate in their society through their shopping process. When you leave Thailand, you will take with you not only some unique experiences and memories but also quality products that you will certainly appreciate for years to come.

Our focus on the **shopping process** is important for several reasons. The most important one is the fact that few non-Asians are prepared for Asian shopping cultures. Shops may be filled with familiar looking goods, but when there are no price tags on items, the process of acquiring them can be difficult if you do not understand such basic processes as bargaining, communicating, and shipping. What, for example, will you do if you want a suit made but you have never worked with a tailor and the tailor speaks little English? What type of fabric, cut, lining, lapel, pockets, buttons, and stitching do you want? Can you explain in detail exactly what you want? What should you do when you find a lovely piece of jewelry but no price tag is displayed? How do you know you are paying a "fair" price? More important, how do you know you are getting exactly what you bargained for in terms of quality and authenticity? And if you buy large items, how will you get them back home? The answers to these "how" questions go beyond the basic "what" and "where" of shopping to ensure that you have a successful and rewarding trip to Thailand.

We have not hesitated to make qualitative judgments about the best of the best in Thailand. If we just presented you with shopping and traveling information, we would do you a disservice by not sharing our discoveries, both good and bad. While we know that our judgments may not be valid for everyone, we offer them as **reference points** from which you can make your own decisions. Our major emphasis is on quality shopping, dining, accommodations, sightseeing, and entertainment, and in that order. We look for shops which offer excellent quality and styles. If you share our concern for quality shopping, as well as fine restaurants and hotels, you will find many of our recommendations useful to your Thailand and beyond adventure.

Buying items of quality does not mean you must spend a great deal of money on shopping. It means that you have taste, you are selective, you buy what fits into your wardrobe and home. If you shop in the right places, you will find quality products. If you understand the shopping process, you will get good value for your money. Shopping for quality may not be cheap but neither need it be expensive. But most important, shopping for quality in Thailand is fun and it results in lovely items which can be enjoyed for years to come!

Throughout this book we have included "tried and tested" shopping information. We make judgments based upon our experience—not on judgments or sales pitches from others. Our research was quite simple: we did a great deal of shopping and we looked for quality products. We acquired some fabulous items, and gained valuable knowledge in the process. However, we could not make purchases in every shop nor do we have any guarantee that your experiences will be the same as ours. Shops close, ownership or management changes, and the shop you visit may not be the same as the one we shopped. So use this information as a start, but ask questions and make your own judgments before you buy.

We wish to thank the many individuals and organizations that contributed to this book. Northwest Airlines (*www.nwa.com*) took us safely to Thailand. This fine airline has a well deserved reputation for convenience, comfort, and service. The

Tourist Association of Thailand (TAT) provided useful travel information and local assistance as well as photos.

Whatever you do, enjoy Thailand. Its people, products, and service will charm you. While you need not *"shop 'til you drop"* in Thailand, at least shop it well and with the confidence that you are getting good quality and value for your money. Don't just limit yourself to small items that will fit into your suitcase. Be adventuresome and consider acquiring larger items that can be safely, conveniently, and inexpensively shipped back home. As we note in the section on shipping, don't pass up something you love because of shipping concerns. Shipping is something that needs to be *arranged*, which is relatively easy to do in the case of Thailand.

We wish you well as your prepare to experience Thailand's many treasures and pleasures. The book is designed to be used on the roads, streets, and lanes of Bangkok, Chiang Mai, Chiang Rai, Maesai, Lampang, Lamphun, Mae Hong Son, Ayutthaya, Pattaya, Phuket, and Ko Samui. It also includes references to neighboring Laos, Cambodia, and Vietnam along with a separate chapter (14) on politically incorrect shopping in Myanmar.

If you **plan** your journey according to the first four chapters, **handle the shopping process** according to the next three chapters, and **navigate** the streets of Bangkok, Chiang Mai, and beyond based on the final seven chapters, you should have an absolutely marvelous time. You'll discover some exciting places, acquire some choice items, and return home with many fond memories of a terrific Thailand adventure. You, too, may go home fat, happy, and broke as well as experience that unexplained urge to return to Thailand next year. If you put this book to use, it will indeed become your best friend—and passport—to the many unique treasures and pleasures of Thailand. Enjoy!

Ron and Caryl Krannich
krannich@impactpublications.com

Liabilities and Warranties

WHILE THE AUTHORS HAVE ATTEMPTED TO provide accurate and up-to-date information in this book, please be advised that names, addresses, and phone numbers do change and shops, restaurants, and hotels do move, go out of business, or change ownership and management. Such changes are a constant fact of life in ever-changing Thailand. We regret any inconvenience such changes may cause to your travel and shopping plans.

Inclusion of shops, restaurants, hotels, and other hospitality providers in this book in no way implies guarantees nor endorsements by either the authors or publisher. The information and recommendations appearing in this book are provided solely for your reference. The honesty and reliability of shops can best be ensured by **you**—always ask the right questions and request proper receipts and documents. Chapters 3, 5, and 7 provide useful insights on how to best do this in the case of Thailand as well as neighboring countries.

The Treasures and Pleasures of Thailand provides numerous tips on how you can best experience a trouble-free adventure. As in any unfamiliar place or situation, or regardless of how trusting strangers may appear, the watch-words are always the same—*"watch your wallet!"* If it's too good to be true, it probably is. Any *"unbelievable deals"* should be treated as such. In Thailand, and elsewhere in Southeast Asia, there simply is no such thing as a free lunch. Everything has a cost. Just make sure you don't pay dearly by making unnecessary shopping mistakes.

THE TREASURES AND PLEASURES
OF THAILAND

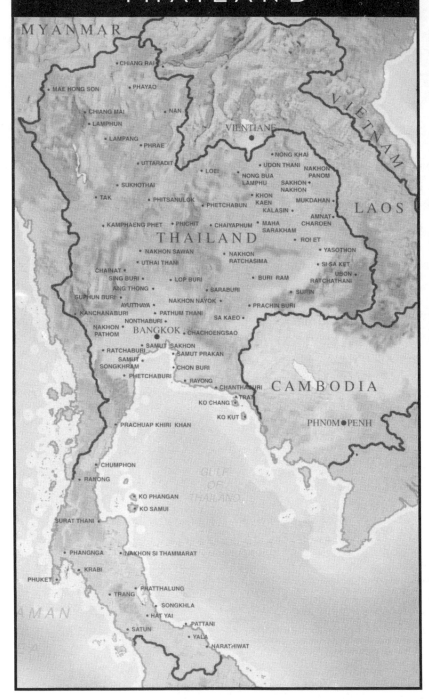

THAILAND

Welcome to
Seductive Thailand

Welcome to one of the world's most fascinating and seductive places. You've made a wise decision in selecting Thailand as your next travel destination. Charming, exotic, colorful, and chaotic, Thailand is filled with unique treasures and pleasures that will touch your life forever. If you approach it properly, it should yield some very special travel experiences you'll remember for years to come. Best of all, you'll want to return again and again to what is one of the world's most exciting travel and shopping destinations.

AN INTRIGUING LAND

If this is your first visit to Thailand, you're in for a real treat. You'll discover an intriguing land of exceptionally friendly and gracious people, talented craftspeople, bustling cities and towns, picturesque countrysides, idyllic beaches and villages, colorful festivals, exciting cuisine, gorgeous hotels, and fascinating cultures. It's a land where you can literally *"shop 'til you drop"* and still want to come back for more. Thailand will surely touch you forever with its many unique treasures and pleasures.

From the chic boutiques, dazzling jewelry stores, awe inspiring antique shops, and colorful markets of Bangkok to the dusty shophouses and cluttered factories of major destinations beyond Bangkok, let us take you on a very special adventure of a lifetime as we fly, drive, and walk to some of the world's most exciting places. Come with us and we will share with you a Thailand largely absent in the enticing tourist brochures, travel books, and advertisements aimed at bringing you to another mystical, mysterious, and magical world of Southeast Asia!

A TRIP WELL WORTH TAKING

Thailand is one of the world's most interesting travel destinations. Known as the "Land of Smiles," for its friendly and jovial people, and the "Land of the Free," for its ability to avoid Western colonization, Thailand is a delightful place to shop, sightsee, and indulge your gastronomic and entertainment fancies. Visit Thailand and you will likely return home with wonderful memories and a treasure-trove of products to enhance your home and wardrobe.

❑ Thailand is a delightful place to shop, sightsee, and indulge your gastronomic and entertainment fancies.

❑ Thai service is simply outstanding—the best you will encounter in all of Asia.

❑ Thailand is best appreciated by travelers who love spontaneity and can tolerate charming chaos.

Thailand proudly displays its long historical, cultural, and religious traditions to visitors. Better still, it offers shoppers a unique variety of quality arts and handicrafts expressive of these traditions. Particularly sensitive to foreigners, the Thai are gracious hosts who genuinely want you to enjoy your every moment in their charming and colorful country. When you visit Thailand, you will encounter a kaleidoscope of wonderfully exotic travel experiences. If you miss Thailand, you will miss a truly fascinating adventure.

GETTING TO KNOW YOU

We highly recommend Thailand for many reasons. Offering a great deal to visitors, Thailand is one of today's best kept travel secrets. It's a relatively inexpensive destination, especially since the extreme devaluation of the Thai currency (the baht) attendant with the collapse of the Thai economy in June 1997. The people are friendly, delightful, and relatively honest to deal with. Thai service is simply outstanding—the best you will encounter in all of Asia. Displaying a unique service ethic, punctuated by extreme deference, you will be pampered with polite, considerate, and spontaneous people who are genuinely concerned that you, their guest, are *"having a good time"* in their country. Thais put their best face forward for your convenience and enjoyment. If you come directly from Hong Kong—where the people tend to be more formal, reserved, and at times rude—Thailand is a paradise of personable people who try hard to make your visit most enjoyable.

But Thailand is best appreciated by travelers who love spontaneity, a bit of painless adventure, and can tolerate charming chaos. It is for those who are open to new experiences rather than tourists who seek to reconfirm their notion that the world should always be well organized and orderly—just like back home. The Thais do not organize themselves like many Westerners, nor do they disorganize themselves like many of their neighbors. Thais generally lack strong and efficient organization, but they prize individualism, tolerate the unique, and permit a high degree of individual autonomy. It's a country exhibiting a great deal of spontaneous and makeshift organization, where everything seems to be in the process of being completed—or further complicated. It has a certain worn, dilapidated, makeshift, yet charming look about it, in spite of impressive new high-rise office buildings, hotels, and banks that punctuate its ever changing urban landscapes with innovative and adventuresome Thai architecture.

CHARMING CHAOS

Thailand exhibits a certain degree of disorderliness, chaos, unpredictability, and adventure that also makes it such a delightful and charming place to visit—once you overcome your initial reluctance to venture forward into its many congested roads, streets, and lanes. Indeed, you first become disoriented by the visual chaos of its streets. Then you become captivated by the serendipity, charm, contrasts, contradictions, and spontaneity of the Thai who seem to adjust so well to everyday inconveniences with their *mai pen rai* ("never mind") attitude toward daily inconveniences inherent in their country of muddling chaos.

Thailand, its people, and its products grow on you—if you let them. But you must first be open to them rather than force them into preconceptions or a tidy plan to be quickly followed. While Hong Kong's and Singapore's do-it-yourself organization and conveniences allow you to quickly implement your travel plans, Thailand is not designed for people in a hurry. In Thailand you need time, flexibility, a sense of humor, and a little help to get things done. Going from one point to another in Bangkok, for example, can become a nightmare of traffic congestion, requiring you to rethink what may become an unrealistic plan.

Thailand will charm you with its many pleasures. While your memories of Hong Kong will center primarily on your purchases, the crowds, the harbor views, and the efficiency of the city and its people, your memories of Thailand will turn to its gracious people, fine food and service, unique shopping, beautiful hotels, glittering temples in the midst of chaotic neighborhoods, a charming river and canals graced with lumbering barges, speeding long-tail boats, and numerous funny and serendipitous experiences. After a while, you forget the heat and pollution and mainly recall the positive treasures and pleasures experienced in this exotic and friendly country.

> ❏ Bangkok, a bustling city of over 8 million people, is a shopper's paradise.
>
> ❏ Bangkok and Chiang Mai are the country's major centers for fashion, design, production, trade, marketing, transportation, and communication.
>
> ❏ Chiang Mai is to Thailand what Bali is to Indonesia—a truly unique cultural center which is also one of Asia's major cottage industry centers for producing handcrafted items.

Whatever you do, don't miss Thailand. It's a very special place. We know since we've lived there for nearly five years and have returned there frequently over the past 33 years. In many respects, Thailand is our second home. The sites, hotels, restaurants, and shopping are marvelous, and you will enjoy its wonderful people. But you must approach Thailand right and give it enough time to grow on you. Like many other travelers who have discovered the delights of this country, you should leave Thailand with a very special set of memories and some wonderful purchases that confirm the wisdom of having visited this exotic place.

SURPRISING COMMUNITIES

Experiencing the treasures and pleasures of Thailand primarily involves making trips to shopping centers, hotel shopping arcades, department stores, shophouses, factories, markets, towns, and villages located in and around Thailand's two major cities—Bangkok and Chiang Mai. These are the country's major centers for fashion, design, production, marketing, transportation, trade, and communication. Here you also will find most of Thailand's best travel amenities—fine hotels, restaurants, entertainment, and tourist sights. At the same time, you will discover some unique shopping opportunities in small towns and villages where you can purchase local products either not available in the city shops or less expensive than elsewhere. Most of these towns and villages are located in the northern region within a one- to four-hour drive of Chiang Mai. You will quickly discover the best quality shopping is found in Bangkok and, to a lesser extent, Chiang Mai. Indeed, most other cities in Thailand are relatively small and nondescript provincial towns. Some of these places attract visitors to annual tourist festivals. Except for a few resorts located south and southeast of Bangkok, few other cities can sustain more than a few hours of interest for most travelers.

Bangkok, a bustling city of over 8 million people, is a shopper's paradise. Stroll through the Emporium, Peninsula Plaza, River City Shopping Complex, World Trade Center, The Promenade, and Oriental Place and you will quickly discover some of the best quality shopping in all of Southeast Asia. Shop after shop offer exquisite jewelry, clothes, antiques, art, and home decorative items for discerning shoppers with an eye for quality. Venture into the Chatuchak Weekend Market, Pratunam, Banglompoo, Chinatown, and the vendor stalls lining Patpong, Silom, and Sukhumvit roads and you will find great bargains on inexpensive clothes, souvenirs, and copy watches, handbags, briefcases, and belts. The city brims with thousands of shops that will literally keep you busy shopping for days.

While chaotic Bangkok may not be everyone's favorite city, it does offer wonderful opportunities and amenities unmatched by any other city in the country. As some old Thai hands occasionally sum it up, *"Bangkok may not be Thailand, but thank God it's close!"* Despite its often unsavory reputation, we still love Bangkok. Stay at one of the many luxury hotels along the Chao Phraya River and you, too, may fall in love with this charming ugly duckling of a city!

Chiang Mai, Thailand's second largest city of over 200,000 people, is located approximately 700 kilometers north of Bangkok. The size of this city says a lot about the role of Bangkok vis-a-vis the rest of Thailand as well as indicates where you may want to expend most of your travel energy. Bangkok, which is nearly 50 times the size of the next largest city, Chiang Mai, remains the world's most extreme case of urban primacy.

Chiang Mai is a city of legendary charm and beauty. It is to Thailand what Bali is to Indonesia—a truly unique cultural center which is also one of Asia's major cottage industry centers for producing handcrafted items. Known for its gentle and friendly people, beautiful scenery, pleasant winter climate, diverse attractions, and a major staging area for nearby adventure travel forays, especially trekking and eco-tours, Chiang Mai is a shopper's paradise for antiques and locally produced, as well as imported Southeast Asian, handcrafted products that make lovely home decorative items: woodcarvings, textiles, furniture, silver, basketry, celadon, lacquerware, and umbrellas. Explore the small shops and stalls in the downtown Night Bazaar, shopping centers, and shophouses as well as in the many factory shops along nearby Chiang Mai-Sankamphaeng Road and adjacent to the town of Hang Dong and you will leave Chiang Mai with a treasure-trove of lovely handcrafted items at relatively inexpensive prices. Indeed, you will be shopping in many of the same places dealers from Bangkok and abroad come to buy items for their shops. If you shop Chiang Mai right, you can save 50-200% on the same items that appear in the shops of Bangkok.

Numerous other places in Thailand also offer wonderful treasures and pleasures. Chiang Rai, Lampang, Lamphun, Maesai, and Mae Hong Son in the North; Phuket, Krabi, and Samui Island in the South; and Ayutthaya, Hua Hin, and Pattaya near Bangkok remain some of our favorite destinations. While great places for sightseeing and enjoying the outdoors, these places offer some shopping opportunities. If this is your first visit to Thailand and you have limited time, we recommend spending most of your time in Bangkok and Chiang Mai. These two places represent Thailand's finest treasures and pleasures. If you want to spend some time relaxing on the beach, we recommend including Phuket and Samui islands in your travel plans.

APPROACH IT RIGHT

If approached in the right manner, Bangkok and Chiang Mai offer wonderful treasures and pleasures not found in other Asian cities and countries. To be most rewarding, Thailand must be approached differently from other places in Asia. For example, formerly a rapidly developing Third World country which recently graduated to the status of a dynamic Newly Industrialized Country (NIC), Thailand has a long, continuous, and proud history with unique traditions and a distinctive culture. These are clearly expressed in Thailand's art and handicrafts. Moreover, since the neighboring countries of Myanmar (Burma), Laos, and Cambodia still do not attract many tourists or businesspeople, Thailand functions as the major middleman for acquiring and marketing beautiful arts, antiques, and handicrafts—most of which are compatible with contemporary Western homes—from these surrounding countries.

Despite continuing international political pressure to eliminate copyright and trademark violations, Thailand is still one of the world's leading producers of inexpensive reproductions and copies of antiques, designer label clothes, and accessories. Although the quality of copies varies greatly—from outstanding to poor—individuals not interested in paying high prices for authentic and copy-protected goods and wish to do some "fun shopping" will indeed find Thailand to be a shopper's paradise! But be forewarned that you also will be in violation of laws which have yet to be consistently enforced.

Wherever you go in Thailand, you will find plenty of unique opportunities to learn about and acquire Thailand's many treasures. Thai craftspeople are some of Asia's most talented and prolific artisans who still produce good quality products at reasonable prices.

Our recommendation: Visit Thailand as soon as possible before the craft skills decline in response to Thailand's developing urban service and industrial economy and before prices increase substantially due to rising labor costs.

TREASURES OF QUALITY AND VALUE

The Treasures and Pleasures of Thailand is a different kind of travel book for a very special type of traveler. It is not another smorgasbord of popular sites and sightseeing tours nor does it promote cheap travel nor the latest travel fads. You'll find plenty of excellent travel guides—most of which are ostensibly revised annually—that already cover such travel preferences. We, on the other hand, primarily focus on quality shopping, dining, and accommodations as well as special tours for people who wish to experience the best of the best of what Thailand has to offer discriminating travelers.

The book is designed to provide you with the necessary knowledge and skills to enjoy this country's many treasures and pleasures. Going beyond typical sightseeing tours of Bangkok and Chiang Mai, or visits to popular temples and museums, we focus on how you can acquire Thailand's many treasures by becoming a savvy shopper. We especially designed the book with three major considerations in mind:

- Learn a great deal about Thai society and culture by meeting its many talented artists, craftspeople, and shopkeepers and exploring its cities, towns, and islands.

- Do quality shopping for items having good value.

- Discover unique items that can be integrated into your home and/or wardrobe.

As you will quickly discover, this is not a book on how to find great bargains in inexpensive Thailand, although we do show you how to bargain (Chapter 5) as well as where and how to find bargains. Nor are we preoccupied with shopping in weekend and night markets for cheap goods—places we often find disappointing and, with a few exceptions, a waste of precious travel time. And we are not particularly interested in shopping for expensive brand name luxury goods—imported from Europe or manufactured locally under licensing arrangements—which appear in many shops in response to the shopping preferences of Japanese, Taiwanese, and Korean tourists and to Bangkok's wealthy residents. These items tend to be overpriced and reflect an "imported" shopping culture of little appeal to us since we are primarily interested in finding quality local products expressive of local cultures.

❑ Focus on quality shopping for unique items that will retain their value.

❑ When in doubt, go for quality products–you will enjoy them much more in the long run.

❑ Good craftsmanship everywhere in the world is declining. The general trend in Thailand is to move from producing high quality arts and crafts to creating fakes and copies as well as to mass producing contemporary handicrafts for tourists and export markets.

While you will find bargains in Thailand and prices still seem inexpensive, this book focuses on quality shopping for unique items that will retain their value. As such, we are less concerned with shopping to save money and to get great bargains than with shopping for local and unique products that can be taken home, integrated into one's wardrobe and home decor, and appreciated for years to come. Rather than work with a cheap tailor or purchase an inexpensive piece of jewelry or art, we prefer finding the best of what there is available and selectively choose those items we both enjoy and can afford. If, for example, you buy one finely tailored suit, a single piece of exquisite jewelry, or a special work of art that can be nicely integrated into your wardrobe or home, chances are these purchases will last much longer, and you will appreciate them for many more years to come than if you purchased several cheap pieces of jewelry or tourist kitsch that quickly loose their value and your interest.

Our general shopping rule is this: *A "good buy" is one that results in acquiring something that has good value; when in doubt, go for quality because quality items will hold their value and you will enjoy them much more in the long run.*

Indeed, some of our most prized possessions from Thailand are those we felt we could not afford at the time, but we purchased them nonetheless because we knew they were excellent quality items and thus they had great value. In retrospect, our decisions to buy quality items were wise decisions because these items are things we still love today.

We have learned one other important lesson from shopping abroad: good craftsmanship everywhere in the world is declining due to the increased labor costs, lack of interest among young people in pursuing traditional craft skills, and erosion of traditional cultures. Therefore, any items requiring extensive hand labor and traditional craft skills—such as woodcarvings, textiles, silver and bronze work, ceramics, furniture, basketry, tribal artifacts, and handcrafted jewelry—are outstanding values today because many of these items are disappearing as fewer craftspeople are trained in producing quality arts and crafts. As elsewhere in the world, the general trend in Thailand is to move from producing high quality arts and crafts to creating fakes and copies as well as to mass producing handicrafts for tourists and export markets.

Throughout this book we attempt to identify the best quality shopping in Thailand. This does not mean we have discovered the cheapest shopping nor the best bargains. Our search for unique shopping and quality items that retain their value in the long run means many of our recommended shops may initially appear expensive. But they offer top value that you may not find in many other shops.

UNFORGETTABLE PLEASURES

The second half of our travel equation consists of Thailand's pleasures. And Thailand has many unforgettable pleasures that will remind you of this delightfully exotic country for many years to come. The number one pleasure is the Thai people themselves. An exceptionally polite, cultured, and fun-loving people who seem to thoroughly enjoy life, you will especially like Thailand because of these people. Thailand's other pleasures include its many lovely beaches, landscapes, sightseeing attractions, hotels, and restaurants.

You won't get bored here. Just the sights and sounds are enough to fascinate most visitors. There's plenty to see and do in Thailand. In addition, you'll discover some of the world's best hotels in Thailand, from the Regent, Oriental, Shangri-La,

Peninsula, and Sukhothai in Bangkok to the Regent Resort in Chiang Mai and the Amanpuri in Phuket. If you judge a country by it's food, you'll love Thailand. You'll be pleasantly surprised by all the wonderful restaurants serving everything from outstanding Thai food to fine French, Italian, German, Chinese, Japanese, and Korean cuisine. This is a country that seems to be perpetually eating from early morning to the wee hours of the next morning, whether along the street and in shopping malls or at home and in restaurants. Best of all, some of Thailand's finest restaurants are also found in its best hotels. If where you stay and what you eat are major travel concerns, then you should enjoy our many "best of the best" hotel and restaurant recommendations in Chapters 11 and 12.

❏ If you judge a country by it's food, you'll love Thailand.

❏ Thailand's finest restaurants are also found in its best hotels.

❏ We recommend initially spending at least four days in Bangkok.

SELECT YOUR CITIES

If you decide to include all of the places outlined in this book, you will want to start your adventure in Bangkok. However, should you enter Thailand after first visiting Singapore and Malaysia, you may want to initially stop in Phuket and Samui islands and then proceed on to Bangkok before going on to Chiang Mai and other areas of the northern region.

We recommend initially spending at least four days in Bangkok where you will have a chance to survey shops, products, prices, and shipping arrangements prior to visiting other areas of the country. If you plan to make many purchases that would require a sea freight shipment from Thailand—at least one cubic meter in volume—Bangkok will become your central shipping point. It's best to begin making shipping arrangements in Bangkok before venturing on to other parts of the country where you may make additional large purchases that will need to be consolidated into a single sea freight shipment from Bangkok.

We recommend making Chiang Mai your next stop after Bangkok. This is Thailand's craft center where you will find many items appearing in the shops of Bangkok for sale in the Night Bazaar and in the numerous factory shops in and around Chiang Mai. If you visit Phuket before Chiang Mai, you may discover you are purchasing many items made in Chiang Mai at twice the Chiang Mai prices. From Chiang Mai you can rent a car to visit Chiangrai, Maesai, Lampang, and Lamphun. If you wish to visit Mae Hong Son, it's best to fly from Chiang Mai rather than make the grueling 11 hour drive. If you plan to visit Myanmar, Laos, Cambodia, or Vietnam, you may have to return to Bangkok for direct international flights to these destinations; however, a few international flights now connect Chiang Mai with Myanmar, Laos, and Cambodia.

You will probably want to return to Bangkok for a few days before continuing on to Ayuthaya, Pattaya, Phuket, or Samui. From Phuket you can travel to Malaysia, Singapore, Indonesia, or the Philippines. These countries also offer wonderful shopping opportunities. Should you decide to include them in your travel plans, we recommend three other volumes in our "Impact Guides" series: *The Treasures and Pleasures of Singapore and Malaysia, The Treasures and Pleasures of Indonesia,* and *The Treasures and Pleasures of the Philippines.*

PLACES, PRODUCTS, AND PRICES

You may or may not get better buys on handcrafted items in northern Thailand than in Bangkok. The theory that goods are always cheaper at the production source is not always true. While many of the handcrafted items in Bangkok are made in Chiang Mai, they are not necessarily available in Chiang Mai to most visitors. Many Bangkok shops work directly with factories in Chiang Mai by having pieces commissioned to their own design and color specifications. On the other hand, many dealers from Bangkok buy handcrafted items off the open market in Chiang Mai—the Night Bazaar, Chiang Mai-Sankamphaeng Road, and Hang Dong— places you are likely to visit. In these cases you might be able to buy the same handcrafted items in Chiang Mai for one-half the price asked by shops in Bangkok.

❏ Shops in Bangkok tend to have the best quality items.

❏ If you see something you love, buy it now; if you wait to find it elsewhere, chances are you won't find a comparable item, and the one you left behind may be gone when you return.

In general, however, we find shops in Bangkok tend to have the best quality items; their buyers seem to pick the best of what is available in Chiang Mai and other areas in the North. Designs and displays in Bangkok shops are far superior to any found in shops outside Bangkok. When you consider the costs of traveling to Chiang Mai, as well as the cost of shipping items from Chiang Mai to Bangkok, you may do just as well by making purchases in Bangkok. Our general rule for doing comparative shopping in Bangkok, Chiang Mai, and other areas in Thailand is this: *If you see something you love, buy it now; if you wait to find it elsewhere, chances are you won't find a comparable item, and the one you left behind may be gone when you return.*

Visit Chiang Mai and other areas in Thailand if you have the time. Chiang Mai has many lovely one-of-a-kind items not available in Bangkok. Better still, prices in Chiang Mai can be very good if you know how to properly shop this city and its hinterland. It's also a delightful and charming place to visit.

ORGANIZE FOR THAILAND AND BEYOND

The chapters that follow primarily take you into the best shops, hotels, restaurants, and sites in Bangkok and Chiang Mai. We also include a few other attractive locations. In so doing, we've attempted to construct a complete user-friendly book that first focuses on the shopping process but also includes the best of Thailand's many other treasures and pleasures.

The chapters are organized as one would organize and implement a travel and shopping adventure to Thailand. Each chapter incorporates basic details, including names and addresses, to get your adventure started in each city.

Indexes and table of contents are especially important to us and others who believe a travel book is first and foremost a guide to unfamiliar places. Therefore, our index includes both subjects and shops: the shops are printed in bold for ease of reference; the table of contents is elaborated in detail so it, too, can be used as another handy reference index for subjects and products. By using the table of contents and index together, you can access most any information from this book.

The remainder of this book is divided into four parts and 13 additional chapters. The three chapters in Part I—"**Traveling Smart**"—assist you in preparing for your Thailand shopping adventure by focusing on the "how-tos" of traveling. Chapter 2, "Know Before You Go," takes you through the basics of getting to and enjoying your stay in Thailand, including international and domestic transportation and the promises and pitfalls of local travel. Chapter 3, "Prepare For Your Adventure," surveys key pre-trip preparation concerns—costs, customs regulations, money management, packing, and shipping arrangements. Chapter 4, "Arrival and Survival," takes you into Thailand and examines major concerns in getting around with ease—customs, immigration, money, transportation, tours, food, restaurants, accommodations, and safety.

The next three chapter in Part II—"**Acquiring Unique**

Treasures"—introduces Thailand's shopping world by examining critical "what" and "how" questions. Chapter 5, "Shopping, Bargaining, and Shipping Rules" prepares you for Thailand's distinct shopping culture where knowing important shopping rules, pricing practices, bargaining strategies, and shipping do's and don'ts are keys to becoming an effective shopper. Chapter 6, "Major Shopping Choices," surveys the major products you will encounter in your Thailand shopping adventure. Chapter 7, "Gems, Jewelry, and Tailoring Tips," examines three problematic shopping areas that are often the bane of shopping in Thailand and the main sources of most shopping complaints.

The three chapters in Part III—**"Surprising Bangkok"**—examine the "how" and "where" of shopping in Bangkok. Here you will learn how and where to best shop for different products as well as enjoy your stay in one of Asia's most exotic cities. This chapter identifies names, addresses, and telephone numbers of Bangkok's top quality shops.

Part IV—**"Exotic Chiang Mai and Beyond"**—examines the many treasures and pleasures of Chiang Mai. It also surveys a few other cities in Thailand as well as explores the neighboring countries of Cambodia, Laos, Vietnam, and Myanmar.

BEWARE OF RECOMMENDED SHOPS

Throughout this book we concentrate on providing you with the necessary **knowledge and skills** to become an effective shopper in Thailand. We prefer not recommending and listing specific shops and services—even though we have favorite shops we use when shopping in Thailand. We know the pitfalls of doing so. Shops that offered excellent products and service during one of our visits, for example, may change ownership, personnel, and policies from one year to another. In addition, our shopping preferences may not be the same as yours. As a result, we do not include extensive lists of "recommended" shops because we believe it is much more important for you to **know how to shop** than to be told where to shop.

Our major concern is to outline your shopping options in Thailand, show you where to locate the best shopping areas, and share some useful shopping strategies that you can use anywhere in Thailand, regardless of particular shops we or others may suggest. Armed with this knowledge and some basic shopping skills, you will be better prepared to locate your own shops and determine which ones offer the best products and service in relation to your own shopping and travel goals.

However, we also recognize the "need to know" when

shopping in Thailand. Therefore, throughout this book, we list the names and locations of various shops we have found to offer good quality products. In many cases we have purchased items in these shops and can also recommend them for service and reliability. But in most cases we surveyed shops to determine the type and quality of products offered without making purchases. To buy in every shop would be beyond our budget, as well as our home storage capabilities! When we do list specific shops, we do so only as reference points from which to start your shopping. We do not guarantee the quality of products or service. In many cases we have found our recommendations to be shops of exceptional quality, honesty, and service. We believe you should have the advantage of this information, but we also caution you to again evaluate the business by asking the necessary questions.

If you rely solely on our listings, you will miss out on one of the great adventures of shopping in Thailand—discovering your own special shops that offer unique items, exceptional value, and excellent service.

Should you encounter any problem with these recommendations, we would appreciate hearing about it. We also welcome recommendations and success stories! We can be contacted through our publisher:

Drs. Ron and Caryl Krannich
IMPACT PUBLICATIONS
9104 Manassas Drive, Suite N
Manassas Park, VA 20111-5211
Fax 703-335-9486
E-mail: *krannich@impactpublications.com*

While we cannot solve your problems, future editions of this book will reflect the experiences of our readers.

You also may want to stay in contact with the publisher's travel Web site:

www.ishoparoundtheworld.com

This comprehensive site is designed to complement the Impact Guides with numerous additional resources and advice. The site includes travel and shopping tips, updates, frequently asked questions, links to useful travel sites (airlines, hotels, restaurants, tourist offices, tour groups, maps, publications), recommended resources, a message board, and an online travel bookstore. If you have questions or comments, you may want to address them to us at this site.

EXPECT A REWARDING ADVENTURE

Whatever you do, enjoy your shopping and travel adventure to Thailand. This is a very special country that offers unique items that can be purchased and integrated well into many Western homes and wardrobes.

So arrange your flights and accommodations, pack your credit cards, ATM card, and traveler's checks, take your sense of humor, wear a smile, and head for one of the world's most delightful shopping and travel destinations. You should return home with much more than a set of photos and travel brochures and a weight gain attendant with new eating habits. You will acquire some wonderful products and accumulate many interesting travel tales that can be enjoyed and relived for a lifetime.

Experiencing the treasures and pleasures of Thailand only takes time, money, and a sense of adventure. Take the time, be willing to part with some of your money, and open yourself to a whole new world of treasures and pleasures. If you are like us, your shopping adventure will introduce you to an exciting world of quality products, friendly people, and interesting places that you might have otherwise missed had you passed through these places only to eat, sleep, see sights, and take pictures. When you travel and shop in exotic Thailand, you learn about some exciting places by way of the people, products, and places that define this country's many treasures and pleasures.

PART I

Traveling Smart

2

Know Before You Go

THE MORE YOU KNOW ABOUT THAILAND BEFORE you depart on your adventure, the better prepared you should be to enjoy its many delightful treasures and pleasures. However, given numerous and somewhat radical changes within the past three years, it's increasingly difficult to give an accurate snapshot of today's evolving Thailand. At best, we can provide you with an orientation that should be useful in preparing for Thailand's changing realities.

NEW AND CHANGING REALITIES

Rapid changes are especially evident in Thailand's economic and tourist infrastructure. Indeed, during the past decade, Thailand has experienced economic highs and lows which have had a significant impact on tourism, an industry that periodically goes through amazing boom and bust cycles. During the 1980s, for example, Thailand experienced one of the highest economic growth rates in the world. New office buildings, hotels, and shopping centers seemed to sprout up everywhere in Bangkok, Chiang Mai, and a few other regional cities and resort communities. Hundreds of new cars poured onto these city's already overtaxed road systems, exacerbating Thailand's legendary urban chaos.

By 1990, Thailand's booming tourism industry was the envy of most countries, indeed, a model for many developing countries. During much of the year hotel occupancy rates were in the 90 to 100 percent range; the domestic airline was normally fully booked on the Bangkok-Chiang Mai run; and inbound tour services, shops, and restaurants reported a booming business.

Unfortunately for most visitors, the Thai tourism industry responded to this brief boom by steeply increasing prices; in the case of many hotels, room rates nearly doubled and tripled within a 12-month period! Within a two-year period, Thailand's tourist infrastructure had become severely strained as millions of tourists flocked to discover what was reputed to be one of Asia's best kept, and inexpensive, travel secrets. Tourists were advised to book their hotels and domestic flights well in advance.

But as prices sharply increased, Thailand began to lose one of its major attractions and advantages—its reputation as an inexpensive to reasonably priced destination. Hotel prices peaked in late 1990 with some deluxe hotels charging US$250 and more per night double occupancy—up from US$100 the previous year.

The worldwide recession of early 1991, coupled with the Iraq-Kuwait war in the Middle East, brought a terrible shock to the booming Thai tourism industry. It literally went bust in early 1991 as hotels experienced record low occupancy rates; in peak season, when hotels were normally fully booked, many major hotels reported 30 to 40 percent occupancy rates. At the same time, more new hotels where opening in anticipation of accommodating the 12,000+ visitors attending the annual World Bank meeting in Bangkok and a continuing booming tourist industry. The World Bank group came and went, but the tourism industry failed to return to the booming pre-1991 period. Fueled by a wild good-ole-boy financial sector, the Thai economy continued to boom for the next five years as evidenced in the construction boom that fundamentally altered Bangkok's skyline with many new high-rise commercial buildings and condominiums that lacked many occupants. New expressways began lacing the city in efforts to alleviate the worst aspects of urban chaos—unrelenting traffic congestion that further exacerbated the city's noxious air and deafening noise pollution. The ubiquitous yellow construction crane became the symbol of national prosperity.

But these booming go-go days all came to a screeching halt when Thailand received some shocking economic news on June

30, 1997—its highly speculative and corrupt financial house of cards literally collapsed overnight. On the eve of splendid ceremonies in Hong Kong—which marked the turnover of this long-held British colony to the People's Republic of China—the Thai currency, the baht, took a nose-dive, losing more than 50 percent of its value, as the Thai economy began spiraling out of control; it quickly slumped into a depression. The Thai financial crisis soon spread to neighboring countries, especially Malaysia and Indonesia, that joined the newly depressed economies of Southeast Asia. Even Hong Kong, South Korea, and Japan felt the impact of Thailand's unprecedented economic fall as their economies, too, declined. In Thailand, once booming businesses closed and unemployment increased accordingly. Hundreds of construction projects, including many high-rise commercial buildings and condominiums, were literally abandoned in response to the financial crisis.

By 2000, Bangkok's skyline had a distinct boom/bust look to it—fabulous high-rise buildings constructed in the pre-1997 decade surrounded by the skeletons of buildings yet to be completed. It was a surreal landscape of the good, the bad, and the ugly of Thai economic development. If there was a silver lining in this crash, it was the short-lived respite from Bangkok's horrendous traffic. The city's traffic markedly improved as fewer and fewer local residents took to the always congested streets for shopping and work. In December 1999 the new Skytrain, a much needed elevated rail transportation system planned during Thailand's economic boom times, finally opened to further alleviate the street congestion. Tourist arrivals also declined, especially Asian tourists who had contributed disproportionately to the continuing growth of the tourism industry.

The good news for visitors to Thailand is that airline seats and hotel rooms are now much easier to find and hotel rates have actually declined since 1997. Given the devaluation of the Thai currency, coupled with the declining prices of hotels, Thailand once again has developed a reputation as one of the best travel values in the world. As expected, tourism is now on the increase—up 10 percent from 1998 to 1999—as more and more people discover this fascinating but temporarily wounded country. Not surprisingly, hotels are expected to soon ratchet up their prices in anticipation of another booming period for Thai tourism. Indeed, the tourism industry is now the country's best performing economic sector. Thailand is well on its way to recapturing its booming pre-1991 levels of tourism. Our advice: *Get there soon if you want to take advantage of some great travel and shopping bargains!*

Thailand's most serious tourism problem remains Bangkok's continuing nightmare of traffic congestion, accompanied by noxious fumes, air pollution, and high levels of noise. Each year, for the past 20 years, we've said the traffic and transportation inconveniences can't possibly get worse. And each year they actually did—that is, until 2000. With the opening of the new elevated rail system, Skytrain, it's now relatively easy to get from one part of Bangkok to another, especially along the heavily congested Sukhumvit Road and Silom Road corridors. Trips that might take one hour by taxi, can now be made by Skytrain within ten minutes. Our advice: *Learn to use the Skytrain as soon as you arrive in Bangkok; you'll save lots of time and headaches if you do!*

If there is one thing you will find most unattractive about Thailand, it is Bangkok's traffic and pollution. Chiang Mai is not much better. While the government has ostensibly taken some bold measures to literally elevate the problem in Bangkok —with a series of expressways and Skytrain—the streets can still be a nightmare of traffic congestion. Consequently, where you stay in Bangkok, and whether or not you use the river and Skytrain for transportation, will make a significant difference in how much you enjoy this city as well as your feelings toward Thailand and the Thai people in general. If you stay near the central shopping areas, you can walk to most places and thus avoid the hassles of being continuously stranded in creeping traffic. Indeed, if you take only one thing from this book, let it be our hotel recommendations. Our advice: *Please stay in a relatively sane and convenient area for shopping—and frequently use the river taxis and Skytrain!*

CHALLENGING INFRASTRUCTURE

Please keep in mind that Thailand is an advanced Third World nation that entered the ranks of the Newly Industrialized Countries (NICs), such as Hong Kong, South Korea, Taiwan, and Singapore, during the 1980s and then quickly retreated in 1997. As such, it exhibits signs of a boom/bust economy centered in and around Bangkok, with its once large middle-class and affluent upper-class, and a severely strained infrastructure trying to handle a huge and entangled population that commutes long distances each day for school, work, and shopping.

The infrastructure problem is especially evident in Bangkok, despite the recent economic downturn. From crowded port and shipping facilities to overloaded transportation, communication, and energy systems, Bangkok is a challenge to navigate. Its numerous inconveniences are often offset by its many shopping and dining oases, as well as its delightful people who often take such inconveniences in stride. Today's Thailand still exhibits some rough edges which contribute to its exotic image and, in turn, appear as inconveniences for many foreign visitors. Yet, it's an amazing place that captivates many visitors who fall in love with this unique place. If you do Thailand right, you'll want to return again and again to further enjoy its unique treasures and pleasures. You, too, may be seduced by people, culture, shopping, and sights.

We do not hesitate to strongly recommend what has become one of our favorite travel destinations. We have traveled to and from Thailand numerous times during the past three decades; lived and worked in its many cities, towns, and villages; and ventured into nearly every one of its 73 provinces. We've been seduced, and we don't mind it at all! If you're like us, you'll have a love affair with this country. You're fondest travel memories will center on Thailand, and you'll want to return again and again to this fascinating place.

Thailand always surprises us with its changes from year to year. Today, it's once again an excellent travel buy. It's a convenient country to get to and, except for Bangkok's entangled infrastructure, it's a relatively convenient country to get around in. But don't neglect Bangkok—despite its inconveniences, it's a fabulous place. After all, the really "good stuff" for travelers—from hotels and restaurants to shops and sites—is disproportionately found in Bangkok.

LOCATION AND AREA

Thailand is located in the heart of mainland Southeast Asia, south of China, west of Laos and Cambodia, east of Myanmar, and north of Malaysia, Singapore, and Indonesia. Extending nearly 1,000 miles from north to south and 500 miles from east to west, its 200,000 square miles make Thailand approximately the size of France or the state of Texas. Its population of 60 million is primarily rural (80 percent).

❑ Population of 60 million.

❑ Located in the heart of mainland Southeast Asia.

❑ About 1,000 miles from north to south and 500 miles from east to west.

❑ Nearly 200,000 square miles or about the size of France or Texas.

The largest city is the capital, Bangkok, with a population of over 8 million. The second largest city, Chiang Mai in the North, has a population of over 200,000. These two cities are the primary destinations for most tourists and the areas for the most exciting shopping adventures. Except for a few beach resorts in the Southeast and South and a few towns in the North, other cities and towns are relatively nondescript places primarily functioning as administrative and commercial centers for Thailand's highly centralized government. Some of these towns host annual tourist festivals, such as the Elephant Roundup (Surin) and the Rocket Festival (Yasothon).

CLIMATE, SEASONS, WHEN TO GO

For many visitors from temperate climates, Thailand appears to have three similar seasons: hot, hotter, and hottest!

But in reality there are three distinct seasons which vary somewhat in different parts of the country, especially in the South where the rainy season extends into a six month period. The hot season occurs between March and May, with temperatures ranging from 86°F to 104°F. The rainy season begins in May and lasts through October. A highly unpredictable season, it is marked by frequent rains, high humidity, and sporadic flooding in Bangkok. March through June can be the most miserable months of the year; the hot and rainy seasons meet in what is often an oppressive combination of hot and sticky days and nights, where the only relief is escape into air-conditioned buildings or your hotel swimming pool.

Thailand's cool season begins in November and ends in February. The temperatures are more pleasant, skies are clear, and the humidity is relatively low. During the cool season temperatures are known to drop into the low 30s(°F) in the North, but normally the temperatures are in the low to mid-80s throughout Thailand. This is the best season to visit Thailand and, not surprising, it is the peak tourist season for visitors.

Thailand's year-round tropical climate is relatively easy to prepare for in terms of clothing. You should take lightweight clothes, preferably loose fitting cottons, for most of the year. If you plan to visit during the cool season and travel to the North, be sure to pack a sweater or jacket, warm socks, and gloves. While it rarely freezes, the combination of cool temperatures and high humidity can be extremely chilling.

COPING WITH HEAT AND HUMIDITY

If you visit Thailand during the hot and humid season, be sure to prepare yourself accordingly. Even the hottest seasons in

Thailand are not much worse than summers in such places as Chicago, St. Louis, Houston, New York, Washington DC, Atlanta, Miami, or New Orleans. The difference is more in how one's lifestyle relates to the climate. Back home, for example, you may confine yourself to air-conditioned places when the weather is very hot and humid. But as you shop and sightsee in Thailand, you will be outside, doing a great deal of walking, on such hot and humid days.

Assuming you will feel Thailand's heat and humidity more than back home, you can best prepare for this climate by following these basic rules on how to cope with Thailand's heat and humidity:

- Wear lightweight clothes made primarily from natural fibers, preferably cotton.

- Carry a collapsible hand fan and use it when and wherever necessary.

- If you visit during the rainy season, take an umbrella with you at all times.

- Wear a hat on sunny days.

- Plan to be indoors, especially in air-conditioned areas, during the heat of the day.

- Do few things that require a great deal of walking.

> ❏ The rainy reason begins in May and lasts through October.
>
> ❏ March through June can be the most miserable months of the year.
>
> ❏ Cool season begins in November and ends in February—the best season to visit Thailand.
>
> ❏ Take lightweight clothes for most of the year.

- Use public transportation for even short distances, especially river taxis and the new Skytrain.

- Slow down your walking pace—shorter stride at one-half your normal walking speed.

- Drink plenty of fluids.

- Change your best laid plans whenever necessary—welcome to the land of serendipity!

By making a few of these adjustments in your lifestyle, you should be able to take the heat and humidity after a while. But if you insist on walking everywhere at a frantic pace, the heat and humidity will seem oppressive and will quickly run you down and ruin your trip. You'll quickly learn the easier you take Thailand, the easier it will be on you.

GETTING THERE

Getting to Thailand is relatively convenient. Most visitors enter Thailand by way of Bangkok International Airport, located just north of Bangkok. Serviced by 60 international airlines, this is a relatively efficient, although increasingly crowded, airport. Plans are underway to construct a new international airport.

Air connections to Bangkok are relatively good. It is best to fly the Pacific route if you originate in the U.S. or Canada. From New York City, you can fly directly to Bangkok in about 24 hours—depending on the airline and routing. It's a long one-day journey, but it goes surprisingly fast if you take a good book with you and plug in the head phones for viewing what hopefully may be some good movies!

During our last two trips to Thailand, we flew **Northwest Airlines**. We found their schedules to be the most convenient, the flights very comfortable, the service attentive, and the food well prepared. We have often appreciated the good service we find as we travel in Asia. We found the attentive, but not obtrusive, service on Northwest compared very favorably with what we have experienced traveling overseas. The flight attendants went out of their way to make passengers comfortable and well cared for. We really enjoyed our Northwest flight and were impressed with several innovative programs that should appeal to anyone interested in ecology. Northwest has been cited for the second consecutive year as the most eco-friendly airline. Indeed, Northwest developed the first in-flight recycling program, and it pioneered a program to allow passengers to choose their food items from an a la carte service which both pleases passengers and has cut food waste by 20 percent.

If you fly frequently, consider membership in Northwest's WorldPerks^{SM} (frequent flyer) and WorldClubs^{SM} (airport lounges and special services) programs. For more information on the **WorldPerks**^{SM} frequent flyer program which also is partnered with KLM, contact Northwest by phone (1-800-447-3757) or mail: Northwest Airlines Customer Service Center, 601 Oak Street, Chisholm, MN 55719. For information on the **WorldClubs**^{SM} program, contact Northwest by phone (1-800-692-3788), fax (612-726-0988), or mail: Northwest Airlines, Inc., WorldClubs Service Center, 5101 Northwest Drive, Department A5301, St. Paul, MN 55111-3034. Also, be sure to visit Northwest Airline's Web site for detailed information on flights and services: *www.nwa.com*. You may want to make these contacts before doing your ticketing.

For most travelers from North America and Europe, the flight to Thailand is a long one. Thus, you may wish to upgrade your ticket to "Business Class" for more room and comfort. You will pay more for this upgrade but the increased comfort may be well worth it.

While we usually arrive by air, a wonderful way to enter Thailand is by **train**. There are no rail connections between Thailand and the neighboring countries of Myanmar, Laos, Cambodia, or Vietnam, although regularly scheduled international flights do connect these countries with Bangkok, and a few road connections are sometimes open with Myanmar (Maesai and Maesot) and Laos (Vientiane). One of the world's most delightful and romantic rail trips originates in Singapore, transverses the length of the Malay Peninsula, enters southern Thailand, and ends at the Hualampong Railway Station in Bangkok. Along the way you may wish to stop in Kuala Lumpur and Penang—two large Malaysian cities offering some good shopping opportunities for Malay handcrafted and duty-free items (see another Impact Guide entitled *The Treasures and Pleasures of Singapore and Malaysia*). The Singapore-Bangkok Express takes about 54 hours. Along the way you will get a quick glimpse of rural and urban Southeast Asian life. The first-class cars are more than adequate, but you are well advised to take along some snacks and buy bottled drinks, fruits, and well cooked foods from vendors at the various stops along the way. This trip is best enjoyed in the privacy of your own air-conditioned sleeping compartment. It's worth paying a little extra to really enjoy this wonderful rail trip. If you really want to do this trip in style, take the luxurious Orient-Express which originates in Singapore and completes its five-star journey in Bangkok. For information on this unique trip, contact Abercrombie & Kent, 1520 Kensington Road, Oak Brook, IL 60521-2141, Tel. 1-800-323-7308 or Fax 630-954-3324 (*www.abercrombiekent.com*).

You can also drive a **car** from Singapore to Bangkok, but we do not recommend such an adventure, especially through southern Thailand. The road systems are excellent in Singapore and Malaysia and good in Thailand, but the rules of the road— or lack thereof—change dramatically as soon as you enter Thailand. Indeed, many Malaysians go through culture shock in Thailand, much of which is directly attributed to Thai driving habits. Malays fear driving in Thailand where only one rule seems to govern roads: the faster and more aggressive the better. Unless you have adapted to the Thai defensive driving style and follow the local rule that *"signaling your intention means losing the advantage,"* driving in many parts of Thailand is both dangerous and insane. And should you get into an accident, you will likely be detained. This could mean an interruption to your otherwise marvelous trip. Nonetheless, we usually rent a car and drive when we travel outside Bangkok. In Chiang Mai, Phuket, and Samui, we usually rent a car through Budget or Avis at the airport.

Finally, you can enter Thailand by **bus**, but only from the South. The tour buses operating in southern Thailand are relatively convenient and efficient. However, their small seats make them uncomfortable for many Westerners, and they are dangerous with accidents frequently occurring. Unless you want to live dangerously on the edge of Thailand's local transportation system, we recommend avoiding buses. Whenever possible, fly or take the train in Thailand.

GOOD TRAVEL DEALS

If you use the Internet, you can easily make reservations on-line by using several on-line ticketing groups. The four major reservation services are:

www.expedia.msn.com *www.previewtravel.com*
www.itn.net *www.travelocity.com*

Other popular on-line reservation services, with many claiming discount pricing, include:

www.air4less.com *www.moments-notice.com*
www.airdeals.com *www.onetravel.com*
www.airfare.co *www.priceline.com*
www.bestfares.com *www.smarterliving.com*
www.biztravel.com *www.thetrip.com*
www.cheaptickets.com *www.lowestfare.com*
www.concierge.come *www.travelscape.com*
www.etnlinks.com *www.travelzoo.com*

However, while these on-line ticketing operations may appear to be convenient, we've found many of them can be more expensive than using a travel agent, especially one who works with consolidators. You'll get the best rates through consolidators, which may be 30 to 40 percent less than the major on-line ticketing operations. Consolidators often have small box ads in the Sunday travel sections of the *New York Times*, **Washington**

Post, Los Angeles Times, and other major newspapers. Some of them, such as International Discount Travel, also provide price quotes on the Web: *www.idttravel.com.* Other popular consolidators specializing in discount ticketing include Airtreks.com (1-800-350-0612, *www.air-treks.com*), Air Brokers International (1-800-883-3273, *www.airbrokers.com*), and World Travellers' Club (1-800-693-0411).

You should consider a package tour to Thailand regardless of whether you are a first-time visitor or a seasoned traveler. Many tours, as well as several airfare/hotel combinations packages, are very good buys—for under $1,600 for 7 days in Thailand. Some tours concentrate on Bangkok while others include two or more other locations, such as Chiang Mai, Phuket, and Samui. Most of these tours include round-trip air transportation (coach class), transfers to hotels, accommodations in deluxe and first-class hotels, Western-style buffet breakfast, and various tours. It is very difficult to beat these prices by arranging your own flights and hotels. Paying the rack rate alone at a first-class Bangkok hotel (US$200+ per day) can equal the total price of the special shopping tour package. And if you have already done the tours, which are included in the package, you can gracefully bow out and go off to do your own thing. Consult your travel agent, check several Internet sites, and survey the travel sections of the Sunday *New York Times, Washington Post, Los Angeles Times,* and other major city newspapers for special packages to Thailand. West coast newspapers, especially the *Los Angeles Times,* will often carry ads for special shopping tours to Asia which include Thailand. You may be pleasantly surprised at what you find.

ANTICIPATED COSTS

Thailand is one of those wonderful places that gives you a full range of travel choices, from extreme budget to fabulous luxury. Here, you can easily travel on a limited budget or splurge to your heart's content, depending on both your budget and comfort orientation. The country is still a favorite destination for independent budget travelers who go through an interesting class and attitudinal transformation. Many pack their *Lonely Planet* guidebook and live a low-class travel life on US$15 to US$25 a day by staying in basic guest houses and hotels for US$5 to US$15 a night and eating from small restaurants and food stalls for US$7 to US$10 a day; many of these travelers frequent the dingy guest houses that constitute a kind of budget travelers' ghetto along Khao San Road near Democracy Monument in Bangkok. If that's the way you like to travel, you'll find lots of company at Thailand's train and bus stations and in budget hotels, guest houses, and food stalls. You'll find Thailand most accommodating to this style of travel.

On the other hand, if you like things to be just as good as back home, or even much better, Thailand will not disappoint you with its upscale hotel and dining choices and wonderful service. Indeed, these choices will give you a different perspective on Thailand and the Thai people—from economy class to super luxury class. You'll find some of the world's best hotels, resorts, and spas in Bangkok, Chiang Mai, and Phuket with rooms going for US$150 to US$450 a night—Oriental, Regent, Peninsula, Shangri-La, Sukhothai, Grand Hyatt Erawan, Le Royal Meridien, Sheraton Grande Sukhumvit, Regent Resort, Amanpuri, and Le Royal Meridien Phuket Yacht Club. In these places you can dine at some of Asia's finest restaurants for US$30-50 per person. You will likely be pampered in a style you may not be accustomed to but which you will find most acceptable. To travel to Thailand without sampling such choices is to miss out on some of Thailand's greatest pleasures which are still reasonably priced compared to many other countries.

Your biggest expense is likely to be for shopping treasures. Here, we cannot give you specific guidelines other than the general observation that you should take enough cash, personal checks, and traveler's checks, as well as sufficient credit card limits, in anticipation of finding plenty of treasures . If you love good quality gems and jewelry or are a serious collector of art, antiques, and home decorative items, you may quickly find yourself in financial trouble given the large number of quality items you may want to purchase in Bangkok and Chiang Mai!

PACKAGE TOURS OR ON YOUR OWN

Since Thailand is a popular travel destination, many tour packages include Thailand in their Asian itineraries. **TBI Tours** (Tel. 1-800-221-2216, Web site: *www.generaltours.com*), for example, is a well-known Asian tour operator. If you're looking for a very special experience, contact **Global Spectrum** for either individualized or group tours to Southeast Asia:

Global Spectrum
5683 Columbia Pike, #101
Falls Church, VA 22041
Tel. 1-800-419-4446
Web site: *www.vietnamspecialists.com*

Thai Airways offers the "Royal Orchid Holidays." They include international transportation and local arrangements. The packages are very flexible, enabling individuals to structure their own visit to Thailand without having to join an organized tour group. For further information, contract your travel agent or visit the Thai Airway Web site: *www.thaiair.com.*

If you want to travel deluxe class, consider the services of Abercrombie & Kent and Travcoa.

❑ **Abercrombie & Kent:** 1520 Kensington Road, Oak Brook, IL 60521-2141, Tel. 1-800-323-7308 or Fax 630-954-3324. Web site: *www.abercrombiekent.com.*

❑ **Travcoa:** 2350 SE Bristol, Newport Beach, CA 92660, Tel. 1-800-992-2003 or Fax 949-487-2800. Web site: *www.travcoa.com.*

If in doubt about your travel and tour options to Thailand, contact your local travel agent for information.

Should you decide to do Thailand **on your own**, you can easily arrange your own transportation and accommodations. We recommend booking your hotels in advance—especially if you are arriving during the peak tourist season. Once you arrive, you will find numerous tour services available to assist you with your stay. Most, however, focus on seeing sights in and around Bangkok. None of these services focus on shopping. With this book and a few other key resources, you will be well prepared to shop Thailand on your own and have a marvelous time doing so.

DOCUMENTS

Thailand is a relatively easy country to visit if you plan to be there less than two months. Most foreign nationals who plan a week or two in Thailand need only a valid passport and a confirmed ticket for onward passage. Upon arrival you receive a 30-day "transit visa" which normally cannot be extended. If you plan to stay longer, you should apply for a 60-day "tourist visa" from a Thai embassy or consulate prior to departure.

ON-LINE AND OFF-LINE RESOURCES

Numerous useful travel resources are available on Thailand—both print and electronic—but they are not well distributed outside Thailand, except for the Internet.

Most of the off-line resources are maps and travel guides focusing on sightseeing, restaurants, hotels, culture, and crafts. Much of what is written about Thailand for tourists and budget travelers is centered on accommodations, restaurants, and the typical tourist attractions found in Bangkok and Chiang Mai—questions already addressed by package tours.

For an overview of Thailand, examine the *APA Insight Guide: Thailand* and the *APA Cityguide: Bangkok*. Heavy on color photography, these books give a brief overview of the history and culture of the country as well as insightful summaries of travel to the various regions. The final *"Guide in Brief"* sections provide useful information on hotels, climate, language, and holidays. Read these books before going to Thailand; they are big, bulky, and heavy—not good travel companions.

Most major travel guides on Asia and Southeast Asia devote a brief chapter to Thailand. The chapters give a basic sketch of hotels, restaurants, and sightseeing opportunities. Some of the most popular guides on Thailand are Knopf's *Thailand*, Fodor's *Thailand*, Fielding's *Thailand*, and Moon's *Bangkok*. Baedeker produces a city guide entitled *Bangkok*. For budget travelers, the Lonely Planet's volume—*Thailand: A Travel Survival Guide*—gives good advice on how to do Thailand on the cheap. It also includes useful information on navigating Thailand on your own. For an interesting collection of stories relevant to travelers, we highly recommend James O'Reilly's and Larry Habetgger's *Travelers' Tales Thailand* (San Francisco: Tryveers' Tales). The book consists of 55 short stories or excerpts examining different aspects of Thailand. Gault Millau's *The Best of Thailand* is an ambitious attempt to identify Thailand's best restaurants, hotels, and shops. However, it omits many of Thailand's best places and elevates some mediocre ones. Many of these and other relevant guides are available in local bookstores or they can be ordered through Impact Publication's on-line travel bookstores: *www.impactpublications.com* or *www.ishoparoundtheworld.com*.

Once you arrive in Thailand, you will find several useful guides and maps. Two "must buy" resources are Nancy Chandler's *Map of Bangkok* and *Map of Chiang Mai*. Both colorfully illustrated maps are filled with information on shopping areas, shops, sights, hotels, restaurants, recreation, and transportation. The maps are available in major bookstores and hotel sundry shops. Chandler's maps will quickly become your best travel companion for Bangkok and Chiang Mai. However, you may want to acquire these maps prior to arriving so you can include them in your pre-trip planning. The maps can be ordered directly from the publisher by mail, fax, or e-mail:

Nancy Chandler Graphics
9th floor, Bubhajit Building
20 North Sathorn Road
Bangkok 10500, Thailand
Fax (662) 266-6579
E-mail: nancychandler@yahoo.com
Web site: *www.nancychandler.net*

The publisher accepts money orders or credit cards (Visa or MasterCard). Money orders should be made payable to: NCG Marketing Ltd. The maps also are available through Impact (see their ad on page 362 or visit their on-line bookstores: *www. impactpublications.com* or *www.ishoparoundtheworld.com*.

Also look for *The Groovy Map* to Bangkok which is available in Bangkok bookstores and hotel shops. The company that produces this map also maintains a Web site with lots of useful information on hotels and restaurants: *www.groovymap.com*.

One of the best local guides to Bangkok is the *Bangkok Guide* published by the Australian-New Zealand Women's Group. Designed for expatriates living in Thailand, it's filled with useful information on living and shopping in Thailand. It includes everything from where to buy ballet shoes to how to shop for jewelry. The book is available in major bookstores in Bangkok, with the best supply found in Asia Books at 221 Sukhumvit Road (between Soi 15 and 17). Also, look for Robin Brown's *A Guide to Buying Antiques, Arts & Crafts in Thailand* (Times Books) which is available in some bookstores, especially Asia Books. Somewhat dated (1989), nonetheless, this is a very useful illustrated guide. Pat Nervo's *Factory Outlet Shopping Bangkok Style* is still available at Asia Books. Somewhat dated and mistitled, this book is primarily an annotated listing of all types of shops. Thailand has a few markets, but it simply does not have factory outlets in the sense of Hong Kong.

A great deal of tourist literature is available at the airport, hotels, and from travel agents in Bangkok. Thailand's national tourism organization, the Tourism Authority of Thailand (TAT), provides lots of useful on-line information and advice:

www.tourismthailand.org

TAT works with the Thai Gem and Jewel Traders Association and its 47 affiliate "Jewel Fest Club" members to ensure the quality of gem and jewelry shops (*www.tat.or.th/do/gemo.htm*). TAT also prints handouts on individual cities, festivals, and tours, such as the Elephant Roundup in Surin and the Rocket Festival in Yasothon, as well as sponsors a few tours. You may wish to visit their **TAT Information Counters** at these locations:

Arrival Hall Donmuang Airport
Terminal 1, open daily 8am-midnight

Arrival Hall Donmuang Airport
Terminal 2, open daily 8am-midnight

4 Ratchadamnoen Nok Avenue
Bangkok, open daily 8:30am-4:30pm

10th floor, Le Concorde Building (TAT's main office)
202 Ratchadapisek Road, Huai Khwang
Bangkok, open Monday to Friday, 8:30am-4:30pm
Chatuchak Weekend Market, Phahonyothin Rd.
Bangkok, open Saturday and Sunday, 9am-5pm

TAT's 24-hour Tourist Service Centre at 4 Ratchadamnoen Nok Avenue (Tel. 1155) assists tourists by providing general information as well as handles complaints and emergencies. In Chiang Mai you may want to visit the TAT office at 105/1 Chiang Mai-Lamphun Road, just south of the Narawat Bridge, or call them at 248-604 or 248-607.

Most major hotels will have copies of several free weekly and monthly publications designed to assist you during your stay in Thailand. The major ones include *Lookeast*, *Thaiways*, *Where*, and *Bangkok Timeout*. While some of these publications may be difficult to find, especially the informative *Lookeast*, ask your hotel concierge for information on these city publications.

One of the first English-language magazines we always look for is the hip *Bangkok Metro*. It identifies Bangkok's top restaurants, nightlife, shopping, travel, and much more. It's widely available in most bookstores and hotel sundry shops. Best of all, you can browse this magazine's excellent Web site as part of your pre-trip planning:

www.bkkmet.com

Other useful gateway Web sites for accessing information on Thailand include:

www.sanuk.com
http://th.orientation.com/eg/
www.siam.net
http://dir.yahoo.com/Regional_Information/Countries/
   Thailand

The two major English-language newspapers published in Bangkok are widely available in major cities and towns throughout the country: *The Bangkok Post* and *The Nation*. In addition to providing basic coverage of international news, these newspapers include calendars of upcoming events, performances, and specialized tours sponsored by such organizations at TAT, The Siam Society, and the National Museum. You can access these newspapers on-line by going to these gateway sites:

> *www.ecola.com/news/press*
> *www.newslink.org/news.html*
> *www.newspapers.com*

Alternatively, go directly to their URLs:

> *www.bangkokpost.net*
> *www.nationmultimedia.com*

Other useful publications in Thailand that can be accessed on-line include:

Business Day	*http://bday.net*
Welcome to Chiang Mai	*www.chiangmai-chiangrai.com*
Samui Guide	*www.samuiguide.com*
Phuket Gazette	*www.phuketgazette.net*
Sawasdee	*www.thaiair.com/flying/ sawasdee/cover/htm*

Since the most useful travel guides, books, maps, and magazines on Thailand are difficult to find outside Thailand, or are too academic and specialized for travelers, your best starting point for background reading before arriving in Thailand is the *APA Insight Guide: Thailand* and *APA Insight Cityguide: Bangkok*. Remember, these are not practical trip planning guides—they give you a sense of *"setting"* with their lovely color photographs and discussions of history and culture. Like most other volumes in the APA Series, this one is available worldwide through APA Publications in Singapore or through Prentice-Hall in the United States. For more practical travel information in planning your trip, you may want to survey the various Asian travel guides published annually by Fodor's, Fielding, Baedeker, American Express, Lonely Planet, Frommer, Rough Guides, and Moon. Check out these Websites for useful on-line information relating to travel guidebooks:

www.fodors.com
www.lonelyplanet.com
www.away.com (excerpts Moon guidebooks)
www.fieldingtravel.com
http://travel.roughguides.com
www.ishoparoundtheworld.com

As soon as you arrive in Thailand, you should make a quick trip to one of Bangkok's best bookstores—**Asia Books**. Several branches of this store have excellent collections of general and specialized resources on Thailand. The main Asia Books store is located at 221 Sukhumvit Road, between Soi 14 and 17 (Tel. 252-7277 or 250-1833). It is conveniently located just east of the huge Ambassador Hotel restaurant and shopping complex on Sukhumvit Road. Its branch stores are found on the second floor of the pleasant Peninsula Plaza shopping arcade on Rajadamri Road, next to the Regent Hotel (Tel. 253-9786 thru 8)—a great place to start your whole shopping adventure in Thailand—and in the Landmark Plaza (attached to the Landmark Hotel on Sukhumvit Road) and in the Thaniya Plaza (between Silom and Suriwongse Roads near Patpong).

Other good bookstores in Bangkok include **Books Kinokuni-ya** (Emporiurm, Sukhumvit Road), **D.D. Books** (32/9-10 off Soi 21 Sukhumvit Rd., Tel. 258-3703), the **Bookseller** (81 Patpong Rd., Tel. 233-9632 or 233-1717), **Robinson Book City Yajimaya** (222 Soi 1 Siam Square, Tel. 251-5433 and 250-0710), and the bookstores in the five branches of the **Central Department Store**, but especially their major distribution center on Silom Road.

When you visit these bookstores or your hotel newsstand and sundry shop, you should look for copies of *Sawadii* and *Living in Thailand* magazines. You should also find copies of two books on Thailand which make wonderful light reading: Carol Hollinger's *Mai Pen Rai* and William Warren's *Jim Thompson: The Legendary American of Thailand*—both of which can be found in some libraries abroad or obtained through the publisher, Houghton-Mifflin (Boston). If you fall in love with Thai food, these bookstores also stock a good collection of English-language Thai cookbooks, many of which are written for Western kitchens.

If you are interested in arts and crafts but know little about Thailand, don't worry. Once you arrive in Thailand you can quickly learn a great deal about traditional Thai arts, crafts, culture, and religion. One of the best books covering all areas of Thai arts and culture is the special bicentennial issue of *Sawadii* magazine—*Sawaddi Special Edition . . . A Cultural Guide to*

Thailand. A collection of important articles on different facets of Thai art and culture, this book is available at some bookstores in Bangkok or directly from the American Women's Club of Thailand, 33 Rajadamri Road—a short walk from the Peninsula Plaza and Regent Hotel. Two special issues of *Arts in Asia* magazine are devoted to Thai arts and handicrafts: May-June 1978 and November-December 1982 (*Bangkok Bicentennial Issue*). For additional information on Thai arts and handicrafts, visit **The National Museum** (next to Thammasat University and across from Pramane Ground on Naprathat Road). A good way to see and understand this interesting museum is to take the special one-hour English-language tours available at 9:30am, Tuesday through Thursday:

Tuesday:	*Thai Art and Culture*
Wednesday:	*Thai Buddhism*
Thursday:	*Early Thai Art*

The Siam Society also has displays, as well as a great deal of literature and special tours, on Thai arts and crafts. You may want to include their library and museum on your tour of Bangkok: The Siam Society, 131 Soi Asoke, Sukhumvit Road, Tel. 258-3491 or 391-4401.

Many visitors become fascinated with the hilltribe handicrafts. For excellent introductions into the hilltribes and their handicrafts, look for these two books in Bangkok's major bookstores: Paul and Elaine Lewis' *Peoples of the Golden Triangle* (London: Thames and Hudson), and Margaret Campbell's *From the Hands of the Hills* (Hong Kong: Media Transasia).

If you are interested in shopping for home decorative items in Thailand, be sure to get a copy of *Thai Style* (Bangkok: Asia Books/Singapore: Times Edition). This beautifully illustrated book is filled with examples of Thai architecture as well as demonstrates the tasteful use of Thai home decorative items, especially antiques, woodcarvings, and handicrafts. You will find other books that specialize on different types of Thai handcrafted items, from textiles to pottery. For those interested in Lao textiles now widely available in Thailand, be sure to pick up a copy of Patricia Cheesman's *Lao Textile: Ancient Symbols —Living Art* (Bangkok: White Lotus Co.). If your interests include Burmese lacquerware, look for Sylvia Fraser-Lu's *Burmese Lacquerware* (Bangkok: The Tamarind Press). An excellent resource for understanding the unique Burmese tapestries called *kalagas* is Mary Anne Stanislaw's *Kalagas: The Wall Hangings of Southeast Asia* (Menlo Park, CA: Ainslie's). Most of these books are available at Asia Books as well as at a few antique and home decorative shops such as the Elephant House in Bangkok. In the United States, many of these and other books on Thailand are available through Oceanie-Afrique Noire (9 East 38th Street, New York, NY 10016, Tel. 212/779-0486) or the Cellar Book Shop (18090 Wyoming, Detroit, MI, 48221, Tel. 313/961-1776). Write or call them for copies of their most recent catalogs. If you are in the Washington, DC area, be sure to visit the Banana Tree (1223 King Street, Alexandria, VA 22314, Tel. 703/836-4317). This shop carries a good selection of books on Thailand amongst its many quality arts, antiques, and home decorative items from Thailand.

TOURISM AUTHORITY OF THAILAND

The Tourism Authority of Thailand (TAT) is Thailand's official government agency responsible for promoting tourism. This organization has offices in 16 countries which provide information on traveling to Thailand. They also maintain branch offices in 22 of Thailand's 73 provinces. If you contact their offices, they can provide you with brochures and answer any questions you might have concerning travel to and within Thailand. Some of these offices may be able to help you with shopping questions. The TAT overseas offices are found in following locations:

ASIA AND THE PACIFIC

Suite 22.01, Level 22, Menara Lion
165 Jalan Ampang
50450 Kuala Lumpur **MALAYSIA**
Tel : (007 60 3)216-23480; Fax : (007 60 3)216-23486
E-mail: *sawatdi@po.jaring.my*
Covers: Malaysia, Brunei, India, Middle East

c/o Royal Thai Embassy, 370 Orchard Rd.
Singapore 238870, **SINGAPORE**
Tel: (65)235-7694; Fax: (65)733-5653
E-mail: *tatsin@mbox5.singnet.com.sg*
Covers: Singapore, Indonesia, Philippines, South Africa

401 Fairmont House
8 Cotton Tree Drive
Central, **HONG KONG**
Tel: (852) 2868-0732; Fax:(852) 2868-4585
E-mail: *tathkg@hk.super.net*
Covers: Hong Kong, Macau, People's Republic of China

13 Floor, Boss Tower
No. 111 Sung Chiang Rd.
TAIPEI 104
Tel: (886 2)2502-1600; Fax: (886 2)2502-1603
E-mail: *tattpe@ms3.hinet.net*
Covers: Taiwan

Coryo Daeyungak Center Bldg.
Rm. No. 604, 6th Fl., 25-5, 1-Ka
Chungmu-Ro, Chung-Ku
Seoul 100-706, **KOREA**
Tel: (82 2)779-5417; Fax: (82 2)779-5419
E-mail: *tatsel@soback.kornet.nm.kr*
Covers: Republic of Korea

Yurakucho Denki Bldg.
South Tower, 2F.
Room No.259, 1-7-1
Yurakucho, Chiyoda-ku
Tokyo 100, **JAPAN**
Tel: (81 3)3218-0337; Fax: (81 3)3218-0655
E-mail: *tattky@crisscross.com*
Covers: Northern Areas of Honshu Island: Tohoku,
Kanto, Hokkaido Island

Technoble Yotsubachi Bldg., 3F.
1-6-8 Kitahorie Nishi-ku
Osaka 550-0014, **JAPAN**
Tel: (81 6)6543-6654; Fax: (81 6)6543-6660
E-mail: *tatosa@ca.mbn.or.jp*
Covers: Southern Area of Honshu Island: Kinki,
Chugoku, Chubu

El Gala Bldg., 6F.
1-4-2, Tenjin, Chuo-ku
Fukuoka 810-0001, **JAPAN**
Tel: (8192) 725-8808 Fax: (8192) 735-4434
E-mail: *tatfuk@asahi-net.or.jp*
Covers: Kyushu Island, Shikoku Island, Okinawa

2nd Floor, 75 Pitt Street
Sydney 2000 **AUSTRALIA**
Tel: (61-2) 9247-7540; Fax: (61-2) 9251-2465
E-mail: *info@thailand.net.au*
Covers: Australia, New Zealand, the South Pacific

Europe

Thailandisches Fremdenverkehrsamt
Bethmannstr. 58 D-60311
Frankfurt/M., **GERMANY**
Tel : (49 69) 138-1390; Fax: (49 69) 281-468
E-mail: *tatfra@t-online.de*
Covers: Germany, Austria, Switzerland, Eastern Europe

49 Albemarle Street
London WIX 3FE, **ENGLAND, UK**
Tel:(44 171) 499-7679; Fax:(44 171) 629-5519
E-mail: *info@tat-uk.demon.co.uk*
Covers: United Kingdom, Ireland, Finland, Scandinavia,
South Africa

Office National du Tourisme de Thailandais
90 Avenue des Champs Elysees
75008 Paris, **FRANCE**
Tel: (33 1) 5353-4710; Fax: (33 1)4563-7888
E-mail: *tatpar@wanadoo.fr*
Covers: France, Belgium, Luxembourg, Netherlands

Ente Nazionale per il Turismo Thailandese
Via Barberini 68, 4th Fl.
00187 Roma, **ITALY**
Tel:(39 6)487-3479; Fax:(3906)487-3500
E-mail: *tat.rome@iol.it*
Covers: Italy, Spain, Greece, Portugal, Israel, Egypt,
Turkey

The Americas

611 North Larchmont Boulevard, 1st Floor
Los Angeles, CA 90004 **U.S.A.**
Tel: (1-323) 461-9814; hotline 1-800-Thailand (for
U.S.A. and Canada); Fax: (1-323) 461-9834
E-mail: *tatla@ix.netcom.com*
Covers: Alaska, Arizona, California, Colorado, Hawaii,
Idaho, Kansas, Montana, Nevada, New Mexico, North
and South Dakota, Oklahoma, Oregon, Texas, Utah,
Washington, Wyoming, Guam Island and all Central and
Southern American countries, all west Canada: Alberta,
British Columbia, Manitoba, Northwest territories, Sas-
katchewan, and Yukon.

1 World Trade Centre, Suite 3729
New York, NY 10048, **U.S.A.**
Tel.: (1-212) 432-0433; hotline 1-800-Thailand (for
U.S.A. and Canada); Fax: (1-212) 912-0920
E-mail: *tatny@aol.com*
Covers: Washington DC, New York, New Hampshire,
Vermont, Maine, Pennsylvania, Connecticut, Massachu-
setts, Rhode Island, Virginia, West Virginia, Maryland,
New Jersey, Delaware, North and South Carolina, Ten-
nessee, Alabama, Georgia, Florida, Puerto Rico, Bahamas

If you're traveling outside Bangkok, you may want to visit
these local TAT offices for information and advice:

NORTHERN REGION

105/1 Chiang Mai-Lamphun Rd., Amphoe Muang
Chiang Mai 50000
Tel: (66 53) 248-604; (66 53) 248-605
Covers: Chiang Mai, Lamphun, Lampang, Maehongson

448/16 Singhakhlai Rd., Amphoe Muang
Chiang Rai 57000
Tel : (66 53) 717-433; Fax: (66 53) 717-434
Covers: Chiang Rai, Phayao, Phrae, Nan

209/7-8 Surasi Trade Centre
Boromtrailokanat Rd., Amphoe Muang
PHITSANULOK 65000
Tel: (66 55) 252-743; Fax: (66 55) 252-742
Covers: Phitsanulok, Phetchabun, Sukhothai, Uttaradit

193 Taksin Rd., Tambon Nong Luang
Amphoe Muang
TAK 63000
Tel: (66 55) 514 341 3; Fax: (66 55) 514-344
Covers: Tak, Phichit, Kamphaeng Phet

CENTRAL REGION

Saeng Chuto Rd., Amphoe Muang
KANCHANABURI 71000
Tel: (66 34)511-200; Fax: (66 34) 511-200
Covers: Kanchanaburi, Nakhon Pathom, Samut Sakhon,
Samut Songkhram

500/51 Phetkasem Rd., Amphoe Cha-am
PHETCHABURI 76120
Tel: (66 32) 471-005-6; Fax: (66 32) 471-502
Covers: Phetchaburi (Cha-am), Ratchaburi,
Phrachuap Khirikhan

382/1 Mu 10 Chaihat Rd.
Amphoe Bang Lamung
Pattaya City, CHONBURI 20260
Tel: (66 38) 427-667; Fax: (66 38) 429-113
Covers: Pattaya

153/4 Sukhumvit Rd.
Amphoe Muang
RAYONG 21000
Tel: (66 38) 655-420-1; Fax: (66 38) 655-422
Covers: Rayong and Chanthaburi

100 Mu 1 Trat-Laem Ngop Rd.
Tambon Laem Ngop, Amphoe Laem Ngop
TRAT 23120
Tel: (66 39)597-255; Fax: (66 39)597-255
Covers: Trat and its islands

108/22 Mu 4, Tambon Pratuchai
Amphoe Phra Nakhon Si Ayutthaya
Phra Nakhon Si **AYUTTHAYA** 13000
Tel: (66 35)246-076-7; Fax: (66 35)246-078
Covers: Phra Nakhon Si Ayutthaya, Saraburi, Angthong,
Suphanburi, Pathumthani, Nonthaburi

H. M. The Queen's Celebration Bldg.
(temporary office)
Narai Maharat Rd., Amphoe Muang
LOPBURI 15000
Tel: (66 36)422-768-9; Fax: (66 36)424-089
Covers: Lopburi, Nakhonsawan, Uthaithani, Chainat,
Singburi

182/88 Suwannason Rd.
(temporary office)
Amphoe Muang
NAKHON NAYOK 26000
Tel: (66 37) 312-282; Fax: (66-37) 312-286
Covers: Nakhon Nayok, Sa Kaeo, Prachinburi,
Chachoengsao

NORTHEAST REGION

2102-2104 Mittraphap Rd.
Tambon Nai Muang
Amphoe Muang
NAKHON RATCHASIMA 30000
Tel: (66 44) 213-666; Fax: (66 44) 213-667
Covers: Nakhon Ratchasima, Buriram, Chaiyaphum

264/1 Khaun Thani Rd.
Amphoe Muang
UBON RATCHATHANI 34000
Tel: (66 45) 243-770; Fax: (66 45) 243-771
Covers: Ubon Ratchathani, Amnat Charoen, Sisaket
Yasothon

15/5 Prachasamosorn Rd.
Amphoe Muang
KHONKAEN 40000
Tel: (66 43) 244-498-9; Fax: (66 43) 244-497
Covers: Khonkaen, Roiet, Mahasarakham, Kalasin

184/1 Soontornvijit Rd.
Tambon Nai Muang, Amphoe Muang
NAKHON PHANOM 48000
Tel: (66 42) 513-490-1; Fax: (66 42)513-492
Covers: Nakhon Phanom, Sakon Nakhon, Mukdahan

16/5 Mukmontri Rd., Amphoe Muang
UDONTHANI 41000
Tel: (66 42) 325-406-7; Fax: (66 42) 325-408
Covers: Udonthani, Nong Bua Lamphu, Nongkhai, Loei

SOUTHERN REGION

1/1 Soi 2 Niphat Uthit 3 Rd.
Hat Yai, SONGKHLA 90110
Tel: (66 74) 231-055, 238-518; Fax: (66 74) 245-986
Covers: Songkhla (Hat Yai) and Satun

Sanam Na Muang
Ratchadamnoen Rd., Amphoe Muang
NAKHON SI THAMMARAT 80000
Tel: (66 75) 346-515-6; Fax: (66 75) 346-517
Covers: Nakhon Si Thammarat, Trang, Phatthalung

Tourist Information Center 102/3 Mu 2
Tambon Kaluwonuea, Amphoe Muang
NARATHIWAT 96000

Sungai Kolok Tourist Information Centre
Asia 18 Rd., Amphoe Sungai Kolok
NARATHIWAT 96120
Tel: (66 73)516-144; Fax: (66 73)522-412
Covers: Narathiwat, Yala, Pattani

73-75 Phuket Rd., Amphoe Muang
PHUKET 83000
Tel: (66 76)211-036; Fax: (66 76)213-582
Covers: Phuket, Phangnga, Krabi

5 Talat Mai Rd., Ban Don, Amphoe Muang
SURAT THANI 84000
Tel: (66 77) 288-818-9; Fax: (66 77) 282-828
Covers: Surat Thani, Chumphon, Ranong

Prepare for Your Adventure

WHILE THAILAND IS A RELATIVELY COMFORT-
able and convenient place to travel, it requires some
basic pre-trip preparation if you really want to enjoy
this country's many treasures and pleasures. You will
especially want to anticipate the most important aspects of any
trip to this part of the world by budgeting overall costs, checking on Customs regulations, managing your money, gathering
essential shopping information, packing right, and anticipating
shipping alternatives and arrangements. Once you've done this,
you should be well on your way to having a terrific adventure
in Thailand and beyond.

MINIMIZE UNCERTAINTY

Preparation is the key to experiencing a successful and enjoyable shopping adventure in Thailand. But preparation involves
much more than just examining maps, reading travel literature,
and making airline and hotel reservations. Preparation, at the
very least, is a process of minimizing uncertainty by learning
how to develop a shopping plan, manage your money, determine the value of products, handle Customs, and pack for the
occasion. It involves knowing what products are good deals to

buy in Thailand in comparison to similar items back home. Most important of all, preparation helps organize and ensure the success of all aspects of your adventure.

DEVELOP AN ACTION PLAN

Time is money when traveling abroad. If you plan to include all shopping areas identified in this book, you will need to do some detailed planning. Given the near full capacity operation of some Thai Airways routes, we highly recommend making any domestic air reservations at least six weeks in advance of your arrival in Bangkok. This is especially important if you plan to visit Chiang Mai during the high season.

The better you plan and use your time, the more time you will have to enjoy your trip. If you want to use your time wisely and literally hit the ground running, you should plan a detailed, yet tentative, schedule for each day. Start by doing the following:

- Identify each city, town, island, or other area you plan to visit.

- Block out the number of days and/or hours you plan to spend in each place.

- List those places you feel you "must visit" during your stay, including many of the "best of the best" shops we identify.

- Select accommodations that are conveniently located near the places you plan to visit as well as near the major public transportation arteries, especially close to the new Skytrain stations in the case of Bangkok.

- Leave extra time daily for unexpected discoveries and for rewarding yourself.

Keep this plan with you and periodically revise it in light of new and unexpected information.

At a minimum, we recommend 5-7 days in Bangkok; 3-5 days in Chiang Mai; 2-3 days if your itinerary includes Chiang Rai, Maesai, Lampang, and Lamphun; 2-4 days for Phuket; and 2-3 days for Ko Samui. You may also want to include another week or two to visit other areas, such as Mae Hong Son, Tak, and Phitsanoluk in the North; Sukhothai, Ratburi, and Kanchanaburi, and Pattaya in the Central region; Nakorn Ratchasima (Korat) and Khon Kaen in the Northeast; and Nakorn Si Thammarat, Songkla, and Hatyai in the South. While these areas do not offer as many shopping opportunities as the main areas covered in this book, they are interesting areas to visit. The Tourism Authority of Thailand will be able to give you information on these areas. As we noted in Chapter 2, the head office in Bangkok sometimes sponsors tours to these and other locations outside the major tourist destinations.

CREATE YOUR OWN GOOD LUCK

Thailand is a very special place where you are likely to encounter a great deal of good luck. It's a great place for dashing well designed plans, altering expectations, and experiencing serendipity. The funniest and most unexpected events usually arise in Thailand to make any travel and shopping adventure to this country a most rewarding and memorable one.

But just how much pre-trip planning should you do? Planning is always fine, but don't overdo it and thus ruin your trip by accumulating a list of unfulfilled expectations. Planning needs to be adapted to certain realities which often arise and become the major highlights of one's visit to Thailand.

Good luck is a function of good planning: you place yourself in many different places to take advantage of new opportunities. You should be open to unexpected events which may well become the major highlights of your travel and shopping experiences.

> ❏ Do as much research as possible before your depart.
>
> ❏ Network for information and advice.
>
> ❏ Ask "who," "what," "where," "why," and "how" questions.
>
> ❏ Write, call, fax, or e-mail TAT for information.
>
> ❏ Once in-country, contact the local TAT offices.
>
> ❏ Your hotel concierge should have information on the best restaurants and sightseeing— but not shopping.

If you want to have good luck, then plan to be in many different places to take advantage of new opportunities. Visit, for example, many different shopping centers, hotel shopping arcades, factories, and markets in both Bangkok and Chiang Mai if you want to experience a truly rewarding shopping adventure. Expect to alter your initial plans once you begin discovering new and unexpected realities. Serendipity—those chance occurrences that often evolve into memorable and rewarding experiences—frequently interferes with the best laid travel plans. Welcome serendipity by altering your plans to travel plans. Welcome serendipity by altering your plans to accommodate the unexpected. You can do this by revising your plans each day as you go. A good time to summarize the day's events and accomplishments and plan tomorrow's schedule is just before you go to bed each night.

Keep in mind that a plan should be a means to an end—experiencing exciting travel and shopping—and not the end itself. If you plan well, you will surely experience good luck on the road to a successful adventure in Thailand!

CONDUCT RESEARCH AND NETWORK

Do as much research as possible before you depart on your Thailand adventure. A good starting place is the Internet. You'll discover several gateway sites that lead to all types of travel information, including many useful chat groups that discuss the latest travel developments in Thailand and its neighboring countries. You may want to start with these large travel gateway sites and then explore more specific sites focused on Thailand:

www.citynet.com	*www.yahoo.com*
www.mytravelguide.com	*www.travel-guide.com*
www.travel.com	*www.Travel-Library.com*
www.travelnotes.org	*www.vtravel.com*

We cover these and several hundred additional travel Web sites in our forthcoming companion volume, *Travel Planning on the Internet* (Impact Publications, October 2000).

When you begin focusing specifically on Thailand, start with these gateway sites:

www.tourismthailand.org
www.sanuk.com
www.sawadeethailand.com
http://th.orientation.com/eg/
www.siam.net
http://dir.yahoo.com/Regional_Information/Countries/
Thailand

If you're interested in restaurants, entertainment, nightlife, and other aspects of Bangkok life, be sure to visit the monthly *Bangkok Metro Magazine's* on-line site: *www.bkkmet.com*. Also check out *www.groovymap.com* and *www.bestinbangkok.com*.

If you're planning to visit Chiang Mai, Phuket, and Ko Samui, check out these useful Web sites:

www.chiangmai-chiangrai.com
www.phuketgazette.net
www.samuiguide.com

If you're not using the Internet, you may want to write, call, fax, or e-mail the TAT office nearest you. We've included the necessary contact information on pages 38-44.

We also recommend **networking for information and advice**. You'll find many people, including relatives, friends, and acquaintances, who have traveled to Thailand and who are eager to share their experiences and discoveries with you. They may recommend certain shops where you will find excellent products, service, and prices. Ask them basic who, what, where, why, and how questions:

- **Where** (cities) did you find the best shopping?
- **What** shops did you particularly like?
- **What** do they sell?
- **How** much discount could I expect?
- **Whom** should I talk to?
- **Where** is the shop located?
- **Is** bargaining expected?
- **Do** they pack and ship?

List serves, news groups, and travel discussion groups on the Internet can provide a great deal of useful information and advice. Explore these groups for starters:

Newsgroups:	*www.deja.com* *www.digiserve.com*
List Serves:	*www.liszt.com* *www.egroups.com*
Travel sites:	*www.fodors.com* *www.lonelyplanet.com* *www.ishoparoundtheworld.com*

Once you arrive in-country, be sure to gather information from local sources, especially those identified in Chapter 2.

CHECK CUSTOMS REGULATIONS

It's always good to know Customs regulations before leaving home. If you are a U.S. citizen planning to return to the U.S.

from Thailand, the U.S. Customs Service provides several helpful publications which are available free of charge from your nearest U.S. Customs Office (or write P.O. Box 7407, Washington, DC 20044). Several also are available in the "Traveler Information" section of the U.S. Customs Web site: *www.customs.ustreas.gov/travel.htm*:

- *Know Before You Go* (Publication #512): Outlines facts about exemptions, mailing gifts, duty-free articles, as well as prohibited and restricted articles.

- *Trademark Information For Travelers* (Publication #508): Deals with unauthorized importation of trademarked goods. Since you'll find many copies of trademarked items in Thailand, this publication alerts you to potential problems with U.S. Customs prior to returning home.

- *International Mail Imports* answers many questions regarding mailing items from foreign countries back to the US. The U.S. Postal Service sends all packages to Customs for examination and assessment of duty before they are delivered to the addressee. Some items are free of duty and some are dutiable. The rules have changed on mail imports, so do check on this before you leave the U.S.

- *GSP and the Traveler* itemizes goods from particular countries that can enter the U.S. duty-free. GSP regulations, which are designed to promote the economic development of certain Third World countries, permit many products, especially arts and handicrafts, to enter the United States duty-free, but only if GSP is currently in effect. If not, U.S. citizens will need to pay duty as well as complete a form that would refund the duties once GSP goes into effect again and is made retroactive—one of the U.S. Congresses' annual budgetary rituals that is inconvenient to travelers and costly for taxpayers. Most items purchased in Thailand are allowed to enter duty-free when GSP is operating.

MANAGE YOUR MONEY WELL

It is best to carry traveler's checks, two or more major credit cards with sufficient credit limits, U.S. dollars, and a few personal checks. Our basic money rule is to take enough money and sufficient credit limits so you don't run short. How much than not enough when shopping in Thailand.

We increasingly find **credit cards** to be very convenient when traveling in Asia. We prefer using credit cards to pay for hotels and restaurants and for major purchases as well as for unanticipated expenses incurred when shopping. Most major hotels, restaurants, and shops honor American Express, Master-Card, Visa, and Diner's cards. It is a good idea to take one or two bank cards and an American Express card. You may also want to take your ATM card which is readily accepted in Bangkok and to a lesser extent in Chiang Mai and Phuket, although beware of transaction fees.

It's a good idea to take **traveler's checks** in U.S. denominations of $50 and $100. Smaller denominations may seem expensive to cash after a transaction fee is deducted. If you only need to change ten or twenty dollars, it is often cheaper to change cash than traveler's checks. Most major banks, hotels, restaurants, and shops accept traveler's checks, although some do add a small service charge. Money-changers and banks will give the best exchange rates, but at times you'll find hotels to be more convenient because of their close proximity and better hours.

❑ Use credit cards to pay for hotels and restaurants and for major purchases.

❑ Carry one or two bank cards and an American Express card.

❑ Consider requesting a higher credit limit on your bank cards.

❑ Take plenty of $50 and $100 traveler's checks.

❑ Keep one personal check aside to pay Customs should you have dutiable goods when you return home.

❑ Carry an "emergency cash reserve" primarily in $50 and $100 denominations.

❑ Keep a good record of all charges in local currency— and at official exchange rates.

Personal checks can be used to obtain traveler's checks with an American Express card or to pay for goods to be shipped later—after the check clears your bank. If you are a U.S. citizen returning to the United States, consider keeping one personal check aside to pay Customs should you have dutiable goods when you return home and you don't wish to use your charge card for such payment.

Use your own judgment concerning how much **cash** you should carry with you. Contrary to some fearful ads, cash is awfully nice to have in moderate amounts to supplement your traveler's checks and credit cards. It especially comes in handy when visiting Myanmar which has an interesting "cash and carry" economy (see Chapter 14). But of course you must be very careful where and how you carry cash. Consider carrying an "emergency cash reserve" primarily in $50 and $100 denominations, but also a few 20's for small exchanges.

USE CREDIT CARDS WISELY

Credit cards can be a shopper's blessing. They are your tickets to serendipity, convenience, good exchange rates, and a useful form of insurance. Widely accepted in Thailand, they enable you to draw on credit reserves for purchasing many wonderful items you did not anticipate finding when you initially planned your adventure. In addition to being convenient, you usually will get good exchange rates once the local currency amount appearing on your credit slip is converted by the bank at the official rate into your home currency. Credit cards also allow you to float your expenses into the following month or two without paying interest charges. Most important of all, should you have a problem with a purchase—such as buying a piece of jewelry which you later discover was misrepresented or has fake stones, or antiques which you later learn are expensive reproductions—your credit card company **may** assist you in recovering your money and returning the goods. Once you discover your problem, contact the credit card company with your complaint and refuse to pay the amount while the matter is in dispute. Businesses accepting these cards must maintain a certain standard of honesty and integrity. In this sense, credit cards may be an excellent and inexpensive form of insurance against possible fraud and damaged goods when shopping abroad. If you rely only on cash or traveler's checks, you have no such institutional recourse for recovering your money.

The down-side to using credit cards is that some businesses in Thailand will charge you a "commission" for using your card, or simply not go as low in the bargaining process as they would for cash or traveler's checks. Commissions will range from 2 to 6 percent. This practice is discouraged by credit card companies; nonetheless, shops in Thailand do this because they must pay a 4-5 percent commission to the credit card companies. They merely pass this charge on to you. When bargaining, keep in mind that shopkeepers usually consider a final bargained price to be a "cash only" price. If you wish to use your credit card at this point, you will probably be assessed the additional 2 to 6 percent to cover the credit card commission or lose your bargained price altogether. Frequently in the bargaining process, when you near the seller's low price, you will be asked whether you intend to pay cash. It is at this point that cash and traveler's checks come in handy to avoid a slightly higher price. However, **don't be "penny wise but pound foolish."** You may still want to use your credit card if you suspect you might have any problems with your purchase.

A few other tips on the use and abuse of credit cards may be useful in planning your trip. **Use your credit cards for the things that will cost you the same amount no matter how you pay,** such as lodging and meals in the better hotels and restaurants or purchases in most department stores. Consider requesting a higher credit limit on your bank cards if you think you may wish to charge more than your current limit allows.

Be extremely careful with your credit cards. Although rare, some restaurants and shops in Thailand have been known to alter credit card amounts or make duplicate charge slips. Be sure merchants write the correct amount and indicate clearly whether this is U.S. dollars or Thai baht on the credit card slip you sign. It is always a good practice to write the local currency symbol before the total amount so that additional figures cannot be added or the amount mistaken for your own currency. For example, 3,800 Thai baht are roughly equivalent to 100 U.S. dollars. It should appear as "B3800" on your credit card slip. And keep a good record of all charges in local currency—and at official exchange rates—so you don't have any surprises once you return home!

SECURE YOUR VALUABLES

Thailand is a relatively safe place to travel if you take the normal precautions of not inviting potential trouble. We have never had a problem with thieves or pickpockets in Thailand but neither have we encouraged such individuals to meet us. If you take a few basic precautions in securing your valuables, you should have a worry-free trip.

Be sure to keep your traveler's checks, credit cards, and cash in a safe place along with your travel documents and other valuables. While money belts do provide good security for valuables, the typical 4" x 8" nylon belts can be uncomfortable in Thailand's hot and humid weather. Our best advice is for women to carry money and documents in a shoulder bag that can be held firmly and which should be kept with you at all times, however inconvenient, even when passing through buffet lines. Choose a purse with a strap long enough to sling around your neck bandolier style and keep a firm grip on it. Purse snatching is not a common occurrence in Thailand, but it is best to err on the side of caution than to leave yourself open to problems that could quickly ruin your vacation.

For men, keep your money and credit cards in your wallet, but always carry your wallet in a front pocket. If you keep it in a rear pocket, as you may do at home, you invite pickpockets to demonstrate their varied talents in relieving you of your money, and possibly venting your trousers in the process. If your front pocket is an uncomfortable location, you probably need to clean out your wallet so it will fit better.

You may also want to use the free hotel safety deposit boxes for your cash and other valuables. If one is not provided in your room, ask the cashier to assign you a private box in their vault. Remember, most hotels assume no responsibility for thefts from in-room safes. Always double-check them for possible malfunctioning. Indeed, we recently encountered an in-room safe that was anything but safe—after setting it with our unique code, we discovered any other combination of numbers would also open it! Under no circumstances should you leave your money and valuables unattended in your room, at restaurant tables, or in dressing rooms. You may want to leave expensive jewelry at home so as not to be as likely a target of theft.

If you get robbed, chances are it will be in part your own fault, because you invited someone to take advantage by not being more cautious in securing your valuables.

Take All Necessary Shopping Information

We recommend that you take more than just a copy of this book to Thailand. At the very least you should take:

❑ A prioritized "wish list" of items you think would make nice additions to your wardrobe, home decor, collections, and for gift giving.

❑ Measurements of floor space, walls, tables, and beds in your home in anticipation of purchasing some lovely home furnishings, tablecloths, bedspreads, or pictures. Thailand is a great place for lovely home furnishings.

❑ Photographs of particular rooms that could become candidates for home decorative items. These come in handy when you find something you think—but are not sure— may fit into your color schemes, furnishings, and decorating patterns.

❑ Take an inventory of your closets and identify particular colors, fabrics, and designs you wish to acquire to complement and enlarge your present wardrobe.

❑ If you think you will have tailoring work done, be sure to take pictures or models of garments you wish to have made. If you have a favorite blouse or suit you wish to have copied, take it with you. It is not necessary to take a commercial pattern, because Thai tailors do not use these devices for measuring, cutting, and assembling clothes.

DO COMPARATIVE SHOPPING

You should also do comparative shopping before arriving in Thailand. This is particularly important in the case of gems and jewelry—two popular items that are the most frequent subjects of scams—which are available elsewhere in the world and which can be easily appraised for their international market value. Other Thai products tend to be unique and thus difficult to compare with shops in other countries. However, the general rule of thumb we discovered is that most unique Thai items, such as antiques and home decorative items, as well as some gems and jewelry, found in shops outside Thailand cost at least five times what they would cost in Bangkok and Chiang Mai.

Items that originate in Chiang Mai will sell for about half what they will cost in Bangkok shops. Prices among shops within cities and towns can vary as much as 500%!

If you are a true comparative shopper, you should first make a list of what you want to buy and then do some "window shopping" by visiting local stores at home, examining catalogs, checking the Internet, and telephoning for price and availability information. While such comparative shopping is especially useful and easy when pricing electronic goods and cameras, these are not products you will want to purchase in Thailand because they are expensive given the duties placed on them by the Thai government.

Jewelry, one of Thailand's great shopping buys, begs comparative shopping as well as some minimal level of expertise for determining authenticity and quality. Read as much as you can on different qualities of jewelry and visit jewelry stores at home where you can learn a great deal by asking salespeople questions about craftsmanship, settings, quality, pricing, and discounts. In most of Bangkok's major bookstores and hotel sundry shops, for example, you will find a useful guide to this subject: John Hoskin's *A Buyer's Guide to Thai Gems and Jewelry* (Bangkok: Asia Books). At the same time, you should review our gem and jewelry buying advice in Chapter 7 as well as visit this Web site to learn about gems and jewelry: *www.modera.com*. Also, be sure to review the gem and jewelry buying advice on TAT's Web site: *www.tourismthailand.org*. This site provides useful buying advice, especially the importance of shopping at the many reliable jewelers who are members of the "Jewel Fest Club" sponsored by the Thai Gem and Jewel Traders Association, as well as Thailand's huge Free Trade Zone for diamonds, gems, and jewelry manufacturing and exporting—**Gemopolis** (located 30 kilometers east of Bangkok).

You can get good buys on gems and jewelry in Thailand **if** you know what you are doing. Most people, however, are simply overwhelmed by the choices confronting them. Novices shopping for gems and jewelry in Thailand can end up with much less than they bargained for. Many think they are getting a "steal" and then later discover it was the shop or street vendor that got the real steal!

KEEP TRACK OF ALL RECEIPTS

Be sure to ask for receipts and keep them in a safe place. You will need them later for providing accurate pricing information on your Customs declaration form. Take a large envelope to be used only for depositing receipts. You may want to organize your list for Customs as follows:

Receipt #	Item	Price (Baht)	Price (US$)
1. 72143	white silk blouse	B2700	$36.84
2.			
3.			
4.			

When you go through Customs with your purchases organized on a separate list in this manner, you should sail through more quickly since you have good records of all your transactions.

PACK RIGHT AND LIGHT

Packing and unpacking are two great travel challenges. Trying to get everything you think you need into one or two bags can be frustrating. You either take too much with you, and thus transport unnecessary weight around the world, or you find you took too little.

We've learned over the years to err on the side of taking too little with us. If we start with less, we will have room for more. Your goal should be to avoid lugging an extensive wardrobe, cosmetics, household goods, and library around the world! Make this your guiding principle for deciding how and what to pack: *"When in doubt, leave it out."*

Above all, you want to return home loaded down with wonderful new purchases without paying extra weight charges. Hence, pack for the future rather than load yourself down with the past. To do this you need to wisely select the proper mix of colors, fabrics, styles, and accessories.

You should initially pack as lightly as possible. Remember, except for the winter months in the far north of the country, Thailand's climate is usually hot and humid. Take only light-weight clothes made primarily of natural fibers. Avoid garments made of polyester or wool. Since dress in Thailand is very casual, you need not take suits unless you are going on business. However, if you plan to dine in one of Thailand's top restaurants—the Oriental Hotel's Normandie Grill—men must wear a coat and tie. This dining experience is actually worth taking a coat and tie with you to Thailand!

Items you are likely to pack but which are readily and inexpensively available in Thailand include clothes, suitcases, bags, maps, stationery, and CDs. You may want to take a minimum number of such items since you can always buy more along the way. But do take all the shoes, specific medications, and makeup you will need on the trip. These items may be difficult or relatively expensive to find in the brands you desire.

Since you will do a great deal of walking in Bangkok, take at least one pair of comfortable walking shoes and one pair of dress shoes. Break these shoes in before you leave home. Wearing new shoes for lengthy periods of time can be uncomfortable. Take only essential shoes which will coordinate with all of your outfits. Should your shoes become damaged, they can be repaired inexpensively and quickly in Thailand.

CHOOSE SENSIBLE LUGGAGE

Whatever you do, avoid being a slave to your luggage. Luggage should be both **expandable and expendable**. Flexibility is the key to making it work. Get ready to pack and re-pack, acquire new bags along the way, and replace luggage if necessary.

Your choice of luggage is very important for enjoying your

shopping experience and for managing airports and airplanes. While you may normally travel with two suitcases and a carry-on, your specific choice of luggage for shopping purposes may be different. We recommend taking two large suitcases with wheels—perfect if one fits into another; one large carry-on bag; one nylon backpack; and one collapsible nylon bag.

If you decide to take hard-sided luggage, make sure it has no middle divider. With no divider you can pack some of your bulkier purchases. This type of luggage may appear safer than soft-sided luggage, but it is heavier, limited in space, and not necessarily more secure. A good soft-sided piece should be adequately reinforced.

Your **carry-on bag** should be convenient—lightweight and with separate compartments and pockets—for taking short trips outside major cities. For example, if you plan to visit Mae Hong Son or Chiang Rai in the North, you can leave your large luggage pieces at a hotel in Chiang Mai and only travel with the carry-on bag for a few days before returning to Chiang Mai.

> ❏ Take at least one pair of comfortable walking shoes.
>
> ❏ We recommend taking two large suitcases with wheels.
>
> ❏ Your carry-on bag should be convenient for taking short trips outside major cities.

We also recommend taking a small nylon **backpack** in lieu of a camera bag. This is a wonderfully convenient bag, because it can be used as a comfortable shoulder bag as well as a backpack. It can hold cameras, film, travel books, wind-breakers, umbrella, drinks and snacks and still have room for carrying small purchases. When you find your hands filled with purchases, your backpack can go on your back so your hands are free for other items.

A collapsible **nylon bag** also is a useful item to pack. Many of these bags fold into a small 6" x 8" zippered pouch. You may wish to keep this bag in your backpack or carry-on bag for use when shopping.

If your second suitcase will be relatively empty as you leave home, it's a good idea to fill it with bubble-wrap and other packing materials which should come in handy when you later repack in Thailand.

THROW IN A CALCULATOR

Since you will be doing a great deal of shopping, take a small battery operated calculator for adding your purchases and converting currency equivalents. Using a calculator when bargaining also impresses upon shopkeepers that you are a serious shopper who seems to know what you are doing. Solar calculators may be convenient to carry, but you may have difficulty operating them in dimly lit shops. Several brands of "conversion calculators" are now available, usually found at your local luggage shop. Once you enter the conversion factors for the foreign currency, its easier to calculate the equivalents. These conversion calculators also aid you in converting meters to yards and Celsius to Fahrenheit.

A currency conversion chart also can be a time-saver for figuring currency equivalents. You can make your own by listing the equivalent amounts for several standard US$ amounts ($5, $25, $60) on a small piece of heavy paper or on a business card; keep a copy in your pocket for quick reference.

CHECK THE LIST

While we recommend traveling light, you may want to take some of the following items with you. If you take everything on this checklist, you'll indeed travel heavy! Before you close your suitcases and bags, check to see if you have packed everything you need by reviewing this checklist:

OVERALL PACKING

❑ Included only the essentials for the trip
❑ Kept total weight to a minimum
❑ Completed packing process 24 hours before departure

LUGGAGE

❑ Two suitcases
❑ One carry-on with one change of clothes, toiletries, cosmetics, and documents
❑ One or more collapsible bags
❑ Small nylon backpack (for camera and maps)
❑ Can carry all baggage by myself without the assistance of a porter or a pushcart

PACKING MATERIALS

❑ Plastic bubble-wrap for wrapping delicate items
❑ Scissors and/or pocket knife (be sure to pack these items in your check-through luggage)
❑ Wrapping cord and strapping tape
❑ Carrying strap

FILM/CAMERA

❏ Camera and accessories for purse and/or backpack
❏ Sufficient film

ELECTRICAL APPLIANCES

❏ Hair dryer (converts to 220-volt)
❏ Curling iron (220-volt or butane)—can buy in Bangkok
❏ Plug adaptors
❏ Voltage converter
❏ Shaver (converts to 220-volt)

PURSE AND WALLET

❏ Shoulder bag with outside pocket (women)
❏ Clutch purse (women)
❏ Wallet, purse, and clutch includes only essential items needed for this trip

CLOTHES

❏ Coordinated wardrobe
❏ Light-weight clothes with high cotton fabric content
❏ One dressy outfit
❏ Swim suit

SHOES

❏ One or two pair of comfortable walking shoes
❏ One pair of dress shoes (comfortable too!)
❏ Slippers or shower thongs

SECURITY

❏ Flashlight
❏ Burglar/fire alarm
❏ Padlocks or security strap for luggage

READING MATERIALS

❏ Paperback book(s)
❏ Travel guides
❏ Envelope with travel information

ODDS-AND-ENDS

- ❏ Travel alarm clock
- ❏ Aspirin, cold remedies, medicated ointment for cuts
- ❏ Medication for diarrhea
- ❏ Prescription drugs
- ❏ Prescription for eyeglasses
- ❏ Sunglasses
- ❏ Band-aids
- ❏ Notepad, pens, paper clips, rubber bands
- ❏ Sewing kit and safety pins
- ❏ Ziplock bags
- ❏ Shampoo
- ❏ Collapsible umbrella
- ❏ Calculator
- ❏ Suntan lotion with sunscreen/Solarcaine
- ❏ Deodorant
- ❏ Cosmetics
- ❏ Small mirror
- ❏ Moist towelettes or handi-wipes
- ❏ BenGay
- ❏ Nail clippers, file, and emery board
- ❏ Retractable tape measure
- ❏ Laundry soap
- ❏ Skirt hangers

SHIP WITH EASE

One of the worst nightmares of shopping abroad is to return home after a wonderful time to find your goods have been lost, stolen, or damaged in transit. This happens frequently to people who do not know how to ensure against such problems. Failing to pack properly or pick the right shipper, they suffer accordingly. This should not happen to you in Thailand.

You should not pass up buying lovely items because you feel reluctant to ship them home. Indeed, some travelers only buy items that will fit into their suitcase because they are reluctant to ship larger items home. But you can easily ship from Thailand and expect to receive your goods in excellent condition within a few weeks. We seldom let shipping considerations affect our buying decisions. We know we can always get our purchases home with little difficulty. For us, **shipping is one of those things that must be arranged**. We have numerous alternatives from which to choose, from hiring a professional shipping company to hand carrying our goods on board the plane. Shipping may or may not be costly, depending on how much you plan to ship and by which means. It is seldom a hassle in Thailand.

Before leaving home, you should identify the best point of entry for goods returning home by air or sea. Be prepared to specify the "Port of Entry." For example, in Virginia our port of entry can be Baltimore, Norfolk, or Richmond. We usually specify Baltimore for ocean freight and Washington Dulles International Airport for air freight. Once you are in Thailand, you generally have five alternatives for shipping goods home:

- Take everything with you.

- Do your own packing and shipping through the local post office (for small packages only).

- Have each shop ship your purchases.

- Arrange to have one shop consolidate all of your purchases into a single shipment.

- Hire a local shipper to make all shipping arrangements.

Taking everything with you is fine if you don't have much and you don't mind absorbing excess baggage charges. If you are overweight, ask about the difference between "Excess Baggage" and "Unaccompanied Baggage." Excess baggage is very expensive while unaccompanied baggage is much less expensive, although by no means cheap.

❏ Shipping is one of those things that must be arranged.

❏ Before leaving home, identify the best point of entry for goods arriving by air or sea.

❏ Most major shops are skilled at shipping goods for customers. They often pack items free and only charge for actual postage or freight.

❏ Be sure to insure your shipments against both loss and damage.

Most major shops are skilled at shipping goods for customers. They often pack the items free and only charge you for the actual postage or freight. Many of these shops use excellent shippers who are known for reasonable charges, good packing, and reliability. If you choose to have a shop ship for you, insist on a receipt specifying they will ship the item and specify that you want the shipment insured for both loss and damage—frequently called "all-risk."

If you have several large purchases—at least one cubic meter—check with local shippers since it is cheaper and safer to consolidate many separate purchases into one shipment which is well packed and insured. Choose a local company which has an excellent reputation among expatriates for shipping goods. Consult the Yellow Pages under the headings "Shipping" or "Removers." Do some quick research. If you are staying at a good hotel, ask the concierge about reliable shippers. He should be able to help you. Personnel at the local embassy, consulate, or international school know which companies are best. We also identify in Chapter 5 (Bangkok) and Chapter 12 (Chiang Mai) the names, addresses, and telephone numbers of a few shippers considered reliable by local expatriates.

Sea freight charges are usually figured by volume—either by the cubic meter or a container. **Air freight** charges are based on a combination of size and weight. For a sea shipment there is a minimum charge—usually one cubic meter—you will pay even if your shipment is of less volume. There are also port fees to be paid, a broker to get the shipment through Customs, and unless your hometown is a major seaport that handles freighters, you will also pay to have your shipment trucked from the port of entry to your home. On air freight you pay for the actual amount you ship—there is no minimum charge. You can usually have it flown to the international airport nearest your home and avoid port fees altogether. However, there will be a small Customs fee.

If your items are less than three feet in length and you don't wish to hand-carry them home, consider sending them by **parcel post**. This is the cheapest way to ship and parcel post tends to be reliable, although it may take four months for final delivery. Most shops will take care of the packing and shipping for parcel post.

If you buy any items that are less than three feet in length and you don't wish to hand-carry them home, consider sending them by **parcel post**. This is the cheapest way to ship. Parcel post tends to be reliable, although it may take three to six months for final delivery. Most shops will take care of the packing and shipping for parcel post. Small and light weight items, such as inexpensive jewelry, can be reliably and inexpensively shipped from Thailand by **Express Mail** or through one of the major international delivery services, such as UPS, Federal Express, or DHL, with the expectation of arriving within three to four days. In fact, don't be surprised to find small brown UPS boats plying the waters of the Chao Phraya River, just like their brown truck counterparts back home!

If you have items that are too large for parcel post, but nonetheless are small and relatively lightweight, air freight may be a viable option. Consider air freight if the package is too large to be sent parcel post, but much smaller than the minimum of one cubic meter, and does not weigh an excessive amount relative to its size. Air freight is the transportation of choice if you must have your purchase arrive right away. Sea freight is the better choice if your purchase is large and heavy and you are willing to wait several weeks for its arrival. When using air freight, contact a well established and reliable airline.

We have tried each of these shipping alternatives with various results. Indeed, we tend to use these alternatives in combination. For example, we take everything we can with us until we reach the point where the inconvenience and cost of excess baggage requires some other shipping arrangements. Sometimes we arrange to have all our large purchases consolidated with a Bangkok shipper that takes care of all packing and shipping. They pick up the items from the shops, repack, and combine them in a single sea shipment. At other times we work with one shop which agrees to consolidate all our purchases. This shop takes care of all packing and then arranges to have the items shipped in a single sea shipment. Such approaches require trusting a few key shops, making a long distance telephone call or two, and using Bangkok as the central consolidation and shipping point. While our approaches may seem complicated at first, in practice they work very well and we receive our goods with little or no problem.

When you use a shipper, be sure to examine alternative shipping arrangements and prices. The type of delivery you specify at your end can make a significant difference in the overall shipping price. If you don't specify the type of delivery you want, you may be charged the all-inclusive rate. For example, if you choose door-to-door delivery, you will pay a premium to have your shipment clear Customs, moved through the port, transported to your door, and unpacked by local movers. On the other hand, it is cheaper for you to just have the shipment arrive at your door; you do your own unpacking and carting away of the trash. If you live close to the point of delivery, you can easily clear Customs and pick up the shipment yourself. By doing this, you can save US$100 to US$125 that a local broker will charge to clear Customs and move the shipment out of the port; you may save another $300 to $500 in local transportation and delivery charges—depending on the size of the shipment.

We simply cannot over-stress the importance of finding and establishing a personal relationship with a good local shipper who will provide you with services which may go beyond your immediate shipping needs. A good local shipping contact will enable you to continue shopping in Thailand even after returning home!

Arrival and Survival

AFTER PREPARING FOR YOUR ADVENTURE, THE next step is to face the realities of arrival and survival. You're going to Thailand on what will certainly become a marvelous shopping and travel adventure you will fondly recall for many years to come.

FLYING IN

The flight into Bangkok gives you a glimpse of what lies ahead. If you arrive from Tokyo, Hong Kong, or Taipei, your plane crosses Vietnam, Laos, and the parched plateau of Northeast Thailand. Within 40 minutes of Bangkok International Airport, the plane clears the final mountain range on the edge of the Korat Plateau and begins descending toward Bangkok.

If you arrive during daylight and on a clear day, you begin seeing Thailand's breadbasket—the flat, fertile Central Plain divided into a checkerboard of rice fields, punctuated by small villages, and outlined by country roads, rivers, canals, and highways. So far Thailand looks flat, green, wet, and sparsely populated. Within 20 minutes of landing you get a good glimpse of the muddy Chao Phraya river which empties into the Gulf of

Siam and the small boats and freighters working their way to and from Bangkok's busy harbor. It's as if your map has just come alive. As your plane descends onto the runway, you get a quick glimpse of Bangkok's sprawling airport with Thai military planes at one end of the tarmac and golfers playing with their toys near the edge of the runway. Until you land, there is no hint of what lies ahead in the streets of Bangkok.

AIRPORT

The Bangkok International Airport is located approximately 20 kilometers north of the city center, adjacent to the old Don Muang International Airport and the domestic air terminal. Completed in 1988, this is one of Asia's busiest airports; indeed, plans are underway to construct a new international airport further east of Bangkok to handle increased demands for passenger and freight services. Currently servicing over 60 international carriers, Bangkok International Airport handles nearly 10 million passengers a year. It has everything a modern airport terminal should and also includes some extras normally associated with Thai service—jetways, moving walkways, escalators, elevators, baggage carts, informative signs and television monitors, efficient Immigration and Customs officials, clean and well lighted facilities, restaurants, shops, money exchange booths, and information and reservation desks. Designed to speed visitors through entry formalities with the maximum of ease, during peak periods of the week the airport can become very congested. In general, the most heavily trafficked times of the week are Friday, Saturday, and Sunday, 9am to noon and 4:30pm to 10pm. When we arrive during off-peak periods, we normally walk from our plane and complete Immigration, baggage retrieval, and Customs procedures as well as exchange money and arrange for a taxi within 30 to 40 minutes—one of the fastest airport entry-exit systems in all of Asia.

AIRPORT PROCEDURES AND SERVICES

Depending on where you deplane, the walk from the jetway to the Immigration booths can be a long one. If you have much hand luggage, use one of the free push carts that are conveniently available as soon as you leave the jetway. You will walk through a long corridor and turn into another corridor which has moving walkways to ease your journey. If you deplane on the tarmac and are shuttled to the terminal building by bus, you will enter the terminal near the row of Immigration booths.

The **Immigration** booths are located to your left. Except during heavily trafficked periods when several international flights arrive or few Immigration officials are available to man the booths, Thai Immigration procedures are relatively efficient— more so than in Hong Kong although less so than in Singapore. They merely process your paper work with the usual reading and stamping procedures.

Your next stop will be the **baggage claim** area. After completing Immigration, take the escalator directly to the lower level where you will find the baggage claim area. As you ride down the escalator, look ahead for the board at the front of the hall which lists the baggage carousel for your flight number. Baggage carts are conveniently located under the stairway and behind the baggage carousels.

Customs is located directly in front of the baggage retrieval area. The procedure is very simple. If you have nothing to declare, head for the green exit sign. Custom officials will take your Customs Declaration Form, look it over quickly, and probably let you proceed to the exit and service hall. If you declare anything, go to the section marked in red where Customs officials will inspect your declaration form and bags and determine if you need to pay any duties. In general, we find Thai Customs officials in Bangkok to be very accommodating and efficient.

- ❏ Bangkok International Airport is a very modern and convenient airport.

- ❏ The most heavily trafficked airport times are Friday, Saturday, and Sunday, 9am to noon and 4:30pm to 10pm.

- ❏ Thai Immigration procedures are relatively efficient.

- ❏ Baggage carts are conveniently located under the stairway and behind the carousels.

- ❏ If you have nothing to declare, head for the green exit sign.

- ❏ Purchase tickets at the Airport Taxi window in the arrival hall to get a special taxi that runs between the airport and hotels. Then go outside and stand in the queue.

- ❏ Use the free hotel service if you need a hotel.

- ❏ We do not recommend booking tours at the airport. You can always arrange tours later.

- ❏ The Money Exchanges at the airport give the same rates offered by other banks in the city and much better rates than you will get at hotels.

- ❏ Be wary of anyone who wants to rush you into buying a service or give you something "free" such as a free shopping tour. There is no such thing as a free tour.

After Customs, you enter directly into the **Arrival Hall**. Here you will find several convenient services as well as many helpful airport personnel ready to assist you with all of your local arrangements. Immediately ahead and to your right is a row of service desks to assist you with airport to city transportation, hotel and tour arrangements, tourist information, and money exchange.

This service section of the airport is a welcome sight for many first-time and seasoned travelers to Thailand. You may wish to use several of these service desks:

- **Airport Taxi:** Stop here to get information and purchase tickets for a special taxi service that runs between the airport and hotels. You have two choices: purchase a 650B regular car or 750B executive car. The regular car is fine in most cases; use the executive car if you have four or more people in your party or you have a lot of luggage. You pay at this desk, receive a receipt, and take your receipt outside to queue, more or less, for an Airport Taxi. This is an excellent service offering clean, efficient, and safe taxis. These taxis, however, cost from 80B to 120B more than other types of taxis arranged through a nearby taxi stand or along the road adjacent to the airport terminal. We recommend paying a little more for this service because the taxis are bigger, cleaner, and more comfortable than the less expensive alternatives and the drivers tend to be more careful.

- **Thai Hotel Association:** Personnel at this desk can assist you with hotel reservations should you arrive without a booking. They will show you a list of hotels with varying price ranges from which you can select accommodations most appropriate for your budget. They will call hotels to make a reservation. This is a free service you should use if you need a hotel. Trying to phone a hotel on your own from the airport is not worth the bother given this convenient service.

- **Tour Services:** This desk is operated by one tour company which has an airport concession—Travel East Co. Ltd. It is not sponsored by the Tourism Authority of Thailand, although you may be led to believe it is. Since we know nothing about this company and we are generally suspect of companies that have monopoly concessions on tourist services, we are very hesitant to recommend their services. The personnel will show you an illustrated loose-leaf notebook that outlines several popular tours. You select your tours and make reservations by paying for them in full. The tour company will then arrange to pick you up at your hotel at your designated time. However, you may or may not wish to use this service. There are many other ways to join organized tours as well as several other excellent tour companies which way be better for you than signing up at the airport. You can easily arrange for tours through your hotel or tour companies in the city. We have over the years used many excellent local tour companies, such as Tour East and Greylines, but we always arrange these tours through hotel tour information desks. If this airport desk were organized by a tour company association representing different tour companies, we would not hesitate to recommend using their services. For now, our recommendation is not to book tours through this desk immediately upon arrival. Instead, take a look at the tour options offered by this company, pick up a copy of their color brochure, and go directly to your hotel where you will be in a better position to survey additional tour options and compare prices. Should you later decide this company is the best for you, call their local number which appears on their brochure. Our experience is there is no need to be in a hurry to arrange a tour at this time. You can always arrange a tour later, after you have a better idea what you want to do—in addition to shopping in Bangkok!

■ **Tourist Information Counter:** Open daily from 8am to midnight, this desk is operated by the Tourism Authority of Thailand. The personnel will answer your questions and provide you with maps and tourist literature. Be sure to stop at this desk since they may have useful information you cannot find at your hotel. A stop here should save you a trip to the two TAT offices in the city which are not located near the major hotels and shopping areas.

■ **Left Baggage:** If you have baggage you wish to store at the airport, use this service desk. You can leave bags here for 25B per item per day.

■ **Money Exchange:** You will find four money exchanges in various locations in this Arrival Hall. Operated by major Thai banks, these exchanges give the same rates offered by other banks in the city and much better rates than you will get at hotels. You may do a little better at some banks in the city, but the difference is so small that it may not be worth the bother to use valuable time trying to save a few pennies.

You may also encounter personnel in this Arrival Hall who will come up to you and ask if you need assistance. Most of these people work for the airport or the airlines and are genuinely helpful. Others work for the tour information desk or taxi company and attempt to steer you into buying their services. While the airport authority has done an admirable job in discouraging the presence of annoying touts and taxi middlemen that used to plague the airport arrival section, occasionally a tout will wander into this area or approach you while you queue for a taxi to offer you his "special" services. Some of these people may misrepresent their affiliation; none of them are officials with the Tourism Authority of Thailand. Some will be very helpful in easing your entry and exit from the airport. Others may want to sell you their services. Use your own judgment as to whom you should trust—but be careful.

In general, be wary of anyone who wants to rush you into buying a service or give you something "free" such as a free shopping tour. There is no such thing as a free tour and such people invariably are working for commissions derived from your spending habits.

AIRPORT TO CITY TRANSPORTATION

Your trip from the airport to the central hotel sections of the city, especially along the river (Peninsula, Shangri-La, Oriental, Royal Orchid Sheraton), can take anywhere from 20 minutes to 90 minutes, depending on the time of day and routing. For example, if you arrive on a Sunday and take the expressway, you may be amazed to find the trip only takes 20 minutes! However, should you arrive at other times and your taxi or car does not take the expressway, you may find yourself stuck in traffic for more than an hour. Be sure to pay extra to take the expressway since you'll save lots of time getting into the city.

Your transportation alternatives from the airport to the city include hotel car, airport taxi, regular taxi, bus, and train. Several of the major hotels have their own cars waiting for incoming guests. However, these are not free. They cost from 700B to 1200B for a one-way trip from the airport to the hotel. They are usually new cars, clean and driven by relatively careful drivers. As you move through the arrival hall, look for your hotel sign being waved in the midst of the crowd that congregates at the left end of the hall. Ask your hotel representative about their transportation service, especially the cost.

One of the fastest and most convenient services is the **Airport Taxi** service. This service consists of a fleet of special taxis that only operate between the hotel and city. Costing 600B to 700B per vehicle, these taxis are clean and roomy and their drivers are polite, courteous, and relatively safe operators.

You can reserve an Airport Taxi at one of the two service desks on the right in the Arrival Hall.

A cheaper alternative to the limousine is to catch a **regular taxi**. While airport authorities discourage tourists from using these taxis, they are available if you know where to look for them. In fact, you may be approached inside the arrival hall by someone who offers you a ride to the city in one of these taxis which they claim are cheaper than the airport taxis. These vehicles are found to the right of the arrival hall exit as well as along the highway in front of the airport. Local residents will use the taxis because they are cheaper. You can save anywhere from 100B to 200B on the airport to hotel ride if you take one of these vehicles. However, be prepared for a few inconveniences and potential problems. These regular taxis tend to be much smaller and less comfortable than the airport taxis. You may have difficulty communicating with the driver who most likely does not speak much English, and the ride itself may be somewhat frightening should bad luck land you a driver who is a speed demon!

If you choose this local curb-side transportation and your taxi driver refuses to use his meter or claims it is broken, expect to be quoted several different—and equally outrageous—prices. The first quoted price may be an attempt to see if you know better. Unless otherwise indicated, you are assumed to be new in town and thus a rich and naive tourist ready for plucking. Expect someone to ask for 600B, then 450B, 400B, and 350B. If you wait a little and persist, you might be able to rent the whole car for 300B. If it is not raining (rain is worth an extra 50B) and if there are few other customers waiting, you may even get the ride for 250B. Such a price brings feigned moans and groans, exaggerated expressions of shock, and claims of poverty (*"But my family must eat!"*) from these entrepreneurs and con artists. Be good-humored about this haggling game by noting that you are a *"poor tourist who loves Thailand."*

You can also get from the airport to the city by **bus or train**. While not the most convenient ways to get to your hotel—especially if you have much luggage—and not recommended unless you are on a tight budget, since you will have to take a taxi once you get into the city, they are the cheapest ways to make the trip—costing less than 100B. Ask at the service desk for directions to the bus stand and the train station. You will have to walk across the main highway (take the overhead walkway) to get to the train stop. The train will eventually stop at the main railway station in downtown Bangkok—Hualampong Railway Station. From there you can take a taxi to your hotel, a ride that should not cost more than

100B. You might also consider catching the new Skytrain which has a station at Mo Chit (N6), just north of the Chatuchak Weekend Market on the way to the airport.

If you arrive in Bangkok by **train**, you will most likely get off at the main Hualampong Railway Station. This station is centrally located within a short distance of most major Bangkok hotels and shopping areas. There are plenty of air-conditioned taxis and open-air, motorized trishaws (*rot tuk tuk*) to take you to your destination. Most rides cost 100B to 120B, and you should not have to pay more than 150B. Like the airport, some cabs may not have meters, the driver may not want to use the meter, or he claims the meter is broken. In such cases the driver may try to rip you off by quoting 200B and 300B prices. Be persistent and insist on 80B or 100B but be willing to give in at 120B. When in doubt about a fair price, walk a few hundred feet to the main street, Rama IV Road, and motion for a metered cab. The metered cabs will probably cost 80B to 90B, depending on your destination.

Our airport to city recommendation: take the 600B to 700B Airport Taxi service or a car from your hotel. You will pay more, but the additional comfort, convenience, and perhaps safety are well worth the extra amount. After all, it costs less than US$20 which is still inexpensive for a 20 kilometer, 45 minute to one hour taxi ride.

CUSTOMS AND EXPORTS OF ANTIQUES

You must complete a Customs clearance form prior to entering Thailand. It's a standard form with the usual set of questions and prohibitions. For example, you are permitted to bring into Thailand duty-free 200 cigarettes or 250 grams of tobacco, one quart of wine or liquor, and your personal effects. You are prohibited from importing narcotics, obscene materials, firearms and ammunition, and some fruits, vegetables, and plants.

You are required to observe certain rules on exporting Thai Buddha figures larger than those worn as amulets, arts, and antiques. The law prohibits the export of Buddha figures without special permits; arts and antiques need government certification for export. These documentation requirements are observed to varying degrees. During the past ten years the Thai government has taken a special interest in closely scrutinizing the export of large Buddhas as well as partial Buddhas. In fact, a few antique dealers have had trouble over the illegal export of such items.

If you are interested in purchasing such items, know beforehand that you may have a problem with export permits. Ask your shopkeeper about potential export problems **before** making a sensitive purchase. Most shopkeepers are well aware of the changing political climate that may or may not permit the export of the Thai cultural and religious heritage. However, much of what gets exported from Thailand as arts and antiques really comes from Myanmar or Cambodia—two countries and heritages the Thais have been instrumental in exploiting for centuries and thus feel no particular obligation to protect today —except for some Khmer art which may actually come from Northeast Thailand rather than Cambodia. The whole permit process takes time and is an inconvenient bureaucratic obstacle for many serious shoppers. Don't try to secure the necessary permits on your own. Your time is worth more than the little money involved in having someone else arrange the permits. Most shopkeepers will take care of the certification requirements for you, or they will recommend how best to ship your goods trouble-free. Suffice it to be said that most anything can be exported from Thailand for a price.

One important word of caution before you encounter potential export problems. If you purchase Buddha images or antiques from dealers outside Bangkok, especially in Chiang Rai, hand carry those items with you to a reputable shipper in Chiang Mai or Bangkok rather than rely on the shop to ship and handle the certification and export permit requirements. Some of our readers have had delivery problems with Buddha images purchased from shops in the Thai-Myanmar border town of Maesai in the northern province of Chiang Rai. They trusted small shops to take care of all shipping and certification. While some shops may be dishonest, others simply aren't equipped to deliver like the experienced international dealers in Chiang Mai and Bangkok. When in doubt, take your purchases with you to a reputable shipper.

AIRPORT TAX AND LOOSE CHANGE

The airport departure tax on all international flights is 200B (US$5.26) per person. This is paid when you check in for your departure flight. Make sure you have enough baht set aside for this tax.

If you have extra baht left, consider "making merit" by dropping it in one of the charity boxes conveniently located in the departure lounge. The donations go to very worthwhile causes.

Currency and Credit Cards

The baht (B) is the currency of Thailand. As we go to press, it is roughly equivalent to US$.026 (US$1 = 38B). Prior to 1997 the baht was relatively stable in relation to the US dollar, but it has fluctuated greatly during the past three years due to Thailand's economic crisis (at one point US$1 = 58B). The baht is divided into 100 satangs and represented by small gold-colored 25 and 50 satang coins. Silver-colored coins are issued in 1B, 2B, 5B, and 10B denominations. The most widely circulated baht notes are in 10B (brown), 20B (green), 50B (blue), 100B (red), 500B (purple), and 1,000B (khaki) denominations. Each bill is easily distinguished by color and Arabic numbers.

❑ Traveler's checks receive a higher exchange rate than notes.

❑ Smaller shops may accept Visa or MasterCard, but many attempt to pass the 4-6% service charge on to the customer.

❑ Expect bargained prices to be "cash prices" unless otherwise agreed.

❑ The biggest problem is traffic—lots of it in all forms, combinations, and speeds!

❑ There is no pressure to tip in Thailand, although tips are widely accepted and appreciated.

❑ Thais generally try to be helpful and accommodating.

❑ Half the fun in Thailand is getting lost and then finding your way to your destination. Never fear. You will seldom get lost for more than 15 minutes.

Banks give the best exchange rates; hotels give the least attractive rates. Banks are in abundance and are open from 8:30am to 3:30pm, Monday through Friday. A few branches are open on Saturday. Money changers keep somewhat longer hours, especially on the weekend. Traveler's checks receive a higher exchange rate than bank notes, but you must pay a small government stamp fee for each check.

Credit cards are accepted in major hotels, restaurants, and shops of Bangkok and Chiang Mai. The most widely accepted cards are Visa, MasterCard, American Express, and Diner's Club. Smaller shops may accept Visa or MasterCard, but many shops will attempt to pass the 4-6% service charge on to the customer if the bargained price is very low. This is an improper practice, but the profit margins of many small shops are so small that they cannot afford to permit customers to use a credit card on bargained prices. Expect bargained prices to be "cash prices" unless otherwise agreed. When the bargaining really gets tough, many merchants will ask whether you intend to pay cash; you'll get a slightly lower price with cash.

If you use an American Express card and a merchant

attempts to add the percentage to your bill, you can either refuse to pay it or ask that it be included as a separate line item on your credit card slip. American Express should reimburse you for the amount as long as it appears as a separate line item. They, in effect, charge the amount back to the merchant since it is against their regulations to charge customers for the service charge under American Express rules.

SECURITY AND SAFETY

Thailand's airport security system is typical for most airports—hand-checks and X-rays of carry-on luggage. Compared to other airports, the Thais are more considerate in handling your personal effects. They are less likely, for example, to tear into your luggage, unwrap packages, and leave you standing with a mess on your hands as often happens in Hong Kong. The present X-ray machines appear to be safe for average speed film. High speed film may be damaged. When in doubt, ask the security personnel to hand inspect your film rather than send it through the X-ray machine. Computer diskettes should be fine when sent through the machines, but it may be best to play it safe with special handling.

Bangkok and most of Thailand are relatively safe for visitors. The biggest problem is traffic. You must be extra cautious when crossing streets and walking along lanes and sidewalks. The buses, taxis, motorized trishaws, motorcycles, and cars can be dangerous if you don't watch them carefully. Many sidewalks are broken or uneven, so watch your step while walking. Thailand does have a crime problem, especially pickpockets and petty thievery, but few tourists are ever victimized. Nonetheless, use common sense on where, when, and how you walk in Thailand. Travelers most likely to encounter crime problems are often those who stay in budget accommodations where security tends to be lax or those who wish to experience Bangkok's low life of bars, massage parlors, prostitutes, and transvestites. The best hotels will have the best security. Consequently, you may find the extra cost of staying at a deluxe hotel is offset by the better security systems.

TIPPING

There is no pressure to tip in Thailand, although tips are widely accepted and appreciated. Tipping rules in Thailand are very flexible and approximate the original intent of a tip—given for good service. However, in international service areas, such as hotels, restaurants, bars, clubs, and hairdressers, 10% tips are expected and often added to your bill as a service charge. Major hotels and restaurants do normally add a 10% service charge and a 11% government tax to your bill. Unless service is exceptional, you need not leave an additional tip in these places.

The general Thai tipping practice in small street restaurants is to leave loose change rather than a fixed percentage of the bill. If, for example, your bill comes to 171B and you pay with two 100B bills, you may wish to leave a bill and a few coins behind. However, always leave at least 5B—less than that is somewhat insulting (remember, 5B is equivalent to US$.13). In small inexpensive open-air restaurants, leaving a 10B or 20B tip on most bills is quite acceptable.

You need not tip taxi drivers since the price you pay is already negotiated or appears on the meter. But on some occasions you may want to give an additional 20B or 30B because you either feel sorry for your driver (he got caught in an extra 20 minutes of traffic) or he was exceptionally helpful. If a driver takes you to one of his recommended shops, don't feel obligated to tip him for this "extra" service; he probably received a 10% commission from the shop on everything you purchased!

Hotel and airport porters should be tipped 10B to 20B per bag, with a 20B minimum. Use your own discretion in tipping all others.

Don't be intimidated if a taxi driver, porter, or guide tries to demand a larger tip, which some are known to do. Not surprising, some people working close to the tourist trade brazenly try to take advantage of tourists. Just ignore them and walk away. Keep in mind that service tends to be excellent in Thailand. It often deserves to be rewarded with a tip genuinely expressing your appreciation for a job well done.

LANGUAGE

Language does present difficulties for some visitors to Thailand. While English is widely spoken in major hotels, restaurants and tourist shops, outside these areas communication at times can present problems. Few taxi drivers, for example, speak English. Few waiters and waitresses outside major restaurants speak or understand English. On the other hand, many restaurants print their signs and menus in Thai, Chinese, and English.

The language barrier, however, should not deter you from

getting around with relative ease. Many Thais, especially those in Bangkok, speak some basic English. Tours are available with English-speaking guides. You can rent a car with an English-speaking driver.

Thais generally try to be helpful and accommodating. They will usually try to understand you through a combination of sign language, writing, and a few English words. On the other hand, don't expect much help from young girls; they tend to be shy, and many will giggle and run away from you when approached.

When bargaining with street or market vendors, speak slowly in English and use your fingers to state your price—each finger representing 10B. Whenever possible, have someone write place names and addresses in Thai, collect name cards in Thai, and take a Thai/English map with you. Although some Thais cannot read Thai, many will ask fellow Thais for help. Some will approach you to practice their English, ask if you need any assistance, and take time to help you. In fact, half the fun in Thailand is getting lost and then finding your way to your destination. Never fear. You will seldom get lost for more than 15 minutes.

BUSINESS HOURS

Most shops are open 10 hours a day—from 10am to 8pm—seven days a week. However, some shops keep shorter hours, closing by 6pm and are closed Sunday. Check with your hotel or call ahead if you plan to visit shops in the evening.

Banks open at 8:30am and close at 3:30pm, Monday through Friday.

In Bangkok, post offices are open 8am to 6pm, Monday through Friday, and from 9am to 1pm on Saturday. Post offices outside Bangkok close at 4:30pm.

Government offices are open from 8:30am to 4:30pm, Monday through Friday, with a noon-to-1pm lunch break. The best time to conduct government business is from 9am to 11:30am.

TRANSPORTATION AND TAXIS

A fascinating variety of transportation is available for your pleasure—and displeasure—in Thailand. Indeed, the modes of transportation are often as interesting as the trips themselves, and your choices may determine how much you enjoy your travel and shopping adventure in Thailand.

In Bangkok you can choose among hotel cars, taxis, buses (air-conditioned or regular), motorized trishaws, rental cars, motorbikes, boats, and the new elevated train system called the Skytrain. We recommend using only the Skytrain, taxis, and hotel cars. They are convenient, air-conditioned, inexpensive, and plentiful—our basic requirements for decent transportation. Buses are overcrowded, uncomfortable, and extremely slow. The motorized trishaws are cute novelties, but they are uncomfortable, unsafe, and dirty. Try them once for the novel experience, but use them often and you may get a bad case of black lung, along with a nice coating, from head to toe, of black pollutants. The same is true for the taxi motorbikes which should only be used if you are in a real hurry; they will weave in and out of the traffic and occasionally take to the sidewalk to get you where you want to go! Renting and driving your own car or motorbike is an adventure in latent suicide; do so only if you are well insured, your children have already graduated from college, or you feel a lack of excitement in your life. Hold your breath. Welcome to Bangkok's roller coaster on wheels!

The general rule for choosing transportation in Bangkok is to go with what is quick, comfortable, and reasonably priced. The most convenient way to travel is to hire a **hotel car**, with an English-speaking driver, by the hour, half-day, or full-day. If you intend to accomplish a great deal in one day, this will be your best choice. It will be more expensive than a regular taxi, but for comfort and convenience you cannot do better. You will especially appreciate a car and driver when you go shopping in the lanes and neighborhoods that have few taxis. It's always good to know you have a car waiting, and it will be able to accommodate your purchases. And the prices of a car and driver in Thailand are very reasonable compared to other cities in the world.

Two words of caution when hiring a car and driver: make sure your driver does not use your shopping time to request commissions from the shops you visit nor take you to his

---

❑ We recommend using only hotel cars and taxis in Bangkok.

❑ You will especially appreciate a car and driver when you go shopping in the lanes and neighborhoods.

❑ Except during rush hour, a taxi should find you within 1-2 minutes. Just stand along the curb and wave for a taxi.

❑ Make sure the driver engages the meter and the air-conditioner is working properly.

❑ Feel perfectly free to correct any irritants—loud radio, excessive speed. Most cab drivers will politely accommodate.

❑ Boats are a great way to get around various sections of Bangkok that border the river.

recommended shops. Remember, he's not a shopping expert. Ask the hotel to give you a "commission-free" driver and make sure he doesn't accompany or follow you into the shops. If he does, chances are he's requesting from the shop a 10-30% commission on everything you buy, which means you won't be able to bargain for as low a price as otherwise. Also, be skeptical about any driver's shopping recommendations. Drivers are not quality shoppers; many steer tourists into only those shops that give them commissions. Consequently, they avoid—some will even bad-mouth (*"Jim Thompson too expensive—I'll take you to much better place"*)—quality shops that do not participate in the commission game.

Taxis are available everywhere in Bangkok. They cruise the streets and lanes like an army of frantic ants. Since most drivers rent their cabs by the day and are not confined to zones, they are free to roam wherever they can find a fare. They are the ultimate example of free enterprise run amuck!

Most taxis in Bangkok are metered, although some drivers will refuse to use their meter if you look like a newly arrived tourist who doesn't know any better. Always insist that the taxi driver engage the meter once you get into the cab—and before you take off. If not, you will most likely be in for a big surprise when you arrive at your destination and are told you owe 500B for a ride that should have cost 100B! If the driver refuses to use his meter, or says it's broken, just open the door to leave; he'll quickly get the message and then engage his meter or quickly fix it. Whatever you do, don't be intimidated by such taxi drivers. They're playing a game. If you fall victim to such a scam by having failed to negotiate the price or check the meter, just throw some banknotes at him (usually 100B to 150B for a 20 minute ride) and leave in a hurry. You'll be gone by the time he picks them up. Unfortunately, many tourists get taken by such drivers who plague the tourist industry.

All you need to do to get a cab is wave your hand or stand near the curb looking in need of transportation. Except during rush hour, a taxi should find you within 1-2 minutes. As soon as a taxi stops, the driver will either roll down his window, or you can open the door to tell the driver where you want to go. Since most taxis are metered, all you need to do is to get into the cab and make sure the driver engages the meter (pushes a button to start it). Depending on a state of traffic, some drivers may refuse to take you to particular destinations or they insist on negotiating a price rather than using the meter. For example, during rush hour traffic or during a heavy rain, a driver may refuse to take you to a place that would normally cost 100B on the meter. He may demand 200B for the ride. If you encounter this situation, or one in which the taxi does not have a meter or the driver claims the meter does not work, you will need to negotiate the price before getting in. A standard negotiation scenario is both a verbal and nonverbal exchange. Successful ones go something like this:

YOU: *"Siam Centre. How Much?"* (Or you point to Siam Centre on your Thai-English street map).

DRIVER: *"100 baht"* (or he sticks 10 fingers in the air).

YOU: (Start to respond nonverbally by looking like you are thinking over this offer. Next, look a little disappointed with this price. Finally, respond verbally) *"60 baht. Okay?"*

DRIVER: *"80 baht."*

YOU: *"70 baht"* (Now start to look away toward some other cabs as if you are prepared to negotiate with someone else).

DRIVER: *"Okay"* (Or he may just motion for you to come into the cab, which means agreement).

If your cab driver does not speak a word of English, do not despair; you can still communicate. Once he understands your destination, then you can conduct the price negotiation by using your fingers. When in doubt on what constitutes a fair price, insist on 80B, but be willing to settle for 90B or 100B depending on both the distance and the time involved. Most short distance taxi rides in Bangkok cost 80B to 90B; longer distance rides usually run 120B to 150B. Most of our rides cost around 80B. You should never take a taxi without first making sure the meter works and is engaged (some drivers conveniently forget to push the button) or establishing a negotiated price.

Bangkok's taxis can be both intimidating and irritating. Many vehicles are rusty; some rattle, weave, and hiss. Most are air-conditioned, but the air-conditioning may or may not be functioning properly—either too hot or too cold. Few cabs have seat belts. Worst of all, many drivers use a noxious air fresher that sits on the dashboard—you may have roll down the windows to escape this overpowering smell! Many of the drivers race their cabs from one stop light to another—a frightening experience for visitors who are used to a different set of road rules. And some drivers operate their radios and cassettes so loud that you can hardly hear yourself think!

But it's easy to overcome the intimidation and alter such irritants. Don't be afraid to assert yourself. Before getting into the cab, for example, be sure to check if the air-conditioner is working properly. If not, you may be in for a miserably uncomfortable ride in Bangkok's heat and humidity. Pick another cab with good air-conditioning. Once you get into the cab, feel perfectly free to correct any irritants. Ask the driver to please turn the air-conditioning up or down, drive slower, or turn down the volume on the electronics. Use sign language, such as pointing to the air-conditioner or radio, to make your point. Most cab drivers will politely accommodate your requests.

The new **Skytrain** (***www.bts.co.th***), which opened in December 1999, is now one of the fastest ways to cut through much of Bangkok's notorious traffic. It's fabulous for visitors and local residents alike! Indeed, Bangkok will never be the same since Skytrain. This elevated mass transit system is especially convenient for shoppers who want to go from Sukhumvit Road to Silom Road, a trip that can take up to an hour by taxi but which is now only a 10-15 minute Skytrain ride. The Skytrain links most major hotels and shopping centers by encompassing these key roads: Sukhumvit, Ploenchit, and Rama I running east and west; Rajadamri, Silom, and Sathorn running south; and Phyathai and Phaholyothin running north. You can now quickly get to the popular Chatuchak Weekend Market by getting off at the northern Skytrain station (N7). The newest maps of Bangkok now include the Skytrain routes and stations. If you are unclear how Skytrain operates, be sure to check with your hotel concierge on the routes and stations. Have him mark on your map where you can enter and exit the stations. Better still, be sure to pick up the latest edition (2000) of Nancy Chandler's wonderful *Map of Bangkok* which includes the Skytrain routes and stations in relation to Bangkok's major hotels, restaurants, shops, and sights, as well as *The Official BTS Skytrain Map* produced by Groovy Map Co. The Skytrain opens a whole new transportation, sightseeing, and shopping world to Bangkok. Our advice: *At least try the Skytrain before wasting your time stuck in a taxi trying to navigate Bangkok's highly congested, polluted, and noisy streets.*

Boats are a great way to get around various sections of Bangkok that border the Chao Phraya River. They have become increasingly popular with tourists who wish to avoid the horrendous travel congestion in the southwest section of the city. If you wish to go from the Peninsula, Shangri-La, Oriental, or Royal Orchid Sheraton hotel areas to the Grand Palace and Wat Phra Keo area near Thammasat University and the National Museum, it's much quicker to get there by boat than by bus, taxi, or private car. Indeed, the boat trip will take about 20 minutes whereas the road trip may take up to 50 minutes, depending on the traffic situation. This river route is also a very pleasant and entertaining way to see a different aspect of Bangkok. The water traffic is extremely entertaining—at times charming and amazing —for many first-time visitors. Water taxis, which depart every 5 to 10 minutes, are readily available along various sections of the river and they are relatively inexpensive.

Transportation outside Bangkok will vary depending on the particular regions and cities you visit. If you travel between Bangkok and Chiang Mai, you can go by plane, train, bus, or rental car. Again, we do not recommend driving a rental car unless you are used to Thai-style defensive driving. The road system is excellent, but the truck and bus traffic is dangerous for inexperienced drivers. On the other hand, you may want to drive a car within the northern region—between Chiang Mai, Maesai, Chiangrai, Lampang, and Lamphun. The traffic here is less intense and driving seems much safer, although you still need to drive defensively. We also do not recommend taking a bus, be- cause most—including the air-conditioned luxury tour buses—- are uncomfortable for people over 5'4" and they do have accidents. The road trip to Chiang Mai is 697 kilometers and takes about 9 hours.

If you have time, the **train** from Bangkok to Chiang Mai is a good way to travel. Thai trains are relatively efficient, clean, safe, and comfortable. Several trains leave daily for the 759 kilometer, 14 to 16-hour trip. The daily Express is the best train. Two Express trains leave Bangkok—one at 6pm and another at 7pm—and arrive in Chiang Mai 14 hours later. Reserve your tickets ahead of time since these popular trains are often fully booked. Slower trains leave during the day and allow you to see much of the colorful countryside, bustling train stations, small towns, and villages of the flat central plain and mountainous northern region. The first-class air-conditioning can be frigid, so take a sweater and jacket with you for the chilling night ride.

Air connections between Bangkok and Chiang Mai are excellent. Flights are frequent, the planes are comfortable, and the pilots have an excellent safety record. The flight to Chiang Mai takes about one hour. Be sure to make your reservations well in advance. In fact, the air traffic is so heavy that Thai Airways often flies 747s between Bangkok and Chiang Mai on weekends! Also, make sure you get to the domestic airport in plenty of time. This relatively new airport is often overcrowded and check-in lines can get long.

Transportation within towns and cities outside Bangkok also varies depending on the region and town. In Chiang Mai, taxis are mainly available to transport you between towns. You can purchase a taxi seat along with four or five other passengers, or you can rent the whole taxi for yourself. You also can rent a car with a driver for a private tour.

Within the city of Chiang Mai, the major means of transportation are human powered trishaws (*samlor*), motorized trishaws (*rot tuk tuk*), buses (*rot mae*), and minivans (*song thaew*). The buses are slow but cheap. The minivans are very convenient although somewhat uncomfortable and confusing for visitors who have no idea as to their routing. Most rides cost 8 baht, and the minivan will normally take you where you want to go. Since Chiang Mai is a university town with a relatively well educated and sophisticated local Thai and expatriate population, enough people speak some English to help you get around should you feel confused or lost.

You can also rent a motorbike or car to tour Chiang Mai and the surrounding area. Except for the congested downtown section, it is relatively easy to do your own driving. However, it is still most convenient and relatively inexpensive and stress-free to rent a car with driver. While the driver may not speak much English, it is usually enough to get you where you want to go. You can arrange for a car and driver at your hotel (front desk, bell boy, or doorman), negotiate with drivers who station themselves in or around the major hotels—be sure to bargain hard—or contact one of several rental companies near your hotel. If you plan to do a lot of shopping, be forewarned that many drivers in Chiang Mai expect 20-40% commissions from the local shopkeepers. If you make major purchases, you can save a lot of money by driving your own rental car.

We usually rent a car in the north through Avis or Budget car rental. They have offices in both Bangkok and Chiang Mai. If you reserve ahead of time through their Bangkok offices, you can have a car waiting for you upon arrival at the Chiang Mai International Airport.

TOURS AND TRAVEL DEALS

You will have no problem arranging tours and travel within and beyond Thailand. Several tour agencies—as well as the Tourism Authority of Thailand—offer a variety of tours within Bangkok and Chiang Mai as well as to other towns and resort areas throughout the country. Most of the tours are well organized, inexpensive, convenient, and comfortable. Your hotel should have brochures outlining the various tours and will help make the necessary scheduling arrangements. Some of the major tour groups include **Diethelm Travel** (Tel. 255-9150), **East West Siam** (Tel. 256-6153), **Orientours** (Tel. 229-4300), **Siam Express** (Tel. 236-5970), **Tour East** (Tel. 259-3160), **Turismo Thai** (Tel. 245-1551), and **Success Travel** (Tel. 935-7057).

Numerous travel agencies in Bangkok offer bargain air fares to major cities throughout the world, including neighboring China, Myanmar, Laos, Cambodia, Vietnam, Malaysia, Singapore, and Indonesia. Watch the classified ads in the English-language newspapers—*Bangkok Post* and *Nation*—as well as the monthly travel magazines, such as *Where*, for special air fares. For example, Bangkok-based *www.cheaptickets.net* offers some very good air deals within and beyond Thailand.

FOODS, DRINKS, AND RESTAURANTS

Thailand is our favorite Asian destination for food, drinks, dining ambiance, and restaurant service. It is a food and beverage paradise. You can find almost every type of food to satisfy your gastronomic desires. Bangkok, and to a lesser extent Chiang Mai, includes the usual international fast-food establishments, such as Pizza Hut, McDonald's, KFC, and A&W Root Beer as well as numerous French, Continental, Italian, Middle Eastern, Indian, Japanese, Korean, and Chinese restaurants.

Thai food has a well-deserved reputation for being spicy hot. It is a unique blending of Indian, Chinese, and indigenous cuisines. It is particularly noted for the use of hot spices, sugar, peanuts, coconut milk, and local ingredients, such as lemon grass. Unless you have already sampled Thai food, you should be cautious what you order. Thai foods can be flaming hot for the uninitiated. Small green peppers, for example, have the biggest kick. Eat one of these and you may feel you are having cardiac arrest! Should you be so unfortunate to sample the wrong peppers and spices, seek relief by placing sugar on your tongue; water tends to inflame the heat. The sugar technique usually works well in combating the worst effects of Thai cooking ingredients.

If you have never tried Thai food, you may want to start with some relatively tame dishes and gradually move on to more challenging selections. Thai-Chinese dishes, such as *nua phat naman hoei* (a meat and vegetable dish with oyster sauce) and *muu phat priew wan* (sweet and sour pork), are always good starters. You will most likely enjoy the *muu satay* (grilled skewered pork with a spicy peanut sauce), *kai jat sai* (stuffed omelet), *kai jang* (barbecued chicken), *penang nua* (beef in peanut-based sauce), and *kaeng masaman* (Indian beef curry with peanuts). For the more adventuresome, try *tom jam kung* (lemon grass soup with shrimp), *kaeng kai* (yellow chicken curry), and *bai phat krapraw* (meat and vegetable dish laced with basil leaves). Thai noodle dishes, such a *kui tiew phat see yuu*, *phat thai*, and *kui tiew nua sap*, are outstanding and not spicy hot. In fact, you will seldom go wrong ordering any of the Thai noodle dishes.

Thai restaurants are found throughout Bangkok, along its major highways and lanes. A few major hotels and restaurants sponsor Thai cultural shows which include a sampling of Thai food. Some of the best include **Baan Thai** (Soi 32 Sukhumvit Rd., Tel. 258-5403); **Pimarn** (Soi 46 Sukhumvit Rd., Tel. 258-7866); and **Sala Rim Naam** (Oriental Hotel, Tel. 234-8829). For some of the best Thai food, try the following restaurants: **Baan Khanitha** (36/1 Sukhumvit Soi 23, Tel. 258-4181); **Kalpapreuk** (27 Pramuan Road, Silom, Tel. 236-4335); **Busarakham** (Sethiwan Building, Silom Rd., Tel. 266-6312); **Thanying** (10 Soi Pramuan, Silom Rd., Tel. 236-4361); **Lemon Grass** (Soi 24 6/1 Sukhumvit Rd., Tel. 258-8637); **Jit Pochana** (1082 Paholyothin Rd., Tel. 279-5000 or Soi 20 Sukhumvit Rd., Tel. 258-1578); **Spice Market** (Regent Hotel, Tel. 251-6127); and **Thai Pavilion** (Holiday Inn Crowne Plaza, Silom Road).

- ❏ Thailand is a food and beverage paradise.
- ❏ In general the best and most expensive Western and Chinese restaurants will be found in or around major hotels.
- ❏ Try the many noon buffets.
- ❏ Avoid eating from street vendors—a good breeding ground for hepatitis.
- ❏ Imported wines are extremely expensive and should not be automatically ordered with dinner without first checking the price.

In general, the best and most expensive Western and Chinese restaurants will be found in or around major hotels. For fine Continental and French dining, try the **Normandie Grill** (Oriental Hotel, Tel. 234-0021—expensive and men must wear a coat and tie); **Fireplace Grill** (Le Meridian President Hotel, Tel. 253-0444); **Ma Maison** (Hilton Hotel, Tel. 253-0123); **Hamilton's** (Dusit Thani Hotel, Tel. 233-1130); **La Banyan** (59 Sukhumvit Soi 8, Tel. 253-5556); **Auberge Dab** (One Place Bldg., 1/F, Ploenchi Rd., Tel. 658-6222); or **Le Metropolitain** (Gaysorn Plaza, 3/F, Ploenchit Rd., Tel. 656-1102).

Bangkok abounds with excellent Chinese restaurants. Some of the best include: **Bai Yun** (Westin Banyan Hotel); **The**

Chinese Restaurant (Grand Hyatt Erawan Hotel); **Mayflower** (Dusit Thani Hotel); **Xing Fu** (Novotel Lotus Hotel); **Hai-Tien-Lo** (Pan Pacific Hotel); **Jasmin** (Gaysorn Plaza, Tel. 250-0501).

One of the best ways to enjoy eating in Thailand is to try the many noon buffets and brunches. Most are served in major hotels. They are usually good values, ranging from US$10 to US$25, and offering a wonderful variety of international foods. Some of Bangkok's outstanding buffets and brunches include: **Espresso** (Le Royal Meridien Hotel); **The Captain's Table** (Grand Pacific Hotel); **Colonnade** (The Sukhothai Hotel); **The Dining Room** (Grand Hyatt Erawan Hotel); and **Trader Vic's** (Marriott Royal Garden Riverside Hotel). One of our favorite Italian buffets is at **Giorgio's** (Tel. 234-5599) in the Royal Orchid Sheraton Hotel. The river view is wonderful and the widest selection of food is available Saturdays and Sundays. The relaxing **Lord Jim's** (Tel. 234-8621) at the Oriental Hotel serves a great seafood buffet in a beautiful setting overlooking the river—always one of our first restaurant stops in Bangkok!

If you are looking for marvelous breakfast buffets, two of the best are found at the Le Royal Meridien Hotel and the Dusit Thani Hotel (coffee shop). Two other excellent breakfast buffets are found at the Oriental Hotel (**Verandah**—outdoors along the river) and at the Shangri-La Hotel (both indoors and outdoors along the river).

Many Thai and Chinese restaurants are open-air restaurants in lovely water and garden settings. For a good sampling of these restaurants, try one of the numerous open-air restaurant complexes along Asoke-Dindaeng Road, such as **Kum Luang** (560 Asoke-Dindaeng), which are built over ponds. Be sure to apply mosquito repellant or request a mosquito coil for under your table.

Numerous food vendors are found throughout Bangkok and Chiang Mai. They offer everything from a wonderful variety of sweets, such as fried bananas and *roti* (rolled Indian pancake filled with condensed milk), to numerous noodle dishes and drinks. You may want to avoid eating at these tempting establishments. While most of the foods are safe to eat, the dishes and eating utensils are usually washed in dirty, re-used water—a good breeding ground for hepatitis.

If you visit Chiang Mai, you will find numerous Thai restaurants serving northern Thai dishes. For some of the more unique northern foods, try *khao soi* (curried noddle dish), *khao neow* (sticky rice), and *nam prik ong* (minced pork chili sauce eaten with fried pork skins or sticky rice). Avoid the uncooked pork delicacies, *naem* and *lap*, which can give you bad cases of trichinosis and food poisoning—not to mention a flaming digestive system if you encounter one of their small peppers! Hotel restaurants and coffee shops serve Western food as well as numerous Chinese and central Thai dishes. Chiang Mai also has several good French, German, English, and Middle Eastern restaurants. For French food, try **Le Coq d'Or** (Koh Klang Road). For Italian food, **Piccola Roma** (Charoen Prathet Road) is a good choice. The open-air riverside **The Gallery** (Charoen Rat Road) and the **Nang Nual Seafood Restaurant** (Ko Klang Road) are also excellent for Thai, Chinese, and seafood. The **Jasmine** in the Royal Princess serves some of the best Chinese cuisine in Chiang Mai. **The Pub** (88 Huay Kaew Rd.) serves excellent and inexpensive Western food in a cozy atmosphere— one of the best buys in all of Thailand. The noon buffets at the Chiang Inn and Chiang Mai Orchid hotels are good values. Two of Chiang Mai's best Thai restaurants are the **Sala Mae Rim** (Regent Resort) and **Gala Restaurant** (Suthep Road).

Thailand offers an assortment of excellent drinks. Standard international soft drinks, such as Coca Cola and Pepsi, are widely available. Thailand also produces two excellent non-carbonated orange soft drinks—Green Spot and Birelay. The local milks and ice creams, especially under the brand name Foremost, are excellent and safe to consume. Numerous noncarbonated drinks, fruit juices, and flavored yoghurt drinks are available in small dairy cartons.

Coffee and tea are widely available and are often served together—tea being the chaser to a cup of strong Thai coffee laced with condensed milk. Iced Thai coffee (*olieng*) is a delightful sweet drink. But you must acquire a taste for Thai coffee since it is rather thick and strong. Thai tea is served both hot and cold, with or without cream, and is a good drink. Outside major hotels your cup of hot coffee or tea may be served in a regular drinking glass and thus difficult to handle without a pair of gloves! Let it cool before handling the glass, or wrap it in a napkin or handkerchief—if you don't mind drinking it differently from others around you.

Alcohol also is widely available. Thailand produces three excellent robust beers—Kloster, Singha, and Amarit. Mekong is a popular and cheap national liquor which looks like Scotch but tastes best when mixed with Sprite, 7-Up, Coca Cola, or Pepsi (Thais like to take it with soda water). Numerous other local liquors are produced in Bangkok and the provinces. All major international liquors are widely available in grocery stores throughout Thailand and are reasonably priced even after subjected to Thai duties. Imported wines are extremely expensive and should not be automatically ordered with dinner without first checking the price. The wine may cost you more than a dinner for four. Thailand does produce a cheap local wine, but it is not of export quality and we find it primarily useful as a cooking ingredient. Each bottle tends to come in a different color—an obvious quality control problem!

ACCOMMODATIONS AND ACCESS

You may or may not have trouble finding accommodations in Thailand, depending on what time of year you plan to visit. During the past three years, hotel occupancy rates have been below normal because of the economic crisis and because of excess hotel capacity due to over-building in tourist areas. Nonetheless, Thailand's major hotels often operate near 90% occupancy, with the months of November to January being the hardest to find rooms in both Bangkok and Chiang Mai. Many hotels in Phuket are fully booked during much of the year due to both the increasing popularity of this idealic island and an overflow of tourists from the troubled islands of Indonesia.

As tourism continues to grow in the decade ahead, we expect much of the excess room capacity to decline and prices to rise in response to increased demand for accommodations. For now, you should make hotel reservations well in advance and ask about special rates or discounts. You'll discover some fabulous properties, such as the Peninsula, Regent, Shangri-La, Oriental, Sukhothai, Le Royal Meridien, Sheraton Grande Sukhumvit, and Grand Hyatt Erawan in Bangkok; the Regent Resort in Chiang Mai; and the Amanpuri and the Le Royal Meridien Phuket Yacht Club in Phuket. You can still find some terrific bargains at some of the world's most outstanding hotels in Bangkok—comparable in quality to similar properties in Tokyo, Hong Kong, Rome, Paris, or London but at half the price. Indeed, Bangkok is still a great place to splurge on a hotel that may well become one of your most memorable experiences in Thailand.

What Bangkok does offer to travelers is some of the world's finest hotels. Few other cities in the world offer such a large concentration of deluxe hotels offering the finest in service, facilities, restaurants, and shopping arcades. Bangkok's most famous hotels—Regent, Shangri-La, and Oriental—have set standards of excellence that many other newer hotels have attempted to emulate. The result is some of the finest hotels in the world, out-ranking the best of what Hong Kong or Singapore have to offer. For travelers to Bangkok, the hotel scene itself offers a unique opportunity to sample hotel amenities and experience outstanding Thai service. You can easily and quickly become a "hotel hopper" in Bangkok as you go from one hotel restaurant and shopping arcade to another.

The really good news for hotels and shoppers in Bangkok today is the new Skytrain. Most of the major hotels and shopping centers are located in close proximity to the elevated train stations. For example, Station S1 literally stops near the front door of the Regent Hotel on Rajadamri Road; Station E1 services Le Royal Meridien and Grand Hyatt Erawan hotels, World Trade Center, Gaysorn Plaza, and Amarin Plaza on Ploenchit and Rajadamri roads; Station E5 stops near the Sheraton Grande Sukhumvit Hotel and the Emporium Shopping Center on Sukhumvit Road; Station S1 stops near the Dusit Thani, Pan Pacific, and Montien hotels near Silom, Rama IV, and Suriwongse roads; and Station S6 services the Shangri-La Hotel as well as other nearby riverfront properties.

Bangkok, Chiang Mai, Ko Samui, and Phuket boast numerous hotels and guest houses, ranging from inexpensive (US$6 a day) to expensive (US$400 a day). You should have no problem finding properties that best fit both your budget and travel style.

You may wish to treat yourself to a deluxe hotel since they offer outstanding service, facilities, restaurants, and location. They also are great buys in Thailand compared to many other countries the offer comparable quality accommodations. We review several such hotels and resorts in Bangkok, Chiang Mai, Ko Samui, and Phuket in Chapters 11, 12, and 13.

ELECTRICITY AND WATER

Electricity in Thailand is 220-volts, 50 cycle AC power. Thailand uses a two-prong electrical configuration that only accepts rounded rather than flat prongs. Most major hotels have adapters for your appliances. If you use a hairdryer, take one that works with 220 volts since most adapters won't work with hairdryers. Should you need to purchase a 220 hairdryer, local departments such as Central and Robinsons, have several excellent German, Japanese, and Taiwanese models. We also recommend taking an extension cord with you. It may come in handy since electrical outlets in many Thai hotels—especially budget hotels—are often difficult to find, or they are inconveniently located in relation to the mirror you wish to use.

Tap water and ice made from tap water are not safe to consume. When in restaurants and hotels, ask for bottled water —Polaris is widely distributed and reliable—and ice made from bottled water. Most grocery stores offer a good selection of bottled water packaged in a variety of container sizes. Most water and ice served in major hotels and restaurants will be from bottled water. Rooms normally have a thermos filled with boiled or bottled water. Use this water for drinking and brushing your teeth. The municipal water systems treat the tap water, but they have yet to produce an acceptable product for travelers. Drink the local water and you'll risk suffering the consequences!

PART II

Acquiring
Unique Treasures

5

Shopping, Bargaining, and Shipping Rules

S HOPPING IN THAILAND IS AS MUCH A CULTURAL experience as it is a set of buying and selling transactions in unique commercial settings. While many of the shops, department stores, and markets may look similar to ones you shop in back home, they do have important differences you should know about prior to starting your Thailand shopping adventure. Most of these differences relate to certain shopping and pricing traditions that constitute an important set of shopping rules and bargaining skills you can and should learn before you begin making purchases in Thailand.

Many visitors to Thailand love to buy gems and jewelry as well as acquire tailoring services. These also are products and services fraught with numerous problems, from scams to poor workmanship. If you are interested in making such purchases, you should follow the special shopping rules and develop appropriate communication skills outlined in Chapter 7.

CHANGING SHOPPING SCENE

During the past ten years the shopping scene in Bangkok has changed dramatically. The quality and variety of products has improved and the number of shopping areas has expanded considerably in response to Thailand's rapidly developing economy, emerging middle class, and expanding tourist trade. Once tourists were advised to stay close to their hotels, visit the Weekend and Floating markets, frequent a few special shops catering mainly to tourists, buy Thai silk and a few trinkets normally designed for tourists, and shop for cheap prices. This has all changed during the past decade.

Surprising Bangkok and Chiang Mai are both shoppers' paradises. They have challenged such well noted Asian shopping places as Seoul, Hong Kong, Singapore, and Bali. The continuing proliferation of shops throughout Thailand is amazing. Better still, a new generation of shopkeepers, many of whom are the children of Bangkok's and Chiang Mai's successful merchants and who have been educated abroad, have opened quality shops offering product selections, designs, and colors that appeal to Western tourists who have an eye toward quality.

NEW SHOPPING CULTURE

Shopping in Thailand has undergone a major transformation in recent years. If you follow the shopping rules of ten years ago, you may be disappointed with your shopping adventure in Thailand. You will leave without really finding unique and exciting products for your wardrobe, home, or friends.

Thailand, with primarily emphasis on Bangkok and Chiang Mai, has transformed itself into an international shopper's haven. New and exciting shopping venues are being shaped for today's and tomorrow's visitors. Indeed, this is what makes Thailand one of the best kept shopping secrets in Asia.

Today the shopping choices in Thailand have increased tremendously as shopping is more and more concentrated around large shopping arcades, department stores, chic boutiques, and hotel shops with reputations for outstanding quality products and reliability. Many shops now appeal to Thai and foreign tourists alike and carry good quality products which do not have the look of "Made in Thailand For Tourists Only." Several quality shops now maintain branch stores in two or three other shopping areas in Bangkok. Some even have branch shops in Singapore, Hong Kong, the United States, and Europe—complete with export offices and mail order operations. Such changes are reflected in the overall improvement in the quality of products and the increasing presence of designs more appropriate to Western tastes. While major hotels still constitute important shopping areas, offering excellent quality goods, they are only one of many alternative areas for your shopping pleasure.

BEWARE OF WELL-MEANING ADVICE

One problem visitors to Thailand encounter is in communicating their shopping needs to Thais, many of whom do not understand Western tastes nor the dramatic changes taking place in Thailand's shopping scene. While Thais are a very polite and accommodating people who want you to have a good time in their country, they do not necessarily share your same sense of product design, style, color, and quality. They seek to please you, put their best foot forward, and show you where a *"good deal"* can be made. Often overly obsessed with getting a bargain, many Thais shop for the cheapest price rather than for the best quality products. Consequently, they frequently help you get products at a very cheap price, but the designs and quality also may look cheap.

When asked where is the best place to shop, Thais often recommend places where they shop, because they believe you must have a personal relationship with a shopkeeper in order to get the best buy. They're convinced tourists cannot get a good deal by merely walking into a shop and negotiating a price; it's best that you know someone who is a friend or relative of the shopkeeper to get the best buy. Our experience is that this belief is largely a myth on the part of many Thais who are obsessed in using personal relationships and connections in getting their way. Tourists can often do just as well—and sometimes better—on their own without the assistance of well-meaning locals who believe they are doing you a favor by "loaning" you their connections. Time and again we have received better buys on quality items than Thai friends because we walked unannounced into a shop by ourselves; shopkeepers were more willing to give deep discounts precisely because we were **not** locals; they knew we would be here today and gone tomorrow. They were less likely to do so with a local Thai who would be back tomorrow expecting the same discount! Consequently, if someone tells you it is best to go shopping with a Thai who can get you better prices, it isn't necessarily so—especially if you are willing to bargain hard.

When asked where is the best place to shop, many Thais also recommend a typical tourist shop filled with trinkets—many items you neither need nor want in your wardrobe or home. But this is their idea of a "good time" for tourists. After all, you are a tourist and they feel this is what tourists want to shop for when visiting Thailand. They feel they are helping you by showing you where to buy items real cheap rather than send you to places that are *paeng mak* ("very expensive"). Their concepts of design, color, and quality will seldom be the same as yours. As a result, many visitors to Thailand leave disappointed with their shopping experience and purchases. They have difficulty finding nice things they wish to take back home, including the much-praised Thai silk.

TOUTS, CHEATING, AND COMMISSIONS

❑ Throughout Thailand you will encounter the universal tout who preys on tourists. These are the "10-30%" men.

❑ If you are approached by a street tout, do not start a conversation. Ignore him and keep moving.

❑ Lapidaries selling gems and jewelry at inflated prices seem to be the favorite stops for touts who work as tour guides and taxi drivers.

❑ The pattern is always the same. If you are being taken to a special shop, you are indeed being "taken."

❑ If a tour guide or driver takes you to one of his or her recommended shops, at least 10%—and possibly as much as 40%—of the price you pay will go directly into the pocket of this "helpful" individual.

❑ Shops in the major hotel shopping arcades and shopping centers tend to be reputable.

❑ Your best defense is to know what you are doing—and don't be greedy!

❑ Remember, there is no such thing as a free lunch. If a deal sounds too good to be true, it probably is.

Throughout Thailand, but especially in Bangkok and Chiang Mai, you will encounter the universal tout who preys on tourists. These are the "10-30%" men—you are potentially worth from 10% to 30% to them if you buy where they take you. They approach you ostensibly to help you get a good deal on anything from buying jewelry to satisfying your sexual fantasies. They stand on corners and hang around hotels frequented by tourists. If you're holding a map or camera, some of them will innocently approach you to help you with directions. You should always avoid them.

Touts can come in many forms: taxi drivers, tour guides, hotel personnel, and others who ostensibly are helping you find a "good deal" on your purchases. These people only take you to places which give them a 10-30% commission. In fact, the problem has gotten so out of hand in Chiang Mai, especially among shops along Chiang Mai-Sankamphaeng Road, that these people demand commissions of up to 40%. Welcome to Thailand's shopping Mafia! Being taken to a shop by one of these people is no deal when you have paid their commission by purchasing an item for 10 to 40% more than you could have on your own had you not gone with this person.

If you are approached by a street tout, do not start a conversation since you already know their game and you will merely encourage them to further pester you. Keep walking and firmly say *"No, not interested today"* or *"mai ow"* which roughly translates as *"I don't want any."* It's not the nicest thing to say, but Thai touts will think you speak the local language and thus have no interest in trying to fool *"a local."* End the conversation there. If you don't, you'll be heading for trouble which you really don't need and which you may not be prepared to handle.

You also should be weary of tour guides and taxi drivers who want to end your tour or journey by giving you one "extra"—an unscheduled trip to a local factory or shop where they will give you a "very special deal." Lapidaries selling gems and jewelry at inflated prices seem to be their favorite stops. The so-called "special" is most likely you getting ripped-off and the guide getting a 10% to 20% commission on any of your purchases. If and when this "extra" is offered to you, insist that you be returned immediately to your hotel since you do not want to take advantage of this deal. You can be a little more polite and say you or your spouse are feeling very ill—and you will if you purchase something at one of these shops! It's okay to be somewhat ugly at this point: if they persist, demand a refund or threaten to report the tour guide or taxi driver to authorities. The pattern is always the same. If you are being taken to a special shop, you are indeed being "taken." Unfortunately, this same pattern—although more subtle—occurs among guides who work for some of the most respected international tour groups operating in Thailand. Everyone in the industry knows the game, including some international tour guides who participate, and most play it to their benefit. If a shopkeeper refuses to pay the commission, the tour guide boycotts the shop and takes the next group to another more cooperative shop. As a result, many of the so-called recommended shops of tour guides are not necessarily the best shops you should visit—only ones that give them kickbacks.

Remember, if a tour guide or driver takes you to one of his or her recommended shops, at least 10%—and possibly as much as 40%—of the price you pay will go directly into the pocket of this "helpful" individual. You will do everyone a favor, including yourself, if you will ditch this person as soon as possible. At this point it's okay to be obnoxious, belligerent, or an Ugly Foreigner with such human leeches. After all, you're essentially being robbed!

You may also encounter cheating, mostly petty, on occasion. The cheating will range from misrepresentation of goods, such as gems, jewelry, and antiques, to giving you the wrong change or over-charging you for hotels, meals, and transportation. While we have had few problems with cheating in Thailand, we know others who have had such problems. It usually arises when someone is trying to buy something they know little about; they purchase it from a questionable dealer or shop; or they are trying to get something for nothing. Your best defense is to know what you are doing, and don't be greedy! If, for example, you are buying gems and jewelry, know about authenticity and quality of gems and jewelry **before** you go to Thailand. This is not the time to acquire your basic gem and jewelry expertise from strangers along Bangkok's streets! Also, be careful in purchasing items off the street. Shops in the major hotel shopping arcades and shopping centers tend to be reputable. Remember, there is no such thing as a free lunch. If a deal sounds too good to be true, it probably is. When in doubt—but you still want to purchase the item—consider buying the item using your credit card. Even though you may pay a little more, in many cases your credit card company will help you should you become a victim of fraud when using their card. However, the credit card company is not obligated to do this, so be a knowledgeable consumer.

For your convenience, we've compiled in Chapter 7 useful buying advice relating to gems, jewelry, and tailored clothes. Please refer to this chapter before making any such purchases. If not, you may make several elementary shopping mistakes that could prove both disappointing and costly.

SHOPPING BY THE RULES

The structure of shopping in Thailand is such that you should make a few adjustments to the way you normally approach shopping if you are to best enjoy your shopping adventure. The most important adjustments constitute a set of 13 shopping rules we've found applicable to most Thai shopping situations:

1. **The most important shopping areas are concentrated in the central business districts and a few outlying suburban areas.**

   The best products in terms of quality, designs, and colors are found in shopping centers, hotel shopping arcades, department stores, and shophouses concentrated along one or two major streets in the central business districts of most major cities and towns. However, don't expect to find much shopping in rural areas other than at factory shops and cottage industry houses on the outskirts of Chiang Mai, Chiang Rai, Lamphun, and Lampang. Knowing these shopping patterns, it's a good idea to stay at a hotel in close proximity to the main shopping streets in the center of town. Except for Bangkok and Chiang Mai, where you should visit factories and shops outside the central business district, expect to do 90% of your shopping along a few downtown streets.

2. **Concentrate your shopping on a few shopping areas within close proximity of each other each day.**

    While it is relatively easy to get around in Bangkok, Chiang Mai, and other towns, it's best to focus your shopping in particular shopping areas rather than continuously travel from one shop to another between areas. Compile a list of shops or areas you wish to visit, locate them on a map, and each day try to visit those close to one another.

3. **Prepare to walk a great deal within each shopping area, but use transportation to go from one shopping area to another.**

    While most shops, shopping centers, and department stores are located along a few streets in the central business district, these are often very long streets requiring a considerable amount of walking. Take a good pair of walking shoes, slow your walking pace, and take taxis whenever possible.

4. **Use the Skytrain, taxis, or hotel cars when traveling within or between shopping areas.**

    Public transportation in the form of buses and trishaws are inexpensive but often inconvenient for shoppers. Given the high heat and humidity, as well as the long walking distances involved in shopping, avoid extensive walking. Our rule of thumb: *If we must walk more than one kilometer, we take the Skytrain, taxi, or boat, or we rent a hotel car and driver by the hour, half-day, or day.* However, in the case of Chiang Mai, Chiang Rai, Maesai, Lampang, Lamphun, Phuket, Ko Samui, or other places outside Bangkok, you may want to rent a car and drive yourself to the major shopping areas.

5. **Take your rain and sun gear whenever you go out.**

   Unless you know for certain the weather forecast for the day, it's always a good idea to take an umbrella—a small collapsible one is perfect—sunglasses, and hat when you go out during the day and an umbrella at night. Thailand's hot and humid climate is often unpredictable, especially during the rainy season. The umbrella keeps both the rain and sun off our heads. When we forget to take our umbrella, invariably it rains!

6. **Expect to shop in two very different shopping cultures which require different shopping skills.**

   The first world is the most familiar one for visitors—shopping centers, department stores, and hotel shopping arcades. Shops in this culture tend to have window displays, well organized interiors, and fixed prices which may or may not be all that fixed, depending on your ability to persuade shops to discount prices. The second shopping culture consists of the traditional shophouses, markets, and hawkers which tend to be somewhat disorganized and involve price uncertainty and bargaining skills. You will most likely be able to directly transfer your shopping skills to the first culture, but you may have difficulty navigating in the second shopping culture.

7. **The day and night markets can be fun places to shop, but only if you are open to new sights, sounds, and smells not normally found in other shopping sites.**

   Many of the markets combine fresh fruits, vegetables, and meats with hawker food stalls and shop stalls selling household goods. Somewhat chaotic, these markets can be very interesting and colorful places to visit. They tend to cater to a different class of local residents—lower to lower-middle—than the department stores and shopping centers. Many locals prefer shopping in the markets because prices appear cheap compared to other shopping alternatives. While these markets offer few items of interest to visitors, they do provide a cultural experience and are good places for exotic photo opportunities. Other markets primarily offer inexpensive clothes, household goods, electronics, handicrafts, jewelry, and antiques. These, too, are great places to experience the more traditional buying and selling culture. Depending on the market, you may or may not find good quality products in these places. In most markets the emphasis is on buying cheap goods. You may find inexpensive clothes, handicrafts, souvenirs, and fake products to make the trip to these markets worthwhile. Bargaining, with discounts ranging from 20 to 60%, is the only way to buy in these markets. You will be foolish to pay the first price. In Bangkok, the Chatuchak Weekend Market is most popular on Saturdays and Sundays while the night markets along Patpong and Silom roads are favorite destinations for tourists in search of inexpensive clothes, copy watches, and imitation leather goods. Chiang Mai's Night Bazaar is the center for most market shopping of interest to tourists.

8. **Most department stores and some shopping centers primarily cater to the shopping preferences of local residents rather than to foreign tourists.**

Don't expect to find a great deal of quality local products in department stores and shopping centers. Most of these places orient their product lines to the local middle-class with numerous average quality consumer products and imported goods. However, you will find a few exceptional shopping centers in Bangkok that are primarily oriented to foreign visitors and Thailand's upper class— River City Shopping Complex, Oriental Place, Peninsula Plaza, Promenade, World Trade Center, Gaysorn Plaza, and the Emporium. These are "must visit" places.

> ❑ Take a good pair of walking shoes, slow your walking place, and take taxis whenever possible.
>
> ❑ If walking more than one kilometer, take a taxi, boat, or rent a hotel car and driver.
>
> ❑ It's always a good idea to take an umbrella, sunglasses, and hat when you go out during the day.

9. **The best quality products are invariably found in the major hotel shopping arcades and a few shopping centers with reputations for quality.**

There is nothing surprising to discover that the best quality shops tend to congregate near the best quality hotels which cater to the more affluent business travelers and tourists. The shops in these places will offer a mix of expensive imported products—designer label clothes, jewelry, luggage, shoes, and accessories—as well as excellent quality local products, especially antiques, jewelry, textiles, and tailored clothes. The prices in such shops can seem high, but they offer good quality products. The "best buys" will be on high quality local products rather than on upscale imported goods that are available in many other cities and duty-free shops around the world.

10. Expect to get the best prices on locally produced items that use inexpensive labor.

Imported goods will be expensive regardless of their duty-free status. But any products that use inexpensive local labor—textiles, wood carvings, woven handicrafts, handcrafted jewelry—are excellent buys because the cost of labor is going up and many of the handcrafting skills are quickly disappearing with the onslaught of inexpensive plastic materials and machine labor.

❑ Markets tend to cater to a different class of local residents —lower to lower-middle.

❑ Bargaining, with 20-60% discounts, is the only way to buy in these markets.

❑ The best quality shops tend to congregate near the best quality hotels.

❑ You can expect prices of most goods in small shops to be negotiable.

❑ Never accept the first price offered. Always ask for a special discount.

❑ It's simply a myth that tourists can't do as well on prices as the locals.

11. Don't expect to get something for nothing.

If a price seems too good to be true, it probably is. Good quality products, especially jewelry, antiques, and art, may not seem cheap in Thailand. But they are bargains if you compare prices to similar items found in the shops of Tokyo, Sydney, Paris, London, or New York City.

12. Ask for assistance whenever you feel you need it.

At times you may feel lost and have difficulty finding particular shops or products. Whenever this happens, just ask for assistance from your hotel, shopkeepers, and others. The Thai are friendly and will assist you if they can. Hopefully you won't accidently meet a tout!

13. Don't be surprised if some shopkeepers take a great deal of your time in developing a personal and long-term relationship with you.

Business in Thailand is still a personal set of relations, regardless of all the symbols of impersonal efficiency. While some merchants may initially appear distant and suspicious, most are generally inquisitive if you will initiate a conversation that involves their family, work, or country. Many merchants in Thailand are extremely friendly, enjoy learning more about visitors, are willing to share their knowledge about their country and products, and prefer cementing personal relationships with their customers. The lines between buyer/seller may quickly fade as you develop a friendship with the shopkeeper. You may even find some shopkeepers inviting you to lunch, dinner, or their home as well as giving you special gifts. You may even feel you are being adopted by the family! This is usually a genuine expression of interest, concern, and friendship rather than a sales tactic. Such personal encounters may well become the highlights of your shopping adventure in Thailand and they may lead to lasting friendships with these individuals.

You will also discover other shopping rules as you proceed through the many shophouses, shopping centers, hotel shopping arcades, department stores, and markets in Thailand. Many of these relate to pricing policies and bargaining practices that you can and should learn if you want to become an effective shopper in Thailand.

PRICING PRACTICES AND BARGAINING

Bargaining still remains the way of shopping life in most parts of Thailand. Therefore, if you want to become an effective shopper, you need to know something about the basics of Thai bargaining.

Most North American and European tourists come from fixed-price cultures where prices are nicely displayed on items. In such cultures, the only price uncertainty may be a sales tax added to the total amount at the cash register. Only on very large-ticket items, such as automobiles, boats, houses, furniture, carpets, and jewelry, can you expect to negotiate the price. If you want to get the best deal, you must do comparative shopping as well as wait for special discounts and sales. Bargain shopping in such cultures centers on comparative pricing of items. Shopping becomes a relatively passive activity involving the examination of advertisements in newspapers and catalogs.

Expert shoppers in fixed-price cultures tend to be those skilled in carefully observing and comparing prices in the print advertising media. They clip coupons and know when the best sales are being held for particular items on certain days. They need not be concerned with cultivating personal relationships with merchants or salespeople in order to get good buys.

Like a fish out of water, expert shoppers from fixed-price cultures may feel lost when shopping in Thailand. Few of their fixed-price shopping skills are directly transferable to Thailand's shopping environments. Except for department stores and some ads in the monthly tourist literature as well as local newspapers announcing special sales, few shops advertise in the print media or on TV and radio.

COPING WITH PRICE UNCERTAINTY

Goods in Thailand fall into three pricing categories: **fixed**, **negotiable**, or **discounted**. The general trend in Bangkok is toward fixed prices on more and more goods. In the meantime, **price uncertainty**—negotiable or discounted prices—is the standard way to sell most goods and services in Thailand. The general pricing guideline is this: Unless you see a sign stating otherwise, you can expect prices of most goods in small shops to be negotiable. You can safely assume that all stated prices are the starting point from which you should receive anything from a 10% to 60% discount, depending on your haggling skills and level of commitment to obtain reduced prices.

Discount percentages in Thailand will vary for different items and from one shop to another. In general, however, expect to receive at least a 10% to 20% discount on most items in shops willing to discount. Some will discount more.

The structure of prices on certain goods and services varies. The prices on items in department stores are fixed, although the jewelry section may discount up to 20%. Prices for tailors, hairdressers, airport limousines, and medical personnel are fixed. Hotel prices are subject to a variety of discounts for different categories of travelers—VIP, business, government, weekend, and tourist.

When in doubt if a price is fixed, negotiable, or subject to discounts, **always ask for a special discount**. After the salesperson indicates the price, ask one of two questions: *"What kind of discount can you give me on this item?"* or *"What is your best price?"* Better still, ask the classic *"Is it possible?"* question: *"Is it possible to do any better on this price?"* Anything is possible in Thailand! If the person indicates a discount, you can either accept it or attempt to negotiate the price further.

While skilled shoppers in fixed-price cultures primarily compare prices by reading ads and listening to special announcements, the skilled shopper in bargaining cultures is primarily engaged in face-to-face encounters with sellers. To be most successful, the shopper must use various interpersonal skills to his or her advantage. Once you know these and practice bargaining, you should become a very effective shopper in Thailand—as well as elsewhere in Asia.

ESTABLISH VALUE AND PRICE

Not knowing the price of an item, many shoppers from fixed-price cultures face a problem. *"What is the actual value of the item? How much should I pay? At what point do I know I'm getting a fair price?"* These questions can be answered in several ways. First, you should have some idea of the **value** of the item, because you already did comparative shopping at home by examining catalogs and visiting discount houses, department stores, and specialty shops. If you are interested in a ruby or sapphire ring, for example, you should know what comparable quality jewelry sells for back home.

Second, you have done comparative shopping among the various shops you've encountered in Thailand in order to **establish a price range** for positioning yourself in the bargaining process. You've visited a department store in Bangkok to research how much a similar item is selling for at a fixed price. You've checked with a shop in your hotel and compared prices there. In your hotel you might ask *"How much is this item?"* and then act a little surprised that it appears so expensive. Tell them that you are a hotel guest and thus you want their *"very best price."* At this point the price usually decreases by 10 to 20% as you are told this is *"our very special price,"* *"our first-customer-of-the-day price,"* or *"our special hotel guest price."*

Once you initially receive a special price from your first price inquiry, you may get another 10 to 20% through further negotiation. But at this point do not negotiate any more. Take the shop's business card and record on the back the item, the original price, and the first discount price; thank the shop-keeper, and tell him or her that you may return. Repeat this same scenario in a few other shops. After doing three or four comparisons, you will establish a price range for particular items. This range will give you a fairly accurate idea of the going discount price. At this point you should be prepared to do some serious haggling, playing one shop off against another until you get the best price.

Effective shoppers in Thailand quickly learn how to comparative shop and negotiate the best deal. In learning to be

effective, you don't need to be timid, aggressive, or obnoxious
—extreme behaviors frequently exhibited by first-time practi-
tioners of the Asian art of bargaining. Although you may feel
bargaining is a defensive measure to avoid being ripped-off by
unscrupulous merchants, it is an acceptable way of doing
business in many Asian cultures. Merchants merely adjust their
profit margins to the customer, depending on how they feel
about the situation as well as their current cash flow needs. It
is up to you to adapt to such a pricing culture.

Some shopkeepers also adjust their starting prices depending
on the nationality of the customer. The current pecking order
for variable pricing by nationality seems to be the following:
highest prices for the Japanese because they are likely to think
they are still getting a good deal compared to the high prices
back home; higher starting prices for Italians because Italians
want to bargain hard; and lower starting prices for Americans
because they don't like to bargain and thus are likely to walk
away after hearing the first price if it seems too high!

One problem you may soon discover is that every situation
seems to differ somewhat, and differences between items and
shops can be significant. You can expect to receive larger
discounts on jewelry than on home furnishings. For example,
discounts on jewelry may be as great as 50% to 60% whereas
discounts on home furnishings may only be 10% to 20%.

The one major exception to bargaining concerns tailors.
Tailors normally quote you a fixed-price subject to little or no
negotiation; you merely trust that you are getting a fair price
and, after all, it is not a good idea to make your tailor unhappy
by bargaining when he doesn't want to. He may "get even" by
cheapening the quality of your clothes. Only in tailor shops do
we avoid forcing the price issue by bargaining. At best ask for
"your best price," use a common friend's name as reference, or
ask for an extra shirt, but don't risk being short-changed on
quality just to save a few dollars. If you comparative shop
among a few tailor shops, you will quickly identify what should
be the "fair market rate" for tailoring services, assuming the use
of comparable quality materials.

Our general rule on what items to bargain for is this:
**bargain on ready-made items you can carry out of the
shop**. If you must have an item custom-made, be very careful
how you arrive at the final price. In most cases you should not
bargain other than responding to the first price by asking *"Is
this your best price?"* or *"Is it possible to do better on this price?"*
Better still, drop a few names, agree on a mutually satisfactory
price, and then insist that you want top quality for that price.

Except for custom-made items, department stores, and shops

displaying a "fixed prices" sign, never accept the first price offered. Rather, spend some time going through our bargaining scenario. And in some cases so-called "fixed price" shops will also give a discount—at least it doesn't hurt to try!

Once you have accepted a price and purchased the item, be sure to **get a receipt** as well as **observe the packing process**. While few merchants will try to cheat you, some tourists have had unpleasant experiences which could have been avoided by following some simple rules of shopping in unfamiliar places.

GET THE BEST DEAL POSSIBLE

Chances are you will deal with a Thai-Chinese merchant who is a relatively seasoned businessman; he or she is a family entrepreneur who thrives on status and personal relationships. As soon as you walk through the door, most merchants will want to sell you items then and there.

The best deal you will get is when you have a personal relationship with the merchant. Contrary to what others may tell you about bargains for tourists, you often can get as good a deal—sometimes even better—than someone from the local community. It is simply a myth that tourists can't do as well on prices as the locals. Indeed, we often do better than the locals because we have done our comparative shopping and we know well the art of bargaining—something locals are often lax in doing. In addition, some merchants may give you a better price than the locals because you are *"here today and gone tomorrow."* After all, you won't be around to tell their regular customers about your very special price.

More often than not, the Thai pricing system operates like this: **If the shopkeeper likes you, or you are a friend of a friend or relative, you can expect to get a good price.** Whenever possible, drop names of individuals who referred you to the shop; the shopkeeper may think you are a friend and thus you are entitled to a special discount. But if you do not have such a relationship and you present yourself as a typical tourist who is here today and gone tomorrow, you need to bargain hard.

PRACTICE 12 RULES OF BARGAINING

The art of bargaining in Thailand can take on several different forms. In general, you want to achieve two goals in this haggling process: **establish the value of an item** and **get the best**

possible price. The following bargaining rules work well in most negotiable shopping situations.

1. Do your research before initiating the process.

Compare the prices among various shops, starting with the fixed-price items in department stores. Spot-check price ranges among shops in and around your hotel. Also, refer to your research done with catalogs and discount houses back home to determine if the discount is sufficient to warrant purchasing the item abroad.

2. Determine the exact item you want.

Select the particular item you want and then focus your bargaining around that one item without expressing excessive interest and commitment. Even though you may be excited by the item and want it very badly, once the merchant knows you are committed to buying this one item, you weaken your bargaining position. Express a passing interest; indicate through eye contact with other items in the shop that you are not necessarily committed to the one item. As you ask about the other items, you should get some sense concerning the willingness of the merchant to discount prices.

3. Set a ceiling price you're willing to pay—and buy now!

Before engaging in serious negotiations, set in your mind the maximum amount you are willing to pay, which may be 20% more than you figured the item should sell for based on your research. However, if you find something you love that is really unique, be prepared to pay more if you can afford it. In many situations you will find unique items not available anywhere else. Consider buying **now** since the item may be gone when you return. Bargain as hard as you can and then pay what you have to—even though it may seem painful—for the privilege of owning a unique item. Remember, it's only money and it only hurts once. You can always make more money, and after returning home you will most likely enjoy your wonderful purchase and forget how painful it seemed at the time to buy it at less than your expected discount. Above all, do not pass up an item you really love just because the bargaining process does not fall in your favor. It is very easy to be "penny wise but pound foolish" in Thailand simply because the bargaining process is such an ego-involved activity. You may return home forever regretting that you didn't buy a lovely item just because you were too cheap to "give" on the last US$5 of haggling. In the end, put your ego aside, give in, and buy what you really want. Only you and the merchant will know who really won, and once you return home the US$5 will seem to be such an insignificant amount. Chances are you still got a good bargain compared to what you would pay elsewhere if, indeed, you could even find a similar item!

4. **Play the role of an intelligent buyer in search of good quality and value.**

Shopping in Thailand involves playing the roles of buyer and seller. While Thais do prize individualism in certain areas of their life, they are also terrific role players, more so than Westerners. In contrast to many Western societies, where being a unique individual is emphasized, in Thailand individualism is not as highly valued. Thais learn specific sets of behaviors appropriate for the role of father, son, daughter, husband, wife, blood friend, classmate, superior, subordinate, buyer, seller. They easily shift from one role to another, undergoing major personality and behavioral changes without experiencing mental conflicts. When you encounter a Thai businessperson, you are often meeting a very refined and sophisticated role player. Therefore, it is to your advantage to play complementary roles by carefully structuring your personality and behavior to play the role of buyer. If you approach sellers by just "being yourself"—open, honest, somewhat naive, and with your own unique personality—you may be quickly walked over by a seasoned seller. Once you enter a shop, think of yourself as an actor walking on stage to play the lead role as a shrewd buyer, bargainer, and trader. But at the same time, you may encounter a very individualistic shopkeeper who unpredictably decides to give you a special gift or invite you to dinner just because he or she likes you.

5. **Establish good will and a personal relationship.**

A shrewd buyer also is charming, polite, personable, and friendly. You should have a sense of humor, smile, and be light-hearted during the bargaining process. But be careful about eye contact which can be threatening to Thais. Keep it to a minimum. Thai sellers prefer to establish a personal relationship so that the bargaining process can take place on a friendly, face-saving basis. In the end, both the buyer and seller should come out as winners. This can not be done if you approach the buyer in very serious and harsh terms. You should start by exchanging pleasantries concerning the weather, your trip, the city, or the nice items in the shop. After exchanging business cards or determining your status, the shopkeeper will know what roles should be played in the coming transaction.

6. **Let the seller make the first offer.**

If the merchant starts by asking you *"How much do you want to pay?"*, always avoid answering this rather dangerous set-up question. He who reveals his hand first is likely to lose in the end. Immediately turn the question around: *"How much are you asking?"* Remember, many merchants try to get you to pay as much as you are willing and able to pay—not what the value of the item is or what he or she is willing to take. You should never reveal your ability or willingness to pay a certain price. Keep the seller guessing, thinking that you may lose interest or not buy the item because it appears too expensive. Always get the merchant to initiate the bargaining process. In so doing, the merchant must take the defensive as you shift to the offensive.

7. **Take your time, being deliberately slow in order to get the merchant to invest his or her time in you.**

The more you indicate that you are impatient and in a hurry, the more you are likely to pay. When negotiating a price, **time** is usually in your favor. Many shopkeepers also see time as a positive force in the bargaining process. Some try to keep you in their shop by serving you tea, coffee, soft drinks, or liquor while negotiating the price. Be careful; this nice little ritual may soften you somewhat on the bargaining process as you begin establishing a more personal relationship with the merchant. The longer you stay in control prolonging the negotiation, the better the price should be. Although some merchants may deserve it, **never** insult them. Merchants need to "keep face" as much as you do in the process of giving and getting the very best price.

8. **Use odd numbers in offering the merchant at least 40% less than what he or she initially offers.**

   Avoid stating round numbers, such as 700B, 1800B, or 10,000B. Instead, offer 620B, 1735B, or 8100B. Such numbers impress upon others that you may be a seasoned haggler who knows value and expects to do well in this negotiation. Your offer will probably be 15% less than the value you determined for the item. For example, if the merchant asks 2500B, offer 1530B, knowing the final price should probably be 1800B. The merchant will probably counter with only a 10% discount—2250B. At this point you will need to go back and forth with another two or three offers and counter-offers.

9. **Appear a little disappointed and then take your time again.**

   Never appear upset or angry with the seller. Keep your cool at all times by slowly sitting down and carefully examining the item. Shake your head a little and say, *"Gee, that's too bad. That's much more than I had planned to spend. I like it, but I really can't go that high."* Appear to be a sympathetic listener as the seller attempts to explain why he or she cannot budge more on the price. Make sure you do not accuse the merchant of being a thief! Use a little charm, if you can, for the way you conduct the bargaining process will affect the final price. This should be a civil negotiation in which you nicely bring the price down, the seller "saves face," and everyone goes away feeling good about the deal.

10. **Counter with a new offer at a 35% discount.**

    Punch several keys on your calculator, which indicates you are doing some serious thinking. Then say something like *"This is really the best I can do. It's a lovely item, but 1625B is really all I can pay."* At this point the merchant will probably counter with a 20% discount—2000B.

11. **Be patient, persistent, and take your time again by carefully examining the item.**

    Respond by saying *"That's a little better, but it's still too much. I want to look around a little more."* Then start to get up and look toward the door. At this point the merchant has invested some time in this exchange, and he or she is getting close to a possible sale. The merchant will either let you walk out the door or try to stop you with another counter-offer. If you walk out the door, you can always return to get the 2000B price. But most likely the merchant will try to stop you, especially if there is still some bargaining room. The merchant is likely to say: *"You don't want to waste your time looking elsewhere. I'll give you the best price anywhere—just for you. Okay, 1900B. That's my final price."*

12. Be creative for the final negotiation.

You could try for 1800B, but chances are 1900B will be the final price with this merchant. Yet, there may still be some room for negotiating "extras." At this point, get up and walk around the shop and examine other items; try to appear as if you are losing interest in the item you were bargaining for. While walking around, identify a 100B item you like which might make a nice gift for a friend or relative, which you could possibly include in the final deal. Wander back to the 100B item and look as if your interest is waning and perhaps you need to leave. Then start to probe the possibility of including extras while agreeing on the 1900B: *"Okay, I might go 1900B, but only if you include this with it."* The "this"" is the 100B item you eyed. You also might negotiate with your credit card. Chances are the merchant is expecting cash on the 1900B discounted price and will add a 2 to 6% "commission" if you want to use your credit card. In this case, you might respond to the 1900B by saying, *"Okay, I'll go with the 1900B, but only if I can use my credit card."* You may get your way, your bank will float you a loan in the meantime, and your credit card company may help you resolve the problem in case you later learn your purchase was misrepresented. Finally, you may want to negotiate packing and delivery processes. If it is a fragile item, insist that it be packed well so you can take it with you on the airplane or have it shipped. If your purchase is large, insist that the shop deliver it to your hotel or to your shipper. If the shop is shipping it by air or sea, try to get them to agree to absorb some of the freight and insurance costs.

This very slow, civil, methodical, and sometimes charming approach to bargaining works well in most cases. However, Thai merchants do differ in how they respond to situations and many of them are unpredictable, depending on whether or not they like you. In some cases, your timing may be right: the merchant is in need of cash flow that day and thus he or she is willing to give you the price you want, with little or no bargaining. Others will not give more than a 10% to 20% discount unless you are a friend of a friend who is then eligible for the special "family discount." And others are not good businessmen, are unpredictable, lack motivation, or are just moody; they refuse to budge on their prices even though your offer is fair compared to the going prices in other shops. In these situations it is best to leave the shop and find one which is more receptive to the traditional haggling process.

BARGAIN FOR NEEDS, NOT GREED

One word of caution for those who are just starting to learn the fine art of Thai bargaining. **Be sure you really want an item before you initiate the bargaining process**. Many tourists quickly learn to bargain effectively, and then get carried away with their new-found skill. Rather than use this skill to get what they want, they enjoy the process of bargaining so much that they buy many unnecessary items. After all, they got such "a good deal" and thus could not resist buying the item. Be very careful in getting carried away with your new-found competency. You do not need to fill your suitcases with junk in demonstrating this ego-gratifying skill. If used properly, your new bargaining skills will lead to some excellent buys on items you really need and want.

EXAMINE YOUR GOODS CAREFULLY

Before you commence the bargaining process, carefully examine the item, being sure that you understand the quality of the item for which you are negotiating. Then, after you settle on a final price, make sure you are getting the goods you agreed upon. You should carefully observe the handling of items, including the actual packing process. If at all possible, take the items with you when you leave. If you later discover you were victimized by a switch or misrepresentation, contact the Tourism Authority of Thailand as well as your credit card company if you charged your purchase. You should be able to resolve the problem through these channels. However, the responsibility is on you, the buyer, to know what you are buying.

BEWARE OF SCAMS

Although one hopes this will never happen, you may be unfortunate in encountering unscrupulous merchants who take advantage of you. This is more likely to happen if you wander away from recommended shops in discovering your own "very special" bargains or enter the *"Hey, you mister"* shops. While we have never had these problems happen to us, we do know others who have had such misfortunes. The most frequent scams to watch out for include:

1. **Switching the goods.** You negotiate for a particular item, such as a piece of jewelry or a blouse, but in the process of packing it, the merchant substitutes an inferior product.

2. **Misrepresenting quality goods.** Be especially cautious in jewelry, leather, and antique shops. Sometimes so-called expensive watches are excellent imitations and worth no more than US$15—or have cheap mechanisms inside expensive cases. Leather briefcases, purses, and belts are often fake leathers or leather of very poor quality. Precious stones, such as rubies, may not be as precious as they appear. Synthetic stones, garnets, or spinels are sometimes substituted for high quality rubies. Some substitutes are so good that experts even have difficulty identifying the difference. Accordingly, you may pay US$2,000 for what appears to be a ruby worth over US$10,000 back home, but in fact you just bought a US$25 red spinel! Pearls come in many different qualities, so know your pearls before negotiating a price. Real jade and ivory are beautiful, but many buyers unwittingly end up with green plastic, soapstone, or bone at jade and ivory prices. In fact, since it is now illegal to bring ivory into the U.S., you are really better off with carved bone—but at bone prices! The antique business is relatively unregulated. Some merchants try to sell "new antiques" at "old antique" prices. Many of the fakes are outstanding reproductions, often fooling even the experts. Better still, there is a reputable business in fakes. You may want to just shop for fakes!

3. **Goods not included in the package(s) you carry with you.** You purchase several items in one shop. The seller wraps them and presents them to you, but "forgot" to

include one of the items you paid for. You've become distracted in the process of paying for everything and talking with the shopkeeper to the point of forgetting to check your package(s) carefully.

4. **Goods not shipped.** The shop may agree to ship your goods home, but once you leave they, conveniently forget to do so. You wait and wait, write letters of inquiry, fax, make phone calls, and e-mail the shop; no one can give you a satisfactory response. Unless you have shipping and insurance documents, which is unlikely, and proper receipts, you may not receive the goods you paid for.

Your best line of defense against these and other possible scams is to be very careful wherever you go and whatever you do in relation to handling money. A few simple precautions will help avoid some of these problems:

1. **Do not trust anyone with your money** unless you have proper assurances they are giving you exactly what you agreed upon. Trust is something that should be earned— not automatically given to friendly strangers you may like.

2. **Do your homework** so you can determine quality and value as well as anticipate certain types of scams.

3. **Examine the goods carefully,** assuming something may be or will go wrong.

4. **Watch very carefully how the merchant handles items** from the moment they leave your hands until they get wrapped and into a bag.

5. **Request receipts** that list specific items and the prices you paid. Although most shops are willing to "give you a receipt" specifying whatever price you want them to write for purposes of deceiving Customs, be careful in doing so. While you may or may not deceive Customs, your custom-designed receipt may become a double-edge sword, especially if you later need a receipt with the real price to claim your goods or a refund. If the shop is to ship, be sure you have a shipping receipt which also includes insurance against both loss and damage.

6. **Take photos of your purchases.** We strongly recommend taking photos of your major purchases, especially

anything that is being entrusted to someone else to be packed and shipped. Better still, take a photo of the seller holding the item, just in case you later need to identify the person with whom you dealt. This photo will give you a visual record of your purchase should you later have problems receiving your shipment, from being lost or damaged. You'll also have a photo to show Customs should they have any questions about the contents of your shipment.

7. **Patronize shops that are affiliated with the Tourism Authority of Thailand.** They are more likely to treat you honestly since the parent organization does somewhat police its members.

8. **Protect yourself against scams by using credit cards** for payment, especially for big ticket items which could present problems, even though using them may cost you a little more.

If you are victimized, all is not necessarily lost. You should report the problem immediately to the Tourism Authority of Thailand, the police, your credit card company, or insurance company. While inconvenient and time consuming, nonetheless, in many cases you will eventually get satisfactory results.

USE RELIABLE SHIPPERS

Shipping from Bangkok is relatively convenient although it can be expensive. If you see something you really love, don't worry about getting it back home. Shops and shippers can arrange air or sea transportation. It only takes money—not your time.

Most shops will pack your goods and take care of all documents necessary for exporting, insurance, and customs.

If you buy several items from different shops, you can request that one of the shops consolidate your shipments or arrange for the consolidation yourself. Expatriates in Thailand regularly use several shippers with confidence:

❑ **Hong Kong Transpack:** 59/44 Soi 26, Sukhumvit Road (Tel. 259-0085 or 258-6676; Fax 259-4943).

❑ **JVK International Movers Ltd.:** 222 Krungthep Kreethap (Tel. 379-4646 or 379-4643; Fax 379-5050).

❑ **Thai International Moving & Storage Co. Ltd.**: 279 Soi Narasri, 21 Ramkamhaeng, Hua Mark (Tel. 314-2520; Fax 319-8238).

❑ **Schenker (Thai) Ltd.**: 3683 Rama IV Road, Klongtoey (Tel. 259-7640 thru 51).

Be sure to insure your shipment for both loss and damage. Get all receipts, including a packing list. Normally a sea shipment from Bangkok takes about 8 weeks. However, one of our shipments took about 14 weeks due to unexpected delays with the shipping line that went bankrupt while on the high seas! Other shipments have only taken 4-5 weeks.

6

Major Shopping Choices

THAILAND OFFERS A WONDERFUL ARRAY OF PRO-
ducts and services for discriminating shoppers. While
Hong Kong and Singapore are excellent destinations for
acquiring electronics, jewelry, clothes, and accessories,
Thailand's strengths are in the areas of arts, crafts, antiques,
home furnishings, textiles, gems, and jewelry. Thailand's long
and proud traditions in the arts and crafts continue today in the
numerous factories and shops of Bangkok and Chiang Mai. The
Royal Court continues to promote many of the arts and crafts
as do the many families that produce quality products for the
growing tourist and export markets.

SHOPPING STRENGTHS

Thai product markets are constantly changing. Quality, selection, and styles are being continually upgraded, and new shops
and shopping arcades offering unique quality items regularly
spring up and expand in many different areas of both Bangkok
and Chiang Mai.

Thailand's shopping scene seems to transform itself every
five years with new offerings and services. While only a few

years ago Thailand was well known for several typical tourist items—lacquerware, silk, bronzeware, hilltribe handicrafts, woodcarved elephants, precious and semi-precious stones, and temple rubbings—today Thailand offers a dazzling array of additional goods ranging from gorgeous antiques, handicrafts, and home decorative items to dazzling jewelry, designer clothes, and chic accessories. Thailand is well on its way to becoming a world-class shopping center. In fact, it remains one of the best kept shopping secrets in Asia.

Thailand's major shopping strengths for uniqueness, quality, and value include the following products:

- silk and cotton fabrics
- tailored and ready-made clothes
- gems and jewelry
- silver and nielloware
- bronzeware, brassware, and pewterware
- celadon, ceramics, and pottery
- leather goods
- handmade wood and rattan furniture
- paintings, sculptures, and framing
- antiques from Thailand, Myanmar, and Cambodia
- woodcarvings
- handicraft items
- fake designer clothes, watches, and accessories

For discriminating shoppers, Thailand's major strengths are in the areas of decorative items, home furnishings, antiques, handicrafts, gems, and jewelry. Craft work involving extensive fine hand work tends to be a good buy in Thailand. Handmade items from copies of originals are especially good values in Thailand. Thai clothes are plentiful and inexpensive, but they are often disappointing in terms of quality and style, particularly if you have already seen the wonderful selections in Hong Kong. Thailand has yet to adequately respond to Western shopping tastes for clothes with talented designers who understand current Western preferences for particular colors, designs, and quality. While this situation is improving, Thailand will have to make some major changes before becoming a major international market for these goods. Thai design talent tends to be found in the fields of architecture, interior design, crafts, and jewelry rather than in clothes that must compete with major Western designers. Although Thai silk, cotton, tailored clothes, ready-made clothes, and shoes may be good buys and look lovely on many Thai women, they are no bargain if they are inappropriate for your wardrobe back home.

THAI SILK AND COTTON

Thai silk and cotton are world famous, at least according to what you hear in Bangkok. But there is much more to this story if you are particular about your clothes. Thai silk has a rough quality and is heavier than silks found in many other countries. The colors are often very bright and patterns are somewhat traditional—often a floral or flame pattern. The unique *mutmee* silk produced in Northeast Thailand is a rough material with a particular geometric design and is normally produced in muted colors. Most Thai silk is purchased by the meter or yard from which to make tailored dresses, blouses, shirts, suits, and ties.

When worn by Thai women on festive occasions, the Thai silk looks gorgeous. And for one very good reason. The bright colors contrast nicely with the dark hair and golden-toned skins of the Thai who generally tend to have coloring enhanced by these powerful, bright colors. However, less than one-third of Western tourists have coloring complimented by very bright colors. Thai silks and cottons offered by many shops continue to overpower the coloring of many Western tourists.

Many tourists purchase Thai silks and cottons, because they look so beautiful in Thailand. But once they return home, some become disappointed with their clothing purchases. Many of the colors and patterns are not stylish for Western countries decorating preferences nor for one's personal coloring. The fabrics tend to be too heavy for many clothing styles. Indeed, blouses and shirts tend to be very stiff, lacking the grace and elegance associated with the lighter weight Chinese, French, or Italian silks. But Thai silks do work well for evening dresses as long as the skirt is not too full. They also are great for caftans and robes, and are far superior to the lighter weight Chinese silk for home decorating items, such as bedspreads, pillow covers, and frame mats for paintings and carved pieces. As with any silk, Thai silks can be difficult to care for. The colors may run and they may require dry cleaning.

Thai silks and cottons are excellent for decorative items and home furnishings. They are beautiful when used for upholstering sofas and chairs or when made into draperies, pillow covers, napkins, placemats, wall hangings, jewelry boxes, picture frames, and a variety of custom-made handicrafts. If you purchase paintings, antiques, or other items you wish to have framed, the very rough quality Thai silk makes an inexpensive and beautiful framing mat. Many art and framing shops will do this custom work to your specifications. Ironically, standard paper mat selections are very limited in Thailand because they must be imported. Duties on such imports discourage shops from carrying large selections and inventories. But the shops can make gorgeous mats using your choice of silk fabric for very reasonable cost. For art connoisseurs, this is one of the best buys found anywhere in the world. In fact, we often take our purchases from the United States, Hong Kong, Myanmar, Indonesia, and other countries to have them uniquely framed in Bangkok using the Thai silk.

If you wish to purchase stylish Thai silk clothes or fabric for tailor-made clothes, you only need to visit one shop in Bangkok—the **Jim Thompson Silk Company** at 9 Suriwongse Road. This is Thailand's premier silk shop. They sell silk by the meter as well as have a large selection of lovely ready-made clothes for both men and women, pillow covers, matching placemats and napkins, jewelry boxes, picture frames, bags, scarves, neckties, and a variety of other silk items. Their silk prices are some of the highest in Thailand, but you get outstanding quality products for your money. We strongly recommend this shop, because it offers high quality silk. Its talented designers have developed very creative and elegant designs, and their selection of colors are more appropriate for Western homes and clothing than what is found in many silk shops. Jim Thompson's also has

❑ Thailand's major strengths are in the areas of decorative items, home furnishings, antiques, handicrafts, gems, and jewelry.

❑ Thai design talent tends to be found in the fields of architecture, interior design, crafts, and jewelry rather than in clothes.

❑ For many tourists, clothing purchases may be disappointing. Many of the colors and patterns are not stylish for Western countries. Fabrics tend to be too heavy for many clothing styles.

❑ Expect to find ready-made clothes with a decided adolescent look and which are either too bright or too muted in color.

an excellent selection of Thai cottons, upholstery materials, and neckpiece accessories for coordinating your wardrobe. There are also branch shops in the Oriental Hotel, Grand Hyatt Erawan Hotel, Royal Orchid Sheraton Hotel, World Trade Center, and the Emporium shopping center. A few other shops, such as **Design Thai** (304 Silom Road), **Anita Thai Silk** (294/4-5 Silom Road), **Khanitha** (Oriental Place, River City Shopping Complex, and Suriwongse Road), and **Shinawatra** (corner of Sathorn Tai Road and Soi Suan Phlu) also offer quality silk and cotton. **Paya** (961 Suhkumvit Road, between Soi 51 and 53) is especially good for cotton fabrics, rugs, pillows, comforters, napkins, and placemats.

Even if you are not interested in Thai silk, you should visit the Jim Thompson Silk Company just to observe their exquisite materials and designs, examine their home decorative department, experience professional Thai service, and make at least a small purchase just to get one of their gorgeous shopping bags or boxes! You also should explore the building behind the main shop which is devoted to home decorative items, many of which incorporate Jim Thompson silk.

Tailor-Made Clothes

If you purchase Thai silk or cotton for tailor-made clothes, you should be very selective in who makes your clothes. A great deal of the tailoring in Thailand lacks the smooth clean lines and fits associated with quality tailoring found in Hong Kong. The cuts and pressing tend to produce clothes that lack a first-class look. Some look old-fashioned and rumpled. If you plan to visit Hong Kong after Thailand, you may want to take your material with you to have your clothes made there.

If you want to have clothes made in Thailand, follow our shopping advice in Chapter 7 in order to ensure quality tailoring services. Stay near the hotel tailor shops and be sure to take with you a picture, or an example, of what you want made. Thai tailors are very good at copying styles from pictures, although they may not get all the details right. If you have a suit made, insist on three fittings and be sure the item fits right before accepting it. If you have a man's suit made, check to be sure the tailor specializes in men's suits. Some tailors primarily work with women's clothes and occasionally will do a man's suit. The tailoring skills are not the same. As you quickly discover, you tend to get what you pay for. On the other hand, many visitors to Thailand have been pleasantly surprised with their inexpensive 24-hour tailors!

Some of Bangkok's best men's tailors include **Adam's Tailor** (23/3 Thaniya Road, Tel. 233-7857 and Charn Issara Tower), **C. Fillipo** (Shangri-La and Hilton hotels), and **Perry's** (60/2 Silom Road, Tel. 233-9236). Bangkok's best seamstress is probably **Penny's Boutique** (Peninsula Plaza). They have an excellent selection of Thai, Chinese, French, and Italian silks and do quality work. A surprisingly good quality and inexpensive seamstress has been **Michelle 2** (2nd Floor, Amarin Plaza, Tel. 256-9047). The cheapest tailors in town, which offer seemingly unbelievable deals, are found along Sukhumvit Road, especially near the Ambassador Hotel at Soi 11. Many of these shops promise to produce a package of suits, shirts, trousers, and ties for men or a suit, dress, blouses, and skirts for women for only US$130! You'll see their full-page ads in several of the major tourist publications.

If you are looking for some truly unique clothes, you may want to examine hilltribe clothes which are being made into popular designs and sold in boutiques. Stop at the **Golden Triangle** (3rd floor, River City Shopping Complex, Tel. 234-9365, ext. 301) and **Prayer** (197 Phyathai Road, at Siam Centre, Tel. 251-7549).

READY-MADE CLOTHES

The Thai garment industry has been growing by leaps and bounds during the past decade. You will find Thai ready-made clothes in small shops, department stores, markets, and sidewalk stalls and tables, especially in the **Pratunam Market** adjacent to the Indra Hotel on Rajaparop Road, along **Pahurat Road** in Chinatown, at the night markets along **Patpong** and **Silom** Roads, and in the **Chatuchak Weekend Market**. Many of the ready-made clothes in the markets and sold by street vendors, such as polo shirts, are fakes produced under designer labels. These are inexpensive imitations, but the quality tends to be poor. Many tourists like to buy these as gift items, similar to imitation Rolex and Cartier watches and Gucci bags. However, many of these garments deteriorate after a few washings.

Except for ready-made clothes found at Jim Thompson Silk Company and a few other quality shops (Design Thai, Khanitha, Choisy, Ajai Zecha/A Cha) we have not been attracted to Thai ready-made clothes. The designs and colors are unusual and inappropriate for our wardrobes. These clothes are primarily designed for local consumption and do not fit most Westerners. Indeed, Thais in general do not share the same sense of color and design as Westerners. Although neat and pretty as separate pieces, few pieces seem to go together. Expect to find ready-made clothes with a decided adolescent look and which are either too bright or too muted in color.

If you're interested in imported designer label clothes, be sure to visit the Emporium, Gaysorn Plaza, World Trade Center, Peninsula Plaza, and Sogo at Amarin Plaza. Here you'll find such famous names as DKNY, Gucci, MCM, Chanel, Versace, Hermes, Christian Dior, Escada, Celine, Kenzo, Prada, Valentino, Pierre Cardin, and Max Mara.

GEMS AND SEMI-PRECIOUS STONES

Thailand offers some of the world's best values on precious and semi-precious stones. The best buys are found on Thai sap-

phires—available predominately in blue or black in either star
or plain cabochon—or various shades of blue in faceted cuts.
Zircons, garnets, cat's eye, jadeite, nephrite, tiger eye, and
turquoise are also widely available. Another excellent buy are
rubies from Myanmar and Cambodia, but make sure you do
not buy an inexpensive spinel at ruby prices! Many visitors to
Thailand report being cheated on gem purchases. Most, however, create their own self-fulfilling prophecy: they don't know
what they are doing; they are greedy, trying to get something
for nothing; they buy at shops where tour guides, taxi drivers,
or touts take them; or they frequent fast-talking and questionable dealers. Sadly, some write to us asking us to warn other
visitors about this "problem with Thailand." The problem is
not Thailand. Rather, the problem is the naive shopper who
should have known better than to shop in such questionable
places and entrust large sums of money to strangers!

Thailand is also doing a great deal of diamond cutting. More
and more diamonds at good prices should be appearing on the
Thai market as Thailand attempts to become one of the world's
largest diamond cutting centers.

Many visitors prefer to buy loose cut stones and have them
set in Hong Kong or at home. Others prefer to have the stones
set in Bangkok according to their own designs. Most buyers
report savings of 75% on Thai stones compared to similar ones
back home. The quality of the stones, cuts, and settings will
vary from excellent to poor, so be sure you know your stones
and examine them carefully. Several lapidaries in Bangkok
provide tours of their factories. The Tourist Authority of
Thailand lists several recommended establishments which are
supposed to adhere to fair business practices. Some of the most
reliable include **Thai Lapidary** (277/122 Rama I Road,
Tel. 214-2641), **Uthai's Gems** (28/7 Soi Ruam Rudee, Tel.
253-8582), **Gems Gallery International** (Rama 6 Road, Tel.
271-0150), and **New Universal** (1144-46 New Road, Tel. 234-
3514). Many others are found at the new center for diamonds,
gems, and jewelry located 30 kilometers east of Bangkok—
Gemopolis. Most of the Gemopolis shops and factories are
members of the Jewel Fest Club which is sponsored by the Thai
Gem and Jewel Traders Association. Make sure you bargain for
all of these purchases. Avoid the touts, tour guides, and taxi
drivers who steer you to particular shops. In 99% of the cases
they will receive a commission on everything you purchase, and
they will not take you to the most reputable shops.

We cannot over-stress the importance of knowing what you
are doing when you purchase gems and jewelry in Thailand.
Always patronize reputable shops, many of which are located in

five-star hotels. If you don't, you may join the growing list of individuals who report getting swindled on such purchases.

GOLD AND SILVER

Thailand offers excellent buys on gold and silver. If you wish to buy pure gold, visit a Chinese gold shop and ask for the near pure 24-carat gold "Baht Bracelet" or rings. These are convenient ways to buy gold. The gold is sold at the market rate, and you pay primarily for the gold content—not the craftsmanship that goes into making the bracelets or rings. A small mark-up over the price of the gold is normally equivalent to what you would pay over the daily gold price for a new U.S. gold coin.

Gold jewelry can be purchased in different karats. Thais tend to prefer 18-karat (785), although they can make jewelry any karat you want, and some willingly stamp any karat designation you wish to appear on your jewelry.

Since Thai craft labor is so inexpensive, one of the best values is to have your gold jewelry made or repaired in Thailand. If you need to have a wedding ring or bracelet rebuilt, for example, take it to Thailand. You'll be pleased with the price and the workmanship. Thai craftsmen are excellent in copying designs, and the quality of workmanship can be outstanding. Make sure you take pictures of your preferred designs with you so the craftsmen have a model from which to work.

For wonderfully designed gold jewelry, some in beautiful ethnic designs, be sure to visit two upscale jewelry shops in the Peninsula Plaza: **Among Gallery** and **Chailai**.

Lovely yellow and white gold-dipped flowers are widely available in both Bangkok and Chiang Mai. The **Royal Orchid Company** of Chiang Mai, as well as several imitators, produce and distribute these flowers as pins, earrings, and neckpieces. Made from a fascinating nickel, copper, and gold dipping and plating process, this jewelry is relatively inexpensive and it makes lovely trip gifts.

Silver is also widely available in Thailand. The silver is produced in traditional and modern designs as rings, bracelets, earrings, necklaces, accessories, cups, bowls, and a variety of handicraft forms. The workmanship is relatively good, and the intricate traditional designs are truly unique. In Chiang Mai you will find thinly hammered silver bowls with raised Buddhist figures as well as a wide selection of silver hilltribe jewelry. Silver is also used in making Thai nielloware—decorative items produced by a unique Thai silver inlaid process.

JEWELRY AND ACCESSORIES

Thai jewelry shops are not as dazzling as those in Hong Kong, but they offer as good, if not better, value. Many pearls, for example, come from Phuket in the south. Other pearls must be imported into Thailand and are subject to duties.

We have been surprised to find comparable quality pearls to be better priced in Bangkok than in Hong Kong. But you must shop around in Bangkok to find such pearls. **Tok Kwang** (shops at the Regent Hotel and the Emporium Shopping Center) is probably the best place for top quality pearls, especially pearl clasps. If you buy loose pearls in Hong Kong, you may want to have them strung in Bangkok. Again, take a picture of what design you want. If you want a fancy clasp, you may wish to take a clasp with you since selections in Bangkok are limited. Alternatively, you may wish to have the pearls strung at home where you also will find a better selection of clasps. In the case of the U.S., loose or temporarily strung natural pearls without a clasp enter duty free. If permanently or temporarily strung with an attached or separate clasp, you must pay a 6.5 to 11% duty.

❑ Thailand offers some of the world's best values on precious and semi-precious stones.

❑ Thailand offers excellent buys on gold and silver.

❑ The best quality jewelry, with styles appropriate for Westerners, will be found in shops around the major hotels.

❑ Bronzeware tarnishes, is not dishwasher approved, and is a constant headache to keep clean and spotless. If you buy bronzeware, ask for the "nickle bronze" version.

Jewelry shops in Bangkok offer a wide variety of quality jewelry. There are excellent shops; however, many stores offer mediocre jewelry. The designs look old-fashioned and the stones and settings are often poor quality. Part of the problem is that many shops are largely patronized by local Chinese and Thai who are satisfied with the traditional styles and workmanship, and who purchase jewelry, in part, as an investment. This is particularly true of the numerous jewelry shops found in the Chinatown area in and around Yaowarat and Charoen Krung roads.

The best quality jewelry, with styles appropriate for Westerners, will be found in shops around the major hotels. The Dusit Thani, Regent, Oriental, Hilton, Royal Orchid Sheraton, and the Grand Hyatt Erawan hotels, for example, have a few high quality jewelry shops. **The Emporium, Peninsula Plaza, Oriental Place, Charn Issara Tower, Amarin Plaza**, and the **World Trade Center** have several jewelry shops offering exquisite designs and outstanding quality. Many of these shops are patronized by very wealthy Thai and Chinese and foreign tourists who seek international quality jewelry. For examples of some of the best quality jewelry available in Thailand, visit **Blue River Diamond, Karat, Jaa, Petch Boran, Florentine, Franks, Tok Kwang, Pendulum** on the ground floor of the Emporium; **Frank's, Bualaad,** and **Paa** at the Peninsula Plaza; **Yves Joaillier** and **Valda Jewelry** at the Charn Issara Tower; **Alex & Co.** along Oriental Lane; **Sincere Jewelry** on Silom Road and Sukhumvit Road; **D. Diamonds** in the Amarin Plaza; **Peninsula Gems, Lotus Jewellery,** and **Tok Kwang** at the Regent Hotel; **The Collection, The Original,** and **J.P. Jewelry** in the Hilton Hotel; and **Cosmos Jewelry** in the Royal Orchid Sheraton Hotel. **Uthai's Gems** (28/7 Soi Ruam Rudee, Tel. 253-8582) has been popular among expatriates for over two decades. Although Uthai tends to carry smaller and less expensive jewelry than many of the other shops mentioned, he is able to fabricate jewelry "made to order" for clients. The new gem city, **Gemopolis,** is heavily promoted with tourists. **Naga House** (315 Soi Ongkarak, Samsen Road 28, Dusit, Tel. 669-3416) also is popular with upscale tourists who also want a cultural experience in this unique shop's lovely residential setting. Numerous other shops in or near the Shangri-La, Oriental, Royal Orchid Sheraton, Narai, Dusit Thani, Regent, Grand Hyatt Erawan, Le Meridien President, Siam Inter-Continental, Montien, Indra, and Ambassador hotels offer good quality jewelry. Be sure to bargain in all of these shops.

Several Thai shops are beginning to develop accessories in the form of neckpieces and belts using gold, silver, semi-precious stones, and leather. The designs and varieties are still limited, but the prices are relatively reasonable. Some of the best selections and designs are found at **Jim Thompson Silk Company, Tabtim Thai** (Author's Lounge, Oriental Hotel), and **Bee Bejour** (lower level of the Grand Hyatt Erawan Hotel).

The **Royal Orchid Company** produces inexpensive neckpieces which include yellow or white gold dipped flowers with a variety of semi-precious stones. If you visit Chiang Mai, you can stop at their headquarters (9 Charoen Muang Road) and buy from their selection or arrange to have pieces custom-designed to your specifications. Be sure to take pictures or designs with you as well as clasps. Since most clasps must be imported into Thailand and are thus subject to heavy duties, the clasp selection is very limited and some styles are difficult to open and close. We also recommend taking your own stringing materials, especially if you require a color other than white. The quality and color selection of stringing material is very limited in Thailand.

You should watch the local English-language newspaper or ask at your hotel if any gem shows are scheduled in Bangkok during your stay. These shows provide a wonderful overview of good quality gems, jewelry, and accessories available in shops throughout Thailand. You can make purchases at these shows. Again, be sure to bargain.

COPY WATCHES

Bangkok is one of the best places to buy copies of name brand watches. These watches become many tourists' favorite and most memorable purchases. You'll have fun meeting some local entrepreneurs, shopping in a festive setting, practicing your bargaining skills, and feeling you got a real deal without spending much money. This may well become your favorite form of cheap street evening entertainment in Bangkok! After all, where else can you buy a good copy of a $5,000 Rolex for only $35, find that it actually runs better than your $300 watch? And where else can you shop on the black market with relative ease, safety, and confidence of getting a good deal? These purchases are as much fun to make as the products are to wear!

Most of the copy watches in Bangkok are produced in Taiwan, Hong Kong, or Japan, but they often cost less in Bangkok than in the countries of origin. A wide selection of well-known brand name traditional and designer men's and women's styles are available: Rolex, Cartier, Gucci, Patek Philippe, and many more. Many of the watches have excellent Seiko mechanisms. They are good copies that may fool all but the experts or connoisseurs who know that Rolex Oyster watches do not have quartz mechanisms! Most of these watches cost between $12 and $35 and they make fun gifts for friends and relatives. The leather bands—though often fake—on some watches alone are worth the price of the watch.

But before you buy one of these watches, you should be aware of certain potential problems:

- **Not all copy watches are the same quality**. The ones made in Taiwan are reputed to be better than those from Hong Kong or Japan. The best you can do is to ask before buying if the watch is from Taiwan, Hong Kong, or Japan.

- **The gold casing on some watches wears badly or will turn green after repeated wearings**. The facings may be crooked or the hands bent incorrectly. Examine your purchases carefully for obvious flaws. But keep in mind these are cheap copies which will not always be perfect.

■ **Some of the watches stop working after a day or two.** Test them before leaving Thailand. Set the time as soon as you buy one and check it regularly to see if it runs fast, slow, or not at all. If it stops, take it back to the vendor who will usually exchange it. Try to remember from whom you purchased it.

■ **It is not illegal to buy these watches, but it may be illegal to bring them into some countries.** Manufacturers of the real name brand watches, as well as some governments, do not believe "imitation is the highest form of flattery." They consider imitation to be first of all an illegal activity. Indeed, U.S. Customs may seize them as a trademark violation should they find them in your possession. A few other countries may have similar restrictions. But for the most part you will probably travel without any trouble. Despite recent pressure by the U.S. government to end trademark violations in Thailand, the Thai police are their usual tolerant selves by occasionally making half-hearted attempts to stop this trade. Buying these watches is indeed a "black market" adventure which is relatively safe to play. If you like these watches, you may decide to buy now and worry later about how they will pass through customs. You'll probably be successful if you are discrete. Copy watches are most widely available along Patpong Road (off Silom and Suriwongse Roads) just adjacent to The Bookseller bookstore and across from the Queen's Castle (Bangkok's raunchiest nightclub which is also next to a Christian bookstore!) and along Silom Road in and around Silom Village shopping center. Along **Patpong Road** this watch trade is most lively in the evenings, especially beginning around 7pm, when several vendors set up small tables to display their wares. Along Silom Road vendors operate during the day. Be sure to bargain vigorously. The asking price for Rolex watches may be 1500B, but you should be able to buy it for 800B. Cartier and Gucci watches can be purchased for 300B to 500B. However, many of the watches sold along Patpong Road have problems—don't work after a few days, turn color, have bent hands. Other areas for buying these watches are found around the **major hotels**, such as the Oriental and Royal Orchid Sheraton, and a few **temple complexes**, especially the

Temple of the Dawn. Watches sold near the temples have extremely inflated prices—a 800B Rolex may cost 2000B —and vendors do not like to bargain. Avoid making purchases in these areas unless you find a particular style you must have regardless of the inflated price.

■ **The name-brand copy watches are not on display.** Because of the sensitive international political climate concerning Thai trademark violations, most street vendors no longer display name-brand copy watches out in the open. This "illegal" trade has been forced underground— Thai style, which means a lot of window dressing to please the pesky American trademark cops. Most watch vendors now keep the name-brand copy watches in plastic storage boxes located either under the table or in a special bag or box. Some only keep photos of the watches from which you can "special order" your Rolex, Gucci, Cartier, or Patek Philippe from the photo album. They can deliver within a few minutes. Just ask *"Do you have any Rolex, Gucci, Cartier, Patek Philippe, or other major name watches?"* Surprise! Out comes the photo album. Buying the $20 version of a $5,000 Rolex watch really doesn't affect the bottom-line at Rolex. In fact, you might like your fake Rolex so much that some day you will actually buy the real thing.

BRONZE, BRASS, AND PEWTER

The Thais are very skilled in working with bronze, brass, and pewter. They produce a variety of items which make lovely utensils, gifts, and decorative items, such as letter openers, bells, candle holders, cups, plates, bowls, vases, and flatware.

The bronze flatware is very popular, widely available in shops throughout Bangkok, and relatively inexpensive. The flatware comes in several styles and designs, from traditional to modern, and is available with teakwood storage boxes. Chopstick style and black-burnished bronzeware is also available along with more traditional designs. Many American-based companies sell these same items through direct-mail catalogs for five times the price you will pay in Bangkok. You can buy the flatware in any number of pieces desired or purchase sets in boxes ready to go.

Before buying Thai bronzeware, you should be forewarned of the different qualities of bronzeware. The beautiful Thai bronzeware you see in shops has been meticulously polished to attract your eye. But in reality, some of this bronzeware tarnishes, is not dishwasher approved, and is a constant headache to keep clean and spotless. If you buy the bronzeware, ask for the "nickel bronze" version. Nickel bronze tarnishes less and can be run through a dishwasher.

You will find bronzeware in many jewelry shops throughout Bangkok. The bronze letter openers are inexpensive (50B) and make nice little gifts for friends, relatives, and colleagues. You may want to buy 30 or more of these for trip gifts. The bells, key chains, shoe horns, bottle openers, and candle holders also make nice gifts.

Thailand makes some pewterware, but not nearly as much as you will find in Malaysia. Most of the pewter items are similar to the bronze and brass items—vases, cups, plates, candle holders. Many shops that carry bronze and brass items also sell pewter.

For the bronze, brass, and pewter, check with shops in and around your hotel. The major areas with the largest concentrations of shops specializing in such items is found along **Phetburi Road** (between Rama IV and Phyathai roads) and along **Suriwongse Road** (between the Manohra and Trocadero hotels), **New Road**, and **Oriental Lane** leading up to the Oriental Hotel. **Lin Plaza Gems** (2nd floor, 1-7 Chartered Bank Lane, across from Oriental Place) has a good selection of bronze, brass, and pewterware as well as jewelry and tailored clothes—our all-in-one shop. If you want to go beyond the typical tourist styles and are looking for some truly unique patterns and fine quality craftsmanship in bronze flatware, visit **Thai Home Industries** (35 Oriental Lane, Tel. 234-1736) near the Oriental Hotel. Their unique handmade, black-burnished handle flatware is lovely and looks terrific on Western dining tables. Several shops along New Road, between Oriental Lane and the Post Office, sell similar flatware for much less. Other unique bronze flatware patterns are found at **Design Thai** (304 Silom Road). When buying bronze or brass decorative items, ask that they be coated with silicon. This prevents them from tarnishing. Many shops will do this upon request. They will not use silicon on flatware or other utensils which are used for eating. Even the nickel bronze will spot and tarnish, but not as bad as other types of bronze.

ARTS AND ANTIQUES

Thailand is a virtual treasure chest for fabulous woodcarvings and antiques—both old and new. Major department stores in the U.S.—such as Neiman Marcus, Saks Fifth Avenue, and Bloomingdales—are regular importers of these items. They buy everything from wood salad bowls and serving trays to carved decorative animals. You can buy these in Thailand at a fraction of the U.S. prices.

Thai woodcarvings and antiques have moved into a whole new stage of development during the past ten years. Given the stagnating economy and separatist rebellions in Myanmar, coupled with enterprising Thai importers, numerous shops in Bangkok and Chiang Mai are literally museums for some of the most lovely and exotic Myanmar antiques and art works. Temple woodcarvings and panels, lacquerware, and tapestries—both old and new—abound in Bangkok's many shops.

Thailand is particularly well noted for both its old and new antiques. Old antiques mainly come from Myanmar, Cambodia, Laos, China, and Vietnam. Bronze drums, ceramics, silver figures, wood panels, bronze bells, baskets, chests, sculptures, puppets, and tapestries are only a few of the fabulous items you will find digging through Bangkok's many antique shops. Similar items can be found in the antique shops of Hong Kong and Singapore, but prices will be at least double those found in Bangkok.

But it is the reproductions which are of particular interest to many tourists. Thailand has a well deserved reputation for making excellent copies of art and antiques. In fact, Thailand might best be described as a **copycat culture** rather than a creative culture. From very early ages, Thais learn to copy models from all aspects of life. Copies of old Myanmar tapestries— the *kalagas*—are now mass produced and available at very reasonable prices in numerous shops throughout Bangkok.

❑ Thailand is particularly well noted for both its old and new antiques.

❑ Art work in Bangkok is relatively inexpensive and framing is ridiculously cheap.

❑ If you buy very valuable art work which should be mounted on acid-free paper, do not have it framed in Thailand.

If you are not an expert judge of Asian arts and antiques but nonetheless wish to purchase some lovely home decorative items, you should shop for new antiques and woodcarvings. You will find a vast selection of woodcarved animals, temple panels, mirror frames, doors, windows, and mythical scenes which integrate nicely into many contemporary Western homes. However, large woodcarvings often crack when introduced into dry, temperate climates. Because of the large demand for these carvings and the limited amount of dried wood available, many are made with wood that has not properly aged. Newer wood pieces may crack after a few months.

While you can minimize such problems by purchasing older pieces and shopping at reputable stores, even many of the old pieces will crack in temperate climates. Cracking may occur as wood is subjected to heating systems in much drier climates. If this happens to a prized piece, we recommend contacting a conservator who can both restore and conserve the piece. Contact a museum for information on a conservator nearest you. In addition, consider installing a home humidifier system to help preserve your arts and antiques during the dry winter months.

For examples of Thailand's finest old and new antiques and woodcarvings, you should visit **The Elephant House** (286/69-71 Soi Pattana, Suriwongse Road, Tel. 233-6973); **NeOld** (main shop at 149/2-3 Suriwongse Road, Tel. 235-8352 and a smaller shop in the Regent Hotel, Tel. 250-0737); **Peng Seng** (942/1-3 Rama IV Road, on corner of Suriwongse and Rama IV Road and next to the Jim Thompson Silk Company, Tel. 233-1891 or 234-3836); **Lek Gallerie** (1310-1312 New Road, Tel. 234-4184); **The Fine Arts/The Height** (Oriental Place, Tel. 266-0186-95; River City Shopping Complex, Tel. 237-0077, ext. 354/452); Thaniya Plaza, Tel. 231-3164; and the Sukhothai Hotel, Tel. 287-0222); **Sawasdee Antique Co.** (3rd floor, River City Shopping Complex, Tel. 237-007, ext. 314, 319); **Rama Art Gallery** (1238/1-2 New Road 36, Tel. 233-3330); **August 9** (River City Shopping Complex, Tel. 237-0077-8, ext. 431-422 and Oriental Place, 1st floor, 267-0316); **The Ashwood Gallery** (River City Shopping Complex, Tel. 237-0077, ext. 314, and Oriental Place, Tel. 266-0187, ext. 1252); **River Trade Co.** (351 River City Shopping Complex, Tel. 237-0077, ext. 351-352); **Yonok Treasures** (213 River City Shopping Complex, Tel. 237-0077, ext. 213); **Tomlinson** (Oriental Place, 3rd level, Tel. 630-6939); **Artisan's** (Silom Village, 286 Silom Road, Tel. 237-4456); and **Golden Tortoise** (4 Sukhumvit Soi 49-4, Tel. 391-2842). The greatest concentration of shops can be found on the third and fourth floors (Art and Antique Centre) of the **River City Shopping Complex** which is located next to the Royal Orchid Sheraton Hotel along the Chao Phraya River.

Many of the woodcarvings in Bangkok are actually made in **Chiang Mai**. If you plan to visit Chiang Mai, be sure to stop at **Borisoothi Antiques** (15/2 Chiang Mai-Sankhampaeng Road) and **Bang Chang Come** (141 Hang Dong Road; also operates **Arts and Crafts Chiangmai** at 172 Moo 2 Chiang Mai-Sankhampaeng Road)—Chiang Mai's two major antique dealers. Several small shops on the third and fourth floors of the **Chiangmai Night Bazaar** in downtown Chiang Mai offer good se 67/12 Soi Phra Phinit, Soi Suan Phlu, Sathorn Tai

Road lections of antiques, woodcarvings, and handcrafted items. The factories in **Hang Dong**, approximately 12 kilometers south of Chiang Mai, and along **Chiang Mai-Sankhampaeng Road**, just east of the city, are filled with woodcarvings of all shapes, sizes, and motifs. **Chiangmai Banyen**, located adjacent to Jaifah Chiangmai Lacquerware Co. at 209/3 Super Highway (near the airport intersection and the road to Hang Dong), is one of Chiang Mai's most famous and reliable factories supplying numerous shops in Bangkok as well as department stores and shops abroad with quality woodcarvings. Six of Chiang Mai's finest antique and home decorative shops include **Lanna House** (512 Moo 1, Rimtai, at entrance to the Regent Resort), **Chili** (125 Moo 4 Banwhan, Hang Dong), **Yonok Treasures** (130/9 Moo 1 Chang Mai-Hod Road), **Baan Tarin** (3 Moo 2, Hang Dong) **Rattan House** (road to Hang Dong), and **Jirakarn Antiques** (Hang Dong Road, across the road and down a small potholed Soi from Chilli).

ART AND FRAMING

Thailand is not well noted for its paintings. However, you may find some lovely oil paintings, watercolors, or sketches for your home or for gifts. Indeed, some of our favorite purchases in Asia have been Thai paintings. They are available in a variety of styles from traditional Buddhist art to portrait, landscape, and abstract paintings. Thai artists also produce beautiful modern bronze and brass sculptures as well as wood blocks and temple rubbings. Art work in Bangkok is relatively inexpensive and framing is ridiculously cheap.

You will need to shop in several locations for this art. Many shops sell paintings, but much of what you find is mass produced for tourists and looks cheap and gaudy. If you look enough you will find some lovely works in traditional Thai style, depicting Hindu epics and Buddhist scenes, landscapes, portraits, and modern art. We have been particularly drawn to the watercolors of Kit (now deceased former art professor at Silapakorn University in Bangkok) depicting rural scenes in Thailand; they are now hard to find. The value of his paintings has increased tremendously during the past few years.

If you buy art in Thailand you may want to have it framed there too. You should consider framing different types of art purchases, such as wood panels, carvings, lacquer pieces, tapestries, or anything that would look attractive hung on a wall. Many Thai art shops do nice work with silk mattings and frames. Indeed, the mats and frames are often as much a creative work of art as the piece being framed!

The quality of framing is often good and prices are inexpensive. Thai craftsmen can design any type of frame you wish for paintings, carvings, textiles, and lacquer pieces. For example, a framing job that would normally cost you $250 back home may only cost $50 in Bangkok.

While Thai art shops can custom-make frames for you, their selections of stock frames and mattings are limited. Most matting materials must be imported and thus are limited in width size, color selection, and texture. The frame selections also are limited. But you should not focus only on the stock materials. Focus instead on creating some unique custom-made mats and frames. The real strength of these shops is their ability to custom-design mats and frames—something few shops may do back home. Thai shops can make mats by using any silk material you desire. You may, for example, want to visit Jim Thompson Silk Company to select your favorite silk material to be used as a frame matting which might also match upholstery material or pillows you selected for a particular room. On the other hand, most framing shops have silk samples from which you can choose a matting material. As for frames, the present stock design, size, and color selections are limited. Most shops can make frames to your exact specifications.

For examples of quality Thai art and framing, visit **Surawongse Gallery** (287/25-6 Suriwongse Road, Tel. 233-5333, and on the third floor of River City Shopping Complex); **C.V.N. Exotic Ltd.** (131-3/4 Sukhumvit Road, between Sois 7 and 9, Tel. 235-1860); **Sombat Permpoon Gallery** (12 Sukhumvit Soi 1, Tel. 254-6040); and **Sombat Gallery** (The Promenade, Tel. 267-8891 and River City Shopping Complex, called Four Art Gallery, Tel. 235-2972, ext. 215). Several other shops, such as **"A" Framer** (160/12 Soi 55, Sukhumvit Road), **Sathon Framing** (Soi St. Louis, South Sathorn Road), and **Uthai and Sons** (58/5 Soi 21, Sukhumvit Road, Tel. 258-3660), specialize in quality framing. Most of these art shops will arrange for packing and shipping. One of our favorite art shops, which does little framing now, has excellent reproduction art, especially art deco statutes and prints, is **Art Resources** (142/20 Soi Sueksavitaya, off of Silom Road, Tel. 235-4846 and The Regent Hotel, Tel. 250-0723; see Promote Bonyarungsrit who is one of Thailand's most talented art entrepreneurs).

One word of caution is in order. If you are buying very valuable art work which should be mounted on acid-free paper, do not have it framed in Thailand. Acid-free mounts are not available there. In addition, framing shops use plywood for frame backings. This tends to make the picture heavy, and large pieces may warp. Hence, you need to consider whether the monetary savings and custom-design capabilities are worth the additional costs of shipping and possible problems with warping and acid damage. Nonetheless, Thai shops enable you to create some very unique frames and art displays unavailable back home. We have been very pleased with all of our art and framing purchases in Bangkok.

Leather Goods

You will find many goods made from crocodile, lizard, snake, buffalo, and cow hides. The most widely available items are belts, purses, handbags, wallets, key chains, briefcases, jackets, shoes, and boots. We cannot strongly recommend purchasing such items in Thailand, even though some shops are attempting to become fashionable. The quality is at best mediocre, and you may have problems getting some leather through Customs back home.

Ready-made shoes in Thailand are generally of poor quality. The selection of large sizes is limited, many do not fit well, and they quickly deteriorate on Bangkok's rough sidewalks and streets. You can have your shoes and boots handmade. The prices are reasonable, but again the quality is not exceptional. Some of our readers may disagree with this overall assessment since they report being very pleased with these purchases. You'll have to be the judge. Shops such as **Chao Phya Bootery** (266-268 Sukhumvit Road, Tel. 251-3498), **Siam Bootery** (294-4 Sukhumvit Road, Tel. 251-6862), and **Tony Leather** (300-302 Sukhumvit Road, Tel. 251-6861) produce made-to-order shoes and other leather goods. These are reputed to be the best shops for such custom work. On the other hand, you may want to save your money and buy your letter goods in Hong Kong or watch for sales back home. Our advice: you may be pleased with your leather purchases, but don't expect a great deal or excellent quality. Like much of Thai tailoring, Thai leather work still lacks a clean "finished" look which is apparent when comparing with Italian leather products.

If you have problems with any leather goods you bring with you, such as a suitcase or a shoe, Bangkok is a good place to get repairs done inexpensively. You can have your shoes resoled and reheeled for under US$10. Department stores, such as Central, usually have a shoe repair booth ("Mr. Minit") which does good quality work while you wait. Repairs can be completed within 30 minutes. We do not recommend using the repairmen populating the sidewalks and street corners throughout Bangkok. Their makeshift workmanship is very crude; they may do more damage in the process of repairing your leather goods and shoes. Use them only for emergencies (your heel fell off while walking in front of them or you need something glued!).

Nielloware and Bencharong

Two truly unique and lovely Thai art forms are nielloware and bencharong. The nielloware is a special silver inlaid process available in a variety of colors in addition to the traditional black and white. The traditional designs are in the delicate and graceful Thai flame and floral patterns. Nielloware is made into jewelry, small boxes, ashtrays, cigarette lighters, cuff links, and a variety of other items. It is available in some shops in Bangkok. The best quality nielloware is produced in the southern province of Nakorn Si Thammarat.

The less known bencharong is a special Thai pottery made with intricate designs painted in five colors. Its origin is both Thai and Chinese—pottery made in China but colors applied in Thailand. The shapes, designs, and colors of this pottery are so beautiful and delicate that you may quickly become a bencharong collector. The five-color bencharong comes in many different color combinations, several of which may work well with your home decor.

You can find individual pieces of bencharong in many jewelry and handicraft shops as well as in department stores. **Lotus Ceramics** (Soi 3/1 Sukhumvit Road, Tel. 253-004 or 253- 2890) has a large selection of bencharong ware. For uniquely designed pottery which combines bencharong and celadon, visit **Prempracha's** large factory-shop in Chiang Mai (224 Chiang Mai-Sankamphaeng Road, Tel. 331-540).

Celadon and Lacquerware

In recent years the ancient art of Thai celadon has been revived. The celadon has a crackled appearance. It is covered by a thick clear coating. Fired in kilns, Thai celadon is produced in different green, blue, or tan shades. It is made into pottery, cups, plates, bowls, ashtrays, and an assortment of other small decorative items. It is most widely available directly at the factories in Chiang Mai, especially at the famous **Mengrai Kilns** (79/2 Araks Road, Soi Samlarn 6, Tel. 272-063), or you can see it in Bangkok at the **Celadon House** (278 Silom Road,

Tel. 234-3767) and in several small shops selling jewelry and handicrafts.

Thai lacquerware in the distinctive **black and gold** colors makes lovely decorative pieces or trip gifts. It is made into a variety of goods, from serving trays, plates, and boxes to coasters. The Thai designs are traditional flame, floral, and portrait patterns.

Other Thai lacquerware is produced in a distinctive **red** color. Many shops sell lovely baskets, small tables, figures, and a variety of furniture items in the red lacquer. You may find the red lacquer pieces will work much better in your home than the more traditional black and gold lacquerware.

Many shops in Bangkok and Chiang Mai also stock unique **Myanmar** lacquerware pieces. This lacquerware is produced in distinctive rust and green colors with intricate designs etched in different colors. If you don't have a chance to visit even more exotic Myanmar, Thailand is a good place to pick up some lovely Myanmar lacquer bowls, plates, boxes, trays, coasters, tables, and room dividers.

One of the largest collections of antique Thai and Myanmar lacquerware is found at the **Elephant House** (286/69-71 Soi Pattana, Suriwongse Road, Tel. 233-6973) in Bangkok. For excellent quality lacquerware in Chiang Mai, be sure to visit **Maneesinn** (289 Thapae Road, Tel. 236-586). Several shops in the **Night Bazaar** (3rd and 4th floors) also offer good quality lacquerware.

Handicrafts

Thai handicrafts are well represented in the shops of Bangkok and Chiang Mai. They include a large variety of lovely and unique items: baskets, spirit houses, dolls, hilltribe jewelry, quilts, pottery, picture frames, carvings, placemats, Christmas decorations, embroidered items, hats, etc. For a good selection of quality handicrafts, visit the new **Thai Craft Museum** (2nd Floor of Gaysorn Plaza), **Thai Home Industries** (35 Oriental Lane), **Chitralada Shop** (Thaniya Plaza and Oriental Place), **House of Handicrafts** (Regent Hotel), and the handicraft exhibition area on the fourth floor of the Emporium Shopping Center on Sukhumvit Road. Thailand's largest handicraft emporium is the government operated **Narayana Phand** (The Mall, Rajadamri Road). Most major department stores, such as **Central**, **Sogo**, or **Robinson**, have a handicraft section with fixed prices. It's worth browsing in these department stores to get a good overview of selections, prices, and quality.

Two shops specializing in uniquely designed quality handicrafts are **Rasi Sayam** (32 Sukhumvit Soi 23, Tel. 258-4195) and **The Legend** (3rd floor, Amarin Plaza, Tel. 256-9929). Both shops offer some wonderful pottery, baskets, carvings, and boxes that make nice home decorative items and gifts. Serious collectors of quality handicrafts are well advised to visit both shops, especially Rasi Sayam.

Three very interesting shops specialize in handcrafted dolls, Christmas ornaments, and related items: **Bangkok Dolls** (80 Soi Rajatapan, Rajaprarop Road, Tel. 245-3008; and the Peninsula Plaza); **Lao Song Handicrafts** (2045/5 Soi 77 Sukhumvit Road, Tel. 332-5459); and the **Fatima Self Help Center** (Good Shepherd Sisters, 17/65 Asoke Din Daeng Road, Tel. 245-0458).

Outside Bangkok, near the city of Ayuthaya, is the **Royal Folk Arts and Crafts Center** at Bansai. Sponsored by Her Majesty the Queen, this is a training center where young people learn the traditional arts and crafts. They produce furniture, baskets, leather goods, glass figures, woven items, and paintings as well as numerous small display items. In addition to observing the production of arts and crafts in various workshops, you can also purchase the finished products from the main arts and crafts shop. If you plan to travel to Ayutthaya on your own, you may want to stop here along the way. However, few if any tours to Ayutthaya schedule stops at this center, and we would not recommend a trip just to visit this center.

In Chiang Mai you will find numerous handicraft shops in and around the **Night Bazaar** (go to the second and third floors for the best quality) and along **Chiang Mai-Sankhamphaeng Road** (Siam Gifts has one of the largest selections). For good hilltribe handicrafts, visit the **Thai Tribal Crafts** (208 Bumrung Rat Road, Tel. 241-043) and the **Hilltribe Promotion Center** on Suthep Road. **Sarapee Silk Lace** at 2 Rajwithi Road, one of Chiang Mai's and Thailand's most unique shops, produces fine handsewn lace.

TAPESTRIES

In recent years Bangkok has been flooded with the unique, lovely, and exotic Myanmar tapestries, known as *kalagas*. A stunning and mysterious art form originating in Myanmar more than 200 years ago, it disappeared during the 20th century. It has recently been revived, partly in response to tourism.

These tapestries come in numerous sizes, designs, and color combinations. Most are intricately designed with Buddhist scenes and floral patterns, sewn with gold and silver sequins, and stitched with different colored raised cotton, silk, and velvet materials. The fine designs and labor-intensive work is fascinating. Every time you look at a *kalaga* it tends to yield new details.

You can still find some antique Myanmar tapestries in the shops of Bangkok and Chiang Mai, but these rare pieces are very expensive, costing US$1,500 on up. Most of the new pieces are very attractive and extremely inexpensive. For example, a nice 2' x 2' tapestry may only cost about US$20 and can be framed for less than US$25. A 3' x 7' tapestry might cost US$180 and can be framed for US$100. But be sure to bargain hard; expect to receive at least a 20% discount, and maybe as much as 50% from the initial price.

The Myanmar tapestries make interesting trip gifts, or you may want to purchase one as a wall hanging or center piece for a special room. They may appear somewhat gaudy at first, but if you look hard enough you should be able to find one with the right design and colors to work in your home.

Most tapestries in Bangkok are imitations of the old Myanmar tapestries or are newly commissioned designs. The new pieces are very well done. One of the best places to see a wide selection of these tapestries is among the many art and antique shops on the third and fourth floors (Art and Antique Centre) of the **River City Shopping Complex** next to the Royal Orchid Sheraton Hotel.

FURNITURE

Thailand is an excellent place to buy handmade wood and rattan furniture. Several reliable quality factories in Bangkok will make pieces to your specification in a variety of woods and finishes, especially teakwood. The shops will pack and ship for you. All you need to do is bring your designs with you. They can copy from catalog pictures, but the more details you can provide, the better. Many visitors to Thailand have tables, chairs, beds, chests, cupboards, and other items made according to their designs. After you leave Thailand, you can continue to order furniture through the mail by sending the factory detailed designs. The prices are reasonable, even considering the extra costs of shipping, and the craftsmanship is very good. A rosewood dining room set costing $5,000 in the United States, for example, can be copied for $2,000 in Thailand. With shipping costs, you can still save money.

We regularly use furniture makers in Bangkok to add pieces

to our household furniture, many of which have been discontinued by manufacturers. These Thai factories also can make wood display bases and small tables for pottery and other artifacts. Some of the best furniture factories in Bangkok with display rooms are: **Sweet Home** (33 Sukhumvit Road Soi 27, Tel. 258-3419); **Gersons** (287 Silom Road), **Peter's Furniture** (157/6 Mahadlek 2 Rajadamri Road, behind the Regent Hotel, Tel. 252-6727); **Pong Sin** (109 Suthisan, Tel. 277-0355); and **Prinya Decoration LP** (3106-8 New Phetburi Road, Tel. 318-1824).

A few shops also make unique furniture. One of our favorite items and designs are tables made from dark brown antique opium mats with legs and sides finished in red or brown lacquer. Examples of this furniture are found at the **Elephant House** at 286/69-71 Soi Pattana, Suriwongse Road (Tel. 233-6973, and ask for Cherie who is the owner and designer). Similar opium mat furniture is found at **NeOld** at 149-2-3 Suriwongse Road (Tel. 235-8352).

For Tibetan furniture and rugs, be sure to visit **Acala** (312 River City Shopping Center, Tel. 237-0077, ext. 312). For quality Japanese, Korean, and Chinese furniture, visit **Golden Tortoise Deco** (49/2 Sukhumvit Soi 49, Tel. 259-6641).

If you are looking for something very special, be sure to visit **Pure Design** at 30 Ruam Rudee Road (Tel. 253-1719—by appointment only, which is difficult to get!). This is one of Thailand's premiere home decorative and designer shops. They make very unique pieces of furniture. If you are serious about decorating your home with furniture that expresses Thai design and style, some of which has been seen on the pages of *Architectural Digest*, be sure to consult with the designer—Mr. Chantaka Puranananda. His work is well represented in many of Thailand's major hotels and the homes of Thailand's wealthy.

If you are interested in wicker furniture, concentrate your shopping efforts on several shops along **Sukhumvit Road** between Soi 39 and 43, such as **Pacific Design** (779-781 Sukhumvit Road, Tel. 258-8908). This shop also will make furniture to your specifications.

Individuals interested in collecting antique or old furniture should visit **Yesterday Once Again** on Soi Asoke. This rather cluttered shop collects and refinishes old Thai furniture, especially period furniture. This is a favorite shop for many expatriates.

If you visit Chiang Mai, be sure to stop at the furniture factories and showrooms that tend to be concentrated along Chiang Mai-Sankamphaeng Road. Most of the furniture produced in Chiang Mai is in traditional Thai designs—somewhat gaudy and too ethnic for many foreign visitors. To view a large variety of such furniture, stop at **Tusnaporn** on the Chiang Mai-Sankamphaeng Road (Route 1006 directly east of Chiang Mai city). Several other furniture factories also are found along this same road. However, hold on to your wallet! Try to visit these places on your own. Many of these huge factory/show-rooms, and especially Tusnaporn, are notorious for paying drivers and guides 10-30% commissions for bringing clients to their shops. The commissions, of course, are hidden in your "special" price. The quality of this furniture varies, and it seems to get worse each year. Good teakwood furniture is hard to find given the present bans on forestry. You may end up with inferior quality woods which tend to crack in more temperate climates.

THE MORE YOU LOOK

The Thai produce numerous other arts and crafts many travelers find attractive. The more you poke around the many shops of Bangkok and Chiang Mai, the more you discover interesting and unique items. Indeed, the more you look, the more you may get hooked on this shopping paradise. In addition to the major products just discussed, you will find beautiful lamps, wood and stone statues, sculptures, ancient Ban Chiang pottery, textiles, batik, costumes, head dresses, ivory carvings, handmade Oriental carpets, luggage, dolls, stuffed animals, spirit houses, bells, bronze drums, Chinese and Thai ceramics, porcelain, exotic birds, and much, much more. The list simply goes on and on. You will quickly find there is no substitute for wandering around from one shop to another discovering the infinite variety of Thai shopping treasures.

Thailand may not have the glitter and sheer volume of shops found in Hong Kong and Singapore. But these other famous shopping cities have little to compare to the lovely decorative arts and crafts you can only find by going to Thailand and searching on your own.

7

Gems, Jewelry, and Tailoring Tips

M ANY VISITORS TO THAILAND, AS WELL AS TO other parts of Asia, encounter special difficulties when shopping for gems, jewelry, and tailoring services. They make many mistakes. Indeed, the largest number of tourist complaints relate to these products and services. Inexperienced shoppers and lacking sufficient information, many tourists often rely on local salespeople to vouch for quality. In other words, they trust strangers with their money! Not surprisingly, many such tourists are vulnerable to all types of shopping errors, from scams to misunderstanding purchases. The result is often a disappointing shopping experience.

In this chapter we've compiled some basic information and tips on how to best shop for gems, jewelry, and tailoring services. If you are unfamiliar with such products and services, hopefully this chapter will point you in the right direction to at least **ask the right questions** before making such purchases.

BUYING GEMS AND JEWELRY

You walk past a shop window filled with glittering gems. You stop for just a moment—only to look. You are not planning to buy any jewelry, but the glint of a ruby ring catches your eye.

You've heard travelers' tales of the incredible bargains they've gotten in some exotic city. Why not just check on the price. After all, it doesn't cost anything to look!

For every story of an incredible bargain—a traveler who took a chance, made a purchase and took the gemstone home to find it appraised for 5-10 times what he paid—there is another tale. There are many stories of tourists who took their gemstones home to find the so-called fantastic "ruby" they bought was only a red spinel worth a fraction of what they paid. In fact, the largest number of tourist complaints lodged with the tourist associations in many of the countries we visit deal with jewelry and gemstone purchases. Many of these complaints occur in Thailand where some tourists literally get "taken" when they buy gems and jewelry.

If you will learn about gemstones, realize you can't get something for nothing—anywhere in the world—select the store where you buy using specific criteria, and maintain a healthy level of skepticism, you may be able to make a jewelry purchase you will enjoy for years to come and save money in the process.

QUALITIES OF GEMSTONES

A gemstone should have visual beauty, durability, and rarity. **Beauty** is somewhat subjective with various cultures preferring certain gemstones more than others, and gemstones coming and going in popularity over periods of time. Jade, for example, is generally more highly regarded in Asia than in the rest of the world. Pearls have experienced periods of great popularity only to be held in less regard for periods of time and then to regain popularity again! Beauty may be judged by the depth of color in some stones such as rubies, emeralds and sapphires, or by the absence of color as is the case with most diamonds—though the Argyle diamond mines of Australia provide examples of beautiful champagne, cognac, and pink colors.

Durability refers to three aspects of a gemstone: its hardness, toughness and stability. The hardness of a gemstone is defined by a value on Mohs hardness scale. A diamond ranks at the very top of the scale—a ten—the hardest gemstone. A diamond is much harder than the next stone on the list—corundum, the mineral of sapphires and rubies, is a nine. The lower the level of hardness, the more easily a stone is scratched. Gemstones with a hardness of less than seven are easily scratched.

Toughness refers to a stone's resistance to cracking, chipping or breaking. The diamond, by far the hardest stone, lacks toughness. After years of wear, diamonds with exposed edges, for example, those set in Tiffany settings, are likely to have small chipped corners. Obviously a bezel setting that fully encircles the diamond has practical advantages.

Stability refers to a stone's resistance to chemical or structural change. Opals contain water and can lose water in dry air. Now you know why there is often a glass of water in the jeweler's show window. Once water is lost, the opal may crack. Pearls can be damaged by acid, alcohol or perfume. Porous stones, such as turquoise and coral, can pick up oils from the skin or be damaged by harsh cleansing agents.

KARATS AND CARATS

Don't confuse karat, which is a measure of gold purity, with carat, which measures the weight of a gemstone. Most gold jewelry sold in the United States today is either 14 or 18 karat. Once abroad you will find other degrees of purity ranging from 8K in some countries to 22K or higher in much of the Middle East and Asia. In those cultures, where historically much of a family's wealth and certainly a woman's holdings were in jewelry, anything less than 18K gold is not considered as really gold, and 22K and higher is the norm. In much of the world, 14K will be marked as .585 and 18K as .750 which equal the percentages of gold content in the jewelry. In other words, 18K is 75% gold (.750) and 25% base metal.

Remember that pure gold is soft. To be durable it needs to be alloyed with other more durable metals. A large gold pendant fashioned in 22K gold may be fine, but a ring in 22K will be soft. If the prongs of the setting that hold the gemstone are 22K, you run a high risk of eventually losing the stone. Prongs of no higher than 18K gold are best for setting gemstones. The base metals used as alloys and their amount create the different colors of gold from white gold, to rose gold to yellow gold.

NATURAL, SYNTHETIC, AND SIMULATED GEMS

Natural stones are formed by nature over vast amounts of time and as a result of great amounts of pressure. Natural stones are more scarce and have greater value than synthetic stones. **Synthetic stones** are composed of the exact same substance (chemical properties) as the natural mineral, but have been produced by man in the laboratory. Therefore, it is not easy even for a jeweler to discern the difference between the two since the chemical properties are the same. Because it has been formed by an accident of nature rather than the intent of man, a natural stone usually contains some inclusions. A flawless stone—especially in a mineral that usually contains some inclusions, for example, an emerald—should raise suspicion that the stone may be synthetic. There are sophisticated techniques to differentiate a nearly perfect natural stone from a synthetic, but without the appropriate equipment and training it will be impossible.

A natural stone is worth more than a synthetic; a synthetic stone has more value than a simulated stone. In a **simulated stone**, the optical properties closely resemble the real gem, but the chemical properties are different. The stones look alike to the naked eye, but a jeweler would be able to easily tell the difference. An example is the use of cubic zirconia rather than a diamond. Both are real stones, but one has a great deal more value than the other. **Imitation stones** may be made of glass or plastic or they may be composite stones consisting of a thin slice of the gem material under (doublet) or between (triplet) other material of no real value. A synthetic stone can look lovely, but you shouldn't pay a natural gem price for it.

Over the past two decades **"enhancement" of gemstones** has become common. Irradiation may be used to enhance or change the color of many natural stones. Chemical treatment such as bleaching, dyeing, or oiling are used. Heat is used to deepen the color of some gems or improve clarity, a common practice in Thailand. These practices are legal but should be disclosed on request. Often they are not disclosed. This isn't necessarily because the salesperson or shop is dishonest; the seller may not know because the individual who supplied the stone to them did not disclose the fact.

The 4 C's

Assuming the gem is a natural stone, the color, clarity, cut, and carat weight determine its value. The most valuable **Color** varies with the stone, but generally a stone with deep saturation of color will have greater value than a light hue; however, there is a point at which the stone becomes too dark. It doesn't reflect light and loses sparkle. **Clarity** refers to the absence of inclusions. A flawless stone is one in which no imperfections can be seen at 10X magnification. **Cut** varies with the stone and personal preference. Opaque stones, such as jade, turquoise or coral, are rarely faceted. Since light will not be reflected from within, there is no reason to facet. Instead, they will normally be cut and polished with a rounded top—called cabachon. Transparent gemstones are faceted to reflect maximum brilliance. The round brilliant cut, with its modifications—oval, pear, marquise and heart shapes—and the emerald cut are the most popular today. **Carat** refers to the size of the stone, but size is measured by weight. Two different stones may appear to be different in size because of the way in which they are cut, but in fact be the same weight. Because large stones are rare, one three-carat stone is far more valuable than are three stones of one-carat each—assuming the other three C's are equivalent.

NATURAL, CULTURED, AND SIMULATED PEARLS

A pearl is formed when a foreign substance finds its way into an oyster—either by an accident of nature or the intention of man. The oyster attempts to protect itself from this foreign substance which may be a grain of sand, a very small pebble or a piece of shell, by secreting successive layers of the same material of which its shell is composed—eventually resulting in a solid mass of a luminous substance which is the pearl. It is perhaps ironic, that the oyster's attempt to protect itself from this small invading body provides the incentive for a much more invasive intrusion on the part of man.

Natural pearls—those formed as a result of an accident of nature—are quite rare. That's due, in part, because it takes yet another accident for them to be found by man. However, **cultured pearls** are formed in exactly the same way by the oyster's secretions. The differences are that man has purposely inserted a small "bead," usually of shell material, into oysters that have been raised for this purpose; they then place the implanted shells in wire baskets and return them to the sea where they are suspended from rafts or buoys. When it is time to harvest the pearls, it isn't hard to find the oysters! Only about 20% of the "seeded" oysters will produce quality pearls, but that makes them far less rare than the lucky find of a natural pearl. Few pearls in jewelry stores today are truly natural pearls. Cultured pearls are beautiful and valuable, but should not be confused with a true natural pearl.

Simulated pearls like simulated gemstones have the look of the real thing but have an entirely different composition. Many simulated pearls are pretty plastic!

KNOW WHAT YOU PAY FOR!

So how do you avoid paying natural stone prices for a synthetic or simulated stone? Certainly you should visit one or more of the best jewelry stores in your hometown before you leave home. If you reside in a small town, take the time to visit a large metropolitan area nearby and go to one of the best jewelry stores there. Look at some jewelry—especially the stones you think you may have an interest in acquiring as you travel. Look at the settings and the workmanship of the settings. One of the easiest ways to spot cheap imitation jewelry is not by looking at the stone, but by looking at the workmanship of the setting. The cubic zirconia may fool your untrained eye, but the setting is more likely to give it away!

By now it should be obvious that it is difficult for a person untrained in the jewelry trade and without sophisticated equipment at hand to be certain of what he is getting. So what you know about the shop where you make your purchase will be more important than what you know about jewelry.

With this in mind the following are some guidelines that should help you get a fair deal if you decide to make a jewelry purchase. While you should not fool yourself into believing you are an expert, there is no harm in giving the jeweler the impression you are somewhat gem savvy!

- **Never go to a jewelry store with someone who picked you up on the street!** No matter whether he tells you his uncle owns the store and will give a great deal—just for you, or if he wants to practice his English—avoid him like the tout he is. In the first place, you don't want to make a purchase in any store he would take you to. Quality jewelry stores do not deal in this way. In the second place, you will pay more than you should for any purchase you might make. The tout's commission of anywhere from 10% to over 30% of your purchase has to come from somewhere!

- **Choose the jewelry store carefully.** If you have a recommendation from a trusted friend—great. If not, look at jewelry stores in quality shopping areas—the best part of town! The shops within the best hotels or the arcades of the top hotels or in the best shopping malls will have the best jewelers. A good hotel cannot afford having its reputation tarnished by leasing space to a jeweler who misrepresents his goods. This is no guarantee you may not pay a bit more than you need to if you don't ask for a discount or bargain. But you can feel comfortable that the goods are most likely what they are said to be.

- **Patronize gem and jewelry shops recommended by the local tourist organization.** While you may still encounter problems with such shops, at least you can contact the tourist association for assistance in resolving your problem.

In the case of Thailand, the Tourist Association of Thailand recommends nearly 50 shops which are members of the Jewel Fest Club sponsored by the Thai Gem and Jewel Traders Association. While there are many other excellent shops which are not part of this network, you will at least feel comfortable patronizing the recommended shops.

- **Look around at the merchandise in the store.** Does the store sell only jewelry or do they sell souvenirs and other items as well. The best jewelry stores will limit their sales to jewelry and gemstones. The sales staff in a store that only sells jewelry is likely to be far better informed than in the store selling all kinds of merchandise.

- **Do a quick check of the quality of the merchandise you see.** Compare it to the jewelry you saw in the top jewelry store you visited before you left home. Again, remember to look at the settings. Even if you plan to purchase loose stones, look at the gold work on the pieces that are set. It will tell you a great deal about the quality of the shop. If you don't like what you see, move on to another shop.

- **Check whether prices are clearly marked on each item.** What this tells you will vary in different parts of the world. Some places simply don't mark prices on their jewelry, and this is not necessarily a negative about the shop. It may be marked instead with a code that only the jeweler knows. But where prices are clearly marked, you are assured that the price is not set capriciously—even though the amount of the discount may be! Gems and jewelry in Thailand are usually marked with a code rather than a price tag.

- **Look around at the sales staff.** Do they dress and act professional? Do they seem pushy and try to get people to "buy now" and make a sale, or are they helpful in answering your questions but allow you space to consider your purchase?

- **Look around for the presence of what appear to be gemological instruments.** Are there indications, either by such instruments, or certificates from gemological institutes, that they have accredited gemologists on their staff?

- **Look at any stones through a jewelers' loupe.** Hold the loupe in one hand close to the eye, steadying the hand by resting it against your cheek. With your other hand, bring the stone, held with tweezers, toward the loupe until it is in focus. (You may want to practice holding the stone with tweezers with your jeweler before you leave home!). You should move the stones rather than the loupe.

- **If you expect to make a very expensive purchase, try to deal directly with the manager or owner.** The manager usually knows more about his or her inventory and also may have more flexibility in negotiating a price.

- **If you buy, be sure to get a receipt that is very detailed** as to the gemstone, whether it is a natural stone, the carat weight, the clarity, whether it has been enhanced, and the gold content, if it is a set stone. Be wary of any shop that is hesitant to give you a detailed receipt.

- **Get in writing a guarantee from the shop that you can return the gemstone or jewelry within a reasonable but specific period of time** if you later have it appraised and it turns out not be what it was sold to be. It is also a good idea to be able to return or exchange if you are making an expensive purchase of jewelry for someone who is not with you as you shop.

- **If you have questions about the authenticity and value of your gem and/or jewelry purchases, take them to a certified gemologist for an appraisal before you leave the country.** Don't wait until you get home to discover the value—or lack thereof—of your purchases. Assuming you have a detailed receipt which specifies your return or exchange period, it's best to certify the value of your purchase as soon as possible. The local gemologist or jewelry association, or even your hotel concierge, should be able to recommend someone who can give you an independent judgment. In Bangkok, try Rama Jewelry at the corner of Mahesak and Silom roads or the Asian Institute of Gemological Science at 484 Rajadapisek Road (Tel. 513-2112 or 513-7044). Ask for a Gem Origin Report.

If you will follow most of the above recommendations, you are likely to get a fair deal on the gem purchases you make. Buy jewelry because you love it—not solely as an investment. It is difficult to know what the market will do, and because of the mark-up on jewelry (unless you truly are buying at wholesale), it will take a long time before you could sell your jewelry (estate) for what you have paid.

Finally, you may choose to make your purchase using your credit card. Although your credit card company is under no obligation to do so, and they do expect that you, the consumer, take reasonable precautions when making purchases, if you do get home to find that your "ruby" is really a red spinel, your credit card company may assist you in getting the seller to take back the stone and refund your money.

TAILORING TIPS

Time and again visitors to Thailand—like their brethren in Hong Kong, South Korea, and Singapore—come away with disappointing tailored clothes. Invariably tourists are disappointed with their tailored garments: they don't fit properly, they weren't delivered on time, or the final product was not what the buyer expected.

DISAPPOINTING TAILORED GARMENTS

We know the many pitfalls that can trap the unwary shopper who, used to buying clothing off-the-rack at home, decides to indulge in this unique experience and have clothing custom tailored. Having heard from acquaintances who traveled to this part of the world years ago about the great values in custom tailored goods, our traveler is easy prey for unbelievable deals on tailored garments. How does US$110 sound for a suit, 3 extra pairs of slacks, 3 custom-made shirts, 1 bathrobe, and a few other extras? Unbelievable! Indeed, if it sounds too good to be true, it probably is. In the end you get what you pay for. In fact, this experience could cost you plenty if the garments you pay for are so shoddily made that you seldom or never wear them.

First, consider whether you really want to have custom tailoring done. If you are hard to fit—you're an odd size or shape—and can never find anything to fit properly at home, you may be a candidate for tailoring in Thailand. But if you have no trouble buying garments that fit well "off-the-rack," ask yourself if you really want to go through the hassle and risk of custom tailoring. The hassle involves effectively communicating your wishes to the tailor, returning to the shop for several fittings (don't even hope for a good fit without this), and possibly arranging for shipment of the garments to your home if the tailor fails to finish them on time. The risk is that you will have to pay for goods that are not satisfactory and that you would never have selected if you had found them hanging on the rack. In general, you may find that ready-made clothes back home are a better value in terms of quality, design, fit, and cost.

Tailoring Considerations

If you do decide to go ahead with custom tailoring after our warnings, follow these guidelines:

- **Don't expect to get something for nothing.** Quality fabrics and good workmanship cost money anywhere in the world. Go to a good tailor and be willing to pay for quality. The best tailors tend to be located in and around the shopping arcades of Bangkok's deluxe hotels. We identify several of these tailors by name, address, and phone number in Chapter 10.

- **Look at fabrics and examples of finished work carefully.** Are the fabrics of good quality? Are they soft and supple so they will lay smoothly in the finished garment? Go to the racks of completed sample garments. Check the general appearance of garments including top stitching, buttonholes, and button quality, smoothness of darts and pocket application. Hand sewing is one mark of quality custom tailoring. Turn up the collar and examine the underside for the slightly uneven hand stitches which indicate that it was partly hand sewn. Check the way hems are finished. Check women's jackets and coats to see that the chest area is not excessively form fitted with darts which create a fitted look not popular in the West—especially if you plan to wear the jacket unbuttoned and loose.

- **Check garments waiting for first or second fittings.** Next, go to the rack where other customers' unfinished garments are waiting for first or second fittings. Examine the inside construction of several garments to see how well each is constructed. Firm interfacing should be used inside the upper part of jackets and coats and inside the lapels and collar to give support and shape to the garment. Many tailors now use fusible (iron-on) interfacing to save time instead of the more supple woven interfacing which needs to be sewn into place. Fusible interfacing is fine when used in a limited way, but the exclusive use of fusible rather than woven interfacing results in stiff garments. If fabrics have a pattern check to see how well the pattern matches wherever seams meet.

■ **Specify the right style for you.** Be prepared with photos showing the style or combination of styles you want. (Remember, Thai tailors do not work from pre-packaged patterns. You can select a collar from one photo to be combined with a jacket front from another). Men's suits, for example, can be fashioned in three different styles or silhouettes:

✦ **The American Silhouette:** Derived from the Brooks Brothers "sack" suit of the '50s. Cut straight and full with lightly padded natural shoulders, a center rear vent, and medium arm-holes, it is body concealing and conservative.

✦ **The European Cut Silhouette:** This is sleeker and features a more dramatic fit around the chest and hips with padded shoulders, high armholes, narrow lapels, and a generally slim line which looks best on smaller men.

✦ **The British Silhouette:** Often called the Updated American model, this suit has slightly padded shoulders, nipped in the waist, two deep rear side vents, and cuffed and pleated trousers. The jacket pockets are angled and flapped.

You can, of course, specify other styles. But know before you enter a shop what looks best on you. Avoid being swayed by the salesperson to go with the "latest fashion" if it won't fit your lifestyle back home or your shape.

■ **Communicate every detail.** Don't assume your image is similar to the salesperson's image of the finished product. For example, if the fabric you've selected has stripes, specify the direction—horizontal, vertical or diagonal—for the stripes in the finished garment. The rule to follow here is simple: **assume nothing and explain everything!**

■ **Give the tailor enough time to do a quality job.** Expect to have a minimum of two fittings—three is better—for garments in which fit is critical such as suits or slacks. One fitting might be acceptable for a loosely constructed garment such as a blouse. Expect a suit to take at least four days while a blouse might be completed in one or two days. Good work is not done overnight, and usually only *"Hey, you mister"* shops will make such rash promises.

- **Arrange to take delivery of your finished garments no later than the day before you leave.** Leave yourself a little extra time in case the tailor fails to make the scheduled deadline or time is needed to rectify problems you discover when picking up the completed garments and trying them on for the first time.

If you will be wary of potential pitfalls of custom tailoring and follow these guidelines, you will be a smart shopper for tailored garments. Like many other people, you may be pleased with the outcome of having tailoring done in Thailand.

We address custom tailoring at some length, including a separate section (Appendix) on how to ensure proper tailoring in *The Treasures and Pleasures of Hong Kong*. You might want to refer to that book for more "how-to" information on tailoring if you believe you need more specifics than outlined here.

PART III

Surprising
Bangkok

8

Welcome to Bangkok

B ANGKOK IS A CHAOTIC AND UGLY CITY IN THE
eyes of many first-time visitors who expect major cities to
have attractive architecture, skylines, and coherent central business districts. Except for newer hotels, condominiums, shopping malls, high-rise office buildings, and temple
complexes, by any standard Bangkok is not a visually attractive
city. Its beauty lies elsewhere—off the main streets, beneath
surface appearances, and with its people and products.

CHAOS AND CONTRASTS

Bangkok is one of Asia's most exotic destinations. Row after
row of architecturally unexciting two and three-storey Chinese
commercial shops—worn by a mixture of tropical climate, air
pollution, and cheap construction materials—dominate the ever
changing and dynamic landscape of this bustling and sprawling
city of over 8 million people who muddle-through in a typical
Thai fashion of seeming disorganization and chaos which
somehow works.

Bangkok and the Thai have a certain charm not found in
other Asian cities. In the midst of the chaos, pollution, conges-

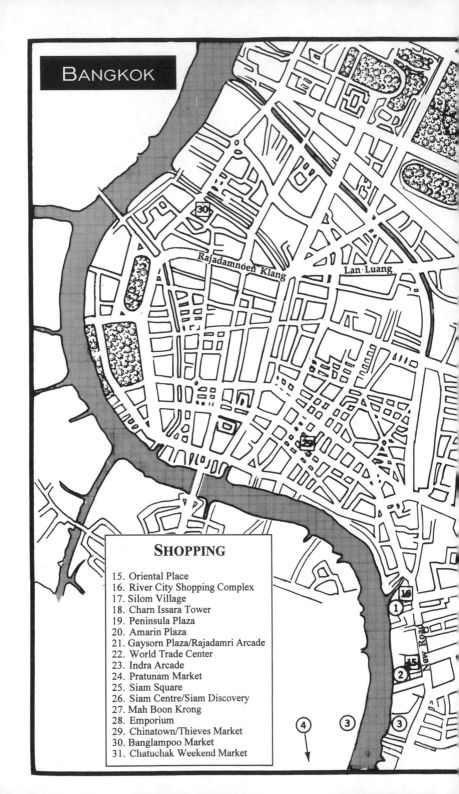

BANGKOK

Rajadamnoen Klang

Lan·Luang

30

29

SHOPPING

15. Oriental Place
16. River City Shopping Complex
17. Silom Village
18. Charn Issara Tower
19. Peninsula Plaza
20. Amarin Plaza
21. Gaysorn Plaza/Rajadamri Arcade
22. World Trade Center
23. Indra Arcade
24. Pratunam Market
25. Siam Square
26. Siam Centre/Siam Discovery
27. Mah Boon Krong
28. Emporium
29. Chinatown/Thieves Market
30. Banglampoo Market
31. Chatuchak Weekend Market

HOTELS

1. Royal Orchid Sheraton
2. Oriental
3. Shangri-La/Peninsula
4. Marriott Royal Garden Riverside
5. Holiday Inn Crowne Plaza
6. Dusit Thani
7. Westin Banyan Tree/Sukhothai
8. Regent/Grand Hyatt Erawan
9. Le Royal Meridien
10. Amari Watergate/Indra
11. Siam Inter-Continental/Novotel
12. Hilton
13. Landmark/Ambassador
14. Sheraton Grande Sukhumvit

tion, heat, poverty, and ugliness of this city stand nearly 400 glittering, colorful, and serene Buddhist temples which punctuate Bangkok's recently developed skyline of modern high-rise office buildings, hotels, and condominiums laced with concrete expressways and an elevated mass transit system, the Skytrain. The ever charming but highly polluted river and canals, filled with colorful long-tail boats and lumbering barges plying the muddy waters of the Chao Phraya River, further add to the contrasts and seeming contradictions of this exotic Southeast Asian city.

A SHOPPER'S PARADISE

While Bangkok is relatively unknown to many travelers, it is one of best places to both shop and travel in Asia. Indeed, it is both a travel and shopping paradise. Just between us, we find Bangkok to be one of the best kept shopping secrets in all of Asia. Most prices are still comparatively reasonable, quality is good, service is excellent, hotels and restaurants are outstanding, and the Thai are the most delightful Asians we have encountered. But to really enjoy this place, you must know the what, where, and how of traveling and shopping in Bangkok. In contrast to other Asian cities, especially the self-contained and densely populated islands of Hong Kong and Singapore, you must work harder at uncovering Bangkok's many treasures and pleasures.

THE STREETS OF BANGKOK

Bangkok can be a truly disorienting yet rewarding experience. Like many other Asian capitals, Bangkok is a large, chaotic, hustling and bustling city frequently choked with horrific traffic that often seems to be going nowhere. From the moment you arrive at Bangkok International Airport and descend into the crowds at the main terminal, to when you first venture from your hotel to cross the street, Bangkok hits you full force with a kaleidoscope of fascinating and often intimidating phenomena. Glittering story-book temples and saffron-robed Buddhist monks walking the streets in early morning—the ultimate signs of exotic Southeast Asia—co-exist amongst an ugly urban jungle of worn commercial buildings, modern high-rise office buildings and condominiums, and fabulous, as well as nondescript, shopping arcades, hotels, and restaurants. Noisy, overcrowded, and polluting buses lumber down the streets alongside rickety *tuk-tuks*, taxis, and chauffeur-driven Mercedes-Benz and BMWs. The mass of humanity plying the maddening streets of Bangkok is so fascinating that one should spend at least an hour just observing and contemplating what makes this city tick. Juxtaposing the old and the new, as well as the beauty and the beast, Bangkok remains a fascinating adventure for many travelers who discover its many unique treasures and pleasures. Whatever you do, don't let surface appearances dissuade you from enjoying this city of charming chaos.

OVERCOMING STREET SHOCK

Tucked away in the midst of this urban jungle is a truly exciting shopping adventure with numerous shops offering a dazzling array of products and bargains. But this shopping experience becomes most rewarding once you overcome what for many visitors is the initial visual shock of a chaotic and intimidating Bangkok. Indeed, standing at the curb of any major intersection can be an extremely disorienting experience as thousands of buses, taxis, and private cars jockey for position before your eyes. The best ways to overcome this shock are to:

❏ Bangkok is a large, chaotic, hustling and bustling city. It hits you full force with a kaleidoscope of fascinating and often intimidating phenomena.

❏ The mass of humanity plying the streets is so fascinating that you should spend an hour just observing and contemplating what makes this city tick.

❏ Avoid making long trips between shopping areas since you will waste a great deal of time in Bangkok's gridlock of slowly moving traffic.

- **Develop a very tolerant attitude toward everything that goes on around you.** View Bangkok as a unique, challenging, and humorous experience rather than as a set of insurmountable problems you must cope with. To really enjoy this city, you should walk its sidewalks, cross its streets, explore its shopping centers and hotels, discover its great restaurants, and happily muddle alongside its masses. This is not the place for neat and tidy minds wedded to plans, schedules, and predictable behavior. It's for the adventuresome traveler who is open to new experiences and enjoys serendipitous situations.

- **Hire an air-conditioned hotel car with an English-speaking driver or take air-conditioned taxis to various shopping areas and city sights.** Unless you are poor, very adventuresome, seek novel experiences, or foolish, do not take buses, *tuk tuks*, or non-air-conditioned taxis, except for very short distances. You will be *"penny-wise but pound foolish"* as you suffer the worst effects of Bangkok's hot and polluted streets.

- **Ride the new Skytrain to and from the major shopping areas.** Literally elevate your transportation whenever possible! If you are not laden down with lots of packages, the Skytrain is the most efficient and convenient way to get around the major shopping areas, especially Sukhumvit Road and Silom Road, and to the Chatuchak Weekend Market. On a heavily street congested day, trips that may take an hour by car or taxi may take only 10 to 15 minutes by Skytrain!

- **Concentrate your shopping on a few shopping areas within close proximity of each other each day.** Unless your hotel is close to a Skytrain station, avoid making long trips between shopping areas since you will most likely waste a great deal of time in Bangkok's gridlock of slowly moving street traffic.

- **Minimize the hassles of traffic by avoiding rush hour traffic which is normally at its peak during 7:30-8:30am and 4:30-6:30pm.** Spend these hours in your hotel, at shops and restaurants, or sightseeing at a particular location, such as along the river or in temples.

- **Ask for assistance whenever you feel you need it.** Thais are a warm and hospitable people who tend to be very helpful and accommodating. If they don't know the answer, or can't understand you, many will try to find someone who can assist you.

- **If you get exhausted, tired, or frustrated with your day on the streets, escape to the peace and quiet of a temple, or the luxury, ambience, and service of a deluxe hotel lobby, restaurant, or coffee shop.** Bangkok offers many wonderful places to escape to for reorganizing your schedule and contemplation. For those moments, we highly recommend staying close to the Regent, Oriental, Royal Orchid Sheraton, Shangri-La, Dusit Thani, Grand Hyatt Erawan, Sheraton Grande Sukhumvit, Siam Inter-Continental, Le Royal Meridien, Novotel, Hilton, or Landmark hotels.

GETTING ORIENTED

Bangkok is one of the few truly Asian cities—spontaneous and largely unplanned—overlaid with numerous traffic arteries and a set of street rules most appropriate for Western cities designed around city plans, zoning regulations, and automobiles. One of the best ways to make sense of this city is to get Nancy Chandler's *Map of Bangkok* (page 32) which includes details on streets, lanes, canals, Skytrain routes, river transportation, shops, shopping centers, restaurants, hotels, and sightseeing. This map, along with this book, may well become your best friends in discovering Bangkok's treasures and pleasures.

The **streets** of Bangkok do have a certain logic. Bangkok's main traffic arteries consist of superhighways/toll roads, streets, lanes, elevated rail (Skytrain), canals, and the Chao Phraya River. Lacking any semblance of urban zoning, commercial and residential areas are mixed together along the streets and lanes. No central city exists—only different government and commercial areas best identified by the names of particular streets, hotels, department stores, shopping centers, commercial buildings, government buildings, and temple complexes.

The **lanes**, or *soi*, are similar to small one-lane streets or alleys found in other countries. They lead into the major streets and are often linked together in a maze of interconnecting lanes. Many of the best shops, restaurants, hotels, and sights in Bangkok—such as Rasi Sayam, Golden Tortoise, Naga House, Asia Heritage and the Gallery, Shinawatra, Fatima Self Help Center, Bangkok Dolls, Royal Orchid Sheraton Hotel, and Jim Thompson House—are found along these lanes. Therefore, you need to look beyond the major hotels, shopping centers, and shops which are most evident along Bangkok's major streets: Sukhumvit, Ploenchit, Phetburi, New Phetburi, Rajaprarop, Rajadamri, Silom, Suriwongse, and New Road. The interior lanes leading from these traffic arteries, especially around the Sukhumvit area, yield some of Thailand's best quality shops.

Canals, or *klong*, used to be the major traffic arteries in Bangkok. Today most canals have been filled with dirt, concrete, or asphalt and are now streets and lanes. The remaining canals are extremely polluted or are charming commercial and residential waterways which many tourists enjoy exploring. But don't expect to do much shopping along these canals. What shopping exists is limited to fruits and vegetables, basic Thai consumer goods, and a few tourist trinkets. You primarily travel the canals to view the exotic lifestyles or to get somewhere quicker than by road.

Most of the canals are found across the river from Bangkok, in the sister city of Thonburi. If you want to enjoy the unique canal experience, buy a copy of Geo-Ch Veran's *50 Trips through Siam's Canals*, which is available at a few major bookstores in Bangkok, or hire your own boat at the dock just adjacent to the Oriental Hotel off New Road, or at the dock next to the Pingklao Bridge near the National Museum. Comfortable 10-passenger boats can be hired for about 400B per hour. But be careful. Some of the middlemen and boatmen may try to take advantage of you by overcharging. Agree on the price **before** getting into the boat and starting the trip; make sure the person repeats the price at least three times; and write the price on a piece of paper in full view of the boatman. If he tries to overcharge you, just leave or say you need to see a policeman (*tamruat*). These actions usually result in getting you what you want. During your trip into the canals, you will see a great deal of commercial and residential activity.

NAVIGATING STREETS AND LANES

Bangkok is divided into a series of administrative districts, but these are relatively meaningless to taxi drivers and shopkeepers. The major locations are identified by particular street names, hotels, government buildings, temples, department stores, shopping centers, or names of tourist sights. If a particular shop is located on a lane, be sure you have the complete address. This includes the name of the main street and the number of the establishment on the particular lane off the main street. For example, "*131/7 Soi 9, Sukhumvit Road*" means the place is located at number 131/7, which is on Soi 9, and Soi 9 connects with Sukhumvit Road. The driver will then go to Sukhumvit Road and turn into Soi 9 to find number 131/7.

As you navigate the streets of Bangkok, going from one shopping area to another, we caution you to be sensitive to certain aspects of these streets, be sure you:

- **Watch where you walk.** In some areas, sidewalks are broken or uneven. Sometimes trees (dying) suddenly appear in the middle of the sidewalk or tree branches hang low—examples of periodic municipal beautification campaigns that that are more nuisances than improvements—planners forgot that pedestrians also use the sidewalks! If you don't watch your feet, you can easily stumble, twist an ankle, walk into puddles, or, worst of all, fall into an open sewer trench—a fate worse than death! If you don't look ahead, you may wrap your body around a tree or bang your head on the branches. And water constantly drips from the roofs of commercial buildings onto the sidewalks, and onto your head—if you don't watch above you. If you are in the Silom-Patpong-Suriwongse Road area at night, beware of the army of feathered creatures that line the overhead wires. Stay clear of the sidewalks or you may be in for an unpleasant volley from Bangkok's bombardier birds—the ultimate sign you have been carousing through Bangkok's sleazy bars at night!

- **Keep your valuables close to you wherever you go.** Like other big cities, Bangkok has its share of thieves and pick-pockets who prey on tourists. This is not a major problem, but it does exist. So don't make it easy for them. Men should keep their wallets in their front pockets, however uncomfortable. Women should hold their hand bags securely; never leave them unattended, even when passing through a luncheon buffet line.

- **Use taxis even for short distances of a mile or less if the traffic is not too heavy and slow.** Walking in Bang-kok's heat, humidity, and air pollution is not good exercise nor a convenient way to get around. It is debilitating and will ruin your day, and your stay. If the Skytrain operates along the same route as a taxi, and stations are convenient, take the Skytrain over the taxi, especially if the street traffic is heavy.

- **Walk only in safe places at night.** Streets and lanes are not well lit at night for your safety against either speeding vehicles or thieves. Use taxis at night whenever and wher-ever possible.

- **Have taxis wait for you in the lanes.** If you take a taxi very far into a lane, you may want to pay the driver to wait. Sometimes it is very difficult to find another taxi to take you out of the maze of lanes. You can easily get lost and spend a confusing and hot 30 minutes or more trying to walk your way out to the main street.

- **Take a small umbrella with you and head for high ground during the rainy season.** When it rains in Bang-kok, it really pours and the city temporarily comes to a halt. Unfortunately, Bangkok's rains come at you from above and below as streets and sidewalks quickly flood during heavy downpours. Deluxe hotels and shopping centers outside the New Road area are good places to seek high ground. .

■ **Use overhead crosswalks, cross streets at intersections, observe the stop lights, and always look to your right as well as to your left.** While Thais are a very polite and considerate people in face-to-face situations, many seem to take on a totally different personality when sitting behind the wheel of a car. Assume you have no rights as a pedestrian, and it is foolhardy to test the traffic with your body. You must walk defensively. It is very dangerous to jaywalk. Use the many overhead crosswalks or cross only at intersections, but always keep an eye on the traffic even though you ostensibly have the right-of-way. Drivers often run stop lights and seldom slow down or stop for pedestrians. Since Thais drive on the left and bus lanes often run against the traffic, make a habit of always looking to your right and then to your left. Many people, including tourists, have been killed or seriously injured by buses, cars, trucks, *tuk tuks*, and motorbikes because they failed to regularly make these cautious observations.

■ **Avoid the Silom-Rama IV Road intersection at the Lumpini Park and Dusit Thani Hotel area whenever possible.** Despite the massive fly-over, this is one of the longest stop lights in Thailand and it is the most congested intersection. Expect to spend 7 to 15 minutes to get across this key intersection. More than one trip through this intersection in a single day will indeed ruin your day. Sometimes it is best to walk across the intersection and then catch a taxi on the other side. Some taxis drivers do not want to take passengers through this intersection, or they will only do so by quoting a high price rather than use their meters.

If you follow some of these basic rules for navigating Bangkok's streets and handling its shopping, you should be able to get around Bangkok with relative ease. Since you want to best use your time for shopping and sightseeing rather than hassle the traffic and discomforts of Bangkok, try to approach this city with a sense of humor and tolerance. Better still, use your time wisely in shopping centers and shops rather than in buses and taxis, or on the streets of Bangkok.

PLAN IT RIGHT

If you come to Bangkok to primarily sightsee, you may be disappointed with your visit, especially after spending so many hours in the traffic trying to go from one site to another. There are sites to visit, but Bangkok's real treasures are found in its many wonderful shops. You'll have a great time discovering top quality products and meeting some very interesting and talented people.

Shopping in Bangkok is especially rewarding if you know the how, what, and where of shopping its many streets, shopping centers, arcades, and department stores.

You should approach Bangkok with a relatively intelligent and flexible plan. Given Bangkok's horrendous traffic situation, **where you stay** will probably be the single most important factor in determining how much you enjoy this city. Believe us. You can easily hate this city if you unwittingly stay in the wrong place. The traffic will quickly kill your enthusiasm for Bangkok as well as Thailand. If you choose a hotel poorly situated in relation to the major shopping centers, you are likely to waste a great deal of time in the traffic trying to go from one shopping area to another. You simply don't need this aggravation by making the wrong hotel choices!

- ❑ Where you stay will probably be the single most important factor in determining how much you enjoy this city.

- ❑ Bangkok's top hotels are good buys compared to comparable accommodations in other countries.

- ❑ Concentrate your shopping in one or two areas each day. If you try to cover more areas, you'll spend most of your day in the traffic!

- ❑ Begin your shopping adventure in the hotel shopping arcades where you will find the best quality products.

- ❑ The trend in Bangkok is to move toward fixed prices on quality products or to give very minimum discounts.

- ❑ Most shops can easily arrange shipping for you.

Our recommendation is to stay in one of four major areas where you can easily walk to the major shopping centers or connect with other centers by means of a short taxi ride:

- ■ **Along or near the Chao Phraya River:** Peninsula, Shangri-La, The Oriental, Royal Orchid Sheraton, Marriott Royal Garden Riverside, or Holiday Inn Crowne Plaza hotels. This remains our famorite location.

- ■ **Near Rama IV, Silom, Suriwongse, and Patpong roads:** Sukhothai, Westin Banyan Tree, Dusit Thani, Pan Pacific, Montien, Tawana Ramada, Plaza, Narai, and the Holiday Inn Crowne Plaza hotels.

- **Near the World Trade Center/Gaysorn Plaza/Amarin Plaza/Peninsula Plaza:** The Regent, Grand Hyatt Erawan, Le Royal Meridien, Le Meridien President, Arnoma Swissôtel, and Amari Watergate hotels.

- **Near the Emporium, Times Square, Landmark, Promenade, and numerous lanes off Sukhumvit Road.** Sheraton Grande Sukhumvit, Novotel Lotus, Landmark, Delta Grand Pacific, Ambassador, and Hilton hotels.

The Siam Inter-Continental and Novotel hotels near the **Siam Centre–Siam Square–Siam Discovery–Mah Boon Krong Centre** complex, and the Indra Regent and Baiyok Sky and Suite hotels near **Pratunam and Rajaprarop Road** are also good choices. For relative peace and quiet, try the Sukhothai Hotel and the Westin Banyan Tree on **Sathorn Tai Road** and the Hilton Hotel at **Nailert Park.**

We also recommend staying at some of Bangkok's top hotels. While expensive (US$150-$350 per night double occupancy), they are still good buys compared to similar accommodations in other countries, and you will love Thailand's high quality accommodations and service.

VISIT ONE AREA EACH DAY

Whatever you do, make sure you concentrate your shopping in one or two areas each day. Except for the Sukhumvit Road area, visiting most shopping areas involves only two taxis rides for the day—one to the area and one back to your hotel—and each area can be easily covered on foot. Trying to cover more than two major shopping areas in a single day will likely put you into the depressing traffic, unless you have planned your shopping around various Skytrain stations. Take it easy. Plan, for example, to spend a day shopping along Suriwongse, Silom, and New Road. On another day head for the Peninsula Plaza, Amarin Plaza, Gaysorn Plaza, and World Trade Center, and maybe also include nearby Siam Centre, Siam Square, and the Pratunam areas. On another day you might want to concentrate only on the Sukhumvit Road area—the Emporium, Times Square, Landmark, the numerous side lanes that define the Sukhumvit Road area, and The Promenade arcade at Nailert Park. But don't try to jump from one of these areas to another in a single day. If you do, you'll spend most of your time in the traffic. And you will quickly learn to hate this city simply because you made such choices!

SET PRIORITIES

The best approach to shopping in Bangkok is to identify the types of items you wish to buy; select your high priority shops in and around major shopping arcades; plan to visit special shops outside these areas; and leave time for serendipity. If you want to take advantage of custom-made clothes, jewelry, and furniture, make sure you bring pictures, examples, or detailed drawings of your designs.

Begin your shopping adventure in the major hotel shopping arcades or centers adjacent to hotels where you will find the best quality products. Start, for example, with Oriental Place (Oriental Hotel), River City Shopping Complex (Royal Orchid Sheraton Hotel), and Peninsula Plaza (Regent and Grand Hyatt Erawan hotels). After surveying the types of goods available, quality, and prices, expand your shopping area to include shops near the major hotel complexes as well as visit quality shops outside these areas. Hire a car and driver to take you to places like the Golden Tortoise Deco, Rasi Sayam, Lao Song Handicrafts, Fatima Self Help Center, and Bangkok Dolls, which are off the normal beaten tourist path.

BARGAIN IF YOU CAN

Be sure you bargain for most items you purchase in Bangkok according to our advice in Chapter 5. Many shopkeepers expect you to bargain and will give anywhere from 10 to 40 percent discounts. However, certain shops have fixed prices or bargain very little. Department stores have fixed prices, but you may receive a 5-10 percent discount on expensive items, such as jewelry, if you ask for it. Prices also are fixed at Jim Thompson Silk Company, Narayana Phand, and a few other shops. And don't expect discounting at high quality antique and art shops, such as NeOld and Elephant House. Jewelry shops, on the other hand, can and do give larger discounts. You will receive the largest discounts—up to 60 percent in some cases—from vendors in markets who both inflate their prices and can operate on small profit margins given their low overhead. You also can receive discounts on hotels, tours, and guides—but only if you ask and only from certain ones at particular times of the year. In general, the trend is to move toward fixed prices on quality products or to give very minimum discounts.

When you bargain in Bangkok, bargain as you would in other countries, but also try to put some additional degrees of light-heartedness and humor into the process. The Thais are very polite, civil, sophisticated, and fun-loving people who enjoy arriving at mutually satisfactory arrangements. You should never raise your voice or act disgusted or insulted. The Thais tend to be responsive to a nice, easy-going, polite, and humorous negotiation process where everyone keeps a good "face" and arrives at a mutually beneficial arrangement.

Thai shopkeepers tend to be rather fair and honest in contrast to similar merchants in many other countries. We generally don't get or feel ripped-off when we shop in Thailand, but of course we avoid the touts and their shops and are generally careful where we shop. Some of our readers have reported problems with their jewelry and antique purchases, but not as a result of following our advice. Indeed, they did just the opposite. Invariably they failed to use good common sense, and they violated the first rule of good shopping—always shop in reputable shops. Whatever you do, please avoid shopping in places recommended by tour guides, taxi drivers, or anyone who approaches you with a "good deal" recommendation. There still is no such thing as a free lunch!

SHIPPING

As we noted at the end of Chapter 5, most shops are familiar with shipping abroad. They will pack your goods and take care of all documents necessary for exporting, insurance, and customs. If, for example, you are exporting Thai antiques, these items require special government export certificates. The shop selling the item, or a shipper, can arrange for this certificate.

If you establish a relationship with a shipper, he will work with you through the mail or by fax or telephone to arrange for additional shipments once you return home. This can be a very useful relationship, especially if you later want to import furniture and antiques from different shops. For example, Sweet Home furniture makers regularly use Hong Kong Transpack for their shipping. If you develop a relationship with both of these companies, you will be well positioned to regularly import furniture and other products by long-distance ordering.

9

Where to Shop

I F YOU ARE LOOKING FOR UNIQUE ITEMS AND
quality goods, you must go beyond the typical tourist paths
and find the best shops for such treasures. Fortunately,
more and more shops in Bangkok are responding to the
tastes of discerning Thai and Western visitors. If you seek
quality shops, you will discover some wonderful treasures that
will make your trip to Thailand especially meaningful.

Before venturing into Bangkok's shopping areas, do what we
recommended earlier—acquire a copy of Nancy Chandler's
Map of Bangkok. It's available in most Bangkok bookstores and
major hotel kiosks or you can get a copy before you leave for
Thailand (see pages 32-33 for order information). Chandler's
map will take you to all the major shopping areas as well as
point you to some of the best restaurants and sites. Detailed
insert maps of the Central Shopping Area (World Trade Center,
Peninsula Plaza, Amarin Plaza, Gaysorn Plaza, Siam Centre,
Siam Square), Sukhumvit Road, Chatuchak Weekend Market,
and Sampeng Lane (Chinatown, Thieves' Market, and Pahurat)
provide many details for conducting your own do-it-yourself
walking tour of these areas. The latest edition also includes the
new Skytrain routes and stations.

Shopping in Bangkok is best approached in terms of different types of shopping locations. These include shopping areas, arcades, centers, department stores, markets, and stalls. Each offers a certain mix of products in varying qualities. Moreover, they offer different styles of shopping.

SHOPPING AREAS

Most of the quality shopping in Bangkok is concentrated along a few major streets and centered around hotels, shopping arcades, and department stores.

SILOM-SURIWONGSE-NEW ROAD AREA

This is Bangkok's major business and financial district. It runs east and west off of Rama IV Road. **Major hotels**, such as the Dusit Thani, Pan Pacific, Montien, Tawana Ramada, and Plaza, as well as two of Bangkok's up-market shopping centers— **Charn Issara Tower** and **Thaniya Plaza**—are found at the eastern end of this area. The infamous Patpong Road area, with its numerous straight, gay, and transvestite bars and lively night market of vendor stalls, is located at the upper end of this district. Excellent shopping is found in and around the hotels, especially the Dusit Thani and Montien hotels. At the upper end of Suriwongse Road, near Rama IV Road, are two of Thailand's finest shops—**Peng Seng** for antiques and **Jim Thompson Silk Company** for quality fabrics, clothing, and decorative items. Next door to Jim Thompson is **Choisy** (9/25 Suriwongse Rd.), one of Bangkok's well established French operated boutiques catering to Western designs. Nearby you will find the **Charn Issara Tower** building (Rama IV Road) which houses several major airline offices as well as three levels of up-scale shops. Except for **Yves Joaillier**, **Valda Jewelry**, **Living Extra** (unique modern unisex jewelry), and **Adam's Tailor**, most other shops here are local boutiques catering to Bangkok's upper class. The designs, fabrics, and colors appeal to few visitors. The nearby **Thaniya Plaza** (off Silom Road) is a center for restaurants, clothing, jewelry, textile, handicraft, art, and antique shops.

Returning back to Suriwongse Road, other good shops, such as **NeOld** (149/2-3 Suriwongse Road) and **Erawan Antiques** (149/8 Suriwongse Road) for antiques and home decorative items, and **Thaipan** (35/6 Suriwongse Road), **Khomapastr** (Suriwongse Road at Montien Hotel), **Khanitha** (Thanom Surawong Center), and **Orano** (149/4-6 Suriwongse Road) for fashionable women's clothes, are found in the area between Jim

Thompson Silk Company and a block past the Tawana Ramada Hotel. Many of the shops in and around the nearby Montien Hotel are also good.

Near the middle of Suriwongse Road—across the street and down a few shops from the old Neilson Hays Library—is one of Bangkok's best antique, furniture, and home decorative shops, **The Elephant House**: 286/69-71 Soi Pattana, Suriwongse Road (Tel. 233-6973).

Toward the lower end of Suriwongse Road (across from the second Toyota dealer sign) you will find **Surawongse Gallery** which has beautiful art work and does nice framing. Also included in this area are numerous tourist shops in and around the New Peninsula, New Fuji, Monohra, and New Trocadero Hotel. Look for **Asian Galleries** (460), **Tai Fah Antiques** (406), and **Ma Peng Seng Antiques** (404) in this area.

Once you reach **New Road**, turn left and explore the numerous jewelry, art, antique, and knickknack shops lining both sides of this street. Half way down this street, on the right, you come to **Oriental Lane** which leads to the Oriental Hotel, Oriental Plaza, Menam Plaza, and the river. Many of the shops in this area offer good quality products, such as **Alex & Co.** for jewelry, **Thai Home Industries** for and handicrafts, **Pagoda Thai Handicrafts**, and **Lin Plaza Gems** for jewelry, bronzeware, and handicrafts. One of the best antique shops in this area is **Arisra Gallery** at 6-8 Oriental Lane (Tel. 630-6131).

Oriental Place is well worth an hour of browsing for jewelry, clothes, antiques, woodcarvings, handicrafts, and paintings. This newly renovated shopping arcade includes some of Bangkok's finest shops. Some of the best shops here include **August 9, The Fine Arts, Capital Antique Galerie**, and **Kee Art Co.** for antiques; **Tomlinson** and **Ashwood Gallery** for antiques and furniture; **Kim, B.H. Jewelry**, and **Sar Jewelry** for jewelry; **Four Art Gallery** and **Royal Gallery** for paintings; and **Khanitha** and **Darlene** for fashionable silk and cotton clothes; **January Co.** for wonderful children's smocked dresses, stuffed toys, and silk; and **Chitralada of the Royal Foundation** for quality handicrafts produced under royal patronage.

Many of the adjacent hotel shops, found in the **Oriental Arcade, Author's Lounge** building, and the **Oriental Hotel** are excellent. In the Author's Lounge of the Oriental Hotel, look for the **Pink Poodle** for haute couture, **Tabtim Thai** for attractive neckpieces, **Sartorial** for tailoring, **Jim Thompson** for silk and cotton, and **Cabochon Jewellers** for exclusive jewelry. Just off the lobby of the Oriental Hotel, adjacent to the Bamboo Bar, is **Royal Thai Gems** with its beautiful gold designs. Just across from the hotel entrance, but attached to the hotel, is a small exclusive and recently renovated shopping area called the Oriental Arcade. Here you will find several excellent clothing, jewelry, and home decorative shops. One of the most exclusive shops is **Lotus** with its unique jewelry designs (also look for their shops at the Regent and Sukhothai hotels in Bangkok, Amanpuri in Phuket, Raffles Hotel in Singapore, and Oberoi in New Delhi). Other nice shops here include **Chedi** for handicrafts, **Kai Kai** for designer clothes, **Private Collection** for Indian jewelry and rugs, **Rangthong Jewelry**, and **Gifts de l'Oriental**, the official Oriental Hotel gift shop with signature clothes, swimwear, and perfumes. The street vendors selling leather goods, watches, polo shirts, paintings, and toys near the Oriental Hotel on Oriental Lane may pester you. They also sell a great deal of tourist junk. Unless you want to be pestered, keep moving and tell them *"I already bought too many."*

At this point you have a choice of returning to New Road or taking a 15-minute hotel ferry to the Royal Orchid Sheraton Hotel and the adjacent **River City Shopping Complex**. We recommend the ferry. It's free and a very pleasant ride. Catch it at the Oriental Hotel's dock at the end of the outdoor dining area and in front of the Author's Lounge. Once you arrive at the River City Shopping Complex, you will find the first and second floor have several clothing, jewelry tailor, handicraft, and shoe stores. Several of our favorite shops on second floor include **January** for children's smocked dresses, stuffed toys, and silk; **Jaana** for uniquely designed jewelry and neckpieces; **Lek Gallerie, Yonok Treasures**, and **Cheng's Collection** for antiques; and **River Mark** for tailoring. Be sure to visit the third and fourth floor shops. This area, also known as the "Art and Antique Centre," has the largest concentration of such shops in Thailand. Some of our favorites here include **The Golden Triangle, Sawasdee Antique Co., Piece of Art, Acala, Ashwood Gallery, River Trade Co., August 9, Beyond the Masks, Heritage Collection, The Fine Arts, The Height, Saowthai, Asia Art**, and **T.K. Art & Antiques**. From River City's second level you can walk directly into the Royal Orchid Sheraton Hotel. You'll be on the second floor where you will find a few jewelry and art shops. **Royal Jewelry, Cosmos Jewelry**, and **Orchid Gems** offer exclusively designed jewelry.

After visiting this area, you can either walk or take the ferry back to the Oriental Hotel or take another ferry to the Shangri-La or Peninsula hotels. If you decide to walk, we recommend taking the less congested **Captain Bush Lane**. Here you will find a few shops offering home decorative items and clothing. **Ben Antiques** at the corner of New Road and Captain Bush Lane has an interesting collection of antiques and home decorative items. Just around the corner, to your right along New Road, is **Betel Nut**, a small shop specializing in unique silver items and beads. If you continue walking along New Road toward the Oriental Hotel, you'll pass the main Post Office and numerous antique and jewelry shops on both sides of the street. One of the most outstanding shops in this area is **Rama Art Gallery** at 1238/1-2 New Road 36 (Tel. 233-3330) with its three floors of exquisite antiques. You will also pass several shops selling bronzeware. For good prices on black burnished flatware—half of the cost at the nearby Thai Home Industries —stop at **Siam Bronze and Thai Products** (1250 New Road).

If you take the ferry back to the Oriental Hotel or wish to go to the Shangri-La Hotel or Peninsula Hotel, board at the River City Shopping Complex. Unfortunately you cannot go directly from the Oriental Hotel to the Shangri-La Hotel, or vice versa, on one of the free hotel shuttle ferries. You must transit at the River City Shopping Complex docks.

If you go to the **Shangri-La Hotel**, you will find several shops in and around this hotel. The main hotel's small shopping arcade has several quality shops: **C. Fillipo** for men's tailoring; **Cotton Corner** and **C.S. Thai Silk** for stylish silk and cotton clothes; **S.S. Gems** for jewelry; and **Pat's Arts & Crafts** for gift items. The Krung Thep wing of the hotel has another shopping arcade with some very nice quality antique, silk, and clothing shops.

If you return to the Oriental Hotel, walk down Oriental Lane and take a right onto New Road. The remainder of this shopping area primarily consists of shops along Silom Road. As you walk down **New Road**, you will see more jewelry, antique, art, and clothing shops. One of Thailand's best antique shops, now converted into two galleries directly across the street from each other, is **Lek Gallerie** at 1310-1312 New Road (Tel. 234-4184). Also look for **Yong Antiques, Somboon Enterprises, From Siam With Love, Maison des Arts, Thai Thong Art Gallery, U-Thong Antiques, Petchburi Gallery, Majestic Art, Artcraft Exports, Alexandra Thai Silk,** and **A. Gallery**.

When you come to **Silom Road**, take a left at the corner antique shop, pass by the small flower market, and begin walking up Silom Road. Many small tourist shops line this street. Within a few minutes you will see the **Holiday Inn Crowne Plaza** on your right. It has a shopping arcade with several jewelry, clothing, and handicraft shops. Within another five minutes you should come to the **Central Department Store, Design Thai, Motif, Anita Thai Silk,** and **Santi's Arts and Antiques**—all worth a stop. Next comes **Silom Village**, a small but nice shopping and restaurant center. The front section is filled with small shops and vendors selling leather goods and souvenirs. A few small home decorative, antique, jewelry, and handicraft shops are found in this shopping area. **Artisan's**, small but good quality and reasonably priced, is one of our favorite art, antique, and home decorative shops; ask to see their nearby furniture warehouse. Also look for **Hill Tribe Products** and **Old Times**. You may want to stay at Silom Village a while to sample some of the Thai food and enjoy the lovely outdoor atmosphere. Directly across the street is **Chai Ma Antiques**.

Further along Silom Road you will see numerous jewelry, clothing, and antique shops catering to tourists, especially around the **Narai Hotel**. Keep an eye on both sides of the street. A few excellent shops, such as **Galerie D'Art**, stand alone across from the Narai Hotel. If you don't look carefully, you will miss some good shops in this area.

From the Narai Hotel you may want to explore two nearby streets that offer out-of-the-way art shops. Look for **Art Resources** at 142-20 Soi Sueksavitaya, North Sathorn Rd. (Tel. 235-4846) for traditional Thai paintings, art deco bronze decorative pieces, and framing. You may need to take a taxi from Silom Road to locate this excellent shop.

Returning to the Narai Hotel, it's a long walk up the remainder of Silom Road. At this point you may want to take a taxi to Patpong Road, Thaniya Plaza, or the Dusit Thani Hotel. During the day **Patpong Road** has little to offer shoppers other than two bookstores and a supermarket. Save Patpong for the evening when this area becomes a huge open air market with vendors selling all kinds of fake watches, clothes, leather goods, audiocassettes, and videos—one of Thailand's most interesting shopping experiences. At the end of Silom is the **Dusit Thani Hotel** with several fine jewelry and clothing shops. On the opposite corner is **Robinson Department Store**. Just down this side of Silom Road you will see **Perry's**, one of Bangkok's best tailors. At this point you have completed this shopping. From here you can cross the busy Rama IV Road to Lumpini Park and then head up Rajadamri Road to the **Regent Hotel** and the adjacent **Peninsula Plaza**.

SUKHUMVIT, PLOENCHIT, RAMA I, RAJADAMRI, AND PHYATHAI ROAD AREA

This is one of the largest and most diverse shopping areas in Bangkok. Sukhumvit Road runs east and west. The confusing aspects of this area are the street names—Sukhumvit Road changes to Ploenchit Road at Soi 1, and then Ploenchit Road changes to Rama I Road at the Rajadamri Road intersection. This shopping area is one long street about 9 kilometers in length, starting with Soi Ekamai (Soi 63) at the far eastern boundary and ending with Phyathai Road at the far western boundary. Sukhumvit, Ploenchit, and Rama I roads are actually one continuous street linking these two boundaries.

Sukhumvit Road and its network of lanes is the major home for many of Bangkok's expatriates. As a result, several stores cater to this group—bookstores, grocery stores, stationery shops, restaurants, furniture stores, shoe stores, etc. In addition, you will find many shops catering primarily to Western and Middle Eastern tourists. Many visitors to Thailand are interested in the wicker furniture shops between Soi 39 and 43 and the shops in and around the huge **Ambassador Hotel complex** at Soi 11. Between the furniture shops and the Ambassador Hotel are a few stores worth noting: **Pacific Design** (779-781 Sukhumvit—wicker furniture), **Santi's Art & Antiques** (178 Sukhumvit Road), and **Asia Books** (221 Sukhumvit Road, between Soi 15 and 17). The Ambassador Hotel has numerous jewelry, antique, silk, and clothing shops along with several restaurants. One of Bangkok's top seamstresses is found here— **Penny's Boutique** (also located at the Peninsula Hotel). Several other good shops, some of Bangkok's best, are located a ways off of Sukhumvit Road, along the lanes, and require taxis to reach them: **Rasi Sayam** (32 Soi 23—unique handicrafts); **Nandakwang** (108/3 Soi 23—lovely cotton products); **Lao Song Handicrafts** (2045/5 Soi 77—for hilltribe handicrafts); **Paya** (961 Sukhumvit Rd., between Soi 51 and 53) for handwoven fabrics and home accessories; and **Asia Heritage and The Gallery** (245-14 Sukhumvit Soi 31) for quality antiques and objets d'art.

Sukhumvit Road Soi 49, also known as Soi Klang, has recently become a new center for antiques and home decorative items. Two of the best places to start here are **Golden Tortoise Deco** (49/2 Sukhumvit Soi 49) and **Golden Antiques and Nim's Tea House** (4 Sukhumvit Soi 49-4) for antique Asian furniture and home decorative items. Also along Soi 49 look for **Pamevo Gallery** (108/2), **Old Wood**, **Botero**, and **Y50**. Adjacent sois include **Native House** (Soi 49-4), **Ispahan** (Soi 49-11), **Sopha Lee** (Soi 49-11), and **Panom** (Soi 49-11).

One of Bangkok's newest and most upscale and popular shopping centers is the **Emporium** at 622 Sukhumvit Road (between soi 22 and 24). If you're looking for designer clothes and accessories, such as **Chanel**, **Versace**, **Hermes**, **Escada**, **DKNY**, **Gucci**, **Prada**, and **Celine**, or some of Bangkok's major jewelry shops, such as **Franks** and **Tok Kwang**, this is the place to shop. Emporium's five levels of shops include Bangkok's two best bookstores (**Kinokuniya** and **Asia Books**), **Jim Thompson** silk shop, **Tower Records**, and a large **Handicraft Center**.

From the Emporium until the end of Sukhumvit Road at Soi 1, you will pass several small shops selling jewelry, leather goods, celadon, handicrafts, and a variety of items for tourists. The largest concentration of interesting shops is between Soi 21 (Soi Asoke) and Soi 1. Next to the Sheraton Grande Sukhumvit Hotel (250 Sukhumvit Road) is the **Times Square Shopping Center** and **Robinson Department Store**. For women's dresses, look for **Koody** and **Infini. C.V.N. Exotic Ltd.** at 131 3/4 Sukhumvit Road has a nice gallery of Thai paintings as well as does inexpensive framing. At Soi 4 you will see the Nana Hotel. Directly across the street are two very good art and jewelry stores, **Galleria D'Art** and **Sincere Jewelry**. Near Soi 3 numerous shop signs are in Arabic as you enter into Bangkok's Arab district. Tailors and tourist trinket shops abound here. You will also come to the **Landmark Hotel and Plaza** with its five levels of shops. Here you will find tailors, leather, gift, souvenir, jewelry, silk, and home decorative shops along with a branch of **Asia Books**.

At Soi 1, Sukhumvit Road becomes Ploenchit Road. Just after crossing the railroad tracks, you come to the **Bangkok Night Bazaar** and **The Tourist Shopping Plaza and Night Market** which are filled with small stalls selling inexpensive clothes and tourist items.

If you turn right at the Ploenchit-Wireless Road intersection, go north to the **Hilton International Hotel** at Nailert Park. The hotel has a few nice jewelry and tailor shops. The adjacent **Promenade** shopping arcade alone is well worth a trip to this hotel. This relatively new but always troubled arcade—shops opening and closing—is one of Thailand's most exclusive upscale shopping centers catering primarily to Bangkok's upper class. Here you will find some of Bangkok's best art galleries (**Nan Naang, Sombat, C.L.**), clothing (**Busadee**), jewelry (**Proud Precious Gems**), and home decorative (**NeOld Hilton**) shops in a beautiful mall setting. Given the recent downturn in the Thai economy, many shops here have closed as fewer and fewer local Thais frequent such upscale shops. As always, this shopping arcade is relatively quiet. It does include some good restaurants for lunch.

If you go straight along Ploenchit Road, you will next come to the **Central Department Store.** This is the largest branch of Bangkok's first department store. It has a handicraft section on the second floor as well as a small bookstore.

After crossing Chitlom Road you next come to one of Bangkok's major shopping complexes—**Le Royal Meridien Hotel–Meridien President Hotel–Gaysorn Plaza–Amarin Plaza** area. The Le Meridien President Hotel has a shopping arcade with several tourist shops offering clothing, jewelry, and knickknacks. Next door and on the corner of Ploenchit and Rajadamri roads is the pleasant upscale **Gaysorn Plaza** with its many fine clothing, accessory, and jewelry shops as well as restaurants, including Planet Hollywood. Look for **Blue River Diamond, Prada, Valentino, Noriko, Max Mara, Bally, Mont Blanc**, and even a **Harley-Davidson** shop! The second floor houses one of the nicest displays of Thai handicrafts found anywhere in Thailand—in a delightful village setting—**Thai Craft Museum**.

If you turn right at the corner of Ploenchit and Rajadamri roads, you will head north to another major shopping area— **Rajadamri Arcade, Phetburi/New Phetburi Road, Pratunam**, and the **Indra Arcade**. We'll return to this area shortly.

Amarin Plaza is located directly across from the Le Meridien President Hotel and Gaysorn. Take the escalator and overhead walkway—if it's working—to enter this plaza. Anchored by Sogo Department Store and next to the huge Grand Hyatt Erawan Hotel, Amarin Plaza has many jewelry, art, clothing, leather goods, and gift shops as well as Bangkok's first McDonald's. Many quality jewelry shops are found here. Some of the best shops include **Thai Pavillion** (nice handicrafts), **The Legend** (unique handicrafts), **Michelle 2** (women's tailoring), **D. Diamonds, Vogue Jewelry**, and **Gemsmond**.

At the intersection with Rajadamri Road, Ploenchit Road becomes Rama I Road. If you take a left at the colorful Erawan Shrine on this corner, you will immediately come to **Sogo** which offers upscale imported and locally-produced licensed designer products. Here you will find such famous designer labels as Gucci, Salvatore Ferragamo, Chanel, Christian Dior, Givenchy, Bruno Magli, Elle, Calvin Klein, Guy Laroche, and Pierre Cardin. This store primarily caters to Bangkok's growing middle and upper classes. You'll find a good food court— "Restaurant Avenue"—on the lower level.

Adjacent to Sogo is the Grand Hyatt Erawan Hotel, one of Bangkok's best hotels. Beginning at the bottom level of this uniquely designed hotel is the **Hyatt Shopping Arcade**. Here you will find several quality shops, including **Bee Bijour** for jewelry and accessories, **Jim Thompson** for silk, **J & A Jewellers**, and a great bakery and two excellent restaurants—Chinese and Italian.

Just a short walk south of the Grand Hyatt Erawan Hotel is

the elegant Peninsula Plaza and Regent Hotel, one of Bangkok's premier shopping areas. **The Peninsula Plaza** has one of the best collections of quality shops selling everything from arts and antiques to high-end jewelry, clothes, and accessories. It is anchored by the Galeries Lafayette Department Store. Some of the best quality shops in the Peninsula Plaza include **Anong Gallery, Frank's, Paa, Bualaad Joaillier, Penny's Boutique, Chailai, Bvlgari, The Hours Glass, Nusra, Gianni Versace, Ermenegildo Zegna, Prasert Collection,** and **Asia Books**. The **Regent Hotel** also has some of Thailand's finest antique, handicrafts, clothing, art, jewelry, and home decorative shops: **NeOld Thai Style, Art Resources, Lotus, Lotus Jewellery, Arts of Asia, Peninsula Gems, House of Handicrafts, Heritage, Lily Art, Pierre Tailor,** and **Tok Kwang**.

If you cross the Rajadamri Road intersection at Rama I Road, you will come to the huge **World Trade Center**. Its four floors of upscale shops have made this one of Bangkok's most popular shopping centers. Combined with several other adjacent shopping centers and hotels, such as the Arnoma Swissôtel Hotel, Le Royal Meridien Hotel, Le Meridien President Hotel, Gaysorn Plaza, Amarin Plaza, Sogo Department Store, Grand Hyatt Erawan Hotel, Peninsula Plaza, Regent Hotel, Rajadamri Arcade, The Mall, Robinson Department Store, Thai Daimaru Department Store, and Narayana Phand, the World Trade Center has virtually transformed this busy intersection into Bangkok's major shopping center. The emphasis here is on upscale shops offering clothes, accessories, jewelry, home decorative items, sporting goods, electronics, toys, and food. The shopping center is anchored by **Zen** (Central) **Department Store** and **Isetan Department Store** and includes a **King Power Duty Free Shop** on the 7th floor. On the first floor, you will find a very nice boutique, **Sonja**, a branch of Penny's Boutique which is also found at the Peninsula Plaza. Other clothing and accessory shops include **Nina Ricci, Calvin Klein, Bernini, Charles Jourdan,** and **Noriko**. However, not everything is imported. Many name brand items, such as Charles Jourdan shoes, are actually produced in Thailand under licensing arrangements. Also look for **Asian Mystique, International Gems, K.R. Jewels,** and **P&P Jewelry**.

If you walk 10 minutes directly west of this intersection along Rama I Road, you will first come to the beautiful Siam Inter-Continental Hotel and then to the huge Siam Centre, Siam Square, Siam Discovery Center, and Mah Boon Krong shopping complex. **Siam Inter-Continental Hotel** has several good jewelry, home decorative, and art shops located in an arcade to the left as you face the hotel. Next door is the four-storey **Siam Centre**. While this center appears to be in de-cline—increasingly dominated by loud and trendy clothing shops for the local youth—it does house a few nice clothing and jewelry shops. Banks, travel agents, restaurants, clothing stores, and gift shops are found throughout this building. Next door is the very youth-oriented **Siam Discovery Center**. Directly across the street from Siam Centre is **Siam Square**. This large shopping center consists of hundreds of small shops, restaurants, theaters, and fast food establishments lining several crowded lanes with the imposing **Novotel Hotel** at its center. Here you will find travel agents, tour companies, antique shops, shoe stores, boutiques, bookstores, sporting goods shops, electronic stores, appliance shops, and a host of other businesses appealing to both Thais and tourists. At the Novotel look for one of Bangkok's best jewelers—**Merlin et Delaunay** —with its exquisite French designs. If you are interested in unique hilltribe clothes and fashions, look for **Prayer** which is located at the corner of Phyathai Road and Rama I Road (very hard to find since it's a small shop—197 Patumwan Circle, Siam Square, Tel. 251-7549).

At the end of Siam Centre and directly across Phyathai Road (and Prayer) stands one of Southeast Asia's largest shopping centers—**Mah Boon Krong**. Connected to Siam Centre by an automated overhead walkway, this center is anchored by **Tokyu Department Store**. It houses hundreds of small shops selling clothes, jewelry, electronic goods, and numerous other specialty items primarily for locals. It's also reputed to be structurally unsound!

RAJAPAROP-RAJADAMRI-PHETBURI-
NEW PHETBURI ROAD AREA

This shopping area parallels the Sukhumvit and Ploenchit shopping area and intersects with it near Gaysorn on Rajadamri Road. Indeed, as new shopping centers open, this area appears to be merging with the World Trade Center, Amarin Plaza, and Peninsula Plaza to create a new mega-shopping area—the closest Bangkok has to a city shopping center. The lines between this area and other shopping areas are no longer as clear as they were seven years ago. This is a very mixed shopping area in terms of types of shops, quality of goods, and variety of products. An extremely crowded, congested, and chaotic area, here you will encounter traditional street vendors, markets, shopping arcades, and department stores. The streets are somewhat confusing because street names change once again: Phetburi Road becomes New Phetburi Road and Rajaparop Road becomes Rajadamri Road at an intersection called Pratunam. To the north of this intersection is Rajaparop Road. It is lined with numerous small shops selling all types of consumer goods. The **Indra Hotel** and adjacent **Indra Arcade** is filled with all types of small shops catering to both locals and tourists: tailors, jewelers, silk stores, gift shops, electronic stores, etc. As you go south on Rajaprarob you come to **Pratunam Market**, an enclosed market area consisting of small consumer goods stalls and surrounded on the outside by numerous street vendors selling food, consumer goods, and tourist trinkets. Here you'll enter into a maze of over 500 small clothing stalls selling inexpensive ready-made garments. This is actually Bangkok's major factory outlet market where you can buy clothes directly from the manufacturers at wholesale prices. However, don't expect to find many clothes that fit (if you are large) since sizes tend to be small and styles and colors may not integrate well with your wardrobe and tastes. Turning right at Pratunam, you head west on Phetburi Road. Immediately next to Pratunam on Phetburi Road is the **City Plaza Department Store**. Across the street is **Pantip Plaza**. The small shops which line both sides of Phetburi Road are largely consumer goods shops or they sell a few tourist items—bronze, leather, dolls, woodcarvings, etc. If you go further west on the left side of Phetburi Road for about one kilometer, or where Rama VI Road meets Phetburi Road, you will come to several bronze shops, such as **Samron Thailand** (302-308 Phetburi Road) selling lots of bronzeware.

If you return to the Pratunam intersection and go east one-half kilometer on New Phetburi Road and then turn left, you will come to a shopping area next to the Empress and Mecure Bangkok hotels. You can also enter this area by taking Makkasan Road off of Rajaparob Road. Shopping along the remainder of New Phetburi Road is very limited given the impact of on-street parking restrictions. Many businesses have declined or moved to other areas of the city since they are no longer easily accessible by car.

If you return again to Pratunam intersection and go south along Rajadamri Road toward the Ploenchit-Rama I intersection, you will come to a very crowded and congested shopping area that eventually flows into the huge Sukhumvit-Ploenchit-Rama I-Phyathai-Rajadamri Roads shopping area where the World Trade Center, Amarin Plaza, and Peninsula Plaza dominate at the intersection of Ploenchit, Rama I, and Rajadamri Roads. To your left you will find **Rajadamri Arcade** and **The Mall**. **Robinson Department Store** and **Thai Daimaru Department Store** serve as the anchors to these two congested shopping centers, selling food, audiocassettes, leather goods, clothes, and a host of consumer and tourist items. Don't miss the huge **Narayana Phand** handicraft emporium that dominates the first two floors of The Mall. Here you will find just about every type of Thai handicraft and gift item available. While the first floor is somewhat disappointing, the second floor is crammed with a good range of varying quality handicrafts. If you walk a little further, you will come to the Gaysorn area which joins with the Sukhumvit-Phyathai Road shopping area.

Other noteworthy shopping areas—older and of less appeal to tourists—are **Chinatown** and **Thieves Market** (along Charoen Krung and Yaowarat roads) and **Banglampoo** (Pra Sumen and Chakrapong roads) in the older western part of the city. You can normally walk along these streets and discover hundreds of shops selling all types of goods for local residents and tourists. However, numerous other quality shops are tucked away on side streets and along the lanes. You need names and addresses and a driver to get to these establishments. Be sure you have a copy of Nancy Chandler's *Map of Bangkok* to explore these areas. The map provides numerous details on products and shops in these areas.

SHOPPING ARCADES AND COMPLEXES

Most shopping arcades and complexes are air-conditioned shopping malls anchored to major hotels or they function as free-standing shopping centers which may or may not be found in air-conditioned enclosures. Since they offer some of the best quality products and prices anywhere, we recommend confining at least 70 percent of your shopping to these areas. Many shops that used to be difficult to find have moved to these arcades for your shopping convenience. While Bangkok has numerous shopping arcades and complexes throughout the city, these are the major ones of interest to visitors:

❑ **Emporium:** Located at 622 Sukhumvit Road (at Soi 24), this is Bangkok's newest and most upscale shopping center. Filled with five floors of jewelry, clothing, accessory, book, music, sports, and home furnishing shops. Anchored by the huge over-staffed Emporium Department Store. Includes a large handicraft display area, restaurants and food court, and five multiplex theaters. Very popular with expatriates. Visit Emporium's Web site for more details: *www.emporiumThailand.com*

❑ **Gaysorn Plaza:** Next to the new Le Royal Meridien Hotel at the corner of Ploenchit and Rajadamri roads, this is another relatively new upscale shopping arcade housing numerous name-brand clothing, accessory, and jewelry stores.

❑ **The Promenade:** Part of the Hilton Hotel complex at Nailert Park, this is one of Bangkok's most upscale shopping arcades. It includes numerous art galleries, home decor, clothing and accessory shops, and jewelry stores along with a few cafes and restaurants. Tastefully done, this shopping arcade has yet to take off as a major shopping area. Consequently, it's often quiet and relatively deserted.

❑ **Oriental Place:** Located just off New Road and near the Oriental Hotel. Filled with excellent quality jewelry stores, antique and home decorative shops, boutiques, handicraft shops, art galleries, tailor shops, and silk stores. Some of Bangkok's best antique and furniture shops are found here. Many other excellent shops are found within a one-half kilometer radius of this shopping center. Always seems quiet and somewhat deserted, although new owners are trying to promote this center more. Like the Promenade, it has yet to take off as a major shopping center.

❑ **Oriental Hotel Shops:** You will find a few exclusive jewelry, antique, art, and clothing shops in three areas surrounding the Oriental Hotel: the **Author's Lounge Building**, **Oriental Arcade**, and the area adjacent to the rear of the **hotel lobby**. Visit these shops while shopping in the nearby Oriental Place.

❑ **River City Shopping Complex:** Adjacent to the Royal Orchid Sheraton Hotel on the Chao Phraya River and connected to the Oriental Hotel as well as the Shangri-La and Peninsula hotels by ferries. One of the best quality shopping arcades. Pleasant setting along the river. Third and fourth floor "Art and Antique Centre" offers a dazzling array of Thailand's finest quality art and antique shops. Other shops offer good quality handicrafts, clothes, jewelry, toys, and souvenirs.

❑ **Shangri-La Hotel Shops:** Located off of New Road along the Chao Phraya River, the Shangri-La Hotel has a small shopping arcade in its main facility (lower level) with shops offering tailored garments, ready-made clothes, gifts, and souvenirs. The hotel's Krung Thep wing has a larger and more attractive shopping arcade with shops offering clothes, gifts, and antiques. Numerous clothing, jewelry, antique, and souvenir shops line the road leading to the main entrance of the Shangri-La Hotel and extending to the ferry dock.

❏ **Holiday Inn Crowne Plaza Shops:** Located along Silom Road (at Surasak/Mahesak roads), this troubled shopping arcade should include more than 50 shops offering everything from clothes and jewelry to souvenirs. However, it has fallen on hard times as many shops have closed. When operational, it's a pleasant arcade offering a wide range of products for the tourist budget.

❏ **Silom Village:** A little hard to find these days because of all the sidewalk clutter. Located between the Narai Hotel and Central Department Store at 287 Silom Road. Small shopping complex with a mix of vendors selling leather goods, tourist knickknacks, jewelry, home decorative items, antiques, and handicrafts. Pleasant open-air restaurants in a water and garden setting. Thai dinner-cultural show presented here at night.

❏ **Thaniya Plaza:** One of Bangkok's newer and more disappointing upscale shopping centers located in the heart of the financial and shopping district just off Silom Road near Patpong Road and the Dusit Thani Hotel. Its four floors of shops offer quality jewelry, clothes, accessories, silk, textiles, antiques, arts, and handicrafts as well as several Japanese, Chinese, and Western restaurants. Includes a branch of Asia Books. Some of Bangkok's best quality shops moved here from the old Oriental Plaza and River City Shopping Complex in 1992, but several of these shops have now moved out because of the lack of shopping traffic and competition from other better located shopping arcades. This is a relatively quiet area. Popular place for business lunches.

❏ **Charn Issara Tower:** A shopping arcade located in one of Bangkok's major commercial buildings on Rama IV Road, between Silom and Suriwongse Road. This is one of Bangkok's most exclusive shopping centers frequented by many of Bangkok's wealthy residents and airline employees who yearn for European styles and quality. The four floors of this shopping center have many jewelry and clothing stores. A popular place for Japanese tourists who seek name-brand items and exclusive jewelry. While some clothing stores position themselves as haute couture, they have a long way to go before they achieve the stylish and finished looks associated with haute couture found in European capitals. An up-market shopping center of disappointing boutiques with pretensions of being "the best."

❑ **Montien Hotel Shops:** Located opposite Patpong Road and just off Suriwongse Road, the Montien Hotel has a small but good quality shopping arcade with shops offering antiques, jewelry, clothes, and gift items. Numerous shops surround the hotel just outside the front door and along Suriwongse Road. This is one of the best shopping areas in Bangkok, especially for fashionable clothes, antiques, and home decorative items. You will find such shops as Jim Thompson Silk, NeOld, and Peng Seng as well as several shops in the Charn Issara Tower and Thaniya Plaza within easy walking distance of the Montien Hotel. This area becomes another type of shopper's paradise from 6:30pm to 11pm every night as over 100 vendors set up tables and stalls among Patpong, Suriwongse, and Silom roads to sell inexpensive clothes, accessories, watches, briefcases, cassettes, videos, souvenirs, and toys in what has become known as the Night Market. Consequently, the Montien is literally a center for non-stop shopping in Bangkok.

❑ **Peninsula Plaza:** Situated next to the Regent Hotel on Rajadamri Road, this is one of Bangkok's most upscale shopping centers. Anchored by Galeries Lafayette Department Store. Filled with excellent quality boutiques, art and antique shops, jewelry and accessories stores, a large bookstore, and restaurants. This is where Elizabeth Taylor used to buy jewelry (Frank's) when visiting Bangkok. Many shops are branches of other shops found at the Emporium, Gaysorn Plaza, Promenade, Oriental Place, River City Shopping Complex, or belong to main shops that are tucked away along Bangkok's many lanes. Nice ambience. A wonderful place to escape from the heat, pollution, and rains.

❑ **Regent Hotel Shops:** Located next to the Peninsula Plaza on Rajadamri Road, this is one of Thailand's best hotels. Its small shopping arcade is one of the best with several exclusive jewelry, art, clothing, antique, home decorative, and handicraft shops. Don't miss this one!

❑ **Hyatt Shopping Arcade:** On the lower level of the Grand Hyatt Erawan Hotel and adjacent to the Amarin Plaza. Includes several exclusive silk, jewelry, clothing, and gift shops along with a famous bakery and two fine restaurants. Top quality shops.

❑ **The Landmark Hotel and Plaza:** Found at the lower end of Sukhumvit Road, across from Soi 3 and just near the railroad tracks, this is one of Bangkok's largest hotel shopping arcades, although by no means remarkable nor particularly special. Strange layout that is confusing to shoppers. Its five levels of shops offer clothes, souvenirs, gifts, antiques, home decorative items, leather goods, silk, and books. Often has special art exhibits in the center of the plaza. Well worth stopping in this air-conditioned plaza if you have been pounding the pavement for a few hours looking for street shops along Sukhumvit Road.

❑ **Siam Square/Siam Centre/Siam Discovery Center:** Found near the Siam Inter-Continental Hotel on Rama I and Phyathai roads. The tall Novotel Hotel stands in the center of Siam Square. Now somewhat worn and extremely crowded with young people, theater goers, and diners, this is one of Bangkok's first major shopping centers. Siam Square consists of a rat maze of hundreds of two and three-storey commercial shops spread over several blocks just north of Chulalongkorn University. Shops offer everything from sporting goods to antiques. Major travel agents, theaters, bookstores, electronic shops, shoe stores, restaurants, coffee shops, and fast food establishments crowded with young people are clustered in this area. You must enter all shops from the hot and congested streets rather than from within an air-conditioned enclosed mall environment. Popular middle-class shopping area for Thais and tourists offering a wide range of varying quality goods and services. Connected to the huge Mah Boon Krong Centre by an overhead walkway which crosses Phyathai Road. The newer Siam Centre across the street is one large four- storey air-conditioned shopping arcade housing over 150 shops which offer a large variety of goods: clothes, jewelry, antiques, handicrafts, silk, electronics, records, CDs, and much more.

Includes banks, travel agents, and restaurants. Tends to be overcrowded with Bangkok's youth cruising the arcade in search of something to do or those shopping for the latest youth fashions. Filled with loud rock 'n roll music. A mixed shopping area with a few good shops (try the Novotel Hotel). We consider this area to be more of a cultural experience than a destination for quality shopping. You may want to avoid it altogether!

❑ **Mah Boon Krong Centre:** Located across from Siam Center at the intersection of Rama I and Phyathai roads, this is one of the largest shopping centers in Southeast Asia. Anchored by the Tokyu Department Store and filled with small shops typical of such shopping centers as Rajadamri Arcade and Amarin Plaza. A popular shopping center for local residents and a favorite hangout for Bangkok youth in search of local action. Another cultural experience offering few items of interest to tourists.

❑ **Le Meridien President Hotel:** Gaysorn was actually one of Bangkok's oldest shopping areas until it was torn down nearly five years ago to make way for a new office, hotel, and shopping complex (Gaysorn Plaza and the Le Royal Meridien Hotel). Located on Ploenchit Road, the Le Royal Meridien and adjacent Le Meridien President hotels have an expansive shopping arcade with tailor, gift, and souvenir shops.

❑ **Amarin Plaza:** Located on Ploenchit Road opposite the Le Royal Meridien Hotel and Gaysorn Plaza and behind the Grand Hyatt Erawan Hotel. Anchored by Sogo Department Store and filled with all types of small shops—jewelry, clothing, shoe, leather goods, gift, art, and electronic goods—and restaurants. Includes several good jewelry and handicraft stores. Popular among middle-class Thai and tourists. Boasts Thailand's first McDonald's.

❑ **Erawan Sogo:** Adjacent to both the Amarin Plaza and the Grand Hyatt Erawan Hotel at the corner of Ploenchit and Rajadamri roads, this store represents Bangkok's first attempt to primarily offer under one roof exclusive designer label men's and women's clothes and accessories (Gucci, Salvatore Ferragamo, Chanel, Christian Dior, Givenchy Bruno Magli, Pierre Cardin, Elle, Calvin Klein, Guy Larouche). Four shopping levels also include a Thai silk section (2nd floor), and home decorative, audio-visual, and art gallery sections on the fourth floor. Lower level is a "Restaurant Avenue" food court consisting of several nice cafes and restaurants. Primarily caters to wealthy Thai and Asian tourists.

❑ **World Trade Center:** Opposite Gaysorn Plaza and Narayana Phand on the corner of Rama I and Rajadamri roads, this imposing commercial center includes one of Bangkok's largest shopping arcades of mixed quality. Anchored by Zen (Central) and Isetan department stores, the first six floors of this massive complex are filled with shops offering clothes, shoes, handbags, jewelry, gold, home decorative items, silk, music, electronics, sporting goods, rugs, and optical goods as well as several restaurants. Includes a terrific supermarket on the lower level (Zen). A pleasant place to escape from the heat and humidity of the congested streets and sidewalks outside.

❑ **Rajadamri Arcade/The Mall:** Located on Rajadamri Road across the street from the World Trade Center and near the Le Royal Meridien Hotel and Grand Hyatt Erawan hotels and Gaysorn Plaza. Consists of several department stores and small shops clustered in a highly congested area. Offers all types of products, but especially geared toward middle-class Thai consumers. Another popular area with Bangkok's youth who cruise for the latest fashions and eat, eat, and eat. Good place to buy audiocassettes and CDs. Rather disorienting shopping arcade but interesting to explore. Vendors lining Rajadamri Road and the lane in front of Robinson Department Store sell leather goods, audiocassettes, clothes, and a variety of other items. Be sure to bargain with these vendors. Also, be sure to visit the huge Narayana Phand handicraft emporium on the first two levels of The Mall.

❑ **Indra Arcade:** Attached to the Indra Hotel on Rajadamri Road just north and east of the Baiyoke and Pratunam markets. Houses over 100 small shops offering everything from clothes and jewelry to knickknacks. Similar in many respects to the Siam Square/Siam Centre and Rajadamri Arcade shopping areas. Crowded with young people and filled with loud music. A mixed shopping area trying to appeal to both local Thais and tourists with consumer goods, theaters, tailors, coffee shops, restaurants, a grocery store, and numerous other middle-class shops. Includes a few quality shops, but tends to have a large number of nondescript tourist shops. Not high on our list of "must visit" places, unless you are staying at the nearby Indra Hotel.

❑ **Ambassador City**: Part of the huge Ambassador Hotel complex on Sukhumvit Road, between Soi 11 and 13. Includes numerous jewelry, clothing, fabric, antique, and handicraft shops along with several specialty restaurants. Hundreds of additional shops offering jewelry, clothes, art, antiques, handicrafts, furniture, and leather goods line Sukhumvit Road just adjacent to Ambassador City. This is an excellent area to roam up and down the street and into a few lanes—especially Soi 19, 21, and 23.

❑ **Seacon Square:** Located on Srinakarin Road. Claims to be the largest shopping plaza in Asia. Includes Robinson, Lotus, Yo Yo Land (an indoor amusement park), skating rink, bowling alley, and an Entertainment Village with 14 theaters.

❑ **Central Plaza:** Located next to the Central Plaza Hotel on Paholyothin Road and near the Weekend Market—a long distance (45 minutes) from the other major shopping areas in Bangkok. Large enclosed air-conditioned shopping center similar to many malls in the United States. Anchored by Central Department Store. Very popular with Thais on weekends. Shops sell a full range of consumer goods, from microwave ovens to toys for children. Pleasant place to explore if you have just come from the nearby Weekend Market.

Shops in and around many other hotels in Bangkok have small shopping arcades offering similar goods. However, the **Emporium, Gaysorn Plaza, Promenade, Oriental Place, River City Shopping Complex, Thaniya Plaza, Charn Issara Tower, Peninsula Plaza, Erawan Sogo, Amarin Plaza, World Trade Center** and shops attached to Bangkok's top hotels—especially The Regent, Grand Hyatt Erawan, Oriental, Sukhothai, Dusit Thani, Montien, Central Plaza, Landmark, and Sheraton Grande Sukhumvit hotels—are the premier shopping areas for the best quality products. Many shops in these arcades are branches of shops in other arcades. When you visit these areas, be sure to look for additional shops within a radius of one-half kilometer. You will discover many interesting shops offering a wide range of quality goods.

DEPARTMENT STORES

Bangkok has gone through a department store building craze in recent years. Indeed, during one weekend in November 1984, six new department stores and shopping centers opened on the same day and nearly immobilized traffic in Bangkok! Ever since then, department stores have continued to expand throughout Bangkok. The department stores primarily cater to the growing local middle-class of Thais. They offer ready-made clothes, cosmetics, toys, and appliances imported from abroad. They are well stocked with restaurants and fast food establishments—all of which seem to do a booming business among Bangkok's avid eaters!

Thai department stores tend to be extremely crowded, cold, and noisy. Many are Japanese department stores which have had to adapt to the local Thai shopping culture. As a result, department stores which initially opened with nice neat behind-the-counter displays with fixed prices now display many goods in typical Thai open-air market fashion—tables in aisles piled high with items and labeled with a special sale sign or guarded by an aggressive salesperson shouting out a sales line, similar to vendors in the traditional markets. It is largely this Thai adaptation to Japanese department stores that makes these places so crowded and congested.

Most tourists do not find Thai department stores of much interest other than as cultural experiences. These stores are primarily designed for the growing Thai middle-class that is increasingly drawn to imported consumer goods and the social status of having shopped at department stores. A few department stores, such as Central, have good book sections and serve wonderful soft ice cream for 10 baht. Some also have handicraft sections, but you may find this section to be too "touristy" for your shopping needs and standards. Except for the handicraft and bookstore sections found in some department stores, you may not want to spend your valuable shopping time in these places.

If you visit department stores, don't expect to do much shopping. Go for the cultural experience, get away from the heat, or find a bite to eat. The major department stores are:

❑ **Central**: One of the first and oldest department store chains in Thailand. Still one of the best. Has an excellent bookstore section at their Silom Road branch. Carries a good selection of Thai handicrafts and handmade furniture at their Ploenchit/Chitlom Road and Central Plaza branches. Also known as **Zen Department Store** at the World Trade Center.

❑ **Robinson:** Similar to Central Department Store. Several large and small branches throughout Bangkok. Largest branches found at the Rajadamri Arcade and on the corner of Silom Road and Rama IV Road.

❑ **Tokyu:** Large Japanese department store anchoring the huge Mah Boon Krong Centre. Filled with all types of consumer goods for Thais.

❑ **Sogo:** Large Japanese department store anchoring the Amarin Plaza. Caters to Thai middle-class with a full range of consumer goods. Another Sogo (Erawan Sogo), located next to the Amarin Plaza and the Grand Hyatt Erawan Hotel, primarily caters to the upper-middle and upper classes with name-brand clothes and accessories— many made locally under licensing arrangements.

❑ **Thai Daimaru:** Anchors the Rajadamri Arcade. One of the first and oldest Japanese department stores. Similar to other department stores designed for middle-class Thai. Crammed with all types of consumer goods.

❑ **Galeries Lafayette**: This large French department store anchors the upscale Peninsula Plaza. An elegant store offering good quality. Includes international brand names such as Christian Dior, Yves St. Laurent, Lancel, and Cacharel.

❑ **Isetan:** A large Japanese department store anchoring the World Trade Center. Good quality products. Includes a Jim Thompson shop. Very popular with young people.

MARKETS, STALLS, AND BAZAARS

Many shopping centers and department stores have characteristics of colorful Third World markets—crowded, chaotic, noisy, and hopelessly disorganized. But certain areas primarily function as traditional open-air markets or enclosed markets with vendors selling goods from small stalls. These places are often crowded, dirty, and smelly, especially if they include a fresh food and fish section. Indeed, we find few such markets are worth visiting, except perhaps for the cultural experience—

which we no longer need since we've seen enough such markets to last a lifetime! The novelty wore off long ago to the point where many such markets are simply a boring waste of time. Nonetheless, we still frequent a few exceptional markets as we search for unique treasures. Indeed, we're hopelessly addicted to both the Chatuchak Weekend Market and the night market or street bazaar along Patpong Road.

While some visitors love to poke around the Thai markets, taking in the unique sights, sounds, and smells, we have yet to become enamored with these places. After you visit one, you may find you have better things to do with your time. Indeed, such markets are best visited as cultural experiences rather than as shopping destinations for finding quality products. You may quickly discover you need no more than 10 minutes to satisfy your curiosity. On the other hand, you may have a great time in these markets mingling with the colorful vendors and making a few interesting purchases. Chances are you will agree with many other visitors to Thailand that only one market is really worth visiting, and it is both a cultural experience and a lot of fun on Saturday or Sunday—**Chatuchak Weekend Market**. Most traditional markets are now facing competition from the more convenient and air-conditioned shopping arcades and department stores. The major markets of interest to tourists include the following:

❑ **Chatuchak Weekend Market:** Also known as "Chatuchak Park" or simply the "Weekend Market." Located on the way to the airport near the Central Plaza Hotel and adjacent Central Plaza Shopping Center, it takes about 45 to 60 minutes to reach this market by taxi. The good news is that the new monorail, Skytrain, stops here (Station N8)! Open every day, the market is most interesting as well as most crowded on Saturdays and Sundays (go very early, by 8:30am, to avoid the crowds and get the best selections), this is the largest traditional market in Thailand. Similar to a flea market, it is loaded with every conceivable household item, including food, clothes, pets, plants, and handicrafts. It also includes antique, porcelain, and hilltribe product sections which can yield some good buys on unique items. Many sections of the market are crowded, hot, and smelly, but the market is exotic and thus worth at least one visit. Go for the cultural experience and to do some "fun" shopping, but don't expect to do much quality shopping here. If you are a pet lover, you may fall in love with the beautiful and inexpensive birds (Cockatoos at US$100), puppies, kittens, and rabbits.

Leave them behind since you will have problems getting them back home. The antique section includes lots of "new antiques", although you can find some good buys on real antiques—but come early on the weekends before the dealers pick over the good stuff. A few vendors sell an excellent selection of hard-to-find beads. You'll find all kinds of inexpensive clothes throughout this market. You might also want to visit the numerous garden stalls that sell inexpensive pots, although not easy to ship home unless you have a sea shipment. If you plan to visit this market, consider stopping across the street at the Jit Pochana Restaurant at 1082 Paholyothin Road. They serve wonderful luncheon buffets in nice indoor and outdoor settings. Eat only **after** visiting the market. Next, proceed on to the Central Plaza Hotel and Central Plaza Shopping Center. This might be the perfect post-market stop as your images of the Weekend Market fade in the aftermath of a great lunch and the air-conditioned splendor of the hotel and shopping complex.

If you plan to visit only one traditional Thai market, be sure to visit this one. It's one of the most interesting cultural experiences in Bangkok, and the highlight of many visitors' trips to Thailand. And you may get lucky and make a few shopping discoveries, especially in the handicraft, antique, porcelain, bead, and hilltribe product sections. For details on this market, see Nancy Chandler's excellent and detailed *Map of Bangkok* which includes a special color coded "Chatuchak Weekend Market" insert.

❑ **Baiyoke Market and Pratunam:** A primarily enclosed shopping area overflowing onto the sidewalks and streets south and east of the Indra Hotel, north of the Amari Watergate Hotel, and southeast of what is reputed to be the world's tallest hotel, the colorful Baiyoke Sky. The numerous stalls here are primarily factory outlet shops selling over-runs and seconds to the public. Unlike Hong Kong, where you can visit garment factories and purchase discounted clothes at factory outlet shops, in Thailand you find this discounted merchandise here at Pratunam as well as at the Chatuchak Weekend Market and various night bazaars. You may find the colors, styles, and sizes of clothing at Pratunam inappropriate for you; much of the merchandise is simply dreadful. However, you may also discover some good buys in this area. Indeed, many shoppers cart away huge bags of clothes and accessories from this wholesale market. To fully explore this market, you must get into the interior area behind the shops which face both Phetburi and Rajaprarop roads. You could get lost in the narrow pathways separating one small stall from another. This area specializes in dry goods, such as cheap shoes, shirts, linens, glasses, and a host of household products. This is another one of those cultural experiences which is also crowded. Not as hot or smelly as the Chatuchak Weekend Market, but just as bewildering for many first-time visitors. Not a good place for people who get claustrophobia in small, crowded, enclosed areas. Like the Chatuchak Weekend Market, this one is loaded with inexpensive clothes and accessories. Be sure to bargain hard for everything! Don't forget to also explore the shops and sidewalk vendors located just outside the market along both sides of Phetburi and Rajaprarop roads. You may also want to wander through the nearby Indra Hotel Shopping Arcade, City Centre Department Store, and Panthip Plaza before heading south to the World Trade Center.

❑ **Thieves Market and Chinatown:** Bordered by Charoen Krung, Yaowarat, Mahachai, and Mitraphan roads. This is an extremely crowded and congested area where you can buy numerous items including jewelry, gold, cloth, antiques, cooking utensils, and colorful funeral supplies. The Pahurat Cloth Market (corner of Pahurat and Chakraphed roads), run primarily by Indian merchants, has a good selection of inexpensive cotton materials sold by the meter. This is a rather crowded and disorienting market but one of the best in Thailand for cotton. Thieves Market (called Nakorn Kasem in Thai and between Charoen Krung and Yaowarat roads at Boriphat Road) is filled with all types of old and new antiques and furniture. This is a excellent place to poke around for Chinese ceramics, bells, bronze drums, carved Chinese panels, and musical instruments. While in Chinatown you can stroll down the famous **Sampeng Lane** (Soi Wanit 1). Enter directly across the street from the Pahurat Cloth Market (Chakraphet Road) or at the other end on Songsawat Road. This lane is filled with small shops selling numerous household goods, clothes, fabric, jewelry, shoes, and tea. If you are looking for gold, the Chinatown area is the place to go. The bright red Chinese gold shops sell gold in all forms—mostly 18K to 22K. The Ban Mo area (Pahurat Road) is a popular market for diamonds and other precious stones. At night Chinatown is brightly lit, reminiscent of Hong Kong's crowded and neon-blazing streets. Nancy

Chandler's *Map of Bangkok* includes a detailed section on products, shops, restaurants, and sights in these areas. We highly recommend referring to this map when visiting this area.

❑ **Banglampoo:** Located along Chakrapong Road, near the National Gallery and not far from Pramane Grounds (*Sanam Luang*) and the Royal Hotel. This is one of Bangkok's larger markets. It is filled with all types of household goods, clothes, fabric, jewelry stores, and food stalls. A very crowded area, it is mainly patronized by local Thai and budget traveler who stay at the nearby Vieng Tai Hotel.

❑ **Floating Markets:** Tourists are normally taken to either of two traditional floating markets along Thailand's colorful and muddy canals. The one most tourists see is in nearby Thonburi. However, this is no longer a worthy attraction since today it mainly functions for entertaining tourists. It's highly congested and the tourist shops awaiting the next boat load of tourists sell tacky souvenirs at highly inflated prices. The second and more interesting floating market is at **Damnoen Saduak**, a two to three-hour drive from Bangkok in the province of Ratburi. The market still has an authentic rural atmosphere, but it has become very commercialized for tourists. If you take a tour, you will stop at the tourist shops along the way. These shops are filled with tourist knickknacks. In addition, everything is over-priced—one of the worst tourist rip-offs in Thailand. You will pay 300% more for many of the products. Our recommendation: buy a banana or orange from one of the boats, take pictures, and enjoy the terrifying speedboat ride. The same and better products are available in Bangkok at much lower prices. Additional floating markets are being opened for tourists in other areas near Bangkok. If you join a tour group, you may be taken to one of these new areas which should be less congested than the two described here.

❑ **Food and Flower Markets:** Numerous food and flower markets are also found in Bangkok. One of the most interesting is the **Bangrak Market** at the end of Sathorn Road. In the evening several portable food stalls are set up and the vendors serve numerous tasty rice and noodle dishes. This is interesting to see, but you may want to pass on the food since the dishes are often washed in dirty water—a source for hepatitis. **Thewarat Market**, adjacent to the river on Luk Luang Road near Banglampoo Market and the National Library, is a nice flower market where you can treat yourself to a dozen roses for only US$2. The **Samyan Market** (corner of Phyathai and Rama IV Road near Chulalongkorn University), **Pak Klong Market** (adjacent to Memorial Bridge), and **Penang Market** (Klong Toei) are all interesting food markets for individuals interested in such cultural and gastronomic experiences.

❑ **Night Bazaars:** Within the past ten years night bazaars have sprung up around Bangkok's major tourist area—Silom, Patpong, and Suriwongse roads. Centered near the Montien Hotel and concentrated along Patpong Road, but also found along Silom Road and Suriwongse Road, the Night Bazaar consists of over 200 vendors who display their wares on makeshift tables. They primarily sell inexpensive clothes, watches, briefcases, leather goods, CDs, audiocassettes, videos, and souvenirs; many are copies or pirated. Given repeated crackdowns on international copyright and trademark violations, many of goods on display no longer have brand names. This does not mean they are not available—they're just not in public view like they used to be a few years ago before the United States put political pressure on Thailand to enforce international copyright and trademark agreements. The brand name goods, especially copy watches, are usually under the table. Just ask to see them and, presto, you've just activated the black market as an eager vendor pulls out a photo album or a plastic freezer box of Rolex, Cartier, Gucci, or Patek Philippe copy watches! A festive atmosphere begins around 6:30pm and continues until around 11pm. Since many of the goods are copies of brand name clothes, watches, and handbags, occasionally the police go through the perfunctory motions of raiding this area which gives shopping an interesting air of adventure. The raids usually dampen shopping for one hour or so, and then it's back to business as usual. If you get caught in one of these raids, don't worry. No one will bother you—just the vendors who are engaged in what is ostensibly an illegal activity.

The Night Bazaar is one of the high points of many individual's visit to Bangkok. The vendors seem to have something for everyone. The Patpong area is the most interesting place to shop given its setting—in the midst of Bangkok's raunchy, neon-blazing topless bars and sex shows (while shopping you'll probably be approached by a tout who will try to sell you—male or female or even with your spouse or friend—on attending his interesting sex show which will probably amaze you for its acrobatics and ingenious choreography!). You will also find smaller but similar bazaar operations at night near some of the other major hotels, such as the Royal Orchid Sheraton, Indra Hotel, and Shangri-La Hotel as well as around Silom Village. Be forewarned, however, that Customs officials in your country may enforce international copyright and trademark conventions by confiscating copies of name-brand goods purchased in Thailand's night bazaars and markets. One or two items for yourself or a novelty gift will usually pass Customs, although we know of individuals who have had the misfortune of being stopped for just one item. It's best not to wear your purchases when passing through Customs.

CRAFT FACTORIES

Bangkok also has its versions of factory outlets. While most arts and crafts in Bangkok shops come from factories in Chiang Mai, a few special craft factories are found in and around Bangkok. You may wish to visit a few of these to observe the craftsmen at work, tour their showrooms, and make direct factory purchases. The major factories welcoming visitors include:

❑ **Thai Lapidary:** 1009-11 Silom Road (Tel. 236-2123). Large factory, cuts and polishes gems.

❑ **S. Samran, Bronze Factory:** 302 Phetburi Road (Tel. 216-7058). Ask at this showroom to be taken to the nearby factory to observe craftsman at work making bronze items.

❑ **Supoj Thai Bronze Factory:** Located across the river from Bangkok in Thonburi (302 Soi 20, Suksawat Road, Bangpakok, Thonburi, Tel. 427-4990). Factory/showroom with craftsmen producing good quality bronzeware.

❑ **Bangkok Dolls:** 85 Soi Rajatapan, Makkasan (Tel. 245-3008). Produces lovely dolls representing the hilltribes and Thai classical dancers. Includes an interesting doll museum for young and old alike.

❑ **Niello Ware, Thai Nakorn Company:** 79 Prachatipatai Road, near Democracy Monument (Tel. 281-7867). Factory producing Thai nielloware.

❏ **Blue & White Potteries:** Located outside Bangkok on the road to the Rose Garden (Surachia Nuparwan, Oom Noi, Samut Sakhon Province). Family produces excellent quality pottery at good prices.

❏ **Tao Hong Thai Ceramics:** Located outside Bangkok in Ratburi Province (234 Chedihak Road Ampur Muang). Produces copies of Sung and Ming pottery. You can visit their Bangkok shop on Soi Sarasin.

❏ **Home Made Silk Factory:** 43 Soi Prom Chai (off Soi 39, Sukhumvit Road, Tel. 258-8766). Displays silk weaving.

OUT-OF-THE-WAY DISCOVERIES

While most of Bangkok's shopping is concentrated in and around major shopping centers and hotel shopping arcades, there are several shops located in hard to find locations. Most of these places are found in residential neighborhoods or in lanes far from the main streets. You will need a taxi or hotel car to get to these places. If you take a taxi, pay a little extra to have the driver wait for you since you may have difficulty finding a cab in these locations. Some of our favorite such discoveries include:

❏ **Rasi Sayam:** 32 Sukhumvit Soi 23 (Tel. 258-4195). Specializes in Thai handcrafted items, but this is not your typical handicraft, tourist knickknack shop. Offers one of Bangkok's most tasteful selections of handcrafted items produced in numerous villages throughout Thailand. Excellent quality and many unique items. Located in an old Thai house.

❏ **Naga House:** 315 Soi Ongkarak, Samsen Road 28, Dusit, (Tel. 669-3416 or 669-3493). Originally opened in 1998 as an upscale house-shop for well-heeled tourists who stay at 5-star hotels, this hard-to-find shop is located in a residential area of Dusit District. It's two floors of quality jewelry and tasteful antiques and handicrafts are nicely displayed throughout several rooms. The emphasis here is on both ambience and quality products. While the prices may seem high, they are generally good considered the quality of the products and compared to shops that offer similar quality jewelry, antiques, and handicrafts. Since the place is so hard to find (drivers get lost), it may be best to call for transportation. They will pick you up at your hotel. You might also consider booking lunch or tea at Naga House. A popular stop for many upscale tour groups.

❏ **Fatima Self Help Center:** Located at 18/65 Asoke Din Daeng Road, this is a popular clothing workshop for expatriates living in Bangkok. Operated by the Catholic Church's Good Shepherd Sisters, the workshop provides training and employment for girls from poor families. They produce a wide range of handsewn items, from pot holders to Christmas decorations. One of the great shopping finds is the beautiful children's smocked dresses or romper suits which can be made to order and shipped to your home.

❏ **Lao Song Handicrafts:** A small shop located at 2045/5 Soi 77 Sukhumvit (Tel. 332-5459 or 311-2277). This is the main outlet for Lao Song hilltribe handicrafts produced in 800 households of 22 villages in northern Thailand. Sponsored by the Church of Christ, the Lao Song produce lovely stuffed animals, placemats, Christmas ornaments, baskets, and pot holders. Many of these designs are now being copied by the House of Handicrafts and the Fatima Self Help Center. Lao Song Handicrafts also exports abroad and has a mail order catalog.

❏ **Bangkok Dolls:** Located at 85 Soi Rajatapan, Rajaprarop (just north of the Indra Hotel), this is a wonderful place to observe the making of the unique and award-winning Thai dolls. While Bangkok Dolls also has a shop at the Peninsula Plaza (Bangkok Dolls Arts & Crafts), it's well worth making the trip to this factory shop to see the selections, museum, and the production process. Appeals to both young and old.

❏ **Art Resources:** Located at 142-20 Soi Sueksavitaya, off Soi Silom 9 (Tel. 235-4846), this art shop is difficult to find because it is located off of both Silom Road and North Sathorn Road—few taxis can find it because of the confusing street names. This is the main shop which does outstanding framing work. We have used the services of Mr. Pramote for over 12 years. The shop sells traditional Thai paintings and European art deco bronze reproductions—its two most popular items. In fact, Art Resources was responsible for much of the art work that is found in the Grand Hyatt Erawan Hotel. You may find it is more convenient for you to visit the Art Resource shop in the Regent Hotel shopping arcade where you will see similar selections.

❑ **The ThaiCraft Association:** 78 Soi 61, Sukhumvit Road (Tel. 714-1649). This volunteer operation sponsors 6-7 craft sales each year on Saturday mornings at various city hotels. Check the local English-language newspapers for specific dates and locations. More than 30 producers display a nice range of baskets, quilts, hilltribe embroideries, cotton and silk fabrics, jewelry, and hand-made paper.

SHOPPING ON LIMITED TIME

If you only have a few days in Bangkok and much of your time is taken up with other activities, we recommend concentrating your shopping in these "must visit" top ten places, and according to this order of preference:

❑ River City Shopping Complex

❑ Oriental Place/Oriental Hotel

❑ Peninsula Plaza/Regent Hotel

❑ Emporium/Sukhumvit Road

❑ Chatuchak Weekend Market

❑ Night Bazaar Patpong Road

❑ World Trade Center/Gaysorn Plaza

❑ Amarin Plaza/Grand Hyatt Erawan

❑ Promenade/Hilton Hotel

❑ Silom Village

These areas alone can take at least four days to cover. To speed up your shopping, be sure to frequently use the Skytrain to get from one area to another. If you don't, you'll find much of your shopping time will be wasted in the traffic. Whatever your plans, chances are you'll quickly discover that you probably did not leave enough time for shopping in Bangkok!

In Search of
Quality

Y OU CAN HAVE A VERY REWARDING SHOPPING
experience by confining your shopping to River City
Shopping Complex, Oriental Place, Peninsula Plaza,
Emporium, Amarin Plaza, World Trade Center, Gaysorn
Plaza, Promenade, Chatuchak Weekend Market and Patpong's
infamous Night Market. However, many other places outside
these areas also offer excellent products and value. Some are
shops while others are homes which also function as shops
tucked away in Bangkok's maze of side streets and lanes.

Some of our favorite shopping discoveries include the following quality shops. Over the years we have found these shops
consistently offer good quality products and are especially
reliable. Many of the owners are wonderful people to deal with
both in Thailand and abroad (by phone, fax, or e-mail).

ANTIQUES, ARTS, FURNITURE,
CARVINGS, HOME DECORATIVE ITEMS

❑ **NeOld:** *149/2-3 Suriwongse Road (Tel. 235-8352 or Fax 662-235-8927) and branch shops in The Regent Bangkok (NeOld Thai Style, 155 Rajadamri Road, Tel. 250-0737) and The Promenade*

(NeOld Hilton). It doesn't get much better than this anywhere in Southeast Asia! This is one of Thailand's premier antique and home decorative shops, the place for the truly discriminating shopper with taste and class. As the name implies—NeOld—this shop specializes in combining the **new** with the **old**. Simply fabulous offerings selected by one of Thailand's top antique dealers and designers—the soft spoken Mr. Chaiwut Tulayadhan. His decorating skills are well represented in the lobbies of major hotels, such as the Oriental, Shangri-La, Hilton, Siam Inter-Continental, Amanpuri Phuket, and Pansea Phuket as well as in many offices and private homes throughout Thailand and abroad. Chaiwut has an incredible eye for quality and knows how to best display and integrate his selections. Offers excellent quality antiques, arts, mirrors, chest panels, tapestries, furniture, wood panels, lamps and smaller items such as ceramics, lacquerware and baskets; most are Myanmar in origin. Gorgeous items which shout quality and will fit into Western decor. Very reliable, very expensive, and very nice. Everything here shouts "class" and "buy me!" The best shop is the main store on Suriwongse Road. If you are a serious collector of antiques with an eye toward decorating, make NeOld one of your first and last stops in Thailand.

❑ **Elephant House:** *286/69-71 Soi Pattana, Suriwongse Road, Bangrak (Tel. 233-6973 or 233-6281; Fax 662-631-4690 or 662-631-4691; e-mail: elephant@ksc.15th.com)*. This remains one of our very favorite shops. We always try to make it one of our first stops in Thailand. Many of our finest antiques and home decorative items come from here. Offers a unique selection of high quality arts, antiques, furniture, objets d'art, and gift items from Thailand, Myanmar, and Cambodia displayed on four floors. Designs own handmade lacquer furniture as well as rattan chairs and tables, and produces own line of lacquerware and attractive rattan baskets and furniture from the owner's factories in Myanmar. The Myanmar owner/designer—Cherie Aung-Kin—knows top quality, speaks excellent English, and is most helpful. Very reliable. Expensive, but you buy quality and can find one-of-a-kind pieces here. Fixed prices. Look for her popular semi-annual sales where most items are discounted at 20%. Does great packing and shipping. Works extensively with dealers in Europe and North America. Somewhat difficult to find, you get to this shop off of Suriwongse Road (just across and down the street from Neilson Hays Library, on the right as you head east toward the river).

❑ **Lek Gallerie:** *1310 and 1275 New Road (Tel. 233-8298, 233-1015 or Fax 662-266-4495). Also has a branch shop at 249 River City Shopping Complex (Tel. 237-0077, ext. 249).* The main shops are located near the Oriental Hotel. Another one of our very favorite shops. Consisting of two newly refurbished shops across the street from each other, although the two are expected to consolidate soon, this gallery specializes in Myanmar and Thai antiques as well as includes a small but stunning collection of old Japanese tapestries. Large selection of Buddhas, panels, lacquer doors, and attractive smaller pieces such as bells and palanquin hooks. Excellent quality, prices, and service. Very reliable and a joy to work with either in Bangkok or from abroad. Does excellent packing and shipping. Contact either Lek or Janya Attakanwong, the very personable husband-wife team that operates these fine shops.

❑ **The Fine Arts:** *452 River City Shopping Complex (Tel. 235-2972-9, ext. 452, Fax 662-237-7548), the Sukhothai Hotel (13/3 Sathorn Tai Road, Tel. 287-0222, and Oriental Place, Tel. 266-0186). Also has shops in other major shopping centers which come under the name of* **The Height** *(Thaniya Plaza #307, Tel. 231-2164, and River City Shopping Complex #354, Tel. 237-0077, ext. 354).* One of Thailand's best and most famous collectors of textiles, Khmer bronzes, and Myanmar antiques. Excellent quality. Also produces unique pieces of furniture, model ships and boats for discriminating collectors, and excellent quality terra cotta reproductions of Khmer reliefs. If you are interested in old textiles, The Fine Arts is the place to go. It is reputed to be Bangkok's largest dealer in old textiles. Operated by a husband-wife team. See the very knowledgeable Mrs. Wallee.

❑ **Peng Seng:** *942/1-3 Rama IV Road (corner of Suriwongse and Rama IV roads and next to Jim Thompson Silk Company, Tel. 233-1891 or 234-3836 or Fax 662- 236-8011).* Outstanding quality art and antique store filled with lovely sculptures, ceramics, tapestries, and bronze pieces. Includes an excellent museum on second floor as well as one of the best selections of art books and back issues of major Asia art magazines. Expensive and reliable. A must visit for the serious antique collector. Well worth a stop to browse.

❑ **Sawasdee Antiques Co.:** *319 River City Shopping Complex (Tel. 237–0077, ext. 319).* Also known as Oriental Commercial House. Operated by the always adventuresome and very knowledgeable Daraluk Chittiboonruam, who personally sources most items, this shop offers a unique collection of Lanna (Northern) Thai arts and antiques. The quality and selections here are outstanding. This is the only shop we know that specializes in the Lanna Thai style. Expensive. Does excellent packing and shipping. The very knowledgeable, helpful, and personable owner, Mrs. Daraluk Satayai, does her own sourcing and collecting with an eye on top quality.

❑ **Golden Triangle:** *301 River City Shopping Complex (Tel. 237-0077, ext. 301).* One of Thailand's most unique quality shops. Excellent selections of hilltribe textiles, silver, and beads. Offers beautifully crafted garments using antique textiles. Nice displays and quality selections and craftsmanship throughout this inviting shop. Operated by the very personable husband/wife team, Chai and Sumiko, and their children. Expensive.

❑ **August 9:** *421-422 River City Shopping Complex (Tel. 237-0077, ext. 421-422). Main shop is located in the River City Shopping Complex. A second shop is located on the first floor of Oriental Place (30/1 Chartered Bank Lane, Tel. 267-0316).* Offers excellent quality antiques and home decorative items, from Myanmar woodcarvings to lacquerware. Always seems to have unique pieces, especially in the Oriental Place shop. Operated by a young couple, Surakit and Neeranart Leeruangsri, who apprenticed under Chaiwut of NeOld. Expensive.

❑ **Tomlinson:** *3rd level, Oriental Place, Tel. 630-6939 or Fax 662-630-6833.* A surprising newcomer to Bangkok with shops in Singapore, Kuala Lumpur, and Manila, this expansive shop on the top floor of Oriental Place showcases one of the best selections of antique furniture and accessories in Thailand. Look for chests, screens, chairs, carpets, and one-of-a-kind objets d'art. As might be expected, everything here is top quality and expensive.

❑ **The Ashwood Gallery:** *3rd (314) and 4th (430) floors of the River City Shopping Complex (Tel. 237-0077, ext. 314 and 430); and ground floor of Oriental Place—GF 24-25 (Tel. 266-0187, ext. 1252).* Offers excellent quality antique Chinese furniture and objets d'art. These two shops are branches of the noted French operated Ashwood Gallery in Hong Kong. Very exceptional quality shops. Expensive but top quality.

❏ **Rama Art Gallery:** *1238/1-2 New Road 36 (Tel. 233-3330 or Fax 662-236-8104)*. Located near the Oriental Hotel, within a five minute walk. A real class operation. This attractive shop is filled with three floors of excellent quality Myanmar, Thai, and Chinese antiques—chests, lacquerware, mirrors, textiles, tapestries, carvings, beds, boxes, and furniture. Wonderful selection of quality items. Expensive.

❏ **River Trade Co.:** *351-352 River City Shopping Complex (Tel. 237-0077, ext. 351-352 or Fax 662-377-3582)*. Offers a very good collection of carved gables, doors, lintels, and marble Buddhas. Moderately expensive.

❏ **Arisra Gallery:** *6-8 Oriental Lane, New Road, Tel/Fax 630-6131*. Very nice collection and displays of Myanmar and Thai antiques, from Buddhas to woodcarvings. Expensive.

❏ **Kee Art:** *Oriental Place, FG-13 (Tel. 266-0186, ext. 1131-1132, Fax 662-235-5720)*. Offers top quality antiques, from woodcarvings to rain drums. Very expensive but also very good quality.

❏ **Yonok Treasures:** *213 River City Shopping Complex (Tel. 237-0077, ext. 213 or Fax 662-711-2068)*. One of our personal favorites which begin in Lampang more than ten years ago, moved to Chiang Mai, and then opened a Bangkok office a couple of years ago. Indeed, we helped name this shop late one evening in Chiang Mai several years ago. The owner, Katha Intrachai, has a good eye for quality antiques, from bronze pieces to woodcarvings. Reasonably priced.

❏ **Acala:** *312 River City Shopping Complex (Tel. 237-0077, ext. 312, Fax 662-639-5788, Web: www.fitzw.com/acala)*. Looking for something very unique in Thailand? Try Tibetan chests and carpets! This is Thailand's only such shop. Very good quality. Owners personally source each piece from their affiliate warehouse in Nepal. Very Web savvy shop with photos of inventory online. You may want to check them out online before visiting their shop in Bangkok.

❏ **Golden Tortoise:** *4 Sukhumvit Soi 49-4 (Tel. 391-2842) and 49/2 Sukhumvit Soi 49 (Tel. 259-6641 or Fax 662-261-8155)*. This is actually two shops under two different names—Golden Tortoise Antiques and Golden Tortoise Deco. The antique shop is filled with very nice quality antique Chinese, Japanese, and Korean furniture and accessories. The home decorative shop includes some antiques but is more oriented toward home furnishings with its nice selection of objets d'art. The second shop also has a charming tea house on the ground floor. Very active in promoting Soi 49 as a center for antiques and home decorative items (see page 177).

❑ **Artisan's:** *Silom Village, 286 Silom Road (Tel. 237-4456 or Fax 662-237-1739).* Two small cluttered but excellent quality shops offer unique antiques, home decorative items, and lots of good furniture. However, appearances can be deceiving since Artisan also has a furniture warehouse nearby (only a two-minute walk). If you're interested in seeing more furniture, ask to visit their warehouse. Moderate prices.

❑ **Pure Design:** *30 Ruam Rudee (off of Ploenchit and Wireless roads, Tel. 253-1719).* One of Thailand's best home designers and decorators involved in major hotel, office, and residential projects. If you are interested in having quality custom work done for your home decorative needs, contact this firm. The owner is one of Thailand's most famous designers. Don't expect to find a shop with a big showroom here. This is a designer's studio. By appointment only. Organized especially for professional designers and serious individuals involved with large, well-financed projects.

❑ **Jim Thompson Thai Silk Co.:** *9 Suriwongse Road (Tel. 234-4900).* Separate building behind the main shop famous for its silk and cotton is devoted exclusively to home decorative items, from furniture and pillows to lamps and accessory pieces. Excellent quality and designs. Expensive.

❑ **Sukhumvit Road, Soi 49:** This is one of Bangkok's newest centers for antiques and home decorative items. Includes ten shops plus restaurants offering everything from antique and modern furniture to carpets and handicrafts: Golden Tortoise Deco, Golden Tortoise and Nim's Tea House, Botero, Ispahan, Old Wood, Panom, Pemavo Gallery, Sophia Lee, The Native House, Y50, White Café, and Do Ri Won. Shops ccasionally sponsor weekend fairs. Also, see page 177.

PAINTINGS AND FRAMING

❑ **Art Resources:** *142/20 Soi Sueksavitaya, off Soi Silom 9 (Tel. 235-4846) and The Regent Bangkok hotel shopping arcade, Rajadamri Road (Tel. 250-0723).* The Soi Sueksavitaya shop

does some of the best framing we have encountered anywhere. However, the owner, Mr. Pramote, does little custom
framing these days. His energies tend to be focused on
producing art deco bronze decorative pieces and traditional
paintings and prints for large hotel, office, and condominium
projects. Both shops have a nice selection of traditional Thai
paintings and bronze sculptures. Visit The Regent Bangkok
shop first to see his work. Moderate prices.

❏ **Sombat Permpoon Gallery**: *12 Sukhumvit Soi 1, Sukhumvit
Road (Tel. 254-6040).* This large gallery represents some of
the leading artists in Thailand. Includes over 10,000 paintings and sculptures of more than 100 local artists.

❏ **Sombat Gallery**: *The Promenade, 2nd Floor, 2 Wireless Road
(Tel. 267-8891) and 215 River City Shopping Complex (called
Four Art Gallery, Tel. 235-2972, ext. 215).* Offers both
traditional and contemporary Thai oils and watercolors.

❏ **Surawongse Gallery**: *287/25-6 Suriwongse Road (Tel. 233-
5533) and third floor of River City Shopping Complex.* Excellent
collection of traditional and modern paintings and sculptures. Good quality and creative framing at reasonable
prices.

❏ **C.V.N. Exotic Ltd.**: *131-3/4 Sukhumvit Road (between Soi 7
and 9).* Large collection of traditional and modern Thai
paintings. Does inexpensive framing.

SILK AND COTTON

❏ **Jim Thompson Thai Silk Co.**: *9 Suriwongse Road (Tel.
234-4900) and small branch shops at the Author's Lounge in the
Oriental Hotel, Royal Orchid Sheraton Hotel, Grand Hyatt
Erawan Hotel, Emporium, World Trade Center, and Jim Thompson Thai House Museum.* One of the world's premier fabric
shops. Offers Thailand's best quality silk and cotton using
excellent designs. Includes ready-made clothes, accessories,
upholstery material, pillow covers, napkins, placemats,
jewelry boxes, picture frames, neckties, and much more. Silk
fabric and gift items found at ground floor, and ready-made
clothes, neck accessories, and cottons on the second floor.
Unfortunately, some of their best colors and designs for
upholstery material are only available in Jim Thompson
designer shops abroad or through local design firms. Colors

and designs are sometimes disappointing, especially for garments. Very expensive.

❑ **Design Thai:** *304 Silom Road (next to Central Department Store, Tel. 235-1553).* Good quality silk and cotton clothes, fabrics, quilted bedspreads, placemats, toys, and numerous gift items. Includes designer bronzeware and some celadon. Also, look for their shops in Hong Kong and Singapore, which carry other designs. Expensive.

❑ **Khanitha:** *Suriwongse Road (Tel. 233-1004), River City Shopping Complex (Tel. 237-0077), and Oriental Place (Tel. 266-0186).* Good quality and fashionable silk. Includes ready-made clothes and jewelry boxes. If you have 3 days or more, they can make a jewelry box to order. Expensive.

❑ **Shinawatra:** *Near Soi Suan Plu, South Sathorn Road (Tel. 286-9991) and Soi 23, Sukhumvit (Tel. 258-0515).* Includes a large collection of silk and cotton fabric as well as ready-made garments, neckties, and scarves.

❑ **Teresa:** *30/1 Oriental Place, Ground Floor (Tel. 266-0186, ext. 1091).* Offers nice quality silk garments as well as produces made to order clothes.

❑ **Paya:** *961 Sukhumvit Road, between Soi 51 and 53 (Tel. 259-2041).* Offers a good selection of upholstery-weight cotton fabrics. Includes rugs, pillows, comforters, placemats, and napkins. Excellent value and prices.

CLOTHES AND TAILORS

❑ **Pink Poodle:** *Oriental Hotel, Author's Lounge (Tel. 236-0400, ext. 3357).* Thailand's most exclusive haute couture designer shop in a class of its own. The owner/designer, Mrs. Yupha Steiner, operates one of the few shops in Thailand that really understands how to work with fabrics, colors, and designs rather than being preoccupied with only offering the highly overrated Thai silk with its inherent limitations. Uses materials from all over the world, but especially Chinese and Indian silks that work much better for many styles than Thai silk. Designs and prints its own materials. Beautifully designed one-of-a-kind garments for those with good taste and lots of money. The shop European and American VIPs go to for something very special. Very exclusive, very unique, and very expensive. See her other shop, **Tabtim Thai**, which is located across the hall, offering attractive neck pieces.

❑ **Penny's Boutique:** *Peninsula Plaza (#111), 153 Rajadamri Road (Tel. 253-4926-7).* Also operates a shop called **Sonja's** in the World Trade Center (A128 Ground Floor, Rajadamri Road, Tel. 255-9531-2). One of Bangkok's best boutiques noted for quality silks (French, Italian, Chinese, Thai) and expert seamstress skills. Uses lighter weight Thai silks for garments than most other shops. If you are interested in having a blouse or dress made in Bangkok, you can't do much better than Penny's Boutique. Expensive.

❑ **Ajai Zecha** and **A Cha:** *Landmark Hotel and Plaza, 3rd Floor (Tel. 252-6911).* Two fashion boutiques operated by Miss Rayib Sathabutr, one of Bangkok's talented fashion designers trained in France. Works with Thai silks (mutmee) and textiles. Knows how to turn ethnic designs and color themes into fashionable garments which appeal to many westerners. Good use of colors.

❑ **Golden Triangle:** *301 River City Shopping Complex (Tel. 237-0077, ext. 301).* One of Thailand's most unique quality shops. Excellent selections of hilltribe textiles, silver, and beads. Offers beautifully crafted garments using antique textiles. Nice displays and quality selections and craftsmanship throughout this inviting shop. Operated by the very personable husband/wife team, Chai and Sumiko, and their children. Expensive.

❑ **Choisy:** *9/25 Suriwongse Road (Tel. 233-7794).* Fashionable designer boutique using Jim Thompson silks and cottons. Offers ready-to-wear garments designed by its French owners.

❑ **Perry's:** *60/2 Silom Road (Tel. 233-9236).* One of Bangkok's best tailors. Does both men's and women's clothes, but watch them carefully when doing women's clothes (they are more tailors than seamstresses).

❑ **Adam's Tailor:** *23/3 Thaniya Road (Tel. 233-7857) and Charn Issara Tower.* Good quality men's tailor. Many consider Adam's Tailor to be the best in town. Expensive.

❑ **C. Fillipo:** *Shangri-La Hotel shopping arcade.* Another good quality men's tailor. Expensive.

❑ **River Mark:** *238 River City Shopping Complex (Tel. 237-0077-8, ext. 238).* Good quality tailor and excellent service. Moderately expensive.

Handmade Furniture

❑ **Gerson & Sons:** *21 off Soi Chaisamarn, Soi 4, Sukhumvit Road (Tel. 253-1638 thru 41).* Produces excellent quality furniture. Reliable.

❑ **Peter's Furniture:** *157/1 Mahadlek 2, Rajadamri Road (behind Regent Hotel, Tel. 252-5236).* Excellent quality and reliable shippers. Includes lots of catalogs from which to choose your own furniture designs.

❑ **Sweet Home:** *155/11-2 Soi Asoke (Tel. 258-3419).* Good craftsmanship on all types and styles of wood furniture. Discuss your plans using either your pictures and drawings or their book of examples. Reliable but sometimes difficult to communicate with salespeople. Get everything in writing and repeat it several times.

❑ **Star House:** *748-52 Sukhumvit Road, near Soi 34 (Tel. 261-0349).* Produces good quality rosewood and teak furniture. Reliable.

❑ **Pure Design:** *30 Ruam Rudee Road (off of Ploenchit and Wireless roads, Tel. 253-1719).* Produces excellent quality furniture in unique designs for those interested in special home decorative pieces.

❑ **Elephant House:** *286/69-71 Soi Pattana, Suriwongse Road (Tel. 233-6973—talk to Cherie).* Also, see page 203. Produces excellent quality lacquer furniture as well as rattan furniture produced in their Yangon, Myanmar factory.

Jewelry, Silver, Accessories

❑ **Lotus** and **Lotus Jewellery:** *Two shops at The Regent Bangkok hotel shopping arcade and one shop in the Oriental Arcade of the Oriental Hotel.* Exquisitely designed jewelry, especially attractive neck pieces. Unique one-of-a-kind pieces fashioned from gold, silver, precious, and semi-precious stones from all over the world. Many combine old items with additions that make the pieces more exquisite than they were originally.

Becoming more eclectic with home decorative items, textiles, and a cigar and wine lounge. These could easily become your favorite shops! Extremely expensive—truly a budget buster!

❑ **Uthai's Gems:** *28/7 Soi Ruam Rudee (Tel. 253-8582).* One of our long-time favorites. Owner/occupant, Uthai, designs jewelry to your specifications. This well established shop has been popular with expatriates, especially U.S. Embassy personnel, for more than 25 years. Reliable. Moderate.

❑ **Frank's:** *104 Peninsula Plaza, 153 Rajadamri Road. (Tel. 254-4528).* Also has shops in The Promenade, Emporium, and Gaysorn Plaza. Beautifully designed jewelry and a favorite shop for visiting VIPs. Specializes in large and elaborate pieces of jewelry that are also very expensive.

❑ **Bualaad Joaillier:** *Peninsula Plaza, first floor, 153 Rajadamri Road.* Exquisite designs, outstanding service, and wonderful shop ambience. Very nice, very expensive, very reliable.

❑ **Paa:** *Peninsula Plaza, first floor, 153 Rajadamri Road* Excellent quality, good designs, and very reliable. Specializes in fine antique jewelry. Very expensive.

❑ **Sar Jewelry:** *Room GF 26, Oriental Place, Tel. 630-6218, ext. 1261.* This small but very reputable shop offers excellent designs and top quality jewelry.

❑ **Tok Kwang:** *The Regent Bangkok (Tel. 250-0735) and Emporium.* Offers excellent quality pearls as well as finely crafted jewelry. Well established family operation.

❑ **Yves Joaillier:** *Charn Issara Tower, 3rd floor 942/83 Rama IV Road (Tel. 233-3292).* One of Thailand's premier French jewelry designers. Produces exquisite designs to your specifications or you can buy from their showcase. Hard to see what's available by looking in the very limited display window. Must go into the shop and talk with the personnel.

❑ **Merlin et Delaunay:** *Novotel Hotel, Siam Square (Tel. 254-3877, 255-6888, ext. 2619).* A long established and reputable French jeweler. Produces attractive and imaginative designs. Contact this shop if you also wish to visit their factory.

❑ **Naga House:** *315 Soi Ongkarak, Samsen Road 28, Dusit, Tel. 669-3416.* See page 199 for more details. Offers uniquely designed jewelry in a pleasant old Thai house. Call for transportation since this place is hard to find on your own.

❑ **Sincere Jewelry:** *Opposite the Narai Hotel on Silom Road (Tel. 234-1241), in the Dusit Thani Hotel, and on Sukhumvit Road.* One of Bangkok's best. Excellent quality designs and very reliable.

❑ **Tabtim Thai:** *Oriental Hotel, Author's Lounge (Tel. 236-0400, ext. 3357).* The owner, Mrs. Yupha Steiner, who also operates the exclusive Pink Poodle boutique, produces unique and attractive neck pieces. Moderate.

❑ **Jim Thompson Silk Company:** *9 Suriwongse Road.* Excellent selection of neck pieces using semi-precious stones, gold, and silver. Go to the second floor display case for examples.

❑ **The Collection:** *The Hilton Hotel, Wireless Road, Tel. 253-0123, Ext. 8683.* Offers beautifully designed jewelry and objets d'art. Uses opals.

❑ **Peninsula Plaza shops:** Houses some of Thailand's best quality shops on the first floor—**Bualaad, Paa, Frank's, Chailai,** and **Anong Gallery**. Very expensive.

❑ **Amarin Plaza shops:** Houses several good quality jewelry shops located on the first and third floors—**Tisa Gems, Chavana, D. Diamonds, Vogue Jewelry,** and **Gemsmond.** Compared to the outstanding Peninsula Plaza jewelry shops, you should find some good quality but more moderately priced jewelry here.

❑ **Gemopolis:** *Located 30 kilometers east of Bangkok (Km. 12, Bangna-Trad highway, off King Kaew Road).* This 300-acre "gem city" includes numerous jewelry shops and factories. Heavily promoted by the Tourism Authority of Thailand as a major tourist destination.

HANDICRAFTS

❑ **Rasi Sayam:** *32 Sukhumvit, Soi 23 (Tel. 258-4195).* This lovely shop housed in in old Thai house offers one of Thailand's finest collections of handcrafted items produced in villages throughout Thailand. Look for pottery, carvings, boxes, baskets, ceramics, etc. The emphasis here is on both quality and unique handicrafts and home decorative items. Excellent designs and good value. Perfect place for serious collectors. Moderate.

❑ **Thai Craft Museum:** *2nd Floor, Gaysorn Plaza.* One of the newest and most ambitious presentations of Thai handicrafts. Laid out as a village, this expansive shop (everything in this so-called "museum" is for sale) offers a huge collection of textiles, ceramics, baskets, clothes, pottery, kalagas, mats, and much more. While this place is somewhat overwhelming, signs throughout the shop explain each product.

❑ **The Legend:** *Third floor of Amarin Plaza (Tel. 256-9929).* Unique collection of excellent quality textiles, porcelain, baskets, and pottery. Many one-of-a-kind pieces, similar in quality to those found at Rasi Sayam. Moderate.

❑ **Chitralada:** *Seven locations: Oriental Place; Royal Thai Decorations Pavilion, Grand Palace; Bangkok International Airport; Vimanmek Mansion, Amporn Palace; Thaniya Plaza; Royal Garden Riverside Hotel Plaza; and Amari Watergate Hotel.* Operated by The Support Foundation of Her Majesty Queen Sirikit of Thailand. Includes a wide range of quality handicrafts, from baskets and hand-embroidered linen to purses, wallets, and belts.

❑ **Narayana Phand:** *In The Mall on Rajadamri Road.* This huge two-floor government-run handicraft emporium offers a very large selection of Thai handicrafts for tourists. Everything from woodcarvings to silver jewelry and paintings. Popular place to send tourists for all their handicraft needs. Highly recommended for last minute shopping and for lots of small trip gifts. Be sure to go up to the second floor. Moderate.

❑ **Nandakwang:** *108/3 Sukhumvit 23 Prasanmitr, Prakhanong (Tel. 258-1962).* Beautiful cotton woven items that make great gifts or additions to one's home decor. Quality placemats, pillows, boxes, toys, and gift items. Hard to find this shop in the maze of lanes off Sukhumvit Road, but persist until you find it! Moderate.

❑ **Thai Home Industries:** *35 Oriental Lane (Tel. 234-1736).* Nice selection of various Thai handicrafts, including baskets, spirit houses, temple bells, wood carvings, and unique bronze flatware. Service is a little slow, but patience pays off. Moderate to expensive.

❑ **House of Handicrafts:** *Large shop in the Regent Hotel (Tel. 250-0724) shopping arcade and small shop in the Amarin Plaza.* Offers a large selection of attractive Thai and hilltribe handicrafts. Moderate.

❑ **Bangkok Dolls:** *Main workshop at 85 Soi Ratapan, off Rajaprarop Road (Tel. 245-3008).* Unique collection of handcrafted Thai dolls reflecting numerous ethnic and cultural themes. Great place for both the young and old to visit. Moderate.

CELADON, BENCHARONG, POTTERY

❑ **Prasart Collection:** *Second floor, Peninsula Plaza, 153 Rajadamri Road (Tel. 253-9772).* Specializes in making gorgeous reproductions of bencharong. The shop has a small inventory which merely represents the type of custom work they can do at their main workshop. And the main workshop is one of Thailand's most interesting museums that houses a fabulous collection of Thai antiques in a large compound which has been designed for preserving Thai arts. If you have time, be sure to visit this museum. It's located near Ramkamhaeng University, via Phetburi Road, approximately 40 minutes from the major shopping areas (9 Soi Krungtepkreetha 4A, Krungtcpkreetha Road, Bangkapi). Take the 1½-2 hour guided tour of the lovely grounds and museum. Open for individuals from 10am to 3pm, Friday, Saturday, and Sunday (300 baht). For more information, contact the Peninsula Plaza shop or call the museum directly—Tel. 374-6328. Very expensive bencharong reproductions but extremely labor-intensive for highly skilled craftspeople.

❑ **Chiiori Bencharong:** *87 Nailert Building, Sukhumvit Road (near Soi 5), Tel. 254-3155.* Offers a wide selection of handpainted bencharong dinner sets, coffee and tea sets, vases, candle stands, and more.

❑ **Celadon House:** *18/7 Sukhumvit 21 (Tel. 258-3920, 259-7744).* Large selection of the light grey-green and dark brown-green celadon. Includes decorative pieces, lamps, and tableware. Has a "seconds" section on second floor.

❑ **Lotus Ceramics:** *Sukhumvit Road, Soi 3/1 (off of the larger Soi 3, Tel. 253-0044 or 253-2789).* Offers a large selection of blue and white pottery.

❑ **Living Art:** *2nd Floor, Oriental Plaza (Tel. 266-0186, ext. 2331).* Includes a beautiful collection of bencharong plates and cups.

❑ **Thai Taworn Brothers Co. Ltd.:** *89/34-35 Rajathavee Cross, Phyathai Road, across from Asia Hotel (Tel. 252-0612).* Large selection of bencharong and blue and white pottery.

BRONZEWARE

❑ **Siam Bronze Factory:** *1250 New Road (Tel. 234-9436).* Large selection of bronze items. Will silicon coat upon request.

❑ **S. N. Thai Bronze Factory:** *157-33 Phetburi Road, Tel. 21-5-8221 or 215-7743).* Large selection of bronze items. Will silicon upon request.

❑ **Lin Plaza Gems:** *Across from Oriental Plaza at 1-7 Chartered Bank Lane (Tel. 233-6592).* Second floor has a good selection of bronze items, from flatware to statues. Good place to buy trip gifts. Also has jewelry.

❑ **Thai Home Industries:** *35 Oriental Lane, off New Road near the Oriental Hotel (Tel. 234-1736).* Offers uniquely designed bronzeware and brass dinner plates.

DUTY-FREE LUXURY GOODS

❑ **King Power Duty Free Shop:** *7th Floor, World Trade Center.* Stocks numerous brand name luxury goods at duty-free prices.

Enjoying Your Stay

B ANGKOK AND THAILAND HAVE MUCH TO OFFER the visitor in addition to shopping. The food is wonderful, hotels are beautiful, service is outstanding, and the sights are truly exotic. We recommend taking time to really enjoy the many pleasures of this fascinating country.

SIGHTSEEING

The major tourist sights in Bangkok center around the history and culture of Thailand. One of your very first stops should be the fabled **Temple of the Emerald Buddha** and the **Grand Palace Complex**. These two adjacent sites are truly awe-inspiring—the highlight of many visitors' trip to Thailand. Few countries in the world have anything to compare to these colorful and exotic places. Another adjacent site, the **Wat Po** temple complex, with its reclining Buddha and traditional massages, is also worth visiting. You also can shop in this area for Thai handicrafts. Since the prices tend to be highly inflated here, bargain hard for as much as 60% discount.

Four other temples are especially worth visiting: **Marble Temple** (Wat Benjamabhopit), **Temple of the Dawn** (Wat

Arun), **Temple of the Golden Mount** (Wat Saket), and **Temple of the Golden Buddha** (Wat Trimitr). These temples should give you a good overview of traditional Thai architecture and Buddhist art themes found in many of Bangkok's antique, arts, and crafts shops.

Several guided tours with English-speaking guides are available for touring the temples and other sights in and around Bangkok. Most are either for a half-day or full-day. Several tour operators, such as **Tour East** and **Greylines**, offer a variety of programs which can be arranged through your hotel. Most of the tours are relatively inexpensive and are taken in the comfort of an air-conditioned bus or minivan. Our favorite tours are:

❑ The Temple of the Emerald Buddha, The Grand Palace, Wat Po

❑ Temple of the Dawn and the Marble Temple

❑ Manohra Song Cruise (two days, Bangkok–Ayutthaya)

❑ The Ancient City

❑ Jim Thompson's House and Suan Pakkard Palace

❑ Ayutthaya and Bang Pa-in (one day, take the Oriental Queen river boat one way)

❑ Vimarnmek Palace

❑ The Floating Market (Damnuen Saduak), Nakorn Pathom, and Salt Flats

❑ The Rose Garden

❑ Bridge on the River Kwai

For a good overview of Thai history and culture, visit the **National Museum** which is located next to Thammasat University, across from Pramane Ground and near the Grand Palace. The private **Prasart Museum** (9 Soi Krungtepkreetha 4A, Krungtepkreetha Rd., Bangkapi, Tel. 374-6328, 374-6384, 10am-3pm, Friday, Saturday, Sunday) also is well worth visiting (see earlier description on page 215).

The river and canals are a delight to experience in Bangkok. You can easily rent your own boat and driver for 400 to 500 baht per hour to tour the river and canals or take the numerous river taxis that ply the muddy Chao Phraya waters. One of the best on-your-own trips is to rent a boat next to the Oriental Hotel or beside the Pinklao Bridge (next to Thammasat University) for a 2 to 3 hour trip through the canals and along the river. Most drivers know where to take you—just tell them you want 2 or 3 hours with a stop at Wat Arun (Temple of the Dawn). It's easy, fun, inexpensive, and you'll have the flexibility to stop to take pictures, see sights, and shop. One of the best times to take this trip is early morning, before the major shopping arcades and shops open and it is cooler.

The Chao Phraya is a fascinating place, especially the stretch from Bangkok to Ayutthaya. One of our favorite river cruises traverses this area and includes an overnight stay on the river in luxurious barge accommodations: **Manohra Song** (Manohra Cruises, 257/1-3 Charoen Nakorn Road, Thonburi, Bangkok 10600, Tel. 662-476-0021 or Fax 662-460-1805). "Manohra Song"—even the name evokes the romanticism of a by-gone era when Thailand moved by rivers rather than roads and the pace of life was slower. Now travelers to Thailand can escape the notorious traffic and enjoy a slower pace on the luxurious Manohra Song—an authentic Thai River Rice Barge that has been converted to luxury yacht standards. With only four air-conditioned staterooms with en suite bathrooms, and beautifully furnished with appointments of teak and Thai fabrics, antiques and art, it comfortably accommodates eight passengers who are served by an attentive on-board crew of four.

The Manohra Song provides a wonderful opportunity for visitors to see the former Thai capital of Ayutthaya and view everyday life along the Chao Phraya River. Most of the cruises are for two days with one night on-board the Manohra Song: others are three-days with two nights on-board. The Up-river Cruise (Bangkok-Ayutthaya-Bangkok) begins when you board the Manohra Song at the Marriott Royal Garden Riverside Hotel pier. As you wend your way up-river, you'll pass the beautiful Temple of Dawn, the magnificent grounds of the Grand Palace, and the boat-house where the Royal Barges are kept. Along with numerous other temples and homes you'll enjoy watching the endless variety of life on the river. From picturesque old rice barges laden with rice, the fast-moving and loud "long-tail" boats, tugs pulling huge barges in a caravan, and every type of small water craft imaginable—all form an unforgettable panorama that makes up the lifeline of Thailand and her people.

You'll arrive at a typical Thai Wat (Temple) in time to be served cocktails on deck as you watch the sunset. With your boat docked at the Wat for the night, you'll be served dinner—a candle-light set menu of Thai cuisine—on board the Manohra Song. The next morning you have the option of "making merit" by gifting the Monks with food and other small offerings provided by Manohra Cruises. After an American breakfast on deck, get underway for Bang Pa-In, the 17th century Royal Summer Palace. This morning you'll see up-country life along the river—children bathing and women doing their daily washing in the river.

When you arrive at Bang Pa-In and the Royal Summer Palace, you'll be met by a private guide who will escort you on a tour of the Palace buildings and grounds and share with you its fascinating history. Later you'll board a "long-tail" boat at the Summer Palace pier for the short journey to the old capital of Ayutthaya where you'll have lunch at a typical Thai riverside seafood restaurant on the riverbank. After lunch, your private guide will escort you on a tour of the old Thai capital of Ayutthaya and its magnificent ruins. You return to the Manohra Song by private car for your return journey to Bangkok. It is also possible to continue to points north: Sukhothai, Chiang Mai, Chiang Rai or Mae Hong Son. Down river cruises are also available with the itinerary reversed so that participants enjoy the same range of sightseeing activities.

We have been to Ayutthaya previously—both by river and by road. But we decided to try this luxury cruise and chose the down-river route. Manohra Song delivered everything we were promised. We were picked up at our hotel by a our own private guide and driver with a Mercedes Benz! We enjoyed chatting with our guide as we journeyed by road to Ayutthaya. Once there, we saw more of the old capital than we have ever seen previously and learned more about its history. We had lunch at a riverside restaurant before traveling by "long-tail" boat to the Royal Summer Palace and Bang Pa-In. While we were sightseeing, our luggage had been transferred to the Manohra Song where it was already in our stateroom when we boarded the boat at the Bang Pa-In pier. We sunned ourselves on deck and watched the life on the river as we floated downstream. we arrived at Wat Bangna where our crew moored us for the night. We enjoyed a private candlelight dinner on board and watched lights flicker in the distance from our comfortable seats on deck.

The next morning we missed the sunrise, but we made offerings to the monks at Wat Bangna and then enjoyed breakfast on deck. We continued our trip downstream—watching the river glide by and occasionally taking our eyes off the scenes unfolding before our eyes long enough to re-read a bit of *Lord Jim*. Too soon, it seemed, we were in Bangkok and after sailing past the Grand Palace and the Temple of Dawn we disembarked at the Marriott Royal Garden Riverside Hotel pier taking with us memories of the Chao Phraya River and its people.

Manohra Cruises offers exclusivity and luxury. All meals on board the Manohra Song as well as lunches on shore are included as are all tours, guides, admissions and intermediate transfers.

A sister rice barge, the Manohra, also beautifully restored by the folks at the Marriott Royal Garden Riverside Hotel, offers nightly dinner cruises. Whether you chose to spend an evening dining aboard the Manohra or spend a night or longer onboard the Manohra Song you will have special memories to take with you when you return home.

ACCOMMODATIONS

Bangkok abounds with some of the world's best hotels. Indeed, hotels such as the Regent, Shangri-La, Peninsula, and Oriental frequently receive international awards at the world's "best of the best" hotels. These properties, in turn, have set a standard that many other hotels seek to emulate.

Since the 1997 economic downturn, Bangkok's hotel prices have fallen considerably. Some of the best hotel deals are found with Bangkok's top five-star hotels.

The following hotels represent Bangkok's very best. For reservations, you can contact the hotels directly, work through your travel agent, or contact an online broker that works with these and other hotels: *www.asiatravel.com, www.entravel.com,* and *www.asia-hotels.com*.

❑ **The Regent Bangkok**: *155 Rajadamri Road, Bangkok 10330, Thailand, Tel. (662) 251-6127, Fax (662) 254-9999.* One of our personal favorite Bangkok hotels, and a frequent winner of travel industry and readers' choice awards, The Regent is centrally located near major business, entertainment, and shopping venues. Large stone elephants greet the arriving guest as the car enters the drive. Cross the stone terrace flanked by lotus pools and enter the lobby which features high ceilings adorned with hand-painted silk panels and a hand painted silk mural flanked by a wide staircase. Beautiful antique wood pieces adorn the lobby, and in the afternoon and early evening a string quintet plays relaxing music from a loft overlooking the lobby as hotel and city residents alike enjoy beverages, light snacks and conversation. The 356 superbly decorated rooms and suites offer every amenity and utmost luxury. The 1997 refurbishment includes an addition of elegant silks from Jim Thompson, handcrafted and comfortable Thai furniture, and Thai accents and antiques. Each guestroom or suite is decorated with a hand-painted silk mural and hand blown glass or hand-crafted northern Thai style lacquer lamps. Guestrooms and suites are spacious and there are a variety of choices —the new cabana rooms and suites, which overlook lush tropical gardens and a 25 meter outdoor swimming pool, offer a "resort" feel in the middle of the city. The marble baths are also spacious with double sinks, soaking tub and separate shower enclosure and stocked with more towels and amenities than you'll probably use. There is a separate dressing area as well. The Regent Club provides additional personal services and 24-hour food and beverage— including a cooked-to-order breakfast along with the traditional buffet—and business services. Shintaro offers contemporary and innovative Japanese food in a casual setting. Even if you don't normally select Japanese restaurants, try this one! The Spice Market is one of the best Thai restaurants in town. Decorated to mimic an old Thai spice shop, this casual restaurant is pleasant for lunch or dinner. Biscotti for Italian food offers contemporary dining within a kitchen concept where guests not only taste, but see the cooking process and smell the "home-cooked" food. As we go to press, Biscotti has been named top restaurant in Bangkok by *Bangkok Metro Magazine*.

MagiNet Laptop Connect provides quick access to Web sites and e-mail eliminating the need for a local internet service provider. Video conferencing service is available. To increase productivity for business travelers, in addition to the superb in-house facilities and a fleet of Mercedes Benz limousines equipped with cellular phones, the Regent offers its *Office on Wheels* which is equipped with TV, VCR, computer, fax, tape recorder, telephone, and removable writing table so the business traveler can be productive while on the road. Shops with a range of exquisite merchandise are located in the Parichart Court. Be sure to at least window shop here as well as in the Peninsula Plaza located across the side street from Parichart Court. *Concierge Best Buys* Regent Hotels' shopping service is a welcome time saver for business travelers and a boon to first-time visitors and serious shoppers alike. In addition to printed material available upon request, the service includes personalized shopping itineraries, securing knowledgeable and trustworthy guides, offering bargaining advice, and assisting with arrangements to ship home bulky purchases too large to carry! If you happen to be at the Regent during December, you'll be treated to one of the best displays of Christmas decorations anywhere. Health Club; Business Center; Meeting and Banquet Facilities.

After a stay at the Regent Bangkok, jet north to charming Chiang Mai, shop for antiques, furniture and handicrafts, and relax for a few days at the Regent Resort Chiang Mai.

❑ **The Peninsula Bangkok**: *333 Charoennakorn Road, Klongsan, Bangkok 10600, Thailand, Tel. (662) 861-2888, Fax (662) 861-1112, Website: www.peninsula.com* A member of The Leading Hotels of the World, The Peninsula is the newest luxury hotel to open in Bangkok. From the imposing W-shaped exterior overlooking the bustling Chao Phraya River to the spacious, well laid-out guestrooms, The Peninsula Bangkok will not disappoint those guests who have enjoyed the famous Peninsula ambience and service in her sister hotels. The hotel design allows scenic river views from each of its 370 guestrooms and suites. Rooms feature the most up-to-date facilities, including a built-in fax machine with a personal phone number, two IDD phone lines with voice mail and a world time clock. Business travelers will appreciate the oversized executive desk with data-port and PC sockets providing an ideal work area—if you can keep your eyes off the river scene below! Splendid marble bathrooms contain two separate sink/vanity areas, a built-in TV above the bathtub, and separate shower and toilet enclosures. Three telephones are conveniently positioned throughout the bathroom with a hands-free phone located near the tub. A foyer area with a luggage bench and closet includes a vanity with easy access to the bath. The noted Peninsula valet box for shoe cleaning and newspaper delivery is provided. Lighting is abundant throughout the guestroom, foyer, and bath, but can be easily dimmed with a touch of a finger on the consoles placed, along with valet call buttons, throughout the room. A selection of suites offer indulgence on a grander scale. Choose from 60 one-bedroom suites, four grand duplex suites, one duplex and one Peninsula suite. Cilantro features an international buffet as well as an a la carte menu; Mei Jiang specializes in classic Cantonese cuisine; and Jesters offers Pacific Rim fusion cuisine in a casual dining setting. Shopping and sightseeing expeditions can easily be arranged from the hotel or on your own. The Peninsula operates a complimentary boat shuttle service to transport guests across the river to and from its private check-in facilities on the Bangkok side of the river or to the River City Shopping Complex—just minutes away by boat—with its four floors of tailors, silk, jewelry and antique shops. Recreation/ Fitness Center; Business Center and Conference Facilities.

❑ **Shangri-La Hotel**: *89 Soi Wat Suan Plu, New Road, Bangrak, Bangkok 10500, Thailand, Tel. (662) 236-7777, Fax (662) 236-8579, toll-free from U.S. or Canada 800-942-5050, Web site: www.shangri-la.com.* Located on the Chao Phraya River and consistent winner of travel industry and readers' poll awards, the Shangri-La combines stunning public spaces, luxurious decor in guestrooms, spectacular views of the river, and service that is attentive without being obtrusive. Each of the 868 deluxe guestrooms and suites combine a modern Western decor enhanced by the rich beauty of Thai decorative motifs and colorful hand-crafted artworks. The marble baths with double vanities offer all the amenities expected in a top hotel. Those who want extra privileges may choose the exclusive Krungthep Wing, where each room or suite has its own private balcony, or select the Horizon Club in the Shangri-La Wing for extra attention and service. On the newly expanded and renovated Club floors, guests enjoy complimentary buffet breakfast each morning and canapes and cocktails each evening; complimentary tea, coffee, and soft drinks are available throughout the day. Late check-out and other complimentary services are extended to Horizon Club guests. Two towers, the Shangri-La Wing (over 650 rooms) and the Krungthep Wing (174 rooms) encircle lush tropical gardens and provide the backdrop for two swimming pools and large sunbathing areas. Angelini, an award winner for both cuisine and architecture, features an open kitchen and pizza oven and serves Italian cuisine from diverse regions of Italy. Shang Palace serves Cantonese cuisine, while Salathip serves Thai cuisine in a romantic traditional setting overlooking the river. Maenam Terrace, set along the river, serves a mix of international barbecue seafoods. The Shangri-La Yacht is available for cruises to Ayutthaya, as well as evening dinner cruises or private charter. Shopping abounds along the road leading to the hotel, and a complimentary boat shuttle service is available between the hotel and River City Shopping Complex with its four floors of tailors, silk, jewelry and antiques shops. Health Club; Business Center and Conference Facilities.

❑ **The Oriental**: *48 Oriental Avenue, Bangkok 10500, Thailand, Tel. (662) 236-0400, Fax (662) 236-1937, toll-free from U.S. or Canada 800-526-6566, Website: www.manda rin-oriental.com.* Long recognized for its ambience and service, The Oriental still ranks with the world's finest hotels. Its 396 luxuriously appointed rooms and suites have river views. Service, service, service is the watchword here. The Normandie, on the top floor, offers a breathtaking view of the Chao Phraya River as well as outstanding Continental cuisine. This is well worth the price for a special night. Lord Jim's overlooking the river on the second floor has a simply outstanding lunchtime buffet. Dinner is a la carte. China House, located across the entryway drive, serves Chinese selections, and Sala Rim Naam, in a Thai style building across the river, serves Thai food and offers a cultural show. Ciao is an outdoor Italian bistro. The two sister river cruisers, Oriental Queen I and II offer day cruises to Ayutthaya and serve a great luncheon buffet on board. A small, but exclusive, shopping arcade is located within the hotel, and across the drive is located another exclusive shopping area—Oriental Arcade. A few steps further is located Oriental Place, a multi-storey shopping center—also exclusive and primarily devoted to shops catering to tourists. Or hop on the complimentary river shuttle, operated by The Oriental, bound for River City Shopping Complex—a four-storey mall with lots of great shops. Thai Cooking School; Oriental Spa; Sports Center; Conference Facilities.

❑ **Sheraton Grande Sukhumvit**. *250 Sukhumvit Road, Klongtoey, Bangkok 10110, Thailand, Tel. (662) 653-0333, Fax (662) 653-0400, or toll-free U.S. or Canada 800-325-3589. Web site: www.sheraton.com.* An ITT Sheraton Luxury Collection hotel, situated three kilometers from the central business district and minutes from the Queen Sirikit Convention Center, its 30-storey tower overlooks the city and a nearby lake. 445 rooms and suites are richly decorated with warm woods, Thai silks and art. Guestrooms are more like studios and are very spacious. Each room has a walk-in dressing area. The spacious bathrooms have a tub and separate shower enclosure. Each room has a compact disc and cassette player and connections for fax and personal computer. Local phone calls, butler service, clothes pressing, and incoming faxes are free to guests. Rossini, a southern Italian bistro, serves seafood, grills and Neapolitan favorites cooked over an open-fire grill as you watch. The Golden Lotus offers classic and traditional Cantonese cuisine. Riva's is a dining venue offering Pacific Rim cuisine along with featured entertainment—a real "happening place". The Orchid Café features an all-day international buffet. The outdoor pool is an attractive area to just sit and relax. Grande Spa and Fitness Center; Business Center; Meeting and Banquet Facilities.

❑ **Le Royal Meridien**: *973 Ploenchit Road, Bangkok 10330, Thailand, Tel. (662) 656-0444, Fax (662) 656-0555. Web site: www.lemeridien-hotels.com.* Centrally located in the business, financial and shopping areas, Le Meridien President Hotel, a longstanding landmark noted for its Thai charm and French flair, opened its new President Tower Wing in 1998 and subsequently renamed the adjacent towering glass property Le Royal Meridien Hotel. Its 758 guestrooms and suites are spacious, luxuriously appointed and provide all the amenities and services expected by the business or leisure traveler. The Royal Club floors offer additional luxury and services. Dining choices include the Expresso café for all-day dining and offers an outstanding lunch-time buffet; the Summer Palace features Cantonese cuisine; Oasis, a 37th floor rooftop restaurant features a fusion grill cuisine; and Shin Daikoku offers traditional Japanese cuisine. Next door at the Le Meridien President, The Fireplace Grill, one of our long-time favorites, offers an array of meats and seafood grilled to perfection. One of Le Royal Meridien's greatest assets is its convention floor, comprising several meeting rooms with various capacities, a ballroom, and a 3500 square meter exhibition area large enough to host up to 2000 delegates—making it Bangkok's largest such facility. The space is enhanced by leading-edge audio-visual systems and computer-enhanced display, monitor and projection systems. Hotel encompasses and adjoins arcades with a variety of name brand shops. Two Health Clubs/Fitness Centers; Business/Convention Facilities.

If you wish to spend a few days relaxing on a tropical island in a luxury resort, Le Meridien also operates Le

Royal Meridien Phuket Yacht Club and Le Meridien Phuket on the Andaman island of Phuket and Le Royal Meridien Baan Taling Ngam on the Gulf of Thailand island of Samui. For an excursion north to Chiang Rai and the area known as the Golden Triangle, Le Meridien Baan Boran enjoys an area noted for its colorful hilltribes and beautiful scenery.

❑ **The Sukhothai**: *13/3 South Sathorn Road, Bangkok 10120, Thailand, Tel. (662) 287-0222, Fax (662) 287-4980. Web site: www.sukhothai.com.* A low rise hotel of stunning architecture and beautifully decorated with Thai antiques, The Sukhothai is a calm oasis amidst the chaos of Bangkok. After driving up the palm-lined drive, you enter the spectacular lobby and feel you have been whisked back to the royal Thai capital of Sukhothai. The spacious guestrooms (146 rooms and 80 suites) feature warm teakwood, Thai silk upholstered chairs and sofas, accented with stone tabletops and wallbase. Lighted niches feature decorative porcelain plates and specially designed wall sconces add a touch of class. The very spacious bathrooms feature teak floors, granite vanities, double sinks, large bathtubs and separate shower and toilet enclosures. Mirrored bathroom spaces abound. The Colonnade is noted for its Sunday brunch featuring a buffet with a wide variety of international selections accompanied by a jazz orchestra. As we go to press The Colonnade was a top selected restaurant by *Bangkok Metro Magazine*. The Celadon serves Thai cuisine in a sala surrounded by a lotus pond and an open-air terrace offers diners a choice of al fresco dining. The extensive a la carte menu offers selections from all over Thailand. La Noppamas serves Continental cuisine in a setting that exudes elegance in the decor and table settings. Terrazzo specializes in Italian cuisine in either air conditioned comfort or al fresco dining next to the swimming pool. All the most up-to-date features for business, comfort and security. Health Club; Conference and Banquet Facilities.

❑ **Siam Inter-Continental**: *967 Rama I Road, Bangkok 10330, Thailand, Tel. (662) 253-0355, Fax (662) 253-2275.* A Bangkok landmark with its huge sweeping roof line reminiscent of traditional architecture, the Siam Inter-Continental is located in the heart of the commercial and business area, and the only hotel in town with 26 acres of landscaped parkland. The 400 guestrooms include 233 rooms—including suites—and Club International within two low-rise Garden Wings, and 177 rooms and suites in a six story Tower Wing. Guestrooms are decorated in Western style with accents of Thai art and furnishings. Some rooms in the Garden Wing have a lovely separate sitting area featuring peacock chairs and enclosed by floor-to-ceiling glass windows from which the guest can watch the peacocks, ducks and other wildlife on the expansive grounds. Club International provides a private accommodation wing, higher levels of personalized service, and upgraded amenities. Avenue One presents Continental cuisine including French, Swiss and Italian, in a relaxing atmosphere. Similan offers the diner an array of fresh seafood to choose from every evening and Thai buffet at lunch. Sivalai is a 24-hour favorite for Thai, Asian and Western specialities offering a buffet breakfast, lunch and dinner. Fitness Facilities; Business and Conference Facilities.

❑ **Royal Orchid Sheraton Hotel & Towers**: *2 Captain Bush Lane, Siphaya Road, Bangkok 10500, Thailand, Tel. (662) 266-0123, Fax (662) 236-8320.* Located on the Chao Phraya River, all rooms overlook the scenic river. With 773 beautifully appointed rooms, including 75 suites, the Royal Orchid Sheraton is a frequent winner of industry and reader's poll awards. The Towers rooms offer many extra amenities and services including sit-down check-in/check-out on the 26th floor; wake-up tea or coffee with daily newspaper; complimentary breakfast and hors d'oeuvres and cocktails in the evening; exclusive lounge and boardroom. Giorgio's serves Italian regional cuisine and features a daily noon buffet and a weekly Sunday brunch. One of our favorites, we especially like the weekend noon buffets. Reserve a table overlooking the terrace and river. The Captain Bush Grill serves traditional Continental cuisine featuring roasts, grilled meats, and prime rib. Benkay serves Japanese cuisine; Thara Thong serves Thai cuisine in a Thai pavilion overlooking the river. Bukhara features Tandoori cuisine. Try the Rim Nam Café for casual dining; the bakery on the ground floor has pastries available for order and take-out. The Royal Orchid Sheraton is connected to the River City Shopping Complex, with its four floors of tailors, silk, jewelry and antique shops, by a 2nd floor enclosed walkway. Fitness Facilities; Business and Conference Facilities.

If you would like to go from your riverside hotel to a

seaside hotel, consider the Sheraton Grande Laguna Beach in Phuket—an hour's flight south from Bangkok.

❑ **Westin Banyan Tree**: *21/100 South Sathorn Road, Bangkok 10120, Thailand, Tel. (662) 679-1200, Fax (662) 679-1199. Website: www.westin.com.* Situated within the business district and near several embassies, The Westin Banyan Tree occupies the first two floors and from the 33rd to 60th floors of Thai Wah Tower II. As an all-suite hotel, it offers separate sleeping and living/working areas —a real plus to the business person who conducts in-room business meetings, and probably serves well for one person traveling alone. However, dividing the space into two distinct separate areas can make each area seem a bit cramped for a couple traveling together. The suites are tastefully decorated and the oversized desk with thoughtful amenities such as paperclips, stapler, and post-it notes will be appreciated by the business traveler. In-room fax machines are available on request. Westin Premier guests enjoy extra amenities and services including special check-in, room amenities based on their stated preferences and breakfast allowance. The Lobby Lounge serves a selection of beverages and light snacks and in the evening there is live entertainment. Rom Sai serves buffet and a la carte Western, Asian and Thai specialities. Bai Yun serves nouvelle Cantonese cuisine from its spectacular rooftop (60th floor) vantage point or try the Compass Rose lounge one floor below for beverages and light snacks. Even if you normally don't use hotels' fitness centers you should try this one—located on the 51st floor! And there are great views from the roof garden heated bubble spa and current pool or Jacuzzi! Spa Fitness Center; Business Center.

❑ **Grand Hyatt Erawan**: *494 Rajdamri Road, Bangkok 10330, Thailand, Tel. (662) 254-1234, Fax (662) 254-6244.* Centrally located in the midst of business and commercial enterprises, the Grand Hyatt Erawan offers 387 luxurious rooms and suites on 22 floors. Rooms are decorated in a contemporary Asian style and bathrooms have a bathtub and separate shower enclosure. The Regency Club executive floors feature extra personalized services. Eight restaurants offer a wide variety of cuisines. A shopping arcade on the lower level has several upscale shops; it also connections to a department store. Health and Fitness Center; Business Center (video conferencing and helicopter service available); Convention Facilities.

❏ **Dusit Thani**: *946 Rama IV Road, Bangkok 10500, Tel. (662) 236-0450, Fax (662) 236-6400.* One of Bangkok's oldest and most prestigious properties. Centrally located in the business and commercial center opposite Lumpini Park, its 530 guestrooms are decorated with rich fabrics, warm woods, and touches of Asian art. Wide range of Cantonese, Japanese, and International cuisines. There is a shopping arcade on the lower level. Fitness Center; Business Center and Convention Facilities.

❏ **Holiday Inn Crowne Plaza**: *981 Silom Road, Bangkok 10500, Thailand, Tel. (662) 238-4300, Fax (662) 238-5289. Website: www.hicp-bkk.com.* Conveniently located in the commercial and business center of Bangkok, The Holiday Inn Crowne Plaza is also within walking distance of shopping and nightlife. The 726 luxurious rooms and suites in two towers offer expected amenities. Five floors of Executive rooms and suites offer deluxe amenities including complimentary continental breakfast in the Executive Lounge, beverages all day with cocktails in the evening, and a library of international newspapers and journals. The Thai Pavilion serves superb Thai cuisine. Ask for a table overlooking busy Silom Road—it's fun to watch the traffic when you're not in it! Tandoor offers Indian selections and Window on Silom serves International cuisine. The Orchid Lounge, in the lobby, serves light snacks and Cheers Pub is popular for evening drinks with live entertainment. Health Club; Business and Conference Facilities.

❏ **Marriott Royal Garden Riverside**: *257/1-3 Charoen Nakorn Road, Thonburi, Bangkok 10600, Thailand, Tel. (662) 476-0021, Fax (662) 476-1120, toll-free from US & Canada 800-228-9290.* A low-rise city resort on the banks of the Chao Phraya River, the 420 rooms have private balconies with river or city views. Pastels of blue, beige and peach mixed with teak wood lend warmth throughout the resort and rooms are appointed for comfort and convenience. Dining options include Benihana, a Japanese-American Steak House; Trader Vic's for a Polynesian dining experience; the Market and Riverside Terrace for seafood and BBQ; The Rice Mill Chinese restaurant or enjoy a dinner cruise on The Manohra—a converted rice barge operated by the Marriott. Away from the hustle and bustle of the city, the river affords a scenic way to commute into the heart of the city. The Marriott's own water taxis make the run from the hotel pier to city center and River City Shopping Complex, with its four floors of tailors, silk, jewelry and antique shops, is only about 15 minutes by boat. Small shopping arcade on premises. Health and Recreation Center; Meeting and Banquet Facilities.

❑ **Manohra Song**: Take an overnight, two-day river excursion to the old Thai capital of Ayutthaya on a classy rice barge that has been converted into luxurious accommodations for this exclusive voyage operated by the folks at the Marriott Royal Garden Riverside. See pages 219-221 for more information.

RESTAURANTS

If you enjoy eating, you should take advantage of Bangkok's numerous restaurants. Many serve wonderful and inexpensive luncheon buffets in lovely settings. Here are some of Bangkok's best buffets in close proximity to key shopping areas:

Buffet	Location	Shopping Area
▪ Expresso (International)	Le Royal Meridien	Gaysorn Plaza Amarin Plaza World Trade Center
▪ Dining Room (International)	Grand Hyatt Erawan Hotel	Peninsula Plaza Amarin Plaza Gaysorn Plaza World Trade Center
▪ Lord Jim's (seafood/Thai Japanese)	Oriental Hotel	Oriental Place, Oriental Lane, New Road
▪ Colonnade	Sukhothai Hotel	Sathorn and Silom Roads
▪ Captain's Table	Grand Pacific Hotel	Sukhumvit Road
▪ Giorgio's (Italian/Thai)	Royal Orchid Sheraton Hotel	River City Shopping Complex
▪ Tiara Room (International)	Dusit Thani Hotel	Upper Silom Road

■ Window on Silom (International)	Holiday Inn Crowne Plaza Hotel, 981 Silom	Silom Road
■ Talay Thong (Thai/seafood)	Siam Inter-Continental Hotel	Siam Centre/Siam Square/Mah Boon Krong Centre
■ Jit Pochana (Thai/Chinese)	1082 Paholyothin Road	Weekend(Chatuchak) Market/Central Plaza
■ President Lounge (International)	Le Meridien President Hotel	Gaysorn/Amarin Plaza/World Trade Center, Rajadamri Arcade
■ Rom Sai (International)	Westin Banyan Tree Hotel	Sathorn and Silom Roads
■ Bon Vivant (International)	Tawana Ramada Hotel	Suriwongse, Patpong, and Silom Roads

Your choices for evening dining are numerous, from elegant and expensive French restaurants to open-air Thai food shops and street vendors. Many are located in major hotels while others are found along the lanes. Some of our favorites include:

THAI

❑ **The Spice Market:** *The Regent Bangkok, 155 Rajadamri Road (Tel. 251-6127). Open for lunch and dinner.* It doesn't get much better than The Spice Market. One of Bangkok's best Thai restaurants and one of our long-time favorites. Charming market ambience and informal dining. Excellent service. Everything here is outstanding but be sure to try the *nam prik ong* (minced pork dip on crispy rice cakes), *thom yum kung* (spicy prawn soup with lemongrass), *nua phad bai kapraow*, (fried beef with chili and fresh basil), and *siew ngap* (red curry with roasted duck in coconut milk). This conveniently located Thai restaurant is one you can easily return to again and again during your stay in Bangkok!

❑ **Baan Khanitha:** *36/1 Sukhumvit 23, Soi Prasanmit (Tel. 258-4181). Open daily 11am-2pm and 6-11pm.* One of Bangkok's most talked about restaurants. Serves excellent spicy Thai dishes in a charming house tastefully decorated with antiques and surrounded by a tropical garden. A real class operation with excellent service. Popular for seafood dishes.

❑ **Mango Tree:** *37 Soi Anuman Ratchathon, across from the Tawana Ramada Hotel on Suriwongse Road and near Coca Suriwongse (Tel. 236-2820). Open 10am-2pm and 6-10pm.* Charming restaurant in an 80-year old Thai house just off one of Bangkok busiest shopping districts. Serves excellent Thai dishes at reasonable prices. Accompanied by classical Thai music. A delightful surprise!

❑ **Kalpapruek:** *27 Pramuan Road (Tel. 236-4335). Open Monday through Saturday 8am-6pm and Sunday 8am-3pm.* Small restaurant in a house. Authentic Thai cuisine and excellent Western desserts. Try the grilled crispy pork with sticky rice. Reasonably priced. Only accepts cash.

❑ **Celadon:** *The Sukhothai, 13/3 South Sathorn Road (Tel. 287-0222). Open 11am-3pm and 6-10:30pm.* Excellent dishes served in a delightful traditional Thai pavilion set in a water garden. Choice of air-conditioned and open-air terrace dining surrounded by a charming lotus pond. Everything here is good!

❑ **Red Pepper:** *Rembrandt Hotel, Sukhumvit Soi 18 (Tel. 261-7100).* One of Bangkok's best Thai restaurants. Excellent selections and service.

❑ **Lemongrass:** *5/1 Sukhumvit Soi 24 (Tel. 258-8637). Open daily 11am-2pm and 6-11pm.* Long-time favorite of expatriates. Nice ambience in an old Thai mansion decorated with antiques, but not particularly elegant for evening dining. Open for lunch and dinner. We prefer it for lunch. Try the signature lemon grass ice tea.

❑ **Ruen Thai:** *Grand Hyatt Erawan, 5ᵗʰ floor, 494 Rajdamri Road (Tel. 254-1234, ext. 4446). Open 11:30am-2:30pm and 6:30-10:30pm.* This cosy restaurant is surrounding by a garden and pool. Includes a delicious lunch buffet. Dinner accompanied by live Thai classical music.

❑ **Salathip:** *Shangri-La Hotel, 89 Soi Wat Suan Plu, New Road (Tel. 236-7777, ext. 1168). Open 6:30-10:30pm.* Popular Thai-style restaurant in a romantic setting overlooking the Chao Phraya River. Serves excellent Thai dishes. Includes nightly (except Monday) classical Thai dance performances from 7:50pm to 9pm.

❑ **Thanying:** *10 Soi Pramuan, Silom Road (Tel. 236-4361).* An old-time favorite. Fabulous cooking (Royal Court-trained cooks) and very nice ambience in an old house. A class operation. The *kaeng masuman* here is outstanding.

❑ **Bussaracum:** *139 Sathiwon Building, Pan Road off Silom Road (Tel. 226-6312). Open daily 11:30am-2pm and 5:30-10:30pm.* Serves excellent Thai food in a classic royal Thai setting. Menu changes monthly. Tends to cook on the bland side for Westerners.

❑ **D'Jit Pochana:** *1082 Pahonyothin-Lad Prao Intersection (Tel. 279-5000).* A long-time favorite. Offers excellent Thai food as well as an extensive buffet. The perfect place to dine if you're visiting the nearby Chatuchak Weekend Market.

❑ **Harmonique:** No *22 Charoenkrung (New Road) 34 (Tel. 237-8175). Open Monday through Saturday, 11am-10pm.* This small but charming enclosed outdoor restaurant, surrounded by art and antiques, serves excellent Thai dishes. Includes an art and antique gift shop. Reasonable prices and excellent service. One of nicest surprises just off of New Road with its numerous art, antique, and jewelry shops. A little hard to find, but your persistence will be rewarded!

CHINESE

❑ **Mei Jiang:** *The Peninsula Bangkok, 333 Charoennakorn Road, Klongsan (Tel. 861-2888). Open lunch and dinner.* Very elegant Cantonese restaurant in one of Bangkok's (Thonburi) newest properties along the Chao Phraya River.

❑ **Bai Yung:** *Westin Banyan Tree, 60th floor, 21/100 South Sathorn Road (tel. 679-1200). Open 11:30am-2:30pm and 6:30-10pm.* Fabulous rooftop restaurant with a breath-taking view of Bangkok. Serves innovative Cantonese cuisine in a contemporary setting known for its elegant surroundings and exceptional service. Excellent dim sum for lunch.

❏ **The Chinese Restaurant:** *Grand Hyatt Erawan, 494 Ratchadamri Road (Tel. 254-1234). Open daily 11:30am-2:30pm and 6:30-11pm.* Elegant Shanghai-deco gourmet restaurant serving outstanding Cantonese cuisine. Noted for its popular dim sum and shark's fin.

❏ **Mayflower:** *Dusit Thani Hotel, Rama IV Road at Silom Road (Tel. 236-0450).* Very elegant Chinese restaurant serving outstanding Cantonese cuisine. Open for dim sum lunch as well as for dinner.

❏ **Hai Tien Lo:** *The Pan Pacific Bangkok, 22nd floor, 952 Rama IV Road Suriwongse (Tel. 632-9000, ext. 4202). Open weekdays noon-2:30pm, weekends 10:30am-2:30pm, and all evening 6:30-11:30pm.* Terrific dim sum and Cantonese cuisine. Popular for sliced Alaskan clams, king prawns, deep-friend pigeon.

❏ **Jasmin:** *Gaysorn Plaza and Times Square.* Noted for its marinated duck, abalone braised with a sea slug, soft-shell crab, and the Monk Jumps Over the Wall (order the day ahead).

❏ **Royal Kitchen:** *16-1 North Sathorn Rd. (Tel. 234-3063). Open for lunch and dinner.* One of Bangkok's best Chinese restaurants in elegant surroundings. Expensive.

❏ **The Empress:** *The Royal Princes Hotel, 269 Lan Luang (Tel. 281-3088). Open daily 11:30am-2:30pm and 6pm-10pm.* This elegant and spacious dining room serves excellent dim sum and Cantonese cuisine. Convenient in relation to the Grand Palace and zoo areas.

❏ **Lee Kitchen:** *Fourth floor Thaniya Plaza, Silom Rd. (Tel. 231-2158).* Considered by many Thais to be one of Bangkok's very best Chinese restaurants. Especially popular with businesspeople for lunch.

❏ **Summer Palace:** *Le Royal Meridien, 973 Ploenchit Road (Tel. 656-0444). Open 11am-2:30pm and 6:30-10:30pm.* Gorgeous dining room, as well as ten private rooms, featuring a fine range of Cantonese cuisine.

❏ **New Great Shanghai:** *648 Sukhumvit Road, near Soi 24 (Tel. 258-7042). Open 11am-2pm and 6-10:30pm.* A long-time favorite offering very good dim sum lunches.

❑ **Shangarila:** *306 Yaowarat Road, Chinatown, near Rat-chawong Road. Open 11am-2pm.* The place to dine if you're in Chinatown. A long-time favorite offering good dim sum lunches.

FRENCH AND CONTINENTAL

❑ **Normandie Grill:** *Oriental Hotel, 45 Oriental Avenue (Tel. 236-0400). Open daily, noon-2pm and 7-11pm.* One of Asia's best restaurants. Wonderful view of the river and Thonburi. Offers outstanding service. Elegant and very expensive. Men need a coat and tie. Reservations required.

❑ **Fireplace Grill:** *Le Meridien President Hotel (Tel. 252-9880). Open daily from 11:30am-2:30pm and 6:30-10:30pm; dinner only on Saturday and Sunday.* Cozy grillroom serving an excellent array of charcoal-grilled meats and seafood accompanied by outstanding service. Always great for Chateaubriand. Still one of our all-time favorites.

❑ **Auberge DAB:** *One Place Building, 540 Ploenchit Road (Tel. 658-6222), 11am-midnight.* Modeled after the famous Paris restaurant, this well appointed restaurant is noted for its imported Atlantic seafood.

❑ **Gourmet Gallery:** *6/1 Soi Promsri 1, Sukhumvit 39 (Tel. 260-0603). Open 11:30am-2:30pm and 6-10pm (except Monday).* This unique Continental restaurant offers excellent home-cooked meals in an art and music-filled atmosphere. Try the baked onion soup and grilled eggplant salad. Good selection of homemade cakes, pies, and ice creams.

❑ **Ma Maison:** *Hilton International, 2 Wireless Road (Tel. 253-0123). Open Monday through Saturday, 11:30am-2pm and daily 6:30pm-10pm.* Very elegant French restaurant offering superb dishes and service. Frequently ranked as Bangkok's best restaurant.

❑ **Le Bistro:** *20/17-19 Ruam Rudee Village, Soi Ruam Rudee (Tel. 251-2523). Open Monday-Friday 11:30am-2:30pm and daily 6:30-11:30pm.* Considered to be one of Bangkok's top five French restaurants.

❑ **Le Banyan:** *59 Sukhumvit Soi 8 (Tel. 253-5556). Open Monday through Saturday 6:30-10pm.* Also considered to be one of Bangkok's top five French restaurants. Pleasant atmosphere and excellent service. Reservations recommended

❑ **La Noppamas:** *The Sukhothai, 13/3 South Sathorn Road (Tel. 287-0222). Open 11:30am-2:30pm and 6:30-10:30pm.* Beautifully appointed and elegant dining room offering an extensive a la carte menu and wine list. Nice view of the hotel's signature stupas and water garden.

❑ **Le Metropolitain:** *3rd Floor Gaysorn Plaza, Ploenchit Road (Tel. 656-1102).* A long-time favorite that has moved to several locations. Always reliable French cuisine served in a 1920s setting.

❑ **Captain Bush Grill:** *Royal Orchid Sheraton, 2 Captain Bush Lane, Siphaya Road (Tel. 266-0123). Open daily 6:30-10am (Towers Breakfast) and 6:30-10:30pm.* Serves traditional Continental cuisine with roasts, grilled meats, prime rib, and table d'hote menu. Includes a special one-hour business lunch and set menu.

ITALIAN

❑ **Biscotti:** *The Regent Bangkok, 155 Rajadamri Road (Tel. 251-6127). Open 6:30-10:30am, 11:30am-2:30pm, and 6:30pm-Midnight (Sunday through Thursday).* Considered by many connoisseurs to be Bangkok's top Italian restaurant since it opened in December 1998 as a home cooking style Italian restaurant. Fun, causal, and contemporary dining in an open-kitchen setting. Everything here is good, from pizzas and pastas to charcoal-grilled meats and desserts.

❑ **Angelini:** *Shangri-La Hotel, 89 Soi Wat Suan Plu, New Road (Tel. 236-7777, ext. 1766), 11am-11:00pm.* An award winning restaurant for its fine cuisine and bold architectural design. Spectacular setting for this three-level modern art decor restaurant with an open kitchen, rotisserie, and pizza oven. Serves excellent pastas, risotto dishes, and seafood followed by wonderful desserts. Includes a popular bar with live band performing nightly (except Monday). Great ambience and first-class presentation and service.

❑ **Rossini:** *Sheraton Grande Sukhumvit, 250 Sukhumvit Road (Tel. 653-0333). Open noon-2:30pm and 6:30-10:30pm; closed for lunch on Saturday and Sunday.* A modern rustic Italian setting with a surprising menu of Southern Italian cuisine. Serves excellent fresh seafood and creative pasta dishes. Very upscale.

❑ **Gianni's Italian Restaurant:** *34/1 Soi Tonson, off Soi Lang Suan, Ploenchit Road (Tel. 252-1619). Open 11:30am-2pm and 6-10:30pm.* Authentic Italian cuisine beautifully presented in a lovely setting. Excellent service and good value. One of Bangkok's very best.

❑ **Giorgio's:** *Royal Orchid Sheraton, 2 Captain Bush Lane, Siphaya Road (Tel. 266-0123). Open daily noon-3pm and 6:30-11pm; Sunday brunch 11:30am-3pm.* An old-time favorite since it first opened in 1983. Features a daily Italian buffet lunch, antipasto buffet dinner, and weekly Sunday Brunch for families with videos, cartoon characters, and games. Excellent fish, shellfish, meat, pasta dishes, and desserts. Prefer the Saturday buffet. Ask for a window table with a terrace and distant river view.

❑ **Pan Pan:** *6-6/1 Sukhumvit Road, near Soi 33 (Tel. 258-9304) and 45 Soi Lang Suan, off Ploenchit Road (Tel. 252-7104). Open for lunch and dinner.* After many years, this is still one of Bangkok's most popular Italian restaurants. Serves excellent pasta dishes, a popular "Chicken Godfather" dish, and Italian-style ice cream.

❑ **Spasso:** *Grand Hyatt Erawan, Lower Lobby, 494 Rajdamri Road (Tel. 254-1234, ext. 3058). Open noon-2:30pm and 6:30pm-2am.* Serves an excellent daily Italian buffet lunch and Sunday brunch. In the evening, Spasso becomes one of Bangkok's hot spots for both dining and entertainment. Live band begins at 9:30pm. Very chic and sophisticated.

❑ **Vito's:** *20/2-3 Ruam Rudee Village, off Ploenchit Road (Tel. 252-7616). Open 11:30am-2:30 and 6-11pm.* Closed lunch Saturday and Sunday. One of Bangkok's most intimate and friendly Italian restaurants offering classic Italian cuisine. Noted for its red tuna tartare, black linguini with lobster, and pappardelle with Tuscan sausage, asparagus, and tomato. Extensive wine selection.

❏ **La Gritta:** *Sukhumvit Soi 19 (Tel. 253-7350).* Offers excellent Northern Italian cuisine. Excellent pasta dishes and beautiful presentations of everything.

❏ **L'Opera:** *55 Sukhumvit Road Soi 39 (Tel. 258-5606).* Serves excellent Italian food in a friendly setting.

SEAFOOD

❏ **Lord Jim's:** *Oriental Hotel, 48 Oriental Avenue (Tel. 236-0400).* Equally excellent for dinner and lunch. Elegant seafood restaurant with superb view of the river. Outstanding service. Try the fabulous mixed seafood grill. Spectacular luncheon buffet with an equally spectacular view of the Chao Phraya River—one of the best in Thailand. Always one of our first dining stops in Bangkok for lunch or dinner.

❏ **Thailand Tonight:** *Royal Orchid Sheraton, Siphya Road (Tel. 237-0022, ext. 3213). Open 6:30-10pm.* Offers a popular Thai-style seafood barbecue buffet along the riverside. Serves deliciously fresh seafood. Includes a cultural show.

❏ **Seafood Market and Restaurant:** *388 Sukhumvit Road, at Soi 21 (Tel. 258-0218). Open 11am-midnight.* Popular with tourists who enjoy a supermarket element to their dining experience—you pick out your favorite catch, along with vegetables and fruits, and proceed through the line and to your table where your dish will be finally presented. An interesting and expensive dining experience.

EUROPEAN/INTERNATIONAL/FUSION

❏ **Espresso:** *Le Royal Meridien, 973 Ploenchit Road (Tel. 656-0444). Open 24-hours a day.* What a fabulous international spread! The luncheon buffet here is awesome with lots of great international and Thai choices. The desserts are some of the best anywhere in Bangkok. Don't plan a busy afternoon after sampling the selections. An all-day East-West dining restaurant offering a la carte and buffets for breakfast, lunch, and dinner.

❏ **Colonnade:** *The Sukhothai, 13/3 South Sathorn Road (Tel. 287-0222). Open 6am-midnight.* One of Bangkok's most popular coffee shops which serves a fabulous luncheon buffet. Especially popular for the Saturday afternoon chocolate buffet and the Sunday brunch. Weekday lunch includes Thai and Japanese selections as well as Continental and Asian specialities. Very elegant setting with live piano music draws a regular suit and tie crowd.

❑ **Neil's Tavern:** *58/4 Soi Ruam Rudee (Tel. 251-5644) and Prime Building, 24 Sukhumvit Soi 21 (Tel. 256-6875). Open Monday through Saturday, 11:30am - 2pm and daily 5:30pm - 10:30pm.* A Bangkok institution for more than 30 years. Offers a relaxing atmosphere and excellent food. Great for Kobe steaks and seafood. Terrific bakery. One of our long-time favorites. Popular with many expatriates who enjoy a pub atmosphere, including candlelight.

❑ **The Dining Room:** *Grand Hyatt Erawan, 494 Rajdamri Road (Tel. 254-1234, ext. 3058).* Offers one of the best breakfast and luncheon buffets in Bangkok with a wide variety of international dishes.

❑ **The Tiara:** *Dusit Thani Hotel, 22nd floor, Rama IV Road, at Silom (Tel. 236-0450). Open daily noon-2:30pm (closed Saturday) and 7-10:30pm.* Terrific view of Bangkok from the top floor of this centrally-located hotel. Daily luncheon buffet offering fusion cuisine along with more traditional Asian and Continental dishes. Try the home-made ice creams. The Sunday Jazz Brunch is especially popular.

AMERICAN

❑ **JW's California:** *JW Marriott Hotel, 4 Sukhumvit Road (Tel. 656-7700). Open daily 11:30am-2pm and 6pm-10:30.* This informal restaurant with its open kitchen turns out excellent soft shell crabs, baked Norwegian salmon, and roast rack of lamb. It's Cal-Asian emphasis offers dishes from China, India, Japan, Thailand, and the U.S.

❑ **Hamilton's:** *Dusit Thani Hotel, 946 Rama IV Road, at Silom (Tel. 236-0450). Open 11:30am-2pm and 6:30pm-10pm.* A long-time favorite that maintains its fine reputation. Serves excellent steaks, U.S. prime rib, grilled Norwegian salmon, and lobster salad.

❑ **T.G.I. Friday's:** *Ploenchit Center, Sukhumvit Soi 2 (Tel. 656-8412) and Kamol Sukosol Building, 317 Silom Road (Tel.*

266-7488). Open daily 11:00am-midnight. Casual dining for burgers, steaks, pork ribs, seafood, Mexican fajitas, and Italian pasta. Good selection of exotic frozen drinks and desserts.

GERMAN

❏ **Bei Otto:** *1 Soi 20, Sukhumvit Road (Tel. 260-0869). Open 11am-3pm and 6-11pm.* Great for pork knuckles. Also includes a bakery and deli shop.

❏ **Paulaner Brauhaus:** *President Park Dome, Sukhumvit Soi 24 (Tel. 661-1111). Open 5:30pm-1:30am.* Has its own brewery. Serves hearty Bavarian specialities. Popular live band.

❏ **Hartmansdorfer Brauhaus:** *2nd Floor, Siam Discovery Center (Tel. 658-0229) and SCB Park Plaza East, Rachadapisek Road (Tel. 937-9301).* Serves own home brewed beer and delicious German food.

VIETNAMESE

❏ **Le Dalat:** *47/1 Soi 23, Sukhumvit Road (Tel. 260-1849).* One of Bangkok's best Vietnamese restaurants. Operated by a noted French-Vietnamese-Lao family and owner of Asian Heritage and Gallery antique shop (Soi 31,Sukhumvit Road). Great ambience with lots of antiques and a lush garden. Eclectic Vietnamese menu.

❏ **Le Dalat Indochine:** *14 Sukhumvit Soi 23 (Tel. 661-7967). Open 11:30am-2:30pm and 6-10pm.* Operated by the sibling of the Le Dalat owner whose popular restaurant is located just across the street. Located in a beautiful old house. Try their signature crab fish dish.

❏ **Tien Duong:** *Dusit Thani Hotel, 946 Rama IV Road, at Silom (Tel. 236-0450).* Classy restaurant offering excellent dishes and good service.

❏ **Thang Long:** *82/5 Soi Lang Suan, Ploenchit Road (Tel. 251-3504).* Serves an excellent combination of Vietnamese and Thai cuisine.

❏ **Sweet Basil:** *1 Srivieng Road (off Soi Pramuan) Silom (Tel. 238-3088). Open 11:30am-2pm and 5-10pm.* Offers fine

Vietnamese/Thai Yai cuisine in a charming 1930's King Rama IV's atmosphere. Try the Hanoi Marbles, steamed shrimp rolls, and beef and noodle soup.

JAPANESE

❑ **Shin Daikoku:** *32/8 Sukhumvit Soi 19 (Tel. 254-9980). Open daily 11am-2pm and 6-10:30pm.* This long established restaurant housed in a lovely Japanese-style house offers outstanding Japanese cuisine and excellent hands-on service by its owner, Kenji Tanaka. Dine next to the cool indoor fish pool or in the privacy of one of the tattami rooms. Try the sashimi, grilled eel, tempura, grilled sardines, chawan mushi, matsuzaka beef, and green tea noodles. Delightful setting for a memorable evening.

❑ **Genji Restaurant:** *Hilton International, 2 Wirless Road, at Nai Lert Park (Tel. 253-0123). Open daily noon-2:30pm and 6:30-10:30pm.* One of Bangkok's best Japanese restaurants frequented by Bangkok's many Japanese businessmen. Serves excellent sushi, sashimi, makizuski, seafood, and Kobe beef.

❑ **Shintaro:** *The Regent Bangkok, 155 Rajadamri Road (251-6127, ext. 8111).* This small casual sushi bar with one private dining room replicates a Japanese neighborhood sushi bar. Designed to be fun, interactive, and contemporary. Incorporates traditional and new styles of sushi, sashimi, noodle and tempura dishes with contemporary, colorful, artistic presentations.

INDIAN

❑ **Rang Mahal:** *The Rembrandt Hotel, 19 Sukhumvit Soi 18 (Tel. 261-7100, ext. 7532). Open daily 11:30am-2:30pm and 6:30-10:30pm.* Considered by many connoisseurs to be Bangkok's best Indian restaurant. Wonderful ambience with a 26th floor view of Bangkok. Great for kebabs. Reservations essential.

❑ **Tandoor:** *Holiday Inn Crowne Plaza, 981 Silom Road (Tel. 238-4300). Open noon-2:30pm and 6:30-11pm.* This elegant northwestern Indian restaurant serves excellent kebabs and tandoor dishes, chicken curry, and mutton masala. Try the extensive Sunday brunch buffet of Northern and Southern specialities.

❑ **Himali Cha Cha:** *Sukhumvit Soi 35 (Tel. 235-1569). Open daily 11am-3:30pm and 6-11:30pm.* Now in a new location, this old-time favorite still produces outstanding Indian-Muslim dishes. Don't go here for the decorating—candy striped plastic minarets on the exterior! Famous for its tandoor chicken.

OTHER SPECIALTIES

❑ **Trader Vic's:** *Marriott Royal Garden Riverside Hotel (Tel. 476-0021). Open noon-2pm and 6pm-1am.* Delightful Polynesian style restaurant with huge signature wood-fired oven, nautical themes, colorful paintings, and a riverside view offers and outstanding brunch. Offers the popular "River of King's Jazz Brunch" every Sunday, 11:30am to 3pm, with a live jazz quintet. Serves a little of everything, from lamb baby back ribs to Indian curries and Chinese won-tons.

❑ **Crepes & Co.:** *18 Sukhumvit Soi 12 (Tel. 251-2895). Open Monday through Saturday 9am-midnight and Sunday 8am-midnight.* This popular French-style crêperie offers a wide range of tempting crêpes as well as standard menu items. Serves a very popular Sunday brunch which tends to run all day!

❑ **Senor Pico:** *2ⁿᵈ Floor, Rembrandt Hotel (Tel. 261-7100). Open 6:30 10:30pm.* Considered by many diners to be Bangkok's best Mexican restaurant. Live band. Reservations recommended.

❑ **New Cup:** *3ʳᵈ Floor, Lake Rajada Office Complex, New Rachadapisek Road (Tel. 264-0247). Open Monday through Saturday, 11:30am-2:30pm.* One of Bangkok's best cafes noted for its nice ambience and imported delicacies. Expensive. The place to see and be seen if you are part of Bangkok's status-conscious upper class. Reservations highly recommended.

❑ **Koreana:** *446-450 Rama I Road (Tel. 252-9398), open 11am-10pm; and 28 Sukhumvit Soi 11, Chai Yose (Tel. 253-8894), open daily 11am-2:30pm and 5-10pm.* A long-time favorite Korean restaurant that offers excellent charcoal beef, pork ribs, tempura, and kimchi. Also serves Japanese dishes.

PUBS

❑ **Taurus:** *Sukhumvit Soi 26 (Tel. 261-3991). Open 6pm-2am.* This combination pub, discotheque, and restaurant is one of Bangkok's trendiest places. Enjoy gourmet dining (Thai and International cuisine) while planning your moves on the dance floor—complete with a live band and D.J.

❑ **Delaney's:** *1-5 Sivadon Building, 1 Convent Road, off Silom Road (Tel. 266-7160). Open 11am -2am.* This popular two-storey Irish pub serves an extensive menu of pub fare and a good selection of beers. Serves excellent beef, lamb, and fish. Very noisy and smoke-filled. Live Irish music every Tuesday through Saturday night. Sunday jam session begins at 3pm. Daily happy hours, 4-7:30pm, and daily set luncheons (Monday through Saturday).

❑ **Concept CM²:** *Novotel Bangkok on Siam Square, Siam Square Soi 6 (Tel. 255-6888, ext. 2549). Open 8:30pm-2am.* This combination pub and restaurant is another "in spot" for young people who enjoy dining at a theme restaurant (rice dishes) and disco-dancing to imported live bands. Includes five bars for women, Cantonese music, virtual reality games, videos, wines, and cocktails.

If you enjoy escaping from the streets of Bangkok with a break for afternoon tea, try the following hotels for **high tea:**

❑ **Author's Lounge:** *Oriental Hotel, 48 Oriental Avenue (Tel. 236-0400). Open 2-6pm.* Very classy Old World setting with live music. Old world ambience in the midst of a small but very upscale shopping center.

❑ **Regent Lobby:** *The Regent Bangkok, 155 Rajadamri Road (Tel. 251-6127). Open 2-5:30pm.* Beautiful setting, with painted ceilings and a huge Thai wall mural, for afternoon tea. String quartet plays from the balcony.

❑ **Sukhothai Lobby:** *13/3 South Sathorn Road (Tel. 287-0222). Open 2-5pm.* Serves the unique and popular chocolate buffet with its wonderful chocolate desserts. If you're a chocoholic, you'll think you've died and gone to heaven! Elegant setting with live music.

❑ **Shangri-La Hotel:** *89 Soi Wat Suan Plu, New Road (Tel. 236-7777).* Daily high tea but especially popular after

3pm on Sundays. Light music and ballroom dancing. Get there early.

❑ **Marriott Royal Garden Riverside Hotel:** *(Tel. 476-0021)*. Daily afternoon high tea. Take the free shuttle boat from River City Shopping Complex on the half hour to reach this down-stream riverside resort.

Dinner cruises are especially popular given Bangkok's many balmy evenings. Check with your hotel or call the places directly for information and reservations. Some of the most popular such cruises include:

❑ **Manohra:** *Marriott Royal Garden Riverside Hotel (Tel. 476-0021)*. Converted rice barge offering breakfast, lunch, and dinner cruises. Call for details and reservations.

❑ **Shangri-La Hotel:** *89 Soi Wat Suan Plu, New Road (Tel. 236-7777)*. Regularly scheduled dinner cruises from 7:30pm to 10pm.

❑ **Oriental Queen I & II:** *Oriental Hotel, 48 Oriental Avenue (Tel. 236-0400)*. Call for details, including chartering these sleek boats for private parties of up to 200 people.

❑ **Wan Fah:** *(Tel. 237-0077, ext. 162)*. Departs 7:30pm. Serves seafood and Thai cuisine. Include live Thai music.

Several **dinner theater restaurants** also combine a Thai cultural show with Thai food. These establishments are mainly organized for tour groups and independent travelers, but most serve excellent Thai food and present an entertaining show at reasonable prices. Some of the best such restaurants are:

❑ **Sala Rim Naam:** *Oriental Hotel, 48 Oriental Avenue (Tel. 437-6211)*. Wonderful riverside setting located in a classical Thai-style pavilion across the river from the main hotel complex (take the hotel ferry). Reservations essential.

❑ **Silom Village Trade Centre:** *286 Silom Road (Tel. 234-4448). Open 11am-11pm.* Set within a small shopping center of arts, crafts, and antique (be sure to visit Artisans) shops, this area also includes a restaurant complex consisting of several covered open-air and in-door restaurants serving seafood and Thai dishes. Thai cultural and classical dance show starts at 8pm.

❑ **Baan Thai:** *7 Sukhumvit Road Soi 32 (Tel. 258-5403).*

❑ **Piman Theater:** *46 Sukhumvit Road Soi 49 (Tel. 258-7861).*

❑ **Maneeya Lotus Room:** *518/4 Ploenchit Road (Tel. 251-0382). Open 10am-2pm and 7-10:30pm.*

❑ **Thai Pavilion:** *Holiday Inn Crowne Plaza, 981 Silom Road (Tel. 238-4300, ext. 4372). Open nightly except Sunday.*

ENTERTAINMENT

Bangkok's nightlife remains as lively as ever. Nightclubs, bars, pubs, discos, and massage parlors cater to all types of tastes, from classy to sleazy. **Patpong Road, Soi Cowboy** (off Sukhumvit Road, between Sois 21-23), and **Nana Entertainment Plaza** (Soi 4, Sukhumvit Road) are Bangkok's sleazy entertainment areas of bars, go-go girls, and sex shows. In these areas the best deals may be the copy watches, scarves, and leather goods sold in front of the bars and just watching all the interesting people walk by. The classiest entertainment venues tend to be found in the major hotels.

Many of the major hotels and shopping arcades offer good entertainment. **Jazz and blues bars** are especially popular in Bangkok, with many of them found along Soi Sarasin and Soi Lang Suan near Lumpini Park. Some of the most popular such places include:

❑ **Bamboo Bar:** *The Oriental Hotel, 48 Oriental Avenue (Tel. 437-6211). Open Sunday through Thursday, 11am-1am, and Friday and Saturday, 11am-2am.*

❑ **Saxophone Pub and Restaurant:** *3/8 Phyathai Road, Victory Monument (Tel. 246-5472). Open 6pm-3am.*

❑ **Trader Vic's:** *Royal Garden Riverside Hotel (Tel. 476-0021).* "River of King's Jazz Brunch" every Sunday from 11:30am to 3pm with a live jazz quintet.

❑ **Witch's Tavern:** *306/1 Sukhumvit Soi 55, Thonglor (Tel. 391-9791). Open Sunday through Thursday, 5pm-1am; Friday and Saturday, 5pm-2am; happy hour Monday through Saturday, 5-8pm.* Serves food along with jazz and pop. Jazz Jam Session featured every Sunday, 5-9pm.

❑ **Brown Sugar:** *231/19 Sarasin Road (Tel. 250-0103).*

❑ **Sukhothai Hotel:** *Lobby Lounge, 13/3 South Sathorn Road (Tel. 287-0222).*

❑ **Magic Mushroom:** *Sukhumvit Plaza, Soi 12, Sukhumvit Road (Tel. 251-9791).*

❑ **Jig-Saw:** *Hilton International, 2 Wireless Road (Tel. 253-0123).*

❑ **Dusit Thani Hotel:** *946 Rama IV Road, at Silom (Tel. 236-0450).*

❑ **Garden Lounge:** *Grand Hyatt Erawan, 494 Rajdamri Road (Tel. 254-1234).*

For **live music** in various forms, try:

❑ **Angelini's:** *Shangri-La Hotel, 89 Soi Wat Suan Plu, New Road (Tel. 236-7777).*

❑ **Champagne Bar:** *Dusit Thani Hotel, 946 Rama IV Road, at Silom (Tel. 236-0450).*

❑ **Dickens Pub:** *Ambassador Hotel, Sukhumvit Road, between Sois 11 and 13 (Tel. 254-0444, ext. 1557).*

❑ **Finishing Post:** *Pan Pacific Hotel, 952 Rama IV Road Suriwongse (Tel. 632-9000).*

❑ **Hard Rock Café:** *Soi 11, Siam Square, Rama 1 Road (Tel. 251-0792).*

❑ **Henry J. Bean's:** *Amari Watergate Hotel, 847 Petchburi Road, Pratunam (Tel. 653-9000).*

❑ **Huntsman Pub and The Piano Bar:** *Landmark Hotel, 138 Sukhumvit Road (Tel. 254-0404).*

❑ **Londoner Brew Pub Bistro:** *Basement, UYBCII Building, Soi 33, Sukhumvit Road (Tel. 261-0238).*

❑ **Paulaner Brauhaus:** *President Park Dome, Sukhumvit Soi 24 (Tel. 661-1111).*

If you're in the mood for **nightclubs and discos**, try these popular places:

❑ **Bubbles:** *Dusit Thani Hotel, 946 Rama IV Road, at Silom (Tel. 236-0450).* A long-time favorite—almost a Bangkok institution!

❑ **Spasso's:** *Grand Hyatt Erawan, 494 Rajdamri Road (Tel. 254-1234).* International band and great food. Chic and sophisticated.

❑ **Riva's:** *Sheraton Grande Sukhumvit, 250 Sukhumvit Road (Tel. 653-0333).* International band. Classy.

❑ **Taurus:** *Soi 6, Sukhumvit Road, next door to Four Wings Hotel (Tel. 261-3991).* See "Pub" section on page 244.

❑ **Concept CM²:** *Novotel Bangkok on Siam Square, Siam Square Soi 6 (Tel. 255-6888, ext. 2549).* See "Pub" section on page 244.

❑ **Leo Grotto:** *Liberty Plaza Building, 10900/167 Soi 55 (Thong Lo), Sukhumvit Road (Tel. 332-9589).*

❑ **Peppermint:** *Patpong 1 Road. Open until 4am (no phone).*

❑ **The Cave:** *United Centre Building, Silom Road.*

Pubs have recently come of age in Bangkok. Many function as restaurants as well as popular meeting places for business-people and expatriates. Bangkok also has many respectable bars that function similarly to pubs—none of the go-go girls and sex shows found along Patpong Road. If you're interested in **pubs and bars**, try some of these popular establishments:

❑ **Blue's Bar:** *231/16 Sarasin Road (Tel. 252-7335).*

❑ **Bobby's Arms:** *114/1-4, 2/F, off Patpong Parking Building (next to Foodland), Patpong 2, Silom (Tel. 233-6828).* A long-time favorite of expatriates.

❑ **Bull's Head:** *Soi 33/1 Sukhumvit Road, near Villa Super-market (Tel. 259-4444).*

❑ **Charcoal Grey Pub and Restaurant:** *888/23-24 Ploen-chit Road (Tel. 253-6766).*

❑ **Delaney's Irish Pub:** *1-5 Sivadon Building, 1 Convent Road, off Silom Road (Tel. 266-7160).* See page 244.

❑ **O'Reillys Irish Pub:** *62/1-4 Silom Road (Tel. 632-7515).*

❑ **The Barbican:** *Soi Thaniya, Silom Road (Tel. 234-3590).*

❑ **The Londoner Brew Pub Bistro:** *Basement, UYBCII Building, Soi 33, Sukhumvit Road (Tel. 261-0238).*

❑ **Toby Jug Pub:** *185 Silom Road (Tel. 234-8772).*

Bangkok also has a few **wine bars** that offer a good selection of wines:

❑ **Circle:** *20/27-29 Ruam Rudee Village, Soi Ruam Rudi, Ploenchit Road (Tel. 650-8047).*

❑ **Oriental Wine Bar:** *Lake Rajada Office Complex, New Rachadapisek Road, Oriental Hotel shop (Tel. 264-0931).*

❑ **Guarantee:** *81 Soi 9, Soi 55 (Thong Lo), Sukhumvit Road (Tel. 662-4700).*

❑ **Winbridge:** *Lang Suan Balcony, Soi Lang Suan, Ploenchit Road (Tel. 251-7767).*

❑ **The Wine Pub:** *Swissôtel, Rajdamrı Road (Tel. 255-3410, ext. 7515).*

If you're in the mood for karaoke, try these popular **karaoke bars**:

❑ **BMB Box:** *Holiday Inn Crowne Plaza, 981 Silom Road (Tel. 238-4300).*

❑ **Sensations:** *Novotel Bangkok on Siam Square, Siam Square Soi 6 (Tel. 255-6888).*

❑ **Cat's Eye:** *Le Meridien President Hotel, 971 Ploenchit Road (Tel. 253-0444).*

For the latest information on what's going on in Bangkok in reference to entertainment, it's best to look at the monthly ***Bangkok Metro Magazine***, the daily ***Bangkok Post***, and weekly tourist publications which normally list "What's Up" for entertainment during your stay. Also try these Web sites for useful entertainment, and restaurant, information: *www.bkmetro.com*, *www.bestinbangkok.com*, and *www.grovvymap.com*.

Some of Bangkok's best entertainment is on the streets at night. Several areas in Bangkok are transformed into evening **sidewalk bazaars**. Vendors set up portable sidewalk restaurants which spill into the streets while others display their wares, including fruits and vegetables, on a cloth spread over the sidewalk or on tables. These evening merchants sell all kinds of items, such as knives, pins, cooking utensils, and clothes, similar to the daytime merchants found in and around the Pratunam Market. These are interesting areas to do night shopping and to watch a fascinating kaleidoscope of activity. Some of the major night bazaar areas are found at:

❑ **Patpong-Silom-Suriwongse Roads**

❑ **Banglampoo Market**

❑ **Pratunam Market**

❑ **Bangrak Market** (Sathorn and New Road)

❑ **Sukhumvit Road** (near Soi 1 and railroad tracks)

The Patpong-Silom-Suriwongse roads area is by far the most interesting and lively night bazaar. Some visitors find this to be one of the major highlights to visiting Thailand. Purchasing copy watches, handbags, and clothes in this area is a favorite —if not **the** most fun—shopping activity for many visitors. It's definitely a simultaneous shopping and cultural experience!

Bangkok is also a good place to enjoy a haircut, manicure, and massage. The process is enjoyable and includes a shampoo and neck massage and a great deal of attentive service. Try **The Best** at Soi 21 or near Soi 5 Sukhumvit Road and the Oriental Arcade (Oriental Hotel) for a high-class haircut; expensive, but a wonderful experience. Many of the barbers and beauty shops in and around the hotels are also excellent.

One of the best massages is given by the traditional masseuses at **Wat Po**, next to the Grand Palace and Temple of the Emerald Buddha.

A variety of other massages for men are also available at the numerous massage parlors throughout Bangkok. However, be prepared to loose your innocence in these palatial dens of iniquity which symbolize Thailand's thriving sex trade.

SAMPLING THE TEMPTING SEX

Thailand is well noted as a major male destination for sex—straight and gay. While cheap, tempting, and easily accessible, sex is not a good deal in Thailand. An ostensibly beautiful woman may turn out to be one of Bangkok's infamous transvestites—a shocking revelation and an embarrassing "war story" to take home. Indeed, messing with the local sex is neither good shopping nor a smart health practice; it's Russian roulette of the worst kind—it can kill you! AIDs has arrived in Thailand and with a vengeance; by some estimates, one of every three Thai prostitutes tests HIV positive. Since AIDs is rampant throughout the country, you should avoid sexual contact with the local population. Unfortunately, Thailand has yet to effectively deal with the main transmission villain—widely tolerated prostitution which is institutionalized in its many massage parlors, bars, hotels, and houses of prostitution that employ more than 300,000 prostitutes. Believe us when we say the sex here is simply deadly. You don't need this memory. Spend your money on things you can take home and admire.

PART IV

Exotic Chiang Mai
and Beyond

Discovering
Chiang Mai

C HIANG MAI IS THE MAJOR CITY OUTSIDE BANG-
kok worth visiting if you seek additional treasures and
pleasures. Other towns do offer a few local handicrafts,
but the selections and quality are limited. In addition,
most Thai provincial towns are very small—between 10,000
and 50,000 population—and offer limited accommodations and
sightseeing opportunities for travelers. Most towns are government administrative and commercial centers which look similar
to one another and are relatively boring places to visit, unless
you know someone locally who is prepared to entertain you. A
few luxury resorts in southeastern and southern Thailand are
well worth visiting if your pleasures include lying on the beach
and being pampered or setting sail for day trips in the Gulf of
Siam or the Andaman Sea after you've shopped Bangkok, Hong
Kong, or Singapore.

GETTING TO KNOW YOU

So it's on to Chiang Mai if you want to do more concentrated
shopping in Thailand. Known as both a province and a city (the
two are confused in most travel guides), Chiang Mai is Thai-

land's second largest city after Bangkok with a population of over 200,000. It is basically a large town boasting a regional university, medical school, a college, hospitals, a large missionary and government presence, numerous hotels and restaurants, interesting Myanmar-influenced temples, charming people, beautiful scenery, and a crowded, congested, and bustling downtown center.

Chiang Mai also is Thailand's major handicraft center and one of Southeast Asia's two largest arts and crafts production centers (Bali, Indonesia is the other center). It produces quality handicrafts for shops in Bangkok and abroad as well as serves as the key middleman for coordinating and marketing handicrafts produced by the numerous hilltribes occupying the mountains of northern Thailand as well as the center for beautiful Myanmar art brought across the Thai-Myanmar border via the rebellious Shan State of Northeast Myanmar.

Chiang Mai also is the major gateway city to adventure travel in Northern Thailand. It's a popular center for budget travelers who enjoy trekking through the hills and mountains or just traveling the North on a limited budget.

Going to Chiang Mai is like going to the woodcarving and artist villages of Mas and Ubud in Bali. You will be going to the production source for Thailand's famous silk, woodcarvings, silverware, celadon, and hilltribe handicrafts. The city and surrounding area consists of several cottage industries run by talented families who continue to pass their trades down from generation to generation. You can visit the houses and factories which produce the goods, watch the craftsmen work, and purchase items from the display rooms or special order to your specifications. The major factories and shops are experienced in packing and shipping to Bangkok and abroad.

During the past 25 years the cottage industries have mushroomed throughout Chiang Mai in response to the increasing demand for Thai handicrafts, antiques, and furniture in Bangkok and abroad. The **Chiang Mai-Sankamphaeng Road**, for example, is lined with silver, lacquerware, celadon, pottery, umbrella, furniture, silk, cotton, and antique shops and factories which are open to the public. Here you can observe hundreds of craftsmen at work as well as visit display rooms to purchase the finished products. **Wualai Road** and **Chiang Mai-Hang Dong Road** (also referred to as Chiang Mai-Hod Road) are lined with similar craft shops. You will see the same or similar items in Bangkok shops, but prices are generally less in Chiang Mai.

Going to Chiang Mai also puts you in touch with the **hilltribes** of northern Thailand and their crafts. The uniquely dressed and exotic looking Meo, Akha, Lahu, Lawa, Lisu, Karen, and Yao tribesmen produce several interesting handicrafts—silver jewelry, boxes, pipes, dolls, textiles, blankets, Christmas ornaments, pillow covers, and much more. The styles and patterns have a distinctive hilltribe look. Red, blue, and black colors along with geometric patterns predominate. In recent years hilltribe clothes have become expensive collectibles used in designing casual wear. Old clothes are the specialty of some expensive boutiques in Bangkok. In Chiang Mai you can buy the separate pieces (though often new) and have them tailored to your own designs at a fraction of the prices charged in the boutiques.

While it is an interesting adventure to visit hilltribe villages, don't expect to get bargains on hilltribe handicrafts in such villages. Many of the villages have inflated prices just for the wandering tourists; some of their products may be made in Hong Kong or Taiwan. You may do just as well buying hilltribe handicrafts in Chiang Mai. In fact, you can buy many directly from tribesmen who come to town to sell their goods in Chiang Mai's bazaars at night.

Going to Chiang Mai also puts you in touch with Myanmar and Laos. During the past decade a great deal of **Myanmar arts and antiques** have found their way into the markets of Chiang Mai and Bangkok. Five years ago, a combination of a stagnant Myanmar economy and regional armed rebellions had resulted in Myanmar art being sold at ridiculously low prices in order to support rebels who needed foreign exchange to purchase Thai goods at the border. This situation has changed due to the increased central government (military) control over the rebel areas of Myanmar.

Myanmar temple carvings, gilded panels, baskets, lacquerware, puppets, and tapestries abound in numerous shops in Chiang Mai. During the past decade, these goods came into Thailand at an alarming rate. Much of the quality art and antiques from Myanmar has disappeared and has been replaced by Chiang Mai's copies. However, many quality items from Myanmar occasionally reappear in Chiang Mai depending on the changing political situation in Myanmar and whether or not the border areas remain open to traders and dealers. If you're looking for quality Myanmar arts and antiques, buy when you find something you like. Such items are quickly disappearing and prices are rising accordingly. A similar movement of antiques and arts from Laos is centered in and around Chiang Mai's many shops.

CHIANG MAI

HOTELS

1. Royal Princess
2. Zenith Suriwongse
3. Chiang Inn
4. Pornping Tower
5. Westin Chiang Mai
6. Amari Rincome
7. Chiang Mai Orchid
8. Imperial Mae Ping

SHOPS

9. Chiang Mai Banyen
10. Old Chiang Mai
    Cultural Center
11. Mengrai Kilns
12. Night Bazaar
13. Chiang Inn Plaza
14. Hilltribe Promotion
    Center
15. Sipsong Panna
16. Royal Orchid Collection
17. Iyara Art/Pon Art
18. Borisoothi
19. Siam Celadon Factory
20. Shinawatra
21. Bo Sang (village)
22. Sankamphaeng (town)
23. Hang Dong (town)
24. Pa Sang (village)
25. Lamphun (town)
26. Lampang (town)
27. Chiang Rai (town)

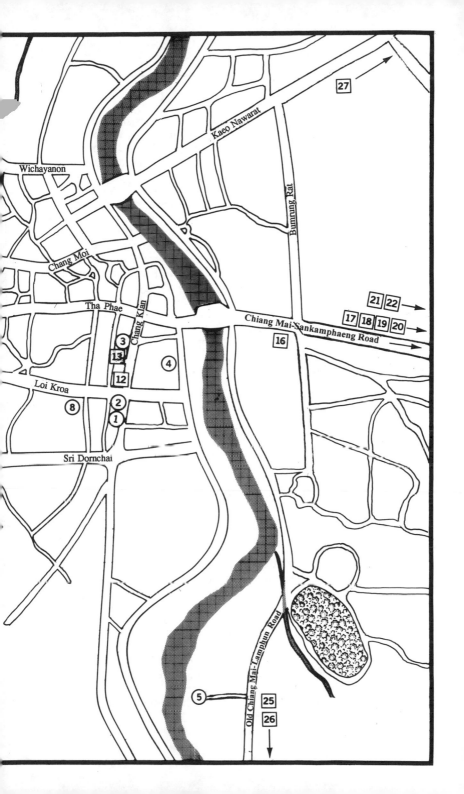

THE STREETS OF CHIANG MAI

Chiang Mai is a city as well as a province consisting of numerous villages and towns. The city of Chiang Mai was originally a walled city with a moat surrounding it. Now a charming and somewhat confusing traffic nuisance, remnants of the wall, gates, and moat are clearly evident and they provide an outline for the city proper. The older commercial, governmental, and residential areas are found within this walled area. But the major commercial and residential areas, as well as some government offices, are located beyond the walls, to the east, north, and west.

The streets and lanes tend to be narrow, crowded, and confusing for first-time visitors. The city proper is very compact and easy to walk around in, especially along the major downtown shopping area along **Chang Klan** and **Tha Phae** roads.

Transportation within the city is relatively convenient, although confusing to many first-time visitors. It's very chaotic. Buses regularly run along the major streets as do minibuses, motorized trishaws and trishaws. The **minibuses** (*song thaew*) are the major means of transportation and cost 8B to 10B for short one-way trips in town. Minibuses are actually small pickup trucks with two benches in the back and covered with a metal roof. The pollution belching **motorized trishaws** (*rot tuk tuk*) are convenient means for two or three people to tour the city and surrounding area; costs vary depending on distance, but expect to pay 30B to 50B for an average ride. The **trishaws** (*samlor*) are man powered. The driver peddles from the front and you sit in back. Samlor are an especially charming means by which to see Chiang Mai at night. You must bargain for each samlor ride; short trips cost 20B to 30B.

There are many shopping areas and sights to visit outside the city proper. Minibuses will take you to areas within a 15 kilometer radius of the city. However, it may be more convenient for you to rent your own minibus by the hour or by the day. If you bargain, you should be able to get one for about 150B to 200B per hour or 1000B and up per day. You also can arrange for a more comfortable car with driver through your hotel, or rent and drive your own car or motorbike. Chiang Mai is fun to tour by motorbike, but you must be careful in navigating through the maddening traffic. We have tried all forms of transportation in Chiang Mai and now prefer to rent a car and drive ourselves. Many tourists prefer to rent a car with driver and not hassle with unfamiliar traffic patterns. It's safe, convenient, clean, fast, and cheap. You should be able to rent a car with driver for 1500-2000B a day, which is about the same as renting a car without driver. You will need this car if you plan to visit the many factories and shops which are located outside the city proper. Budget (189/17-19 Wualai Road, Tel. 202-871), Avis (desk at Airport and the Royal Princess Hotel, Tel. 281-033), and Hertz (90 Sridonchai Road, Tel. 279-474) offer reliable rental cars for 1500-2500B a day. It's best to reserve a car before arriving in Chiang Mai (through the affiliate Bangkok offices), especially during high season months of November, December, and January.

The drawback to renting a car with driver is that in most instances the drivers expect a 10-40% commission from shops where you make purchases. If you expect to make substantial purchases, this could cost you plenty. Many shops say if you'll call them they'll send a car for you. This is workable once you are able to narrow your list to a few shops. But initially if you want to survey the scene, the only way you're sure someone isn't getting a hefty commission on your purchases is to drive yourself or take the minibuses (only ones that drop you off and leave for good).

If you do drive your own car or motorbike, be very careful on the highway outside the city. You must drive defensively—dodging the big 10-wheel trucks and avoiding the pedestrians and bicyclists. The bus and truck traffic is heavy. When they come toward you, get out of their way. They are bigger than you, and they let you know it. It may take you a while to get used to the different types of traffic on the highway

SHOPPING STRENGTHS
AND STRATEGIES

Many Thai products you see in Bangkok can be purchased in Chiang Mai at lower prices. Chiang Mai is especially noted for its silk, cotton, silverware, lacquerware, celadon, antiques, woodcarvings, umbrellas, baskets, and clothes. In contrast to stores in Bangkok, which have limited selections of many different items, in Chiang Mai many stores are very specialized with a wide selection of one or two items only. When you visit a celadon factory and shop, for example, you only find celadon, but it is in many forms: plates, bowls, cups, ashtrays, salt and pepper shakers, chopstick stands, vases, boxes.

When you shop in Chiang Mai, you will most likely visit **factories** with shops attached. The normal procedure is to first tour the factory to see the products being made and then visit the showroom where you can make purchases. Since each factory specializes in a particular product, you need a shopping plan which focuses on specific shops. For example, if you are interested in **antiques and woodcarvings**, visit Chilli, Arts and Crafts Chiangmai, Borisoothi Antiques, Lanna House, Iyara Art, Pon Art Gallery, the Night Bazaar, Hang Dong, and other factory/shops on Tha Phae, Wualai, Chiang Mai-Sankamphaeng, Chiang Mai-Hang Dong, and Ban Tawai roads. If you are interested in **silk**, plan a trip to the towns of Sankamphaeng and Lamphun as well as the village of Pa Sang. In Sankamphaeng, be sure to visit the Shinawatra silk factory, which also has large branch stores in Chiang Mai and Bangkok. If you are looking for **celadon**, you should visit the Mengrai Kilns (79/2 Arak Road, Soi Samlarn 6), Prempracha's Collection (224 Chiang Mai-Sankamphaeng Road), and Siam Celadon Factory (38 Moo 10, Chiang Mai-Sankamphaeng Road). For **furniture** it's off to several shops along the Chiang Mai-Sankamphaeng Road. For good quality **woodcarvings**, visit Letsin and Golden Antiques along Ban Tawai Road in Hang Dong. And if you want to purchase bamboo and rattan **baskets, mats, and hats**, it's off to the village of Hang Dong, 13 kilometers south of Chiang Mai on Highway 108 (Hang Dong Rd.). Refashioned **hilltribe clothes and handicrafts** are mainly found in downtown Chiang Mai at the Night Bazaar (Chang Klan Road) and a few shops along Tha Phae Road. If you are looking for **textiles**, be sure to stop at the Night Bazaar and a few excellent shops scattered throughout the town of Chiang Mai.

The best way to approach shopping in Chiang Mai is to get a good map, a list of names and addresses, and a car and driver to get you from one place to another. Except for strolling down a few streets, such as Chang Klan and Tha Phae, most of your shopping will involve traveling by vehicle between factories and shops.

You should begin your visit to Chiang Mai with a copy of Nancy Chandler's *Map of Chiang Mai*. Similar to her *Map of Bangkok*, this one gives key shops, hotels, restaurants, and sights around Chiang Mai City. You can get a copy of the map in Bangkok, or at hotels and bookstores in Chiang Mai, or purchase it before leaving home (see 33). Armed with this map, you should be able to navigate your way around Chiang Mai with relative ease. You will also find two monthly tourist publications on Chiang Mai: *Welcome To Chiang Mai and Chiang Rai* and *Guidelines: Chiang Mai, Chiang Rai, and the North*. Both publications are free of charge and can be obtained in most hotels. They include maps, travel tips, and advertisements from numerous hotels, shops, restaurants, and tour groups. Before you leave home, you may want to access much of this information online by visiting this useful site for Chiang Mai and Chiang Rai: *www.chiangmai-chiangrai.com*

Most of your shopping will center around four major retail and wholesale shop areas:

- ❑ **Chang Klan and Tha Phae roads** in downtown Chiang Mai (street shops, Night Bazaar, and Chiang Inn Plaza).

- ❑ Small section of **Nimmanhaemin Road** across the street from the Amari Rincome Hotel, near the intersection with Huay Kaew Road.

- ❑ Along the 12-kilometer **Chiang Mai-Sankamphaeng Road**.

- ❑ Along **Chiang Mai-Hang Dong Road**, a 11 kilometer stretch of road south of Chiang Mai, and **Ban Tawai Road** on the outskirts of Hang Dong town.

Additional shopping will be found in special shops and factories in various neighborhoods of the city and in towns and villages within a 20-kilometer radius of Chiang Mai as well as along Wualai Road in the southwest section of the city, along Huay Kaew Road in and around the Chiang Mai Orchid Hotel, and adjacent to the Mae Ping River along Charoen Rat Road. Unlike Bangkok, most shopping in Chiang Mai takes place outside hotel shopping arcades. On the other hand, hotel shopping arcades, such as the popular Chiang Inn Plaza (next to the Night Bazaar along Chiang Klan Road) or the huge (for Chiang Mai) Kad Suan Kaew complex adjacent to the Chiang Mai Orchid Hotel (Huay Kaew Road), are increasingly coming to Chiang Mai and should continue to transform the shopping scene in the coming decade.

Armed with Nancy Chandler's *Map of Chiang Mai* and this book, and ready with a car and driver, you will be well prepared to make Chiang Mai a rewarding shopping adventure. The major shopping areas in downtown Chiang Mai are located along **Chang Klan** and **Tha Phae** roads. Here you will find several shops that sell a variety of local goods, from handicrafts to furniture. The huge **Night Bazaar**, between the Royal Princess, Zenith Suriwongse, and Chiang Inn hotels on Chang Klan Road, offers a good variety of Chiang Mai products at reasonable prices. This colorful and festive area is one you should visit early in your stay. You may want to return there for another night or two. It's a cheap and interesting form of evening entertainment.

WHERE TO SHOP

When you go to Chiang Mai, you must change your shopping strategies altogether. Chiang Mai's shopping facilities and environment are quite different from those you encounter in Bangkok. While in Bangkok much of your shopping centered on shopping arcades, hotel shops, and department stores, in Chiang Mai you must go out into the neighborhoods to find particular factories and shops.

SHOPPING AREAS

Chiang Mai does have a few good hotel shops, small shopping arcades, and department stores. But for the most part these are not significant areas for shopping in Chiang Mai. In Chiang Mai you must go to particular towns, villages, and roads where you will find family factories and shops producing quality goods, or you must look for major markets, such as the popular Night Bazaar along Chang Klan Road.

Most of Chiang Mai's major shopping is concentrated in five major areas:

❏ **Downtown Chiang Mai:** This area is concentrated along the city's two main streets—Chang Klan and Thai Phae—and centered around the Imperial Mae Ping, Zenith Suriwongse, Royal Princess, and Chiang Inn hotels as well as the city market. Here you find Chiang Mai's most popular shopping center—the **Night Bazaar** (also referred to as the **Chiang Mai Night Bazaar Shopping Centre**)—and to a lesser extent the nearby **Vieng Ping Bazaar**. The Night Bazaar is primarily centered in a four-storey **Night Bazaar Building** which includes lots of small shops and vendor stalls. Some of the best shops selling antiques, handicrafts, textiles, and jewelry are normally found on the third and fourth floors of this building. However, the area has been undergoing constant change—shops come and go at amazing speed. This area may or may not yield treasures, depending on who is still in business and what the shops are offering at any particular times. The area is currently in decline as some of the best shops have moved out to other locations or have gone out of business altogether. Nonetheless, you can still find some unique treasures here. For unusual ethnographic pieces, look for two adjacent shops—**The Lost Heavens** and **Under the Bo**. For nice quality lacquerware, visit **Pusaka** and the lacquer shop on the top floor which has no sign (should be **J & D Burmese Antiques**). For excellent quality arts and antiques, and objets d'art, visit **Chilli, Yonok Treasures, Oriental Spirit**, and **Lanna Antiques**. Several nearby shops sell a large variety of handicrafts, textiles, clothes, silver, jewelry, lacquerware, antiques, woodcarvings, and basketry. Don't be surprised if some of these shops have closed recently. The business environment in Chiang Mai is very volatile for these types of shops. Shops in the Night Bazaar, for example, continuously change with many leaving and new ones joining the crowd. Occasionally an act of God— fire—further changes the mix of shops. Nearby is the **Chiang Inn Plaza**. This multi-level air-conditioned arcade includes several excellent shops selling everything from antiques, furniture, and textiles to jewelry and clothing. We especially like the **Product Development Company** for its baskets, trays, and mats and **Nantiya Decor** for uniquely designed traditional and contemporary bleached furniture. Along Tapae Road, look for **Masusook Antiques** and **Maneesinn** for good quality antiques, lacquerware, and baskets.

❑ **Wualai Road:** Located at the southern end of the city, this road is lined with numerous silver factories as well as shops selling a large variety of handcrafted items. Look for **Noparat Silverware, Damrongsilp, Ngern Chiang Mai**, and **Sterling Silver Ornament Factory** for traditional designed silver items; and **Ban Sanpronon** for a nice collection of baskets, lacquerware, instruments, and textiles.

❑ **Neighborhood shops:** A few streets in other areas of the city also have some good shops. For example, along **Nimmanhaemin Road**, across the street from the Amari Rincome Hotel and near the Chiang Mai Orchid Hotel, is a row of very nice quality home decorative, textile, antique silver, clothing, and gift shops well worth visiting: **Gerard Collection, Nandakwang (Homespun Creations), Dararat, Sbun-Nga Collection**, and **Sipsong Panna**. Directly across and up the street (Soi 2) are two interesting art and gift shops: **Tawan Decor** and **Gongdee Gallery**. These are some of Chiang Mai's best quality shops and a pleasant change from other types of shops found in and around Chiang Mai. Not far from this area is **Studio Naenna** (138/8 Soi Changkhian, Huay Kaew Road, Tel. 226-042) which is operated by Pat Chessman, one of Thailand's leading authorities on textiles. She works with nearby villages in creating excellent quality and uniquely designed silk and cotton materials which are primarily sold for export. Dealers interested in importing unique Thai fabrics will especially want to visit this shop. Pat also conducts textile tours for special groups.

On nearby **Huay Kaew Road**, directly across the street from the Chiang Mai Orchid Hotel, is one of Chiang Mai's best silk shops—**S. Shinawatra** (14/4-8 Huay Kaew Road, Tel. 221-076). It also stocks cotton products and handicrafts. Next to the hotel is the huge **Kad Suan Kaew Shopping Arcade** with its numerous small clothing, footwear, music, and electronics shops. Anchored by Central Department Store and filled with small restaurants, this shopping center is especially popular with young people. You probably won't find much of interest here. It does have an excellent supermarket at the lower level (Central) and a Swensen Ice Cream shop.

Along **Bumrung Rat Road** (#208)you will find one of Chiang Mai's major hilltribe handicraft shops—**Thai Tribal Crafts**.

One of Thailand's most unique shops—**Saraphee Silk Lace** at 2 Rajwithi Road (Tel. 214-171)—produces lovely handwoven decorative lace items.

The **Hilltribe Promotion Center** on Suthep Road offers a good collection of hilltribe handicrafts.

Mengrai Kilns at 79/2 Araks Road, Soi Samlarn 6 (Tel. 272-063) produces some of Thailand's best quality celadon and ceramics.

Royal Orchid Collection (Siam Royal Orchid Co.) at 94-120 Charoen Muang Road (Tel. 249-803) offers a unique collection of gold- plated flowers and semi-precious stones made into attractive and inexpensive neck pieces, earrings, pins, and pendants.

Two of the best collections of woodcarvings, furniture, and home decorative items are found at the huge factory emporiums adjacent to each other (family related) at the intersection of the Super Highway (near airport) and Hang Dong Road—**Chiang Mai Banyen** and **Jaifah Chiang Mai Lacquerware Co.** (209/3 Super Highway).

One of Chiang Mai's major antique dealers—indeed, a powerful force in the antique world throughout Thailand and Myanmar—is found at a huge family antique and furniture complex—**Ban Chang Come** (141 Hang Dong Road, Tel. 441-628)—a large teak house on the right just before coming to Ban Tawai Road on your left. It also operates **Arts and Crafts Chiang Mai** (172 Moo 2

Chiang Mai-Sankampang Road, Tel. 338-025).

The Gallery—(located on Charoen Rat Road, just south of the Nawarat Bridge, facing the Mae Nam Ping River, and next to the Riverside and Rim Ping restaurants —is a restaurant that also functions as an art gallery. Its changing monthly exhibits represent the best of modern northern Thai art. Just across the street is one of Chiang Mai's best home decorative shops—**Oriental Style**—located in an expansive turn-of-the-century building that has been attractively restored and shared by the owners' second shop that showcases textiles and antiques—**Vila Cini**. Parking in this area is nearly impossible and somewhat dangerous, so be careful getting in and out of your car or walking on the nearly nonexistent shoulder. These three places are well worth visiting during your stay in Chiang Mai. We highly recommend having lunch or dinner, or just a drink or snack, at one of the restaurants overlooking the river. Great ambience on both sides of the street!

❑ **Chiang Mai-Sankamphaeng Road:** Let's put big "You're About to be Ripped Off!" warning signs all along this famous—although infamous and often outrageous— shopping road. We have a real love-hate relationship with this major shopping area—Chiang Mai's version of a Mafia operation on wheels. One of the most popular shopping areas for tourists, the Chiang Mai-Sankamphaeng Road area, is highly recommended by local touts who ask exorbitant commissions (20-40%) from shopkeepers who, in turn, must inflate prices which are then passed on to tourists. In many respects this is Chiang Mai's best shopping area. On the other hand, it's also Thailand's worst tourist trap where busloads of tourists are taken from one shop to another by drivers and tour guides who are primarily interested in collecting commissions from shops that charge unwitting tourists high prices. They avoid or badmouth the good shops that don't give them payoffs. Unfortunately, the average tourist ends up in mediocre shops that charge high prices. So, if you are taken here by someone, expect to get royally ripped-off—you'll pay at least 30% more than you should, and perhaps much more!

This 12 kilometer stretch of road begins at the intersection of the Super Highway east of the city and continues to the town of Sankamphaeng. Both sides of the road are lined with small factories and shops as well as huge factories and emporiums selling everything from traditional handmade Chiang Mai furniture to silver, antiques, home decorative items, lacquerware, celadon, silk, and umbrellas. One of Thailand's best quality antique and home decorative shops, **Borisoothi** (15/2 Chiang Mai-Sankamphaeng Rd., Tel. 338-460) is located along this road. This is also home for one of Thailand's most famous silk factories— **Shinawatra**. Other good quality shops include **Prempracha's** for cotton, silk, ceramics, woodcarvings, furniture, lacquerware, porcelain, tapestries, silver, and antiques; **Lanna Lacquerware** for lacquer items; **Arts and Crafts Chiang Mai, Iyara Art**, and **Pon Art Gallery** for antiques, woodcarvings, gables, panels, lacquerware, and silver; **Siam Celadon** for celadon; **Kinaree Thai Silk, Chiang Mai Textile & Garment Center, H. M. Thai Silk**, and **Jolie Femme** for all types of silk products; **Chiang Mai Treasure Co.** for large carvings and furniture; **Bo-Sang Handicraft Centre** for a large collection of umbrellas, woodcarvings, dolls, bencharong, lacquerware, baskets, clothes, tapestries, and screens; **Umbrella Making Centre** for beautiful handcrafted umbrellas, dolls, fans, and baskets; **The Emporium of Handicrafts** for a large selection of hilltribe handicrafts; **Siam Gifts** for an excellent range of woodcarvings, tapestries, ceramics, lacquerware, bencharong, leather, ivory, silver, jewelry, jade, and cloisonne. Keep in mind that most of these shops have inflated prices because they live, or die, by paying exorbitant commissions to tour guides, taxi drivers, and other touts.

❑ **Hang Dong:** Located 11 kilometers south of Chiang Mai, this is Chiang Mai's major woodcarving, handicraft, and furniture center. However, few tourists visit here because they are being escorted along the Chiang Mai-Sankamphaeng Road by tour guides and touts who are getting big commissions for steering them into commission-rich shops that may charge two to three times more than the factory/shops in Hang Dong. In fact, many of the shops along Chiang Mai-Sankamphaeng Road procure their products for resale from the factory/shops in Hang Dong. Needless to say, you are better off going directly to the source where you will get better prices and have more fun shopping away from the maddening crowds of tourists and touts. The Hang Dong shopping area actually consists of two areas:

- Factories and shops along both sides of the 11 kilometer Chiang Mai-Hang Dong Road (also called the Chiang Mai-Hod Road), beginning at the intersection of the Super Highway (the Airport Road) and Chiang

Mai-Hang Dong Road and running south to the town of Hang Dong.

■ One narrow road—Ban Tawai Road—located on the left just before entering the bustling small town of Hang Dong (look on the left just before you come to the red and blue flame gas station sign on the right—very hard to find the narrow entrance to this road in midst of the urban congestion). This is the heart of the Hang Dong factory shopping. More than 100 shops line both sides of this road for two kilometers.

The best antique shop along Hang Dong Road is **Ban Chang Come** (#141), a huge Thai house and antique emporium which also operates Arts and Crafts Chiangmai along the Chiang Mai-Sankamphaeng Road (#172 Moo 2). This is Chiang Mai's major antique dealer who at times has controlled large segments of the antique trade throughout Thailand. Also nearby is **Yonok Treasure** (130/9 Moo 1), **Under The Bo**, **Kotchasarn Gallery** (33/16), and **Baan Tarin** (3 Moo 2) for good quality arts and antiques.

Ban Tawai Road is lined with numerous wood carving factories, antique shops, and furniture makers offering some of the best home decorative items in Thailand. Indeed, many shops in Bangkok and dealers from abroad purchase their products here. Some of the best factories and shops along this road include **Chilli** (125 Moo 4) and **Jarakarn Antiques** (look for a small sign that directs you to take a right turn on a side road and then cross a small wood bridge), **Ambiente Chiang Mai**, **Letsin**, and **Golden Antiques**. You can easily arrange to have wood-carvings commissioned here and the factory/shops are experienced in shipping abroad (major shipping companies also are located along this road). Prices here are much better than in Chiang Mai and Bangkok. Off this main road is a terrific stoneware factory, **Korakod Stoneware** (153 Moo 8 Tambol Nongkeaw).

❑ **Doi Suthep:** Located 12 mountainous kilometers from the city, at the foot of Chiang Mai's most famous temple—Wat Prathat—is a shopping center consisting of numerous row shops and vendor stalls selling a wide variety of tourist products. Be careful here. You will find many small stalls selling similar items found in the Night Bazaars in Chiang Mai and Bangkok. Prices can be reasonable if you bargain hard, but some shops charge significantly more than comparable shops in Chiang Mai or Bangkok. Beware of nice air-conditioned jewelry shops that may pamper you with friendly service. This is a big tourist trap with over-priced items of questionable quality.

❑ **Markets:** Chiang Mai abounds with markets. But don't expect to find anything in comparison to Bangkok's huge and diverse Chatuchak Weekend Market. Instead, you'll find lots of fresh fruits, vegetables, meats, fish, and spices along with some dry goods. The largest and most interesting market in Chiang Mai—**Warorot Market**—is located in the heart of the city, near the Mae Ping River and at the corners of Chang Moi, Wichayanon, and Kuang Mane Roads. Here you'll find lots of rattan goods, dried foods, spices, clothes, cosmetics, shoes, crafts, and textiles. The second floor (the escalator may or may not work) includes lots of stalls selling inexpensive clothes, shoes, and hilltribe crafts. Open from 7am to 6pm, this is a very crowded local market with lots of local color. Go here for at least the cultural experience of wandering through a busy local market watching the locals haggle for goods. If you purchased Nancy Chandler's *Map of Chiang Mai*, you'll find a special insert map detailing this market area as well as the adjacent **Lam Yai Market** with its abundance of fresh fruits, vegetables, meats, and fish.

WHAT TO BUY

Shops in and around Chiang Mai offer a wonderful array of products. However, in recent years we have noted a general decline in quality and selection and a progressive increase in prices; shopping is not as much fun as it used to be. Nonetheless, you can easily spend three days exploring the many shops that offer everything from silk, textiles, and ethnic clothes to jewelry, antiques, furniture, and home decorative items. As noted earlier, Chiang Mai is to Thailand what Bali is to Indonesia—the country's major arts and crafts center. Here you will discover factories and meet craftspeople that produce the many lovely products displayed in Bangkok's numerous shops. You should make lots of friends in the process!

JEWELRY

If you are interested in unique inexpensive jewelry and accessories, you should visit the **Royal Orchid Collection** factory and shop at #94-120 Charoen Muang Road (Tel. 249-803) which is located just across the Ping River east of the city. They have a good selection of inexpensive pins, neck pieces, and earrings made from a special gold plating and enameling process using flowers and semi-precious stones. They will make jewelry to your specifications.

Shiraz Co. at 170 Tha Phae Road (Tel. 252-382) offers a wide range of gems (rubies and sapphires) and gold and silver jewelry. This small shop is reputed to be very reliable. For antique and tribal silver, one of the best places is **Sipsong Panna** at 95/19 Nantawan Arcade, Nimmanhaemin Road (Tel. 216-096). Other noted jewelry stores include **Princess Jewelry** at 147/8 Chang Klan Road (across from Royal Princess Hotel, Tel. 828-860) and **Gems Gallery** at 80/1 Moo 3, Sankamphaeng Road (Tel. 339-307) which claims to be the largest jewelry store in the world!

ANTIQUES AND HOME DECORATIVE ITEMS

For antiques, woodcarvings, spirit houses, drums, statues, gilded figures, and lacquerware, you should definitely visit the shops and factories along Hong Dong Road, Ban Tawai Road in Hang Dong, Chiang Mai-Sankamphaeng Road, and the two emporiums at the intersection of the Super Highway and Hang Dong Road.

Chiang Mai's two major antique dealers, especially noted for their quality, are **Ban Chang Come** (141 Chiang Mai-Hang Dong Road, Tel. 441-628; also **Arts and Crafts Chiang Mai** at 172 Moo 2 Chiang Mai-Sankamphaeng Road, Tel. 338-025) and **Borisoothi Antiques** (15/2 Chiang Mai-Sankamphaeng Road, Tel. 338-460). These large shops and factories are well worth a visit during your stay in Chiang Mai. Seven other antique dealers are also well worth visiting: **Iyara Art** and **Pon Art Gallery**, located adjacent to each other on Chiang Mai-Sankamphaeng Road (35/3 and 35/4 Chiang Mai-Sankamphaeng Road); **Chilli** (125 Moo 4 Ban Tawai Road, Tel. 433-281 and 2nd Floor of the Night Bazaar); **Jarakarn Antiques** (137 Moo 8 Ban La Woo, off Ban Tawai Road, Hang Dong, Tel. 248-615); **Yonok Treasure** (130/9 Moo 1, Chiang Mai-Hod Road, off Chiang Mai-Hang Dong Road, Tel. 427308 and 2nd Floor of the Night Bazaar); **Baan Tarin** (3 Moo 2, along Chiang Mai-Hang Dong Road, Tel. 441-623); and **Lanna House** (512 Moo 1, Tambon Rimtai, entrance to the Regent Hotel, Tel. 861-257).

You also will find a few antique and ethnographic shops in the Chiang Mai Night Bazaar in downtown Chiang Mai on Chang Klan Road. You can easily miss the best shops here if you only browse through the first two floors of this building. Be sure to climb the stairs to visit a few of the more interesting shops on the **second and third floors**. Of the few remaining shops, the best include **Pusaka, The Lost Heavens, Under the Bo, Oriental Spirit, Lanna Antiques, Kotchasarn Gallery**, and **Praphan Art**. Other antique shops worth visiting are found along Hang Dong Road and Ban Tawai Road in Hang Dong.

You should also visit the famous **Chiang Mai Banyen** at the intersection of Hang Dong Road and the Superhighway. Previously located on Wualai Road, but leveled by fire in 1989, the new Chiang Mai Banyen will not disappoint you. It's a huge woodcarving factory, emporium, and museum operated by Mrs. Banyen, one of Thailand's most successful and respected entrepreneurs. Banyen employs over 100 craftspeople who make all types of woodcarvings and decorative items. While more expensive than many other factories in Chiang Mai, she does quality work and is very reliable. Banyen was the source used by the famous Jim Thompson over 30 years ago (when Banyen sold antiques) to furnish much of his fabulous house in Bangkok. Her children operate a similar factory and shop next door—**Jaifah Chiang Mai Lacquerware Co.** (209/3 Super Highway).

Style and design are increasingly becoming important themes in Chiang Mai products. Two of Chiang Mai's best home decorative and designer shops are **Oriental Style** (36 Charoen Rat Road, across from the riverfront Gallery Restaurant, just south of the Nawarat Bridge, Tel. 245724) and the **Gerard Collection** (95/23-24 Nimmanhaemin Road, Tel. 220-604). Other good shops are found in the **Chiang Inn Plaza** (visit **Nantiya Decor**) and along Nimmanhaemin Road (try **Tawan Decor** and **Gong Dee Gallery**). For very uniquely designed and fascinating contemporary furniture, be sure to visit Peter Bartlock's **Ambiente Chiang Mai** (169/1 Moo 7 Nongkaew Tawai Road, Hang Dong, Tel. 442-119).

CELADON, BENCHARONG, AND POTTERY

Thai celadon is primarily produced in Chiang Mai. For good quality celadon pottery, visit the **Mengrai Kilns** at (79/2 Araks Road, Soi Samlarn 6, Tel. 272-063) and shop on the Chiang Mai-Sankamphaeng Road. Their celadon pieces are lovely and fit nicely into contemporary art collections of pottery. Other celadon factories produce highglaze celadon dishes and knick-knacks. The **Siam Celadon Factory** at 30 Moo 10 Chiang Mai-Sankamphaeng Road (Tel. 331-526) has a nice showroom for their wares. **Korakod Stoneware** (Tel. 434-105) in Hang Dong produces wonderful stone pots and ceramic elephants.

Prempracha (224 Chiang Mai-Sankamphaeng Rd., Tel. 332-857) produces a wide range of ceramics. They are especially noted for combining celadon and bencharong—producing color combinations and designs only available in this expansive factory-shop. A good place to purchase lovely gift items.

Thailand's famous blue and white pottery is primarily produced in and around the town of Lampang, which is located approximately 100 kilometers southeast of Chiang Mai. You will find nearly 100 factories producing distinct designs in blue and white colors. Some factories also produce celadon and pottery in other colors. The prices are reasonable, perhaps 30% cheaper than the Bangkok shops selling the same items from Lampang!

BASKETS, WICKER, UMBRELLAS

If you are interested in baskets and wicker items, be sure to visit the village of **Hang Dong**, located 13 kilometers southwest of Chiang Mai on the road to Mae Klang waterfall and Doi Inthanon (Highway 108) and the village of **Saraphi**, located about 7 kilometers southeast of the city on the road to Lamphun (Highway 106). Look for the wicker fishtraps which make nice lampshades for hanging ceiling lamps. You also will find baskets and wicker items in the **Night Bazaar** and along **Tha Phae Road** and the **Chiang Mai-Sankamphaeng Road**. Collectors looking for unique items should visit **Maneesinn** at 289 Tha Phae Road (Tel. 282-047). You will find amongst their exquisite lacquerware some older one-of-a-kind baskets.

Many visitors to Chiang Mai like to buy the unique and colorful Chiang Mai **umbrellas**. The place to go for such purchases are the umbrella factories and shops in the "Umbrella Village" (Tel. 331-324) of **Bo Sang**, located on the Chiang Mai-Sankamphaeng Road. Several shops sell their own distinctive style umbrellas. The largest umbrella emporium here is the **Umbrella Making Centre**, located just off the Chiang Mai-Sankamphaeng Road at Bo Sang. Just across the road is another large umbrella factory, the **Bosang Umbrella Maker Community**. Nearby you will find the **Sa Paper and Umbrella Handicraft Centre**. The umbrellas at most shops and factories are inexpensive; the small ones make nice trip gifts for children.

SILK AND COTTON

If you are interested in silk and cotton, primarily in local hues and designs, visit the famous silk town of **Sankamphaeng**, located 13 kilometers east of Chiang Mai. Stop first at the

Shinawatra Thai Silk factory to observe the silk weaving process and explore their sales shop. If you walk down both sides of the main street, you will find several shops that sell silk and cotton material as well as a variety of handicrafts. Since this is a small town, you can easily cover most of the shops in an hour or two by walking along **Mae-On Road**.

Several large shops along the Chiang Mai-Sankamphaeng Road offer varied selections of silk and cotton garments as well as fabric. The major factory/shop here is Chiang Mai's oldest silk producer—**Shinawatra Thai Silk**. Also look for **Prempracha's, H. M. Thai Silk, Kinaree Thai Silk, Chiang Mai Textile and Garment Centre**, and **Jolie Femme**. Within the city of Chiang Mai, look for **Shinawatra Thai Silk's** (18 Huey Kaew) two adjacent shops across the street from Chiang Mai Orchid Hotel.

If you go south of Chiang Mai, you will come to the town of **Lamphun** which also is noted for silk. **Pa Sang**, a village located 10 kilometers southwest of Lamphun, is also well noted for cotton weaving. If you visit Sankamphaeng, Lamphun, and Pa Sang, you will cover most of the factories and shops offering silk and cotton. But don't expect to find the same quality and designs available in the top shops in Bangkok.

CLOTHES AND TEXTILES

Chiang Mai is not noted as a fashion center. However, you will find some interesting clothes and textiles here, from refashioned hilltribe garments to silk clothes. **Studio Naenna** at 138/8 Soi Changkhian, Huay Kaew Road (Tel. 226-042) produces fashionable export quality textiles that can be used for clothing and upholstery. Several shops in and around the **Night Bazaar**, such as **Lanna Collection** (164/98 Chang Klan Road) and **Classic Model** (2nd Floor, Chiang Inn Plaza), as well as a few shops along Tha Phae Road, provide tailoring services and sell refashioned hilltribe garments. For good quality textiles, both old and new, check out several small shops along Loi Kroa Road near Wat Pan Thong: **Indochine** (#35), **Mat Mi Textile Gallery** (#59), **Success Silk Shop** (#56), and **Pa Ker Yaw**. **The Loom** (27 Rajmanka Road, Tel. 278-892) also has a good collection of textiles. The best collection of quality textiles in Northern Thailand is still found with the owner of **Duangjitt House** (serious collectors by appointment only—Tel. 242-291).

Several silk shops along Chiang Mai-Sankamphaeng Road sell ready-made and tailored silk garments. Some of the largest such shops include **Shinawatra, Kinaree Thai Silk, Chiang Mai Textile and Garment Center**, and **Jolie Femme**.

LEATHER GOODS

You will find a few shops and factories as well as vendor stalls selling leather goods. The product range includes handbags, purses, wallets, shoes, and belts. In general, however, we have not been impressed with the quality of Thai leather nor the styles and workmanship. The Thai leather tanning process is still of poor quality. Although the leathers are more supple than we encountered a few years ago, they still lack a finished look and are not particularly stylish. Furthermore, many of the popular tan shoes found in the markets and shops in downtown Chiang Mai are made from elephant leather. We urge you to boycott such items. While a few years ago elephants were being killed for their ivory tusks, today many of Thailand's elephants are being killed for their leather—some of which undoubtedly ends up in these shoes. If you are not picky about quality, workmanship, and style, you can pick up some inexpensive leather items in Chiang Mai. Several shops in the **Night Bazaar** sell leather goods. Along the Chiang Mai-Sankamphaeng Road look for a few factories which both produce and sell leather shoes, handbags, belts, and purses: **San Klang Leather Product** and **Boonkrong Leather Chiang Mai**. Most of these shops do not use elephant leather.

GIFT ITEMS

Most shops in Chiang Mai offer items that will make interesting and lovely gifts back home. We especially like the unique and beautiful selections of woven items—pillows, clothes, tissue boxes, rugs, dolls, placemats—at **Nandakwang** (Homespun Creations) at 95/1-2 Nimmanhaemin Road (Tel. 222-261) and the 3rd Floor of the Chiang Inn Plaza (Tel. 283-090). The items here are both unique and stylish and make lovely gifts appropriate for Western homes. Across the street from the Nimmanhaemin Road shop is **Tawan Decor** (Tel. 894-941) which has numerous decorative items that make great gifts. Just around the corner (Soi 2) is **Gong Dee Gallery** (Tel. 332-783) with its stylish home decorative items. Many shops in the **Night Bazaar** as well as the nearby **Chiang Inn Plaza** also offer a large variety of gift items. You will have to explore the hundreds of shops and stalls in this area to discover just what you need. A few large shops along Chiang Mai-Sankamphaeng Road also offer a large variety of gift items: **Chiang Mai Art, Siam Gifts, Shinawatra, Prempracha, Thai Shop, Bo Sang Handicraft Centre, Umbrella Making Centre**, and **The Emporium of Handi-**

crafts. We especially like **Siam Gifts** and **Prempracha** for their large range of quality items.

SILVER

Chiang Mai also is famous for its silver jewelry and artifacts. The major silver factories with showrooms are located along the **Chiang Mai-Sankamphaeng Road** and in and around **Wualai Road**. Of particular interest to many visitors are the intricately hammered silver bowls with unique Hindu and Buddhist scenes. Silver hilltribe jewelry—necklaces, rings, bracelets, earrings—and silver studded hilltribe clothes are also popular. One of the largest silver factories is **Chiang Mai Silverware** at 62/10-11 Chiang Mai-Sankamphaeng Road (Tel. 246-037). Several shops and vendor stalls sell silver in and around the **Night Bazaar** as well as along Chang Klan and Tha Phae roads. You may find some hilltribe silver available directly from the remaining hilltribe women who operate from the Vieng Ping Bazaar (across from the Anusarn Market which is one street west of Loi Kroh and just off Chang Klan Road near the Night Bazaar). **Sipsong Panna** (95/19 Nantawan Arcade, Nimmanhaemin Road, Tel. 216-096) has a terrific collection of quality antique silver!

LACQUERWARE

Lacquerware is an especially good buy in Chiang Mai with prices nearly one fourth of what you will pay in Bangkok. Several shops on the third and fourth floors of the **Night Bazaar Building** offer nice selections of lacquerware. However, one of the best collections of quality lacquerware for sale in Chiang Mai is found at **Maneesinn** at 289 Tha Phae Road (Tel. 282-047). **Ban Chang Come** (141 Chiang Mai-Hang Dong Road, Tel. 441-628) also has a large collection of lacquerware. **Borisoothi Antiques** (15/2 Chiang Mai-Sankamphaeng Road,Tel. 338-460), **Ancient Crafts** (11/3 Ratchamaka Road, Tel. 278-849), and **Lanna House** (512 Moo 1, Tambon 1, entrance to the Regent Resort, Tel. 861-257) have a few pieces of good quality antique lacquerware. A few shops along Chiang Mai-Sankamphaeng Road produce new lacquerware pieces in a large variety of colors and styles: **Chiang Mai Chaiyapruk Lacquerware** (30/1 Bansanklang, Chiang Mai-Sankamphaeng Road), **Chalerm Lacquerware** (look for sign directing you 50 meters off the Chiang Mai-Sankamphaeng Road), and **Jaifah Chiang Mai Lacquerware Co.** (209/3 Super Highway).

FURNITURE

Handmade teakwood furniture is a major cottage industry in Chiang Mai. Most of the furniture is produced in traditional Thai styles which may or may not fit well with your home decor. The major factories are located along the **Chiang Mai- Sankamphaeng Road**. You may be initially attracted to the first factory on the left—**Tusnaporn**. This famous factory, with its huge showroom of handmade furniture, elephants, and household items, provides a good overview of what most Chiang Mai furniture factories produce. It also will educate you on expected price ranges. However, be very careful here. Once a reliable shop, Tusnaporn has been delisted by TAT for failing to meet TAT service standards. We're not sure what this means, but this shop, as well as other shops affiliated with this firm (Thai Shop next door and Sawaddee at Doi Suthep), have reputations for over-pricing. They also are the major promoters of high commissions demanded by touts and tour guides. Be sure to go here on your own since Tusnaporn does pay guides and touts big commissions; you should expect a significant discount (at least 30%), if you go on your own. Other furniture factories are found on the left side of the Chiang Mai-Sankamphaeng Road. Visitors are welcome to observe the craftspeople and browse through the showrooms. Some of the factories along Ban Tawai Road in Hang Dong also produce furniture, although most of these places primarily produce woodcarvings and home decorative items. These factories are tout-free and thus reasonably priced. One of the most fascinating furniture shops, which produces unique contemporary wood furniture incorporating artistic terracotta pieces, architect/designer Peter Bartlock's **Ambiente Chiangmai** (169/1 Moo 7 Nongkeaw, Tawai Road, Tel. 442-119).

HILLTRIBE HANDICRAFTS

A variety of Thai, Myanmar, and hilltribe handicrafts can be found in many shops in Chiang Mai, but especially in the **Night Bazaar**, located between the Royal Princess and Chiang Inn hotels on Chang Klan Road and around the corner from the Zenith Suriwongse Hotel on Loi Krao Road. We especially like two shops adjacent to each other on the third floor of the Chiang Mai Night Bazaar—**The Lost Heavens** (Thai, Myanmar, and Southern China tribal) and **Under the Bo** (Central and South Asian tribal). For a wide range of hilltribe products, you should visit the **Hilltribe Promotion Center** (also known as **Hilltribe Products**) at 21/17 Suthep Road, located west of the city, just beyond the Chiang Mai University Medical School complex and next to the famous Wat Suan Dok. Also, visit **Thai Tribal Crafts** at 208 Bumrung Rat Road (Tel. 241-043) in the northeast section of Chiang Mai. The **Old Chiang Mai Cultural Center** on Wualai Road also has several hilltribe craft shops.

BEST OF THE BEST

ANTIQUES AND OBJETS D' ART

❑ **Ban Chang Come:** *141 Chiang Mai-Hang Dong Road (Tel. 441-628).* This is one of Thailand's most important antique dealers which has aggressively captured a large portion of the Myanmar market for furniture, ceiling panels, lacquerware, carts, Buddhas, and objets d'art. This huge compound displays only a small portion of inventory, much of which is being restored before it appears on the market in Chiang Mai and Bangkok. Many major dealers from Bangkok and abroad come here to source antiques. Also has had shops under the name Amarawadee Antiques.

❑ **Arts and Crafts Chiang Mai:** *172 Moo 2, Chiang Mai-Sankamphaeng Road (Tel. 338-025).* Owned by the same family that operates Ban Chang Come, this expansive shop displays top quality Buddhas, carved figures, furniture, lacquerware, and objets d'art. See the delightful Ms. Bua who speaks good English and is very helpful.

❑ **Borisoothi Antiques:** *15/2 Chiang Mai-Sankamphaeng Road (Tel. 338-460).* One of Thailand's best known antique dealers who deals with both rare antiques and reproduction furniture and home decorative items. The antiques are always first-class collector's items, including Buddhas, bronzes, and ceramics. The husband-wife owners, Lt. Col. Suwan and Lt. Nandhana, know this business well and are most informative. Don't overlook the back room which includes reproductions and furniture. Borisoothi has its own factory that turns out excellent quality furniture and home decorative items are reasonable prices. Very reliable.

❑ **Chilli:** *20 Night Bazaar (Tel. 818-475); and 125 Moo 4 Ban Tawai Road, Hang Dong (Tel. 433-281).* One of Chiang Mai's best quality antique shops and a supplier to many Bangkok antique dealers. The selections are first rate. Includes a wonderful collection of Buddhas, carved panels, bronze drums, bells, and many unique one-of-a-kind pieces. The Night Bazaar shop provides a small sampling of the larger collection at the Hang Dong shop.

❑ **Lanna House:** *512 Moo 1, Mae Rim-Samoeng Road, Mae Rim, opposite the Regent Resort (Tel. 861-257)*. Very tastefully decorated antique and home decorative shop offering two floors of good quality old and new artifacts. Always something interesting to explore, from lacquerware, boxes, and baskets to Buddhas, silver objects, and weights. Operated by a very friendly and informative Thai-German couple, Lek and Wolfgang Roese. Good prices for such quality items. Be sure to explore the adjacent shops that are partners of Lanna House: **Classic Lanna Thai** for old textiles and classic apparel and **Huen Mai** for handicrafts and decorative art.

❑ **Iyara Art:** *35/4 Moo 3, Chiang Mai-Sankamphaeng Road (Tel. 339-450)*. This impressive Northern Thai-style building houses a unique collection of antique furniture, bronze Buddhas and monks, carved figures, bells, and decorative arts. Includes both large and small items, from oxen carts to jewelry. Always has something new and interesting on display from Myanmar.

❑ **Pon Art Gallery:** *35/3 Moo 3, Chiang Mai-Sankamphaeng Road (Tel. 338-361)*. This place is somewhat disorienting and service always seems absent. Don't worry, you're not invading someone's private quarters! Just walk through the numerous Thai-style buildings connected to each other to discover a large dusty collection of antiques, from furniture and lacquerware to carved panels and huge Northern Thai drums.

❑ **Jirakarn Antiques:** *137 Moo 8 Ban La Woo, off Ban Tawai Road, across from Chilli, Hang Dong (Tel. 441-615)*. Somewhat hard to find, this large and expansive compound is an exercise in chaos! Everything seems to be in the state of repair or disrepair. However, don't let the chaos turn you off to what could be one of your best purchases in Thailand. Jirakarn has a treasure-trove of potentially good stuff—if you have the patience to dig through the "raw materials" and know what to do with them. Has lots of old Northern Thai furniture and panels which can be restored. However, it may be best to take everything with you since Jirakarn's restoration skills may not meet your exacting expectations or standards! May have difficulty communicating in English. Popular place for dealers.

❏ **Yonok Treasure:** *19 Night Bazaar, 2ⁿᵈ Floor (Tel. 818-277); and 130/9 Moo 1, Chiang Mai-Hod Road, Hang Dong (Tel. 427-308).* One of our personal favorites since we first began dealing with the owner, Katha Intrachai, more than ten years ago when he was operating from a tiny shop next to the Asia Hotel in Lampang. Offers an excellent collection of Myanmar antiques and objets d'art, from lacquerware and Buddhas to bronze bells and furniture. Very reliable and helpful. Will also source for anything you need but which is not available in his or others' shops. Also has a shop at River City Shopping Complex in Bangkok.

❏ **Under the Bo:** *22-23 Night Bazaar (Tel. 818-831); and 33/16 Chiang Mai-Hang Dong Road, Hang Dong.* This is one of our favorite shops with an excellent collection of tribal artifacts, jewelry, textiles, and furniture from Thailand, Myanmar, China, Laos, India, and other parts of the world —one of Thailand's truly international art and antique shops. Here you'll find masks, headdresses, jewelry, and numerous unique pieces of furniture. Frenchman Francois Villaret has a sharp eye for good quality. In addition to these two shops, he maintains a warehouse of more treasures, especially furniture. Reasonably priced.

❏ **The Lost Heavens:** *21 Night Bazaar (Tel. 251-555); and 234 Thapae Road.* We've seen this shop grow over the years from a tiny no-name stall offering a few tribal handicrafts to a shop of real substance. Owned and operated by the soft-spoken and adventuresome Goh Michael, this shop offers one of the most unique collections of tribal artifacts from the Yao. If you're into tribal artifacts, this is one of the most interesting shops in Thailand with its jewelry, carvings, and textiles.

❏ **Baan Tarin:** *3 Mu 2, Chiang Mai-Hang Dong Road, Hang Dong (Tel. 441-623).* Popular with dealers, this expansive shop (see warehouse in back) offers good quality antiques, from bells and furniture to small carved items. Little English spoken.

❏ **Pusaka:** *191 Night Bazaar, 2ⁿᵈ Floor (Fax 272-811).* This eclectic antique shop stands out from the rest with its unique collection of artifacts. Look for good quality textiles, lacquerware, carvings from Thailand, China, and Myanmar. The Singapore-Chinese owner (sister of tribal expert Georgia Kan of Tatiana at Tanglin Shopping Centre in Singapore) has a real passion for collecting the best of the best. You are bound to find something special here and learn something new about collecting.

❑ **Oriental Spirit:** *29 Night Bazaar, 2ⁿᵈ Floor (Tel. 273-919).* A very small and attractive shop. Offers many nice antiques, some extremely weathered, from Thailand, Myanmar, and China. Look for lacquerware, woodcarvings, masks, and chofa (wood gables).

❑ **Ancient Crafts:** *11/3 Ratchamaka Road (Tel. 278-849); and 63 Night Bazaar, 3ʳᵈ Floor (Tel. 273-882).* Good collection of old lacquerware, boxes, Buddhas, bells, and silver pieces.

❑ **Kotchasarn Gallery:** *1 Night Bazaar, 2ⁿᵈ Floor (Tel. 819-036); and 33/16 Chiang Mai-Hangdong Road, Hangdong (Tel. 434-267).* Includes numerous objets d'art, from bronze bells, carved figures, Buddhas, and lacquerware to baskets, boxes, pottery, and furniture.

❑ **Paiphan's Collection:** *3 Night Bazaar, 2ⁿᵈ Floor (Tel. 820-764).* Offers a nice collection of antiques, woodcarvings, and lacquerware.

❑ **Maneesinn:** *289 Thapae Road (Tel. 282-047).* This long established shop includes one of the best collections of old lacquerware and basketry. Expensive.

FURNITURE/INTERIOR DECORATING

❑ **Ambiente Chiangmai:** *169/1 Moo 7 Nongkaew, Ban Tawai Road (Tel/Fax 442-119).* Produces contemporary furniture and accessories that incorporate terracotta figures. One of the most unique furniture shops in Thailand with its emphasis on incorporating architectural pieces in furniture designs. The brain child of Dutch architect and furniture designer Peter Bartlock. Does custom work to customer specifications. Includes many interesting pieces in the showroom but also keeps a photo album on numerous other designs. A fascinating and tempting alternative to the typical Thai furniture being made in Chiang Mai.

❑ **Nantiya Decor:** *100/1 Chiang Inn Plaza, 3rd Floor (Tel. 283-092); also has export shop along Ban Tawai Road in Hang Dong (near Chilli).* Produces bleached teakwood furniture in contemporary designs. Perfect for any Western home.

❑ **Gerard Collection:** *95-23-24 Nimmanhaemin Road (Tel. 220-604).* If you've been to Bali and seen the unique bamboo furniture designs of noted designer Linda Garland, you'll instantly recognize this look in furniture. Includes attractively designed bamboo furniture and home decorative items, from sofas to tables and lamps.

❑ **Oriental Style:** *36 Chareon Rat Road (Tel. 245-724).* This has been one of Chiang Mai's first and more inventive home decorative shops opened nearly five years ago. Produces all types of attractive contemporary furniture and accessories using lots of local materials, from rattan to metal. With the departure of its flamboyant Australian designer-creator, the change in ownership also has resulted in a change in direction, especially with the addition of Vila Cini, the adjacent textile and home decorative shop. Housed in a beautifully restored old heritage building, this two-storey shop is delightful to explore. Also includes a restaurant, the Oriental Style Restaurant.

TEXTILES

❑ **Vila Cini:** *The Oriental Textile Co., 30-34 Charoen Rat Road (Tel. 244-025).* This relatively new shop offers a nice collection of locally designed silk and cotton fabrics for designers. While it's not Jim Thompson quality, it is some of the best quality silk we've seen outside Bangkok.

❑ **Nandakwang:** *6/1-3 Nimmanhaemin Road (Tel. 222-261); and Chiang Inn Plaza, 3rd Floor (Tel. 283-090); and the 1st Floor of the Chiang Mai International Airport terminal.* This popular shop includes lots of cotton fabrics and home decorative items, from pillows to placemats. Nice quality and designs. Great gift items for family and friends. Includes five shops in Bangkok.

❑ **The Loom:** *27 Rajmanka Road (Tel. 278-892).* This long-established shop in an old Thai house includes good quality silk and cotton textiles. Popular with collectors, although inventory seems sparse these days.

❏ **Studio Naenna:** *138/8 Soi Changkhian, Huay Kaew Road (Tel. 226-042).* Owned and operated by one of the leading expatriate textile experts, Pat Chessman, who also conducts textile tours in Northern Thailand. Uses all natural fibers in weaving ikat, cotton, and silk using backstrap looms and natural dyes. The Studio functions as a pilot project for training small weaving groups in Thailand, Laos, and Cambodia in the use of environmentally friendly dyeing methods. It also markets the products of a women's weaving group. The small shop includes fabric by the meter as well as ready-made clothes, accessories, handmade ceramics, and books written by Pat on Lao and Thai a textiles. The textiles are all designed by Pat.

❏ **Jolie Femme:** *8/3 Chiang Mai-Sankamphaeng Road (Tel. 247-222).* One of the largest silk and cotton shops in Chiang Mai offering both ready-made clothes and fabric by the meter. Often very busy with bus loads of tourists doing last minute shopping. Includes a factory tour and showroom displays of clothes and accessories, including silk purses, scarfs, napkins, and jewelry boxes

❏ **Classic Lanna Thai:** *512 Moo 1, Mae Rim-Samoeng Road, Mae Rim, opposite the Regent Resort (Tel. 861-257).* Housed next door to Lanna House. Offers old textiles and classic apparel.

❏ **Duangjitt House:** *(Tel. 242-291).* Offers one of the best collections of textiles and silver in Northern Thailand. Used to operate shops along Nimmanhaemin Road and in the Chiang Inn Plaza, but now is available by appointment only for serious collectors. Very expensive.

CELADON, CERAMICS, STONEWARE

❏ **Mengrai Kilns:** *79/2 Araks Road, Soi Samlarn 6 (Tel. 272-063).* For more than 25 years Mengrai Kilns has produced some of the best quality celadon and ceramics in Thailand. Offers attractive green crackled plates, vases, bowls, and figures. Experienced in shipping abroad. Reasonably priced and friendly service.

❏ **Siam Celadon:** *38 Moo 10 Samkamphaeng Road (Tel. 331-526).* Produces traditional celadon as plates, vases, bowls, and figures.

❑ **Prempracha's Collection:** *224 Chiang Mai-Sankamphaeng Road (Tel. 338-540).* This large factory and shop produces a wide range of ceramics as well as unique celadon designs and colors. A very pleasant place to shop near Bosang, the umbrella village.

❑ **Korakod Stoneware:** *153 Moo 8, Tambol Nongkeaw, Hang Dong (Tel. 434-105).* This small factory/shop produces some very attractive pots and ceramic decorative pieces for both indoors and outdoors. If you visit the Regent Resort in Mae Rim and see at the entrance the nicely designed white ceramic elephants (almost signature pieces for the resort) with their trunks held high, now you know where they came from—Korakod Stoneware. They are wonderful elephants that make terrific home decorative pieces. Here at the factory they come in three different colors. Will pack and ship. Very reasonably priced and reliable.

TERRACOTTA

❑ **Ban Phor Liang Muen's:** *36 Prapokklao Road, Soi 2 (Tel. 278-187).* Chiang Mai's first factory to product terracotta plaques, statues, murals, and painted pots. Many of the murals are based on the story from the Ramayana. Interesting decorate art for both indoors and outdoors. Will make to order from their catalog of photos.

JEWELRY AND SILVER

❑ **Royal Orchid Collection:** *94-120 Charoen Muang Road (Tel.249-803).* Produces attractive neckpieces, earrings, and pins made from a special gold plating and enameling process using flowers and semi-precious stones. Primarily exports but you can purchase individual pieces at this business office. Also trades as the Siam Royal Orchid Co.

❑ **Shiraz Co., Ltd.:** *170 Thapae Road (Tel. 252-382).* A popular jewelry shop offering a wide range of gold and silver jewelry as well as selling loose rubies and sapphires.

❑ **Sipsong Panna:** *95/19 Nimmenhaemin Road (Tel. 216-096).* Offers an excellent selection of antique silverware and customized jewelry, opium pipes and weights, and beads from Thailand, Laos, Myanmar, China, and hilltribes.

❏ **Gems Gallery:** *80/1 Moo 3 Chiang Mai-Sankamphaeng Road (Tel. 339-307).* Claims to be the biggest jewelry store in the world—at least in Chiang Mai! Included here because of its size rather than its quality or reliability. Be careful—judge for yourself. This is a branch shop of Gems Gallery International Manufacturer in Bangkok (198/23-24 Rama 6 Road, Phyathai).

ART

❏ **The Gallery:** *25-29 Charoen Rat (Tel. 248-601).* This popular river front restaurant includes an art gallery at the entrance. Displays paintings and sculptures of local artists as well as other art and craft items.

❏ **Tita Gallery:** *68 Moo 6, Mae Rim-Samoeng Road, Mae Rim, opposite the Regent Resort (Tel. 298-373).* Offers a collection of traditional Thai and contemporary paintings by Thai artists.

EXPORT PRODUCT CENTER

❏ **Export Promotion Center:** *29/19 Singharaj Road (Tel. 221-376 or Fax 215-307).* Sponsored by the Department of Export Promotion, Ministry of Commerce, this exhibition hall showcases some of Northern Thailand's best products. If you are dealer or importer/exporter, you should find this center useful. It will put you in contact with the major producers that are export-oriented.

GETTING WHAT YOU WANT

BARGAINING

Getting what you want at a fair price in Chiang Mai requires bargaining. Most important of all, it requires avoiding touts, guides, and drivers. We recommend that you bargain for most things you purchase in Chiang Mai, and ask for special rates on hotel rooms and tours. Shops expect you to bargain, and they typically give 10 to 40% discounts—if you don't arrive with a driver or guide who expects a commission. During the off-season, when hotel rooms are plentiful, many hotels will give discounts if you ask at the front desk. Request a business discount and present your business card if asked for it.

Except for buses and minivans which run regular routes, you should bargain for most transportation in Chiang Mai. Taxis are nearly nonexistent. Most trishaw (*samlor*) drivers, including the motorized ones (*rot tuk tuk*), will reduce their prices by one-third if you bargain; don't accept the first price quoted unless you feel sympathy for these drivers. Few speak English, so use your fingers or show them the bills or coins you are willing to pay. Be sure to bargain for half-day and full-day rentals of cars and motorbikes. You may be pleasantly surprised how much your transportation costs decrease in Chiang Mai by merely countering with an alternative offer.

AVOID THE COMMISSION GAME

You should also avoid the outrageous commissions plaguing much of Chiang Mai's shopping. This problem is particularly pronounced amongst the shops found along the Chiang Mai-Sankamphaeng Road and endemic to tour groups. Many *rot tuk tuk*, *samlor*, minivan, and car drivers as well as tour guides routinely request from shops 10 to 40% commissions on purchases made by individuals they bring to the shops; others may only request 100B to 200B for bringing a group to the shop. Consequently, if you are being taken to a shop by a driver or guide, this individual will probably be getting a huge kickback on everything you purchase. The shop, in turn, adds this commission to the price you pay for the goods. If a shop refuses to give the commission, the driver or guide takes future tourists to another more cooperative shop. Unfortunately, nearly 80% of the shops along Chiang Mai-Sankamphaeng Road have succumbed to this form of blackmail. Shops patronized by large groups of tourists, especially those arriving by tour bus and with drivers, are usually paying the commissions in order to have the customers brought to their shops. Even some of the most reputable international tour groups engage in this practice.

The problem has gotten so serious that it is becoming a crisis of sorts. Prices have become so inflated and the corruption so pervasive that shopping in Chiang Mai may become unattractive. Indeed, in some instances, you may be able to purchase the same items cheaper in Bangkok where you are likely to go into a shop on your own or your driver or guide only requests the standard 10% commission. The 10% commission is the normal going rate in Thailand as well as among touts, drivers, and tour guides in many other countries.

If you rent a car and drive yourself—the best way to avoid the commission game—you will discover the initial asking price will automatically drop by at least one-third—because you came alone—and you may be able to bargain for another 20 to 40% discount. You can also explore many good shops that most tourists never see because they are told by their guides that the shop is *"no good"* or *"it's closed today"* which translates as *"they don't give me a commission there!"*

Another way to get around the commission game is to call the shop and request that you be provided transportation to visit them. They are more than willing to send a car for you, because this means eliminating middlemen who would ask for commissions if they brought you to the shop. You are under no obligation to buy even though the shop has taken the trouble to pick you up. On the other hand, this is an inconvenient and time-consuming way to visit a large number of shops. Some enterprising tourists, who don't want to drive in an unfamiliar town and on the left side of the road, will hire a car with driver for a day or half-day to survey the shops—making no purchases or very small purchases as well as noting shops (request a business card) they wish to return to. After returning to their hotel, they call the shops where they have an interest in making larger purchases and let the shop send a car for them.

Alternatively, if you decide to hire a driver, try to communicate that he is not to take commissions. This means you will have to pay him more for his driving services. But this may or may not work to your advantage. If you don't speak Thai, you can't be sure the driver isn't still getting a kickback, even though he may swear *"No, no, no—I don't take commissions,"* Also, be aware that some drivers will offer you a *"free shopping tour"* or one that is incredibly cheap—100B for four hours! Some tourists think this is a great bargain, equivalent to the proverbial free lunch. They even tell other tourists how they, too, can get a free shopping tour! This is one of those "freebies" you and others are better off not accepting. Remember, there is no such thing as a free lunch, especially when you are paying for it by other means.

DRIVE YOURSELF

You will find driving your own car to be the cheapest way to shop in Chiang Mai. You will have the flexibility to explore Chiang Mai-Sankamphaeng Road, shops found in neighborhoods throughout the city, Hang Dong, and several nearby towns, such as Lamphun, Lampang, Chiang Rai, and Maesai. You will find several car rental agencies in Chiang Rai. We frequently use the reliable **Avis** which has desks at the Chiang Mai International Airport, adjacent to the baggage retrieval area, and in the Royal Princess Hotel (Tel. 281-033). It's best to reserve a car from

Bangkok (the Avis office is located at the Dusit Thani Hotel) and pick it up as soon as you arrive at the airport (call their office if no one is at the desk). You also can call Avis to have them pick you up at your hotel. We've also used **Budget** (189/17-19 Wualai Road, Tel. 202-871) which will arrange to have a car ready for you at the airport and allow you to drop it there when you leave Chiang Mai. Both Avis and Budget are very reliable and responsive. While you'll find many other rental car agencies offering better rates, we prefer using these international firms because of their convenience and reliability, especially the ability to pick up and drop off the car at the airport.

SHIP WITH EASE

You should have no problem shipping goods directly from Chiang Mai. Most large shops are experienced in packing and shipping goods to Bangkok as well as overseas. If you are buying many items from different shops, consolidate them at one shop or use an experienced local shipper. The following companies can assist you with shipping:

Bonsak Cargo Service
1 Soi Kulab, Muang Sat Rd., Nong Hoi
A. Muang, Chiang Mai
Tel. 800-686 or Fax 800707

Carberson (Thailand) Ltd.
152/7 M. 3, Aom Muang Rd., T. Tasala
A. Muang, Chiang Mai
Tel. 308-121

Chiang Mai C. R. Shipping
10/1 Sanlam Rd., Soi 1
A. Muang, Chiang Mai
Tel. 814-300 or Fax 279-447

Schenker (Thai) Ltd.
55 M. 7 Warehouse No. 6
Chiang Mai-Hod Road
Chiang Mai
Tel. 200-301 or Fax 200-303

Translink Express
300/52 Baan Seksurin, Chiang Mai-Lampun Rd.
A. Muang, Chiang Mai
Tel. 424-841

Firms such as **Schenker (Thai) Ltd.** have offices and shipping services in Bangkok. Most shops and shippers can send your goods to your consolidation point in Bangkok.

For fast air shipments, contact the local DHL, UPS, or FedEx offices:

DHL
164/93 Chang Mai Rd., T. Chang Klan
A. Muang, Chiang Mai
Tel. 820-352 or Fax 820-354

UPS
9 Soi 7, Rajdamnoen Rd.
A. Muang, Chiang Mai
Tel. 416-351 or Fax 416-352

FedEx
77/1-2 Sriphum Rd.
A. Muang, Chiang Mai
Tel. 418-451 or Fax 213-568

ACCOMMODATIONS

Chiang Mai offers a wide variety of accommodations for travelers, from very basic to luxury. If you're traveling on a shoestring budget, you should be able to find several inexpensive hotels and guest houses in and around Chiang Mai which cater to the large number of budget travelers who regularly visit Chiang Mai. Indeed, if you pick up the latest monthly issue of *Welcome Chiang Mai and Chiang Rai*, you'll find a relatively complete listing of hotels and guest houses by price range, including guest houses that cost less than US$10 a day. Many of first-class hotels cost between US$45 and US$65 a night.

But the real treat in Chiang Mai is in staying at one of the world's finest resorts—the Regent Resort Chiang Mai. This is a very special property for very special people who wish to indulge in the ultimate pleasures of travel. This resort has literally transformed forever the standard of accommodations, and service, in Chiang Mai as well as upcountry Thailand. Our recommendation: Go for it! Here's what you get if you decide to treat yourself to the "best of the best" in Chiang Mai:

❑ **The Regent Resort Chiang Mai**: *Mae Rim-Samoeng Old Road, Mae Rim, Chiang Mai 50180, Thailand, Tel.(6653) 298-181, Fax (6653) 209-189.* The Regent Resort Chiang

Mai offers luxury, elegance, and unobtrusive service with that special northern Thai warmth and charm that Chiang Mai is justly famous for. It is truly a luxury retreat nestled in the hills—20 minutes north of the city—with its own working rice paddy complete with a water buffalo "family" consisting of Ms. Mud, Mr. Sand, baby Clay and his new brother. This resort, in itself, is enough reason to visit Chiang Mai!

Opened in April 1995, The Regent Resort quickly became a frequent winner of travel industry and readers' poll awards. The Regent consists of 70 lavishly appointed suites reflecting the architectural style of the "Lanna" kingdom of the North. The 64 Pavilion suites are large and show off to advantage the Thai art against the polished teak floors and beautiful cotton fabrics. A separate dressing room leads from the bedroom/sitting area to an oversized bath which overlooks a secluded garden planted with ferns and lush tropical plants. The deep-soaking tub, double vanities and separate shower and toilet enclosures add to the ambience. Additional outdoor seating is provided by a Thai "sala". Six Residences at the Regent are available in combinations of one, two, and three bedrooms. One and two bedroom suites on the lower level feature their own individual plunge pool and terrace. The three bedroom Residence, with a spiral staircase leading to the Penthouse, occupies the entire upper levels and has stunning panoramic views of the nearby mountains (foothills of the Himalayas) and surrounding countryside. All Residences feature polished wood floors, gabled buttresses styled from ancient temples, a fireplace, open plan seating/dining for 10-12 people and a full kitchen with maid's quarters. All Pavilion Suites and Residences include 24-hour room service—outstanding service that is both present but unobtrusive—twice daily maid service, as well as daily and overnight laundry and pressing. Each suite has a personal in-room safe, a compact disc sound system and television with satellite hook-up. *Sala Mae Rim*, the resort's Thai restaurant features the finest in Thai cuisine including Northern specialties. Indoor and outdoor seating is available to take advantage of the sweeping views and gentle evening breezes. An endorsement to the culinary skills of the chef and staff are the many local Thai residents we see dining at *Sala Mae Rim*. The *Pool Terrace and Bar* offer pool-side dining for lunch and dinner in addition to a weekly BBQ dinner. Both Western and Thai dishes are available. *The Elephant Bar* is a casually elegant open pavilion style lounge serving afternoon tea, cocktails and after dinner drinks.

The staff is happy to advise guests where they can purchase some of the lovely furnishings and decorations one is sure to admire around the resort or take a tour of the boutiques and shops—both well established and off-the beaten track—recommended by the Regent. The *Regent Select* Concierge Service provides shopping assistance to interested guests which includes planning personalized shopping itineraries, securing knowledgeable and trustworthy guides, offering bargaining advice as well as assisting with arrangements for shipping of purchases too bulky to carry. If a guest is traveling on to other Regent destinations in Asia, the Concierge can communicate the guest's special shopping needs directly to the next hotel. Upon check-in, the data has been gathered and the guest is handed the shopping itinerary. There is a small gift shop—The Regent Boutique—on premises and a wonderful antique shop, Lanna House, across the road from the entrance to the resort as well as two small shops offering textiles (Classic Lanna Thai) and handicrafts (Huen Mai). Weekly excursions and activity suggestions are available in each guestroom, and range from resort activities of tennis, golf or swimming to the more adventurous activities of river rafting, elephant riding, mountain biking, or hiking. The guest may choose to sun by the gorgeous pool or relax by enjoying a sauna or traditional Thai massage at the Regent Spa.

The Regent Chiang Mai offers conference facilities with seating for groups up to forty people in the Kasalong Pavilion or eighty in the Conference Pavilion. Breakout facilities can be arranged, and an outside terrace adjacent to the Kasalong Pavilion is ideal for cocktail receptions, coffee breaks or informal gatherings. *Exclusively Yours* makes it possible to book the entire resort facilities for conferences. It just doesn't get much better that this! This is definitely our number one choice for accommodations in Chiang Mai. When you leave Chiang Mai after having stayed here, you will have truly fallen in love with Northern Thailand!

Other good hotels in Chiang Mai worth considering include the following:

❑ **Westin Riverside Plaza**: *318/1 Chiang Mai-Lumphun Road, Chiang Mai 50000, Thailand, Tel. (6653) 275-300, Fax*

(6653) 275-299. The Westin is located on the Mae Ping River, a short drive from the main business and shopping district—including the Night Bazaar. The 526 guestrooms and suites feature deluxe amenities. The River Terrace serves international and local dishes in a casual setting overlooking the river. The high ceiling and large expanse of glass make this a bright airy dining area, and an excellent international lunch-time buffet is served daily. The China Palace serves Chinese cuisine with a daily dim sum lunch choice. Castana offers Italian and French cuisine. Health Club and Fitness Center; Business Center and Conference Facilities. Popular with upscale tour groups as well as meeting and conference groups.

❑ **Royal Princess**: *112 Chang Road, Chiang Mai 50000, Thailand, Tel. (6653) 281-033, Fax (6653) 281-044.* Formerly the Dusit Inn, this centrally located hotel is right in the center of Chiang Mai's tourist activities. Step out the door, turn left and you are in the midst of street vendors who set up every evening along the sidewalks. Walk a block further and you are at the Night Bazaar. The 200 rooms are basic—which is the norm for up-country hotels, but clean and comfortable and with expected amenities. Staff is helpful and service is good. The restaurant on the main floor serves a good buffet breakfast and the Chinese restaurant upstairs, Jasmine, is considered one of the best in town! Meeting Rooms.

❑ **Imperial Mae Ping Hotel**: *153 Sridonchai Road, Chiang Mai 50100, Thailand, Tel. (6653) 270-160, Fax (6653) 270-181.* Centrally located in the midst of the tourist activities and only a block from the Night Bazaar, the high rise Mae Ping's 371 rooms are decorated with Thai motifs and deliver amenities to make the guest's stay comfortable. Three restaurants offer Western, Chinese, and Japanese cuisines. Meeting Rooms.

❑ **Chiang Mai Orchid Hotel**: *100-102 Huay Kaew Road, Chiang Mai 50200, Thailand, Tel. (6653) 222-099, Fax (6653) 221-625.* Located next to a local shopping plaza, and a short ride from the Night Bazaar and center of town tourist spots, the Chiang Mai Orchid's 260 guestrooms are tastefully furnished with artwork of Northern Thailand. Considered by local residents to be the best hotel prior to the opening of the Regent Resort and Westin, the hotel is comfortable and offers expected amenities. Continental restaurant, Japanese restaurant, coffee shop serves good Thai lunch-time buffet. Health Club and Business Services.

❑ **Amari Rincome Hotel**: *1 Nimmanhaemin Road (at Huay Kaew Road) Chiang Mai 50200, Thailand, (6653) 221-044, Fax (6653) 221-915.* Located a short ride from the city center and Night Bazaar, the Amari Rincome is across the street from a small, but upscale series of shops and near numerous restaurants. The rooms are nicely decorated with wood carved Northern Thai decorative elements and the lobby features several beautiful antiques.

RESTAURANTS

Chiang Mai has several good Thai, Chinese, French, German, English, and Middle Eastern restaurants along with several coffee shops and fast food establishments. The northern Thai food tends to be spicier than the Thai food in Bangkok. Some of our favorite northern dishes include sticky rice (*khao neow*), a curried noodle dish (*khao soi*), and a wonderful—although sometimes blazing hot—pickled pork chile dip eaten with sticky rice or fried pork skins (*namprik ong*). The local raw pork sausage delicacy called *naem* and a minced pork dish called *lap* are very popular, but they can be very hot and may give you a bad case of trichinosis. And watch out for the small green peppers; eat one of these and you may think you are having cardiac arrest!

You can sample the unique Northern Thai cuisine by attending one of the *khantoke* dinner shows (try the **Old Chiang Mai Culture Center**, 183/5 Wualai Road, Tel. 275-097) or stop at one of the many famous Northern Thai restaurants. For starters, try **Aroon Rai** near the Tha Phae Gate at 45 Kotchasarn Road (Tel. 276-947) in downtown Chiang Mai or **Once Upon a Time** at 385/2 Charoen Prathet Road (Tel. 274-932). But the best and most delightful Thai restaurant in the Chiang Mai area is found at the Regent Resort, the **Sala Mae Rim**. Indeed, many Thai from Bangkok make a special trip to the Regent Resort just to dine at this wonderful Thai restaurant. The *khao soi* doesn't get any better, anywhere!

For good French and Continental cuisine in charming surroundings, try **Le Coq d'Or** at 68/1 Koh Klang Road (Tel. 282-024) and **L'Auberge Chez Gibus** at 42 Kampaengdin Road. One of our long-time favorites is **The Pub** at 189 Huay Kaew Road (Tel. 211-550), just a short walk from the Amari Rincome Hotel. The food here is both excellent and inexpensive.

Good Chinese food and seafood are found at the **Jasmine**

(Royal Princess Hotel), **The Chinese House** (Westin Chiang Mai Hotel), **Panda Palace** (Empress Hotel), and **Ging Pai** (Porn Ping Tower Hotel). Other favorite restaurants include:

❑ **Baan Suan:** *51/3 Chiang Mai-Sankamphaeng Road (Tel. 262-569).* Nicely decorated and situated in a lovely outdoor setting, Baan Suan serves excellent Thai dishes. Frequented by tour groups for both lunch and dinner.

❑ **Piccola Roma:** *3/2-3 Charoen Prathet Road (Tel. 271-256).* Complete with an Italian chef, this is probably Chiang Mai's best Italian restaurant.

❑ **Whole Earth:** *88 Sri Donchai Road (Tel. 282-463).* Excellent Thai, Pakistani, and vegetarian restaurant located in a garden setting.

❑ **The Gallery:** *25-29 Charoen Rat (Tel. 248-601).* This restaurant and bar on the banks of the Ping River also functions as one of Chiang Mai's most interesting art galleries. Located just north of the Nawarat Bridge and next to other pleasant riverside restaurants such as The Riverside and Rim Ping. Across the street from one of Chiang Mai's best home decorative shops, Oriental Style.

❑ **Galae Restaurant:** *65 Suthep Road (Tel. 278-655).* A long-time favorite for outstanding Thai and Northern Thai cuisine. Lovely setting at the foothills of a mountain with a panoramic view of Chiang Mai City.

❑ **Hong Tauw Inn:** *95/16-17 Nimmanhaemin Road (Tel. 218-333).* One of Chiang Mai's best Thai restaurants with a charming country-inn atmosphere.

❑ **Riverside Restaurant:** *9-11 Chorean Rad Road (Tel. 243-239).* Overlooking the Ping River, this popular restaurant serves homestyle Western and Thai food.

❑ **Kaiwan:** *181 Nimmanhaemin Road, Soi 9 (Tel. 221-147).* A long-time favorite garden restaurant near the Amari Rincome Hotel. Serves excellent Thai food. Especially good for *kaeng matsaman.*

❑ **Nang Nuan:** *27/2 Ko Klang Road, Nonghoy (Tel. 281-955).* Located 3 kilometers south of Chiang Mai on the road to Lampang, this river front restaurant is a long-time favorite for fresh seafood and grilled charcoal steaks. Serves really good *tom kha gai.*

The luncheon buffets at the Chiang Inn, Chiang Mai Orchid, and Westin hotels are very good values, although the selections are more limited than at the hotel restaurants in Bangkok.

ENJOYING YOUR STAY

Chiang Mai is much more than shopping, accommodations, and restaurants. It is an intriguing cultural area with wonderful sights and a pleasant atmosphere of people, lifestyles, scenery, and climate. TAT maintains a **Tourist Information Office** (105-1 Chiang Mai-Lamphun Rd., Tel. 248-604 or 248-607) just south of the Nawarat Bridge on the eastern bank of the Ping River (Mae Nam Ping). This office can provide you with maps and information on local tours and attractions. Your hotel also should have information on various tours within and outside the city. Several tour operators offer a variety of tours to the factories, temples, and sights inside the city and to several locations outside the city, such as the Elephant Training Camp, Doi Suthep mountain, Puping Palace, Doi Inthanon, waterfalls, orchid farms, and caves. You also can arrange overnight trips to the interesting province of Chiang Rai and the hill towns of Mae Sariang and Fang or rent a car to explore Lampang and the walled city of Naan.

If you are adventuresome, you can arrange two or three-day trips to the remote province of Mae Hong Son as well as to hilltribe villages. Several companies organize a variety of trekking adventures into the northern hills. We do not recommend wandering into the hills on your own. You may stumble into sensitive areas populated by rebels, drug dealers, or bandits!

The northern Thai culture differs in many ways from the cultures of Bangkok, central, northeastern, and southern Thailand. For an introduction to the diverse lowland and upland cultures of northern Thailand, you should visit the Chiang Mai National Museum, Ladda Land, and the Tribal Research Center at Chiang Mai University as well as attend one of the evening dinner-cultural shows, or *khantoke* shows, sponsored by hotels or at the Old Chiang Mai Cultural Center.

LOOKING BACK

Four days in Chiang Mai should be enough to visit the major factories and shops as well as do some basic sightseeing in this interesting area. Your shopping experience in Chiang Mai will probably be more of an adventure than your shopping in Bangkok. To be effective and truly enjoy shopping in Chiang Mai, you must develop a different shopping strategy which is most appropriate to the structure of shopping and transportation in Chiang Mai. You will do less walking and more vehicular traveling between shops and factories.

You should enjoy the change of pace, the pleasant climate, and the friendly and gracious people in and around this northern city. You will find many items you saw in Bangkok, but you also should discover many antiques and handicrafts not available there. Above all, you will be encounter quality goods, unique items, and reasonable prices.

Chiang Mai should become one of your major shopping highlights in Asia. Chiang Mai—the window to Myanmar, Laos, hilltribes, and the history and culture of northern Thailand—will once again confirm the wisdom of seeking the treasures and pleasures of exotic Thailand!

13

Beyond Chiang Mai, Bangkok, and Thailand

YOU WILL FIND MANY ADDITIONAL TREASURES and pleasures outside Bangkok and Chiang Mai, especially in the northern and southern regions and neighboring Myanmar, Laos, Cambodia, and Vietnam. In northern Thailand, for example, the towns of **Chiang Rai, Maesai, Lampang,** and **Lamphun**—all located within a one to four hour drive from Chiang Mai—are worth visiting for shopping and sightseeing. If time permits, you may also want to visit **Mae Hong Son**, located near the Thai-Myanmar border, an 11 hour drive or 40 minute flight from Chiang Mai.

Ayutthaya, the former 17th century capital of Thailand, is located 86 kilometers north of Bangkok. While it is a major tourist destination for individuals interested in visiting Bang Pa-In Palace and the ruins of the former capital, it offers some unique shopping opportunities.

Pattaya, a popular beach resort southeast of Bangkok, can be reached within three hours driving time; it has a few interesting shops amidst its many restaurants and bars.

Ko Samui, a small island off the east coast of southern Thailand, offers relaxation from the hustle and bustle of shopping and sightseeing in other parts of Thailand. If you love beaches and water sports, this may be your perfect paradise.

Phuket, a major beach and island resort in southern Thailand, offers some interesting shopping opportunities for those who primarily visit this lovely area for sun and surf.

For information on these and other "beyond Bangkok and Chiang Mai" destinations, contact the Tourist Authority of Thailand (see contact information on pages 33-34 and 38-44). Ask for copies of their informative regional brochures which outline the treasures and pleasures of the North, Northeast, Central, and Southern regions. TAT also publishes two useful "Accommodation Guide" booklets which outline details on hundreds of hotels, resorts, bungalows, and guest houses in each of the four regions—the most comprehensive listing available anywhere.

Each of our "beyond Bangkok and Chiang Mai" locations are essentially small towns with populations of fewer than 80,000. Shopping is confined to either the central business district or to shops and factories on the outskirts of town. In each town you should be able to complete your shopping within one to four hours.

GETTING THERE

Getting to these locations is relatively easy. Since they are popular tourist destinations, each town is accessible by air, rail, bus, or car. Tours are regularly organized to the popular towns of Chiang Rai, Ayutthaya, and Phuket. However, it is relatively easy and convenient to rent a car with driver or, if you are a bit adventuresome, drive your own rental vehicle in these towns. In northern Thailand, for example, you may want to rent a car in Chiang Mai and from there drive to Maesai, Chiang Rai, Lampang, and Lamphun and then return to Chiang Mai. This circle trip, including sightseeing and shopping, can be done in two to three days. If you include Mae Hong Son, it's best to fly. In fact, you can take an early morning flight into Mae Hong Son, hire a car and driver to see the major sights and shop, and then take the late afternoon flight back to Chiang Mai where you will still have time to shop Chiang Mai's Night Bazaar. This makes for an interesting one-day trip, but it really doesn't do justice to fascinating Mae Hong Son.

The easiest and fastest way to get to Pattaya is by car. You may want to rent a car with driver to visit Pattaya. If you leave early in the morning from Bangkok, you can see the major sights and shop, and return to Bangkok the same day. However, many visitors prefer staying over in Pattaya for one or two nights.

You will probably want to fly to Ko Samui and Phuket and then rent a car upon arrival at the airports. In Phuket driving allows you to venture into a few nearby provinces, such as Phangnga.

You may want to rent a car with driver in Bangkok to visit Ayutthaya or join one of the regularly scheduled tours to this province and town. One of best ways to see this ancient capital is by taking the overnight Manohra Song cruise from Bangkok (see pages 219-221 for details). Driving in and around Bangkok is much less convenient than driving to "up-country" provinces, towns, and villages.

CAUTIOUSLY EXPLORE THE HINTERLAND

Please do not venture beyond Bangkok and Chiang Mai with the expectation of finding great bargains and quality goods. If you do, you will be disappointed as you waste your precious travel time. The "good stuff" is either in Bangkok or Chiang Mai, with Bangkok by far having the largest range of excellent quality products. The old shopping rule that most *"good stuff flows to the capital"* is especially valid in the case of Thailand. What you will find in these other towns are some very unique items, such as blue ceramics in Lampang and stone sculptures and antique ceramics in Ayutthaya, and some interesting historical and cultural sites. Better still, you will get to see a less urban and more picturesque Thailand than had you just confined your visit to Bangkok and Chiang Mai.

❑ Bangkok offers the largest range of excellent quality products.

❑ Look for blue pottery and other ceramics in Lampang.

❑ Ayutthaya offers stone sculptures and antique ceramics.

❑ Expect to encounter shipping problems with purchases made at border towns. Hand-carry your goods from the shop rather than trust the shop to ship them properly.

❑ Unless you know what you're doing, purchasing gems or jewelry in out-of-the-way places invites scams.

Shops in beach resort communities, such as Pattaya, Ko Samui, and Phuket primarily source their products from Bangkok and Chiang Mai and mark up prices accordingly. If you've already been to Bangkok and Chiang Mai, you may want to pass on the local resort shopping and concentrate instead on the sun and surf pleasures of these delightful places.

If you do shop beyond Bangkok and Chiang Mai, please be careful where you shop and whom you trust with your money and purchases. Most shops and merchants outside Bangkok and Chiang Mai speak little English. Moreover, they are not experienced in documenting, getting permits, packing, and shipping abroad. Some travelers, for example, report shipping problems with purchases they made in the Thai-Myanmar border town of Maesai. However, they forgot the golden rule for shopping in border towns:

> Expect scams to readily operate and unscrupulous mer-
> chants to prey on tourists who mistakenly think *"I'll
> really get a super deal at the border."*

However friendly and enticing, always remember that most border towns tend to be transient communities with popula-tions engaged in all types of legal, illegal, and unethical prac-tices. Remember, if it's too good to be true, it probably is. At the same time, some well-meaning shops agree to do things for buyers—which are considered routine for merchants in Bangkok and Chiang Mai—but in the end they are incapable of perform-ing. For example, some tourists buy antique Buddhas—which are illegal to export from Thailand without proper government permits. Obtaining the permits is an expensive and time-consuming process centered in Bangkok. Unfamiliar with this process, some buyers expect shops in these towns to ship purchases to their home address trouble-free. When their purchases do not arrive in a few weeks, they then write letters of complaint to the shop owners who, in turn, don't read or write English. It is simply foolish to expect shops in such towns to perform these tasks and then further expect them to commu-nicate with you in English.

Our advice for making purchases in such places is both simple and sensible: **hand carry all items you purchase from shops outside Bangkok and Chiang Mai.** You can take them to a reliable shipper, or a central consolidation point, and have them pack and ship everything with the expectation you will receive your goods. **Never ever leave your purchases with a shop in the smaller towns.** To do so invites disappointments. If you purchase a Thai Buddha, for example, be aware you may never get it out of Thailand, regardless of what an enterprising shopkeeper may lead you to believe; take a picture of it since you may never see it again. If you purchase gems or jewelry in out-of-the-way places, especially in border towns such as Maesai, make sure you know what you are doing. An ostensible ruby may turn out to be a beautiful spinel or even a piece of glass! These are expensive lessons you need not learn the hard way. We know, because we've met tourists who have experi-enced such problems through their own naivete.

CHIANG RAI

Chiang Rai, the capital of Thailand's northern most province which borders both Myanmar and Laos, is a small sleepy provincial town located 180 kilometers northeast of Chiang Mai. It can easily be reached within three hours driving distance via a scenic and good paved, yet mountainous and winding, road. Leave Chiang Mai's noisy and polluted rush hour traffic by 7am and you will be in relatively quiet downtown Chiang Rai by 10:00am.

Chiang Rai is becoming one of the north's most popular tourist destinations. Tour buses leave Chiang Mai every day to take tourists into Chiang Rai's land of the "Golden Triangle." Famous for its colorful hilltribe peoples, opium warlords, and Shan rebels from Myanmar, Chiang Rai reminds one of Chiang Mai 20 years ago. The pace of life is slow, traffic is sensible, air and noise pollution are minimal, and the people are both friendly and curious. The area is inherently fascinating because of its natural beauty, diverse population, and history of opium, warlords, rebels, and ancient kingdoms. While one of the most popular tours is to the "Golden Triangle" area northeast of Chiang Rai town, which became famous as a center of opium production in the 1970s, Chiang Rai still retains its colorful reputation as one of Southeast Asia's major opium growing regions—complete with opium warlords, couriers, and middleman who engage in an extremely profitable, adventuresome, and deadly trade.

Shopping in the province of Chiang Rai is primarily centered around the provincial capital of Chiang Rai, the border town of Maesai, and the Golden Triangle area near Chiangsaen. The town of Chiang Rai is a good place from which to explore Maesai and the Golden Triangle area as well as the ancient town of Chiangsaen. While hotel and restaurant facilities are not as deluxe as those found in Bangkok, four relatively new deluxe hotels and resorts have opened during the past ten years in anticipation of a coming surge of tourism to Chiang Rai. Within the city of Chiang Rai are the deluxe **Dusit Island Resort** (Tel. 715-777), **Little Duck** (Tel. 715-620), and **Rimkok Resort** (Tel. 716-446). First-class hotels include the **Wiang Inn** (Tel. 711-533) and the **Wangcome Hotel** (Tel. 711-800). Most tour groups stay at these hotels and resorts which also function as the social centers for the local elite. The hotels have good restaurants as well as small gift shops. In the Golden Triangle area, just west of Chiangsean, is the superbly located and beautifully appointed **Delta Golden Triangle**

Hotel (Tel. 784-001) which overlooks the Mekong River where Myanmar, Laos, and Thailand meet. The nearby 110-room **Le Meridien Baan Boran** (Tel. 784-084) is also a good choice with a wonderful location. Three of our favorite places to stay include the following:

❏ **Dusit Island Resort**: *1129 Kraisorasit Road, Chiang Rai 57000, Thailand, Tel. (66 53) 715-777, Fax (66 53) 715-801.* A luxury resort sitting on an island in the Koh River—a bit outside of the town—some think the Dusit Island Resort has the best location in Chiang Rai. The three wings give all the guestrooms views of the river. Furnished with traditional Northern Thai motifs, the spacious rooms have large marble baths and offer all the amenities of a resort hotel. One dining room serves Western cuisine, a Chinese restaurant serves Cantonese selections, and the Island Café serves a buffet breakfast and a choice of Thai or Western food all day. Health Club; Meeting Rooms.

❏ **Le Meridien Baan Boran Golden Triangle**: *The Golden Triangle, Chiangsaen, Chiang Rai 57150, Thailand, Tel. (66 53) 784-084, Fax (66 53) 784-090, Website: www.infothai. com/lemeridien.* This is one of two luxury resorts in Chiang Rai. A bit outside of Chiangsaen town and sitting on a hilltop, the 106 guestrooms and 4 suites offer all necessary and expected amenities. Appointed in Northern Thai decor, each has a private balcony overlooking the Mekong River. Three restaurants serve Thai and International cuisines. Outdoor activities such as an elephant safari, mountain biking, hiking or trekking. Fitness Center; Conference Facilities.

❏ **Wiang Inn**: *893 Phaholyothin Road, Chiang Rai 57000, Thailand, Tel. (66 53) 711-543, Fax (66 53) 711-877.* Situated in the center of town, the Wiang Inn was the best hotel in town until the resorts outside town opened. Guests can walk to the small (compared to Chiang Mai) Night Market. The lobby is decorated with Northern Thai motifs and spacious guestrooms can look a bit worn—unless you are lucky enough to arrive following a refurbishment. A price list indicates that practically everything from the telephone to the bedspread can be yours if you can't bear to leave it behind! Restaurant serves Western, Thai and Chinese food. Health Club.

Shopping in Chiang Rai should take no longer than two hours. A relatively small and compact town, most of the downtown shops are within easy walking distance from the Wiang Inn and Wangcome Hotel. The main shopping streets are the intersecting streets of **Paholyothin, Ratanacate,** and **Tanalai.** You will find numerous restaurants and shops lining these streets. However, most shops are filled with consumer goods of little interest to tourists. These are interesting shops to browse through, especially at night, to get a sense of what's popular with the local community.

You will find two silver, antique, and craft shops in downtown Chiang Rai worth visiting. **Chiang Saen** at 869/96 Pemavipat Road, just off Paholyothin Road (Tel. 713-535) is Chiang Rai's best antique and handicraft shop. Its three floors are filled with hilltribe clothing, silver, baskets, Buddhas, ceramics, puppets, and lacquerware. The shop has an excellent collection of good quality baskets and Lanna Thai Buddhas. The prices here are also very good—beautiful US$125 baskets in Bangkok sell for US$45 here. Across the street at 869/145 Pemavipat Road is **Chiang Rai Silver Ware** (Tel. 714-764). This shop has a similar range of silver items found in its other shop (Bor Sang Silver Ware) at the village of Bo Sang just off the Chiang Mai-Sankamphaeng Road in Chiang Mai.

One of the major shopping attractions on the outskirts of Chiang Rai is the **Chiang Rai Handicraft Center** (Tel. 713-355), which is located 3 kilometers north of the city, on the road (Phaholyothin) to Maesai and Chiangsaen. Easily recognized by a huge ladle in front of the factory-shop, this is one of the largest handicraft centers in northern Thailand. It's an excellent place to stop and view the making of pottery, ceramics, and silk and cotton material. The showroom is filled with good quality ceramics, clothes, bencharong, woodcarvings, silver, flowers, dolls, lacquerware, puppets, jewelry, paintings, jade, and Myanmar products. This is also a good place to purchase a map of Chiang Rai. All prices here are fixed.

MAESAI

The town of Maesai is by far the major shopping attraction in the province of Chiang Rai. Located 50 kilometers directly north of the town of Chiang Rai, Maesai is one of Thailand's major border crossings with Myanmar. Visitors from all over Thailand—tourists, traders, and itinerant travelers—come here to enjoy the colorful people and shop for bargains. The most interesting side of the border is Maesai—where you can do some interesting shopping at excellent prices—if you are very careful!

Maesai is the type of town you might expect to find at a major border crossing where a very poor country meets a relatively well developed country—somewhat dusty, worn, but busy with people crossing to and from the border in search of products and profits. The Thai side of the border is the prosperous side whereas the Myanmar side is relatively poor, although better off than most upcountry Myanmar towns and villages. Myanmar traders continuously stream across the border to buy basic Thai consumer goods that are difficult to find in rural Myanmar. Thai tourists, in turn, cross the border to purchase traditional medicines and food stuffs as well as witness what life is like on the other side.

Most shopping in Maesai is concentrated along the main street adjacent to the border crossing. Here you will find numerous antique, handicraft, and jewelry shops as well as street side vendors and hawkers selling products from Myanmar. It is a good area to just stroll up and down the street, take pictures from the bridge, visit numerous shops, and watch the colorful tribes people crossing the border and bridge from Myanmar. You can even have your picture taken with the cute tribal children who are real professionals at posing for tourists —and politely asking for payment afterwards. Indeed, "people watching" is as much fun as shopping for inexpensive items from Myanmar.

The shops and vendors in Maesai primarily sell products from Myanmar: gems, jewelry, silver, antiques, lacquerware, tapestries (*kalagas*), puppets, and a variety of other handcrafted items. If you know how to bargain—expect 20 to 60% discounts —prices here are some of the cheapest in Thailand. In fact, many dealers from Chiang Mai, Bangkok, and abroad purchase their antiques, gems, and handicrafts directly from the same shops and vendors you will encounter in Maesai. For example, expect to pay anywhere from one-fourth to one-half the price you would pay in Bangkok for a Myanmar tapestry (*kalagas*) found in abundance in the shops of Maesai. A *kalaga* selling for US$300 in Bangkok and US$200 in Chiang Mai may be only US$100 in Maesai—and a surprising US$1000 in North America and Europe! Myanmar puppets that sell for US$60 in Bangkok and US$40 in Chiang Mai sell for US$15 in Maesai and US$200-400 in North America and Europe. The prices are so cheap that you may find it difficult to restrain your shopping urges.

The reason prices are so cheap here is that Myanmar labor is some of the cheapest in the world. Given the difficult economic situation in Myanmar, which is further exacerbated by the recent economic downtown in Thailand, traders from Myanmar willingly exchange valuable antiques and handcrafted items for the much desired Thai consumer goods. Especially in the case of the *kalagas*, which involve weeks of intensive skilled labor, you will be shocked at the inexpensive prices for these wall hangings. Our advice for shopping in Maesai is to buy now since you may never see these prices—and perhaps the products—again.

We do not have specific recommendations for shops in Maesai. The reason is that most shops and vendors are located next to each other within 150 meters of the border crossing. They all seem to carry the same items. All you need to do is go from one shop and vendor to another to compare products and prices. Once you find something you like, do comparative shopping among the various shops and vendors. As you bargain over prices, play one shop and vendor off the other by mentioning that you can get the same item from another shop or vendor for much less. The competitive nature of this shopping environment will ensure a good price on many products.

Be forewarned, however, that some shops and vendors may misrepresent their goods, and touts may attempt to attach themselves to you in order to get easy shop commissions. A few shops, for example, sell gold and lacquer hats that were ostensibly once worn by Myanmar soldiers. Some shops will tell you these are *"very old— 100 to 200 years"* and try to sell them for US$100-200 each. Don't believe a word they say. These hats may look old, but most were made yesterday; other more honest shops sell them for US$20. Consequently, do your comparative shopping and be skeptical of claims about antiques.

The same is true for gems and jewelry. Maesai is notorious for selling fake gems at genuine stone prices. Many a tourist have left Maesai believing they had purchased a valuable gem at an unbelievably cheap price. And yes, they did get something unbelievable—the gem rather than the price! While you can get good deals on gems at Maesai, please know what you are doing before you make such a purchase. In general, street vendors with mobile carts do not generate a great deal of confidence in any product we might buy that costs more than US$20. If you

❑ Prices in Maesai are some of the cheapest in Thailand but be very careful here.

❑ Merchants and vendors in Maesai are notorious for selling fake gems at genuine stone prices.

❑ Street vendors with mobile carts do not generate a great deal of confidence in any product costing more than US$20.

❑ Be careful at the jade factory. You may not get a good deal.

spend more than US$100 from one of these vendors, don't be surprised if you later learn they were literally "fly-by-night" merchants who sold you a cheap imitation a truly "unbelievable" price!

One exception to our "no recommendation" rule is a shop located along the river adjacent to the border crossing—**Mengrai Antique**. It's noted for offering a wide selection of Myanmar antiques. We have found this shop to be reliable, although some readers report problems with purchases not being shipped as expected or promised. However, we **always** take our purchases with us and would **never** trust this or any other shop in Maesai to ship our goods. We simply expect problems to arise when entrusting international shipments to shops outside Bangkok and Chiang Mai. Mengrai Antique is one of the largest shops in Maesai—three dusty and cluttered floors of antiques and handicrafts. Here you will find an excellent selection of woodcarvings, hilltribe clothes, textiles, antiques, bells, rain drums, lacquerware, baskets, and puppets.

But be your own judge. We're not comfortable making recommendations in Maesai because of the frontier, fly-by-night character of shopping here. You can easily get cheated here if you don't know what you are doing. Remember, this is not Bangkok or Chiang Mai—it's a border town where everyone is out making money on the local border and tourist trade.

To be on the safe side, we recommend starting your shopping at **Mengrai Antiques**. Look over their product selections; ask about prices, but expect to get at least a 20% discount; and then compare their products and prices with other nearby shops and vendors. Two adjacent shops—**Mala Antique** and **Chai Siam**—also offer a large range of antiques, handicrafts, and jewelry. Chances are you will eventually return to Mengrai Antiques to do much of your buying. This shop also sells those US$100-200 "antique" warrior hats for what they are really worth—about US$20—which is indeed an "unbelievable" price!

Maesai also has a jade shop—**Thong Tavee Jade Factory**. Similar to other jade factories, you can observe the jade carving process and then shop at the factory shop. The shop also sells jewelry and silver. And like other jade factories we have visited, prices here seem very high and the quality is not the best. If you purchase anything here, make sure you get a huge discount— nothing less than 60%. We found prices on jewelry here to be about 200% higher than retail shops in Bangkok.

You will also find some shopping opportunities among hilltribe peoples. Several Yao villages sell handcrafted items from stalls near the Hill Tribe Development Center which is located 16 kilometers southwest of Maesai. While a few items are indigenous to the Yao, such as embroidered hats and bags and opium scales, most of the items are imported from shops in Chiang Mai. Be sure to bargain with the Yao, expecting to receive 20 to 50% discounts on most items offered. We don't recommend wandering around too much in this area. We discovered a Rolls Royce and several other extremely expensive cars parked in out-of-the-way-places and speculated about their origins in the heart of opium country. As you may quickly discover in this part of the country, sometimes it is not good to know too much!

As for handling the touts, you may have to look angry and shout at them three or four times before they go away. They are very persistent and often refuse to take "no" for an answer. If you give in to a pesky tout, expect to pay 20-40% more for everything you buy in his company. You don't need such an expensive new friend here or elsewhere in Thailand!

THE GOLDEN TRIANGLE

The popular Golden Triangle area is located northeast of Chiang Rai town or directly east of Maesai. It takes about one hour to get there by car from Chiang Rai town. There's not much to see or shop for here. The ancient town of Chiangsaen is small a quaint town fronting on the Mekong River. It has a few temple ruins dating to the 13th century when Chiangsaen served as a kingdom in northern Thailand. In downtown Chiangsaen you will find one shop (90 Limton) that makes T-shirts, bags using Lao designs, and souvenirs to supply shops near the Golden Triangle Hotel.

The major shopping area is located nine kilometers west of Chiangsaen near the Delta Golden Triangle Resort (222 Golden Triangle) and the marker certifying this to be the "Golden Triangle" area. Here you will find numerous small shops, restaurants, and guest houses catering to the growing tourist trade. More than 30 small shops sell souvenirs, gift items, antiques, T-shirts, lacquerware, silver, pipes, masks, bags, clothes, puppets, gems, and costume jewelry. Two of the better shops in this area are **Phukham** (in front of the Phukham Guest House) and the **Golden Triangle Souvenir** (fronts on river). The huge new shopping center, **Golden Triangle Plaza**, with its impressive river front dock facilities and hovercraft ready to shoot up and down the river, looks out of place since there is little traffic frequenting this area. Indeed, this place was not well planned in reference to future tourist projects, although the local story mentions the important role of drugs (someone has a big bankroll), gambling (projected casino to be opened on the Myanmar side), and warlords (don't ask too many questions about those boats to nowhere, the future casino, and current shopping complex!) in developing this projected future tourist mecca. Nonetheless, you'll find a good antique shop and grocery store on the ground level of this shopping complex, if they are still operational by the time you get there!

Three kilometers further west is the **Wanglao Handicraft Center** where you can observe the traditional weaving process and purchase textiles, black pottery, and bags. Remember, these are tourist areas, so bargain hard for everything you purchase.

LAMPANG

Lampang is a surprise to many visitors. A town of approximately 60,000 people, it is located about 200 kilometers south of Chiang Rai and nearly 100 kilometers southeast of Chiang Mai. Once a sleepy provincial capital best noted for its horse-cart rides and intriguing Myanmar temple architecture, today Lampang is a bustling town which is beginning to offer visitors several shopping options. It boasts beautiful temples, a university (Yonok University), numerous factories for factory outlet shopping, and a very charming urban setting complete with horse-drawn carriages.

Since Lampang is not on the normal tourist itinerary, tourist facilities here are limited but more than adequate for an overnight stay. It has three first-class hotels—**Lampang Wiengtong Hotel** (138/109 Phaholyothin Road, Tel. 225-801), **Wienglakor Hotel** (138/38 Phaholyothin Road, Tel. 228-095), and **Tipchang Hotel** (54/22 Thakrao Noi Road, Lampang, Tel. 226-501)—which offer above average up-country accommodations. The **Lampang River Lodge** (330 Moo 11, Chomphu, Lampang, Tel. 226-922) offers attractive and reasonably priced accommodations in a lovely rural setting. Restaurants are numerous throughout the city.

You are well advised to approach Lampang by first stopping at the **Lampang Tourist Center** which is located adjacent to the Thammasart University Lampang (*Sala Klang Kao*) in the heart of town. There you can view a display of Lampang products, acquire maps and brochures, and ask questions of the personnel who staff the center. Also in this area you will find several vendors selling tourist knick knacks. The town's major market is located only a half block away. Like many other town markets in Thailand, this one is filled with the usual local consumer goods as well as fresh fruits, vegetables, and meats.

Lampang is noted for producing blue and white ceramics, woodcarvings, furniture, and home accessory items. Lampang's blue and white ceramics are found in numerous shops in Chiang Mai and Bangkok. Lampang also produces a distinctive cloisonne which compares favorably with Chinese cloisonne.

Over 50 **ceramic factories** are found in Lampang. You may want to visit a few of these factories. Three of the largest export factories—**Lampang Silpa Nakon, Kittirote,** and **Sang Arun** —are located near each other along the major highway that passes through the town, **Phaholyothin Road.** One of our favorite ceramic factories and shops is **Chour Lampang Earthenware** at 583 Paholyothin Road (Tel. 217-443). They produce a uniquely designed elephant planter with a green ceramic interior—one of the most unusual and interesting items we encountered in Lampang and one that could be exported abroad. You will also find some lovely Bencharong and celadon here as well as porcelain cups, bowls, plates, tea sets, and small ceramic animals. This shop is a little difficult to find since it does not have a sign in English. However, it is on the right-hand side of the road as you go along Phaholyothin Road on your way into the town of Lampang. You will see the ceramics on display in the front of this open shop. Another excellent ceramics factory is **Indra Ceramics** at 382 Lampang-Denchai Road, km. 1 (near Yonok University, Tel. 221-189). Along with the traditional blue and white ceramics they produce some lovely green and peach colored ceramics. They also produce a wider range of products than most factories—pots, plates, napkin rings, and animals.

Lampang also boasts a **cotton** factory—**Bann Fai** (206/2 Muu 2, Pichai, Lampang-Chiang Rai Road, Tel. 224-602). The factory shop offers a good selection of placemats, clothes, pillows, and drapes as well as ceramics and antique silver.

Lampang is especially famous for its **woodcarvings**. The villages of Mae Tha and Ban Luk are well noted for carving large animal figures—elephants, deer, bears, giraffes, lions, masks, horses, and humans—from monkey-pod wood. They also produce much smaller items. Many shops in Chiang Mai and Bangkok buy their carvings from these villages. Indeed, a visit to these villages will give you a fascinating introduction into both family and village woodcarving traditions in Lampang. Each village household is engaged in producing their own carved figures. You can purchase non-commissioned items here or have your own carvings commissioned. The villages are located approximately one hour driving distance southwest of the town of Lampang. Keep in mind that large pieces of wood may crack when taken to dryer climates.

Lampang is also home to one of Thailand's most important **wood factories—Siam Rich Wood Co.** The factory is located at 304 Super Highway (Tel: 218-448), approximately one kilometer north of Phaholyothin Road, adjacent to the first bridge you cross. The factory does good quality work using teak, pine, rubber, beech, and oak woods. Under contract to produce Scandinavian-type wood products for three companies in the United States—magazine racks, tables, chairs, wine racks, bread boxes, cutting boards, coasters, computer disk storage units, ice chests—Siam Rich Wood Co. also operates a small gift shop which is open to the public. The prices here are very good. You may want to stop here to purchase a few gift items. All of their products integrate nicely into contemporary Western homes.

LAMPHUN

The small provincial town of Lamphun is only 40 kilometers southeast of Chiang Mai. If you are returning to Chiang Mai via Chiang Rai and Lampang, you will most likely pass by this town on the Superhighway. Take a left off the main highway and go into this small provincial town. It offers some shopping opportunities as well as a small but interesting historical museum— **Hariphunchai Museum**—in downtown Lamphun.

Lamphun is noted for its cotton and silk weaving and basketry work. The town of Lamphun itself has a few shops selling these items. However, the major shopping area is a small town within Lamphun province called **Pa Sang**. Located half way between Lamphun and Chiang Mai—approximately 20 kilometers in each direction—Pa Sang has one main street with several shops selling cotton and silk garments, throw rugs, comforters, dolls, pillows, bags, hats, stuffed animals, woodcarvings, and baskets. Most of the items are produced in nearby villages. However, some of the woodcarvings are produced in the Lampang village of Ban Luk. Since we are not impressed with either the quality or styling of the products found in Pa Sang, we cannot recommend making a special trip here. If you are on your way to Chiang Mai from Lampang, or vice versa, you may want to stop here along the way. But don't expect to do quality shopping here. You are much better off shopping in Chiang Mai and Bangkok for your cottons, silks, woodcarvings, and handicrafts. Lamphun does have a few interesting temples worth visiting.

MAE HONG SON

Located 368 winding mountainous kilometers (10-12 hour drive) or a 40-minute flight northwest of Chiang Mai, Mae Hong Son is an interesting provincial town located near the Myanmar border and in the heart of hilltribe and opium country. It's best to take the flight from Chiang Mai which departs daily. If you are in a hurry, you can take the early morning flight and return to Chiang Mai late in the afternoon. Unless you are interested in trekking or exploring hilltribe villages (Shan, Karen, Lahu, Meo), there's not a great deal to do in Mae Hong Son. It has some beautiful Myanmar-style temples and a quaint remote small town atmosphere.

You can easily arrange for a car and driver to take you around town as well as visit a few hilltribe villages within 50 kilometers of town and still have time to shop in downtown Mae Hong Son. Once you arrive at the airport, ask one of the porters for information on a car and driver. They can refer you to a tour operator who is near the airport area. Unfortunately, the airport does not have well organized tourist information services. If you ask around, someone will soon assist you.

Shopping in Mae Hong Son is primarily confined to a few handicraft and souvenir shops. One shop, **Thai Folk Arts and Crafts Center**, located just outside town, has a small collection of locally produced hilltribe dolls, lacquerware, pots, wicker furniture, and hilltribe clothes. Within town you will find a few handicraft shops in a two block area selling the same types of products—lacquerware, gems, jewelry, clothes, and textiles. The attractive Myanmar lacquer boxes are especially good buys— five times cheaper than in Chiang Mai and ten times cheaper than in Bangkok!

If you plan to stay in Mae Hong Son, the two best places in town are the **Holiday Inn and Rooks Resort** (114 Khunlum-prapas Road, Fax 611-524) and **The Imperial Tara Mae Hong Son Hotel** (149 Moo 8, Pang Moo, Fax 611-252).

Again, Mae Hong Son and other northern towns outside Chiang Mai are not major shopping destinations. While they do produce some interesting local handcrafted items, they mainly offer interesting historical and cultural sites and friendly small town atmospheres not found in Thailand's larger cities. Plan to visit these places primarily for rest, relaxation, and curiosity rather than for doing quality shopping.

AYUTTHAYA

Ayutthaya, located 86 kilometers north of Bangkok, is the former capital of Thailand that was sacked by the Burmese in 1767. Today, it is a bustling provincial capital hosting thousands of tourists each year who come to visit the interesting ruins and tour the summer palace at Bang Pa-In. At the same time, Ayutthaya offers some unique shopping opportunities for those who have the flexibility to get around the city and surrounding area on their own.

Since most foreign tourists go to Ayutthaya with a tour group, they have little opportunity to do shopping outside the areas catering primarily to tour buses. Nonetheless, you can do some good shopping while on a tour, especially near one of the major tour bus stops—Wat Phra Si Sanphet. You may want to rent a car and drive yourself to Ayutthaya. However, be forewarned the traffic from Bangkok to Ayutthaya can be horrendous and frustrating. You may want to rent a car with driver instead. One of the best, and most picturesque, trips is the daily boat-bus combination tour from the Oriental Hotel (Tel. 236-0400, ext. 3133). You can either arrive or depart Ayutthaya via an air-conditioned luxury cruiser, complete with a buffet luncheon. Alternatively, you may want to stay overnight on the river by taking the charming Manohra Song cruise to or from Bangkok (see pages 219-221 for details). We prefer the Manohra Song approach to this city.

There are three major shopping areas worth visiting in Ayutthaya: Bansai, Wat Phra Si Sanphet, and Si Sanphet Road. **Bansai**, located a few kilometers outside the town of Ayutthaya, is home for the **Royal Folk Arts and Crafts Center**. Under the patronage of Her Majesty the Queen, the Centre trains students over a three to four month period to produce a wide range of handcrafted items. Organized similar to a college campus, each building specializes in the training and production of specific handcrafted items. You will find students producing wood and rattan furniture, baskets, leather goods, toys, display fruits, stuffed animals, and bamboo items. One area is devoted to glass blowing whereas another area is a center for producing traditional Thai paintings. You will also find a small row of thatched huts on a canal where you can purchase items produced at this training center. The prices are good, and many of the items are unique. You can also purchase similar items in the **Chitralada** shops in Chiang Mai, Bangkok, and Pattaya. These shops are also under the patronage of Her Majesty the Queen. If you are visiting Ayutthaya, this stop is worthwhile. You will be able to see the production of handcrafted items as well as do some interesting shopping.

The major tourist shopping area in the town of Ayutthaya is at **Wat Phra Si Sanphet**. Most tour buses stop here so visitors can see this beautiful temple. Adjacent to the temple is a large market area where more than 30 shops and stalls have been erected. Most of the shops and stalls sell the same items—baskets, hats, bells, instruments, fans, jewelry, woodcarvings, knives, dolls, windchimes, bronzeware, and placemats. Much of this area is filled with overpriced tourist kitsch and drinks. However, you will find a couple of antique shops that sell a large range of what appear to be authentic antiques, although we don't know if their claims are true: **Kornkaew Antiquarium** and **Raan Sajam**. We especially like the porcelain, Bencharong, and unique ceramic coasters which ostensibly come from the bottoms of old ceramic bowls. Be forewarned that these and other shops in this area have inflated prices for tourists. Other shops less frequented by tourists, for example, sell the same ceramic coasters for 75B whereas shops here sell them for 350B. Our advice: take a short walk to Ayutthaya's third shopping area.

The third shopping area is located within a five minute walk of Wat Phra Si Sanphet. Several shops along **Si Sanphet Road** sell a large range of antiques, ceramics, stone carvings, bronzeware, woodcarvings, and paintings. Few tourists visit this area because the tour buses only stop at Wat Phra Si Sanphet. This is unfortunate because the selections and prices are much better than at the other tourist shops. If you are with a tour group, the easiest way to find this shopping street is to directly face Wat Phra Si Sanphet, turn around 180 degrees, and walk straight ahead for 5 minutes toward King Uthong Monument. You will quickly come to this street (Si Sanphet) as it is adjacent to the monument. From the shops you can see Wat Phra Si Sanphet and the tour buses. The best shops here are concentrated at both ends of the row of shophouses. We especially like the large range of selections at **Arun-casem Antique** (79/3 Si Sanphet Road). This shop is crammed with stone sculptures, woodcarvings, ceramics, and Bencharong. One of the major specialties of this and a few other shops along this street are stone carvings. If you wish to have a figure commissioned, the shops will be more than happy to assist you with your request. The prices are good and the workmanship is excellent. While you would not want to air freight such heavy items home, they can easily be shipped by sea freight since sea freight charges are figured on the basis of volume. **Porntip Shop** at 79/3-5 Si Sanphet Road also has a nice selection of blue and white ceramics, jars, woodcarvings, and canvas paintings. This is where you can buy those 350B ceramic coasters for 75B!

Be sure to spend time in Ayutthaya visiting the major temples and ruins. This is a very charming town with many wonderful archeological sites. Four major temples and sites are well worth visiting:

- Wat Yai Chai Mongkhon
- Wat Panan Choeng
- Wat Chaiwatthanaram
- Wat Phra Si Sanphet

If you take the Manohra Song down river to Bangkok in the afternoon, you'll have a very pleasant trip. You'll see life along the river, with lots of rice barges, tug boats, fishermen, and children swimming in the busy and rapid flowing river. Best of all, you'll spend the evening dining and sleeping on the fascinating River of the Kings. In the morning, you'll make merit at a local Buddhist temple and then enjoy breakfast on deck as you finish your memorable cruise from Ayutthaya to Bangkok. While your shopping foray in Ayutthaya may not yield great treasures, that's okay. The pleasures of cruising the Chao Phraya River and getting a glimpse of river life in Thailand don't get much better than this!

PATTAYA

Pattaya, located within three hours driving distance southeast of Bangkok, is one of Thailand's popular resort destinations. It has all the amenities expected of seaside resorts—fine hotels, open-air restaurants, beach facilities, water sports, and numerous resort shops. Pattaya also has several bars and entertainment establishments geared toward all sexual persuasions, fantasies, and age groups. While Pattaya tries to appeal to families, it has a well deserved reputation for being Thailand's center for "beach, beer, and broads." It's party-time along the beach at night, and especially when U.S. Navy ships periodically unload hundreds of sailors who find more interesting things to do than go shopping in this beach resort. It is a combination of the French Riviera, Acapulco, Daytona Beach, and Patpong Road all rolled up into one. Pattaya offers good quality family resort amenities along with honky-tonk sex and sleaze. You may or may not like this place. It's very different from such resort areas as Hua Hin, Cha-am, Krabi, Samui, and Phuket.

The easiest and fastest way to get to Pattaya is by car, although buses regularly shuttle between Bangkok and Pattaya. With a car you can easily get around Pattaya and its outlying areas, especially Jomtien Beach which is 9 kilometers south of Pattaya.

Most shops are found along the main streets—Central Pattaya Road, South Pattaya Road, and Pattaya Beach Road. The largest concentration of hotels, restaurants, and shops are found along Pattaya Beach Road. Here you will find numerous small shops and vendors selling typical resort items—T-shirts, souvenirs, copy watches, postcards, sunglasses, purses, wallets, and inexpensive clothes similar to those found along Patpong and Silom roads in Bangkok as well as jewelry, silk, and Thai handicrafts. The prices here are relatively good compared to Bangkok, especially if you bargain hard. It's also fun shopping, similar to the night bazaar along Patpong Road in Bangkok, for copy watches, clothes, and leather goods.

Some of the best shops along Pattaya Beach Road include **Chitralada**. Located next to P.K. Villa Hotel, this small shop offers good selections of colorful and nicely designed handicrafts, bags, straw hats, and clothes. Many are made in Her Majesty the Queen's training project in Bansai, Ayutthaya. **Thaipan**, which is also found in Bangkok on Suriwongse Road, offers three floors of nice silk, cotton, bronze, and toy products. This is the largest of three branch shops in Pattaya. Be sure to visit the third floor which has dresses, stuffed toys, bronze, and brass items. Next door is **World Gems**, one of Pattaya's nicest, friendliest, and most entrepreneurial jewelry stores. They offer loose stones as well as nicely designed jewelry.

Pattaya also has its share of department stores and shopping plazas such as the Royal Garden Plaza, Central Shopping Center, and Mike Shopping Mall.

Other shopping areas worth visiting are centered in and around the resort hotels. The **Royal Cliff Beach Resort** has a shopping arcade with a few shops offering handicrafts, jewelry, and ready-made and tailor-made clothes.

Approximately nine kilometers south of Pattaya, along the rapidly developing Jomtien Beach, is the **Ambassador City Jomtien**. This is one of Asia's largest hotel and shopping complexes which has 3,650 rooms, a convention center seating 5,000 people, 80 shops, and 34 restaurants! Built by the same owner of Ambassador City in Bangkok, it's one of Thailand's most ambitious resort and convention projects. Some observers have doubts about its future success. It is likely to benefit from Thailand's nearby Eastern Seaboard area which continues to undergo development with new factories and port facilities making this Thailand's hottest economic development area. Numerous other shops and vendors are found along the adjacent Jomtien Beach area which has been virtually transformed over the past few years with new condominiums and hotels.

If you plan to stay overnight in Pattaya, some of the best hotels and resorts include the **Amari Orchid Resort** (Tel. 428-175), **Dusit Resort** (Tel. 425-611), **Grand Jomtien Palace Hotel** (Tel. 231-405), **The Montien Pattaya** (Tel. 428-155), **Royal Cliff Beach Resort** (Tel. 250-421), **Royal Garden Resort Pattaya** (Tel. 412-120).

PHUKET

Phuket is one of Thailand's most popular tourist destinations. Located some 900 kilometers south of Bangkok, Phuket is an island, town, and a province. Increasingly tourists are discovering the many pleasures of this west coast island with its generous offerings of sun, surf, sand, and seafood on the Andaman Sea. It's a world unto it's own.

ACCOMMODATIONS

Tourists primarily go to Phuket for the pleasures—the beaches, relaxation, and seafood. During the past twenty years, numerous tours, restaurants, and first-class and deluxe hotels have sprung up to give Phuket a first-class tourist infrastructure and a well deserved international resort reputation. You will find some wonderful hotels here, such as the **Amanpuri, Le Royal Meridien Phuket Yacht Club, Le Meridien Phuket, Banyan Tree Phuket, Dusit Laguna**, and the **Sheraton Grande Laguna Beach**. In fact, some people travel to Phuket just to stay at some of these fine hotels:

❑ **Amanpuri**: *Pansea Beach, Phuket 83000, Thailand, Tel. (6676) 324-333, Fax (6676) 324-100, or toll-free from U.S. 800-447-7462. Amanpuri* which means "place of peace" in Sanskrit, is built on a coastal hillside on Phuket island. From the moment you are picked up at the Phuket airport by one of the Amanpuri Resort's chauffeur driven cars until you are ushered to your pavilion or villa home, you know you are going to enjoy being "spoiled". The main pavilion with its high pitched, thatched roof, is completely open and overlooks a black lined pool surrounded by tall palms. The 40 pavilions are interspersed within a coconut plantation connected by elevated walkways in the midst of lush tropical foliage. The pavilions are elegantly decorated with simple Thai furnishings in traditional style. They feature an outdoor *sala*—a sundeck and dining terrace—separate bath and shower, an electronic safe, and a stereo CD cassette system. Pavilions feature either ocean or garden views. 24-hour room service is available. Adjoining the resort are 30 villa homes managed by Amanpuri and available for rental. Each villa consists of two to six Amanpuri-styled bedrooms, a private pool and living and dining Thai salas. A live-in maid, and a cook who prepares guests meals in their private kitchen, are both part of the package provided with the rental of one of Amanpuri's villas. The *Terrace* restaurant offers casual all day dining featuring both Thai and European specialties. The Tom Ka Kai, a Traditional Thai soup with a lemon and coconut base combined with chicken, is the best we have ever eaten—anywhere! The chef was kind enough to share his recipe with us and we make a pretty good duplication in our kitchen. The *Restaurant* serves Italian cuisine and there are frequent beach BBQ's from November to April. The *Bar* offers poolside drinks and snacks.

For the active guest there are scheduled or private charters to nearby islands on the resort's fleet of vessels which range from the *Aman I*, a 60 foot luxury Bluewater yacht available for half-day cruises to the *Maha Bhetra*, a 90 foot luxury cruiser available for day charters and overnight excursions. There are dive boats, jet boats and runabouts available. The Amanpuri's dive operation is a PADI facility and offers diver certification courses for beginners as well as more challenging dives for experienced divers. Also available to the guest are six floodlit tennis courts or an exercise room located on the beach complete with a three-station weight gym, treadmill, rowing machine, exercise bike and step machine. For those inclined toward a more relaxed pace, the swimming pool glimmers black above the Andaman Sea and beckons the guest. The pool area overlooks the white sand beach reached by a wide sweeping stone staircase. The *Library* offers a wide selection of books and CD's. The *Gallery* is a great small boutique offering jewelry and antiques procured from some of the best Bangkok dealers.

Amanpuri was the first of the Amman resorts to open and it set the standard for the those that have followed: luxury accommodations utilizing, as much as possible, natural materials and architectural forms indigenous to the area, while disturbing as little of nature's surrounding area as possible. Amanpuri is always at or near the top of the list of the reader polls conducted by the international travel magazines. If you like being pampered, enjoy the sea and sand, and appreciate the beauty of southern Thailand, you won't want to go home!

❑ **Le Royal Meridien Phuket Yacht Club**: *Nai Harn Beach, Phuket 83130, Thailand, Tel. (6676) 381-156, Fax (6676) 381-164. Website: www.phuket-yachtclub.com* A member of The Leading Hotels of the World and a frequent travel industry and readers' poll award winner, its 110 luxurious deluxe guestrooms and suites all have private patios, extra large individual sun decks and a stunning seaview. With a nautical decor befitting its name, yet exuding a traditional Thai atmosphere, all the spacious rooms blend natural materials complimented by traditional motifs. The Regatta offers a selection of Italian cuisines; The Quarterdeck offers Asian and International food; La Promenade serves a variety of Mediterranean food. Fitness Center; Conference Facilities.

❑ **Le Meridien Phuket**: *Karon Beach, Phuket 83000, Thailand, Tel. (6676) 340-480, Fax (6676) 340-479.* This second Meridien property in Phuket is situated on a U-shaped bay that promotes watersports. The guestrooms are furnished in rattan and teak and most have views of the sea. Most guests focus on the large swimming pools just outside their door. More family and tour group oriented than the Le Royal Meridien Phuket Yacht Club. This 448 room, 22 suite resort can keep you fully occupied so that you never leave the grounds. Full range of water sports, tennis, air-conditioned squash courts, golf, sauna and massage. Ten restaurants provide a choice of menus from Italian at Portofino to Japanese at Ariake, and of course Thai at Wang Warin. Fitness Center; Meeting Rooms.

❑ **Banyan Tree Phuket**: *33 Moo 4, Srisoonthorn Road, Cherngtalay, Amphur Talang, Phuket 83110, Thailand, Tel. (6676) 324-374, Fax (6676) 324-375.* Thailand's rich culture is reflected in the architecture and decor of the resort's 52 elegant Garden Villas—each with its own private garden, raised king-sized bed and sunken open-air bath. For the ultimate in luxury, there are 46 villas with their own private swimming pools and salas for al fresco villa dining. Four private Spa Pavilions set in tropical gardens offer a variety of therapeutic relaxation opportunities and massages. Savor meals in Saffron from a choice of Asia's best curries and Watercourt for Asian Seafood and Western fare. The Banyan Tree Gallery specializes in indigenous crafts and artifacts from the Asia-Pacific region. Fitness Pavilion; Golf; Watersports; Meeting Facilities.

❑ **Dusit Laguna Resort:** *390 Srisoontorn Road, Cherngtalay District, Amphur Talang, Phuket 83110, Thailand, Tel. (6676) 324-320, Fax (6676) 324-174.* Overlooking the Andaman Sea and flanked by two lagoons, Dusit Laguna offers 226 spacious deluxe rooms—each with its private balcony. Extra Large bathrooms provide full amenities. River Thai Restaurant's menu features selections from the four regions of Thailand; La Trattoria serves Italian dishes and seafood; Laguna Café features a fusion of Eastern and Western cuisines in air-conditioned comfort or outdoor dining. Fitness and Sport/Recreation Facilities; Convention Facilities.

❑ **Sheraton Grande Laguna Beach:** *Bang Tao Bay, Phuket 83110, Thailand, Tel. (6676) 324-101, Fax (6676) 234-369.* Splendid ocean vistas greet guests in the lobby. Boats transport guests to their rooms through a palm-fringed lagoon. Every room has a water view from a private veranda. The Sheraton Grande's 343 rooms, villas and suites all exude a distinctive Thai ambiance through decorations of indigenous art and handicrafts. Most rooms feature a giant sunken bathtub. A 323 meter pool winds through the resort. The guest has a choice of restaurants—one offering traditional southern Thai specialities, one specializing in Cantonese cuisine and a third featuring Italian food. A casual restaurant offers regional favorites and continental selections. Fitness Center; Watersports; Conference/Meeting Facilities.

But Phuket also offers shopping opportunities for visitors who do not plan to visit Chiang Mai or have limited time in Bangkok. Most of Phuket's shops and emporiums sell woodcarvings, handicrafts, silk, cotton, and antiques imported from Chiang Mai and Bangkok. Indeed, some enterprising entrepreneurs from Chiang Mai have opened handicraft emporiums— similar to the ones found along Chiang Mai-Sankamphaeng

Road in Chiang Mai—in and around the town of Phuket. Prices, of course, are higher in Phuket for the same items you will find in Chiang Mai and Bangkok. In addition, the cost of labor in Phuket is high compared to other areas in Thailand.

At the same time, shops in Phuket offer several unique locally produced items. The major products include pearls, beach wear, batik, and shell items. The pearls are especially attractive and can be good buys if you know what you are doing. The colorful Phuket batik is distinctive and attractive.

DOWNTOWN PHUKET

Shopping in Phuket is mainly found in the downtown area along Phang-nga, Rasda, and Phuket roads, at handicraft emporiums outside the town, and in a few resort hotels. Downtown Phuket should be one of your first stops on the island. Here you will find a very helpful **Tourism Authority of Thailand** office at 73-75 Phuket Road (Tel. 211-036). A good place to start shopping is at the corner of Yawaraj Road and Phang-nga Road. Both sides of this street have several shops offering antiques, souvenirs, *kalagas*, nielloware, bronze items, jewelry, woodcarvings, clothes, bronzeware, bedspreads, tablecloths, pewter, and napkin rings.

Rasda Road parallels Phang-nga Road. This street is lined with numerous souvenir, handicraft, silk, and jewelry shops. Check out **Silk Master** (1/3 Satool Road, Tel. 212-221; also at 29/4 Thepkrasattri Road, Kokaew, outside the downtown area) for arts, crafts, jewelry, sourvenirs, cotton, and silk. Look for several shops in the **Rasada Shopping Center** (check out **Creative** for fabrics at 64/9 Rasada Road, Tel. 215-958). Just off of Rasda Road is the **Phuket Shopping Center**. Here you will find a department store as well as several small boutiques and shops along the street. You also will find a few tour companies located in this area.

PEARLS AND JEWELRY

Phuket is famous for pearls which are produced locally in Phuket's pristine waters. Several jewelry shops on the island offer a wide range of jewelry. Some of the most popular places include:

❑ **Kriangsak Pearl Farm:** 83 Ranong Road, Soi Phutom, Tel. 211-707.

- **Multi-Gems International:** 154 Thepkasattri Road, Tel. 212-715.

- **Phuket Gems and Gift Center:** 74/15-20 Phun Phon Road, Tel. 214-946.

- **Phuket International Lapidary:** 22-24 Debuk Road.

- **Phuket South Sea Pearl Center:** 20/20 Maeluan Road, Tel. 235-137.

- **Thai Product Center:** 54/8-9 Montri Road, near Pearl Hotel, Tel. 214-849.

- **V.A. Jewelry Shop:** 98/1 Mu 3 Soi Bangla, Tambon Patong, A. Kathu, Tel. 344-444.

- **V.S.K. Gem:** 26-34 Chana Charoen Road, Tel. 256-193.

- **Wang Talang International Lapidary:** 13/1 Vichitsong-kram Road, Tambon Vichit, Tel. 217-175.

Keep in mind that most of these jewelry and pearl centers primarily cater to tourists. As such, be sure you know your pearls and jewelry before making any significant purchases. Phuket pearls, for example, can be of poor quality. They are not the same quality as the Australian, Japanese, and Tahitian pearls.

Many of the major resorts and hotels also have fine jewelry shops. For example, the **Amanpuri** has a fabulous shop which is stocked with the unique jewelry of **Lotus**, one of Thailand top jewelers.

HANDICRAFT EMPORIUMS AND CENTERS

Two of Phuket's best art, antique, and handicraft emporiums are located near each other along Thepkasattri Road. **Chan's Antique and Art Co.** (26/3 Thepkasattri Road, Khokaew, Tel. 215-229), for example, offers a combination of genuine antiques (on the left side of shop) and reproductions—furniture, Buddhas, ceiling panels, jars, ceramics, rain drums, screens, elephants, and bells. Nearby **Thai Style Antique and Decor** (25/7 Thepkasattri Road, Khokaew, Tel. 215-980) also offers a similar mix of arts, antiques, and handicrafts. The quality and selections here are a little better than at Chan's although they both are respectable competitors. We recommend visiting both shops before making any purchases. If you've been in Chiang Mai and visited the shops along Chiang Mai-Sankamphaeng Road, these two attractive shops will bring back memories of Chiang Mai's emporiums. Both emporiums are open from 8:30am to 6pm.

Other shops offering a good selection of arts, crafts, and souvenirs include: **Srirung Wood Carving** (168 M. 3 Thavee-wong Road, Patong, Kathu, Tel. 295-507; and 69 Prachanukroo Road, Patong, Kathu, Tel. 292-341); **Supremo Gift Shop** (37 Thavornwongwongse Road, Tel. 223-044); and **The Palace of Art** (79/5 Vichitsongkram Road, Tel. 215-670).

HOTEL SHOPS

A few of the major hotels in Phuket also have souvenir and gift shops. The most exquisite collection of jewelry, antiques, and decorative items is found at the **Amanpuri**, Phuket's classiest and most expensive resort. This resort has two hard-to-find shops. The sundry shop is located to the left of the pool while the shop with the most exclusive collection of jewelry and antiques—"The Gallery Shop"—is found under the bar. You may have to request that someone get a key to open this shop which seems to have irregular hours. However, it's worth the trouble. This shop carries a collection of jewelry and antiques from Bangkok's most exclusive shop: **Lotus**. The sundry shop also sells beachwear, jewelry, woodcarvings, and baskets. The jewelry, especially the silver earrings, are nicely designed and reasonably priced. The major problem of shopping here is the hotel security. You may or may not get into the hotel grounds if you are not a hotel guest. Our advice: dress like you belong here; maybe the guards won't ask you many questions! Better yet, make a reservation for lunch at either their Thai or Italian restaurant. The food and view are both outstanding.

Other hotels with a few good shops and small shopping arcades include the **Le Meridien Phuket** and the **Dusit Laguna**. We especially like the small jewelry and antique shop at the Le Meridien Phuket—**Finer Things**. One of the most pleasant shopping areas is found in the Laguna Phuket resort area—the relatively new (1995) **Canal Village Laguna Shopping Center**. Located on a lagoon, this pleasant outdoor shopping center with covered walkways includes a nice mix of handicraft, jewelry, silk, tailoring, and brand name clothing shops.

KO SAMUI

The small island of Samui (Ko Samui), located 560 kilometers south of Bangkok and 84 kilometers off the east coast of southern Thailand (province of Surat Thani) and boasting a local population of 35,000, is a delightful island paradise. It's Thailand third largest island of 247 square kilometers—21 kilometers wide and 25 kilometers in length. Until tourism recently arrived, the sleepy island was most noted for its coconut farming and fishing industry. It's still a major exporter of coconuts—reputed to be the best in the country—sending two million nuts a month to Bangkok. A long-time favorite of budget travelers, during the past seven years the island has been "discovered" by more upscale travelers as a pleasant alternative to the hustle and bustle of Pattaya and Phuket. New resorts have developed to capture the growing number of tourists who include Ko Samui on their visit to Thailand.

GETTING TO KNOW YOU

Getting around Ko Samui is relatively easy. As soon as you arrive at the small but friendly tropical airport, you'll find numerous tour and rental car services as well as lots of free tourist literature such as *Accommodation Samui*, *Samui Guide*, and *Samui Welcome*. In fact, Bangkok Airways begins this whole promotional process in the airport lounge in Bangkok as it passes out maps and brochures on Ko Samui.

Once you arrive in Ko Samui, it's most convenient to rent a car to get around the island, especially if you are staying outside the major beach areas. Most resorts provide round-trip airport to resort transportation. Hertz has an airport rental car desk which is only open when flights arrive.

The three major centers on the island are **Chaweng Beach** and **Lamai Beach** in the northeast and east and **Nathon** town on the west coast. All of these places are relatively small but Chaweng Beach tends to be the honky-tonk area with its noisy restaurants, bars, and discos. The island boasts 24 separate beaches on which numerous resorts, hotels, and bungalows have located. You can easily drive around the island in less than two hours.

Ko Samui is a relatively peaceful and quiet island that lacks the bars, nightclubs, and crowded streets and beaches of Pattaya and Phuket. The question is how long this will last as more and more people discover the pleasures of Samui. Signs of such development are evident in Ko Samui's second major town and most developed section of the island, **Chaweng Beach**. An ugly and noisy place dominated by young budget travelers, here you'll find numerous hotels, restaurants, bars, and discos that line the seven kilometer beach. While the rest of the island is relatively quiet, Chaweng Beach is the place to go if you want to shop, dine, and see what's going on in town. After spending a few hours here, you'll be glad you wisely chose to stay elsewhere on this beautiful island!

SHOPPING

What limited shopping that exists on Ko Samui is largely found in **Chaweng Beach** and in the district town of **Nathon**. The best shop in Chaweng Beach is probably the heavily advertised and promoted **Oriental Gallery and Restaurant** (39/1 Koo 3, Chaweng Beach Road, Tel. 422-200) which offers lots of pricey Myanmar lacquerware, handicrafts, silver jewelry, plantation chairs, and furniture. However, if you've shopped for similar items in Bangkok and Chiang Mai, this shop may underwhelm you. If you've not been to other places in Thailand, this is a good shop to make a few choice purchases. Expatriates Michael, Patsy, and Amanda are very informative and say they can ship overseas. Also, try the attractive Thai restaurant which is adjacent to the shop. Other shops nearby offer the usual arts, crafts, clothes, and souvenirs that primarily appeal to budget tourists. Nothing special here.

Nathon is the island's district center or capital city. A great place to see the traditional "gorlae" fishing boats, Nathon is located on the opposite side (west coast) of the island in relation to Chaweng Beach and Lamai Beach, the island's two major beach communities, Nathon is an especially bustling city at night, when tourists come back from a day at the beach or from sailing and scuba diving. Numerous souvenir shops and restaurants line the major streets of this small town. Look for the **Gems Palace** (main road, Tel. 420-290) and **Naga Pearl Shop** (Thong Krut, Tel. 423-272).

Some of the island's best shopping will be found at the major resorts, especially the **Santiburi Dusit Resort** at Maenam Beach. Here you'll find an attractive hotel shopping arcade with several shops offering beachwear, handicrafts, and silk. The resort includes a **Jim Thompson** silk shop with its signature clothes and accessories. The **Le Royal Meridien Baan Taling Ngam** resort also has a nice Jim Thompson silk shop.

ACCOMMODATIONS

Ko Samai has numerous resorts, hotels, and bungalows to accommodate most any travel budget. Most budget travelers head for the inexpensive accommodations available in Chaweng Beach and Lamai Beach, and the character of the restaurants and shops in these areas reflect the spending habits of such travelers.

If you want to treat yourself to the "best of the best" in accommodations, consider these two fine properties:

❑ **Le Royal Meridien Baan Taling Ngam:** *295 Moo 3, Taling Ngam, Koh Samui, Suratthani 84140, Tel. (6677) 423-019, Fax (6677) 423-220, Website: www.sawadee.com/ samui/meridien/* A member of The Leading Hotels of the World, Le Royal Meridien is located on Ko Samui's secluded and tranquil western coast. Nestled amidst a coconut plantation, the resort gently cascades down to the beach below. Aptly named, "Baan Taling Ngam" translates as, "your home on a beautiful cliff." Whether you choose to stay in one of 32 deluxe rooms, 6 deluxe sala rooms, 7 beach suites, 2 deluxe suites all with individual balconies, or one of the 20 luxurious villas with large private verandahs, you will be treated to a spectacular view of the sea and the islands of Ang Thong Marine National Park. The resort's rooms are decorated in traditional Thai style with warm wood finishes combined with modern amenities to provide a comfortable stay. Complimentary coffee/tea with a convenient pot for self-service enhance the facilities. Bathrooms have double sinks, separate shower and toilet enclosures and an oversized tile tub.

Seven outdoor swimming pools with jacuzzi, fitness room with equipment, sauna, and therapeutic massage rooms are available to pamper the guest. The Dive School is a licensed PADI resort facility and winner of the PADI "Excellence" award. The signature infinity pool may be where you want to spend your time if you are in the mood for a relaxing holiday. From the swimmer's vantage, the water appears to drop off the edge into the Gulf of Thailand, while at night you can dine in the Lom Talay overlooking the pool while a gentle breeze wafts the night air and sets in motion the lighted kratong floating in the pool below. No matter whether you choose one of the pools or the beach, a glass of ice water with lime is delivered within minutes of your arrival. Although most guests visit to enjoy the beauty and tranquility of the resort, there are plenty of activities available to keep guests busy if they choose. From the Thai cooking and carving school, elephant and jeep safaris, sunset cruise, an island kayak tour, or a snorkeling and diving trip, the guest can find plenty of interesting activities. With stunning views, a peaceful setting, and continual service with a smile, a visit to Ko Samui should include checking into Le Royal Meridien Baan Taling Ngam.

❑ **Santiburi Dusit Resort**: *12/12 Moo 1, Tambol Mae Nam, Amphur Koh Samui, Surat Thani 84330, Thailand, Tel. (6677) 425-031, Fax (6677) 425-040, Website: www.dusit. com.* A member of The Leading Hotels of the World, The Dusit Resort is located on a palm fringed white sand beach on the island's tranquil northern tip. Guest accommodations include 59 deluxe villas and 14 suites. The polished wood floors and contemporary Thai furnishings give a warm feel and the spaciousness is enhanced by a glass panel between the living room and the bedroom areas. The large bathrooms have two black vanity sinks, black bathtub and separate black tile shower enclosures. A choice of dining is provided by two restaurants: Sala Thai specializes in Thai cuisine, and Vimarnmek presents a menu of fusion East meets West cuisine. Fitness Center; Sports; Boardroom.

There's much more to Thailand than the places we've briefly described here. If this is your first visit to Thailand, you may want to spend most of your time in Bangkok and Chiang Mai and then spoil yourself at a fabulous beach resort in Phuket or Ko Samui. If you approach Thailand in this manner, you will experience the best of the best. You will acquire some quality treasures and experience pleasures you will remember for many years to come.

LAOS, CAMBODIA, AND VIETNAM

You may want to venture into neighboring Myanmar, Laos, Cambodia, and Vietnam. Indeed, we highly recommend side trips to these countries. Communist countries closed to tourists for more than a decade, Laos, Cambodia, and Vietnam are now open to adventuresome visitors. Myanmar also appeals to adventure travelers. We examine Myanmar in Chapter 14, especially the treasures of Yangon, Mandalay, and Bagan.

Laos, Cambodia, and Vietnam are still reconstructing themselves after more than three decades of war and economic collapse. **Laos** remains a very quiet and charming country which offers basic amenities to travelers. While the sprawling capital, Vientiane, is a relatively small, dusty, and uninteresting town, the charming former royal capital of Luang Prabang should be your major destination in Laos. It's reminiscent of a quaint, mildewed, and crumbling Chiang Mai of 30 years ago. Many visitors fall in love with Luang Prabang, one of Asia's best kept travel secrets. Direct flights connect Bangkok with Vientiane. You can also fly from Vientiane to Phnom Penh in Cambodia, but the plane makes a brief stop in Saigon, Vietnam. We feel comfortable flying Lao Aviation and Air Kampuchea, both of which use good equipment and pilots. However, we recommend visiting Laos with a tour company. They take the hassle out of arranging visas, hotels, and transportation.

Cambodia is both a tragedy and a triumph. Twenty-five years of incredible death and destruction seem strangely absent as you enter its new international air terminal, meet its friendly people, and proceed on to the bustling capital of Phnom Penh. Only 25 years earlier this city was literally emptied by the brutal and infamous Khmer Rouge who managed to exterminate nearly 3 million people in one of history's most genocidal episodes. You'll be reminded of the war when visiting Cambodia's holocaust museum and the Killing Fields, and when you see it's many handicapped beggars and young people.

But the real treasures and pleasures in Cambodia are the huge stone temple and palace complex of Angkor Wat and the National Museum and Royal Palace in Phnom Penh. One of the great wonders of the world, Angkor Wat is indeed impressive. You will stand in awe of the symbolic wonders representing one of Asia's most incredible kingdoms responsible for influencing much of mainland Southeast Asian art and culture. The area is now relatively safe to visit since the Khmer Rouge have all but ended their guerrilla warfare. The town of Siem Reap and the main temples at Angkor Wat are safe; but you should approach them with an experienced local guide and driver who will keep you on the straight and narrow path through Angkor Wat. Do not try to be adventuresome by wandering off on your own as some unexploded land mines may exist in "off the track" places.

Vietnam is relatively easy and inviting country to travel in these days. It's encouraging more and more tourism as part of its economic reconstruction program. In response to increased foreign investment and the movement toward a market economy, during the 1990s, the tourist infrastructure improved considerably as many new hotels, restaurants, shops, and entertainment establishments opened. Travelers could visit Vietnam through many different tour groups as well as travel on their own with relative ease.

This is a good time to visit Vietnam. Since the economic downtown in Southeast Asia, Vietnam has become a real bargain destination. As many expats left and the number of business visitors declined, Vietnam now has more than adequate facilities to handle the current number of tourists. Indeed, many hotels and tour operators are currently offering significant discounts. But this situation will not last long. We expect tourism will continue to increase in Vietnam as more and more people discover its many treasures and pleasures. Indeed, it could well become one of the hottest destinations in Southeast Asia in the coming decade.

A strikingly beautiful country of very friendly people, Vietnam is well worth visiting. While it is by no means a shopper's paradise, it does offer wonderful art, lacquerware, and handicrafts. Most quality shopping is found in **Hanoi** and **Ho Chi Minh City** (Saigon). The city of **Hoi An**, just south of Danang in the central region, offers a good selection of paintings produced by its famous local artist community.

The treasures of Laos, Cambodia, and Vietnam are found in visiting their many Buddhist temples and monuments. The pleasures are their delightful people and beautiful scenery and a few nice hotels. The great hotels and restaurants are in Thailand. After visiting Laos, Cambodia, and Vietnam, you will appreciate the treasures and pleasures of Thailand more than ever!

Some travelers avoid Laos, Cambodia, and Vietnam because of their political climates, the general lack of travel amenities, and the concern for personal safety. However, these countries offer some unforgettable travel experiences, and they are relatively safe to travel in, if approached properly. But don't expect the best of the best in travel and shopping in these countries. These are poor Third and Fourth World countries that are best approached as being on the frontier of adventure travel. They offer few shopping treasures, most of which have found their way into the many antique shops of Bangkok and Chiang Mai.

For detailed advice on shopping and traveling in Vietnam, please look for our forthcoming volume on *The Treasures and Pleasures of Vietnam: Best of the Best* which will be released in October 2001.

If you're interested in visiting these countries, one of the most experienced groups to work with is **Global Spectrum**. They are leading Southeast Asian travel specialists that regularly develop individualized and group tours to Vietnam, Cambodia, Laos, Thailand, and Myanmar. Through their extensive network of local tour guides, they can customize a fascinating shopping, cultural, historical, photographic, ecological, or whatever specialty tour you desire. For more information on their services, visit their Web site or contact them at:

Web site: *www.vietnamspecialists.com*

Mail: Global Spectrum
5683 Columbia Pike, #101
Falls Church, VA 22041
Tel. 1-800-419-4446

14

Myanmar
(Burma)

I F YOU WANT TO VISIT A VERY SPECIAL PLACE, BE
sure to include Myanmar (formerly Burma) in your travel
plans. Boycotted by many Westerners because of the current political situation—a military regime unresponsive to
opposition Western democratic forces—today's Myanmar is
struggling to build its tourist infrastructure as well as attract
more tourists to this extremely charming and friendly country.

POLITICALLY INCORRECT TRAVEL

Our "politically incorrect" advice: *Visit Myanmar as soon as possible before it changes too much!* Even if you dislike the current
military government, you'll probably do more to influence
change by visiting the country than by boycotting it. Indeed,
similar to the situation in Tibet, boycotting this place may
make you feel good, but it has little affect on the situation in
Myanmar. Instead, the more people who visit Myanmar, the
more likely change will take place for the better.

We believe boycotting travel to Myanmar for political
reasons is neither smart travel nor smart politics. Only you will
be worse off for having missed a truly unique and rewarding

travel adventure, unlike any other in the world. In fact, Myanmar may well become your favorite travel destination—even more seductive than Thailand!

THE TRAVEL CHALLENGE

Myanmar continues in a time warp—practicing its own form of socialism which has largely destroyed any semblance of a progressive post-World War II economy. It's a place where time stood still for nearly 50 years. But times are quickly changing as Myanmar attempts to catch up to Thailand and many other once robust Southeast Asian economies. During the past eight years, the government has played "catch up" by opening the country to more foreign exchange and investment in order to rebuild its decrepit economy. Numerous new hotels have recently been constructed in Yangon which has resulted in dramatically improving the quality of accommodations and service. Yangon's refurbished Strand Hotel, now an exclusive Amanresort, is one of Southeast Asia's finest hotels. In November 1995 the upscale Venice Simplon-Orient-Express group began conducting 3, 4, and 7-night luxury cruises along the Ayeyarwady (Irrawaddy) River, between Mandalay and Bagan (Pagan). However, the Myanmar economy continues to struggle due to cutbacks in foreign investment attendant with the overall slowdown in Asian economies—especially amongst its heaviest investors from Thailand, Singapore, and Japan. The result is an excess of excellent quality accommodations in Yangon. Indeed, you can stay at a four-star property for less than half of what it would cost for a comparable hotel in Bangkok.

Despite recent changes, Myanmar's tourist infrastructure remains rough with limited accommodations, transportation, and restaurants. Visas are now good for 28 days and must be secured prior to arriving in Myanmar, unless you are arriving and departing with a tour group that has secured a group visa in advance. Try to get a visa before leaving home, allowing at least two months to complete the process. While you can get a visa in Bangkok, the process is both time consuming and inconvenient; you will waste a great deal of time doing so and you still may not get a visa in time.

Given the sometimes difficult logistics of arranging your own hotels, transportation, and sightseeing in Myanmar, you may want to join a group tour or arrange an individualized tour through Myanmar Travel & Tours, the official government tour agency, or through Global Spectum (Tel. 1-800-419-4446, Web site: *www.vietnamspecialists.com*). Also, review the many ads that appear in *International Travel News*, a very useful monthly magazine geared toward travel to exotic and non-Western places (Call 1-800-486-4968 for a subscription or sample issue). Direct flights do fly round-trip Bangkok/Yangon, and we recommend taking the daily Burmese Airline or Thai Airways flight for this leg of the trip. We highly recommend visiting Yangon (formerly known as Rangoon), Mandalay, Bagan, Inle Lake, and Pegu. You may wish to rent a car with driver or take the train to see the countryside. Even an air-conditioned luxury bus now makes a 16-hour trip from Bagan to Mandalay.

You'll discover a Myanmar undergoing some major economic changes which should fundamentally transform the country within the next ten years. Once a well kept secret amongst budget travelers and backpackers, Myanmar should become a major new travel destination within the next decade. Go there soon before it becomes overrun by tourists. Don't expect to do a great deal of shopping in Myanmar since much of the "good stuff" has found its way to the shops of Bangkok and Chiang Mai. Nonetheless, you'll find some very interesting shops in Yangon, Mandalay, and Bagan. But plan to primarily go to Myanmar for the cultural experience.

SHOPPING MYANMAR AND YANGON

Yangon has a few very good shops and markets that are well worth visiting. If you rent a car and driver, you should be able to cover most of the places in one very long day but more realistically in two days. Here you'll find lots of shops and markets offering Myanmar antiques, art, crafts, furniture, textiles, and jewelry.

Shopping in Yangon, as well as most of Myanmar, follows similar rules as the ones identified for Thailand. However, there are a few very important "Myanmar rules" that can turn your search for treasures into a set of shopping problems and headaches should you fail to observe them. Given the fact that Myanmar has operated for so many years under a "Burmese way to socialism" economy, capitalism as you may know it takes on a different form in Myanmar. Above all, this is a fundamental "cash and carry" economy where the buyer should beware, or at least be aware of potential problems and shopping frustrations.

We've frequently encountered some irritating shopping problems that have led us to formulate five "special shopping rules" or warnings for Myanmar:

1. **Price uncertainty and reselling your stuff from under you:** Prices quoted do not necessarily reflect the true value of an item. Indeed, many merchants seem uncertain about what to ask for an item. They start out very high but may settle for a very low price—most likely whatever the market, or person, can or will bear! Don't assume you should automatically get a 20, 40, or 60 percent discount by bargaining the old-fashioned way (see Chapter 5). It could be more, or even less (places such as the Green Elephant House have fixed prices), depending on the merchant and his or her mood at the moment. But the real maddening aspect of bargaining is that a merchant may actually change the price *after* you have reached agreement—a definite ethical violation of bargaining principles in most countries. They often excuse themselves by saying *"Sorry, I made a mistake."* Alternatively, you may pay for an item and leave it in the shop to be picked up later. Instead of putting it to the side as being sold, it usually remains on display without a "Sold" sign attached. In the meantime, another customer comes in and agrees to pay more. When you return to pick up your item, you discover it has mysteriously disappeared and then you learn, to your dismay, that it was sold to someone else, and always at a higher price. The merchant may try to cover his or her tracks by again saying *"Sorry, I made a mistake."* Lesson: Whenever possible, take an item with you as soon as you pay for it. Leaving it behind invites an unbelievable story that usually end with the polite old *"Sorry, I made a mistake"* routine.

2. **Cash only:** Most shops only take cash. Credit cards and traveler's checks are seldom accepted, although a few shops accept them for jewelry purchases. Those that do accept credit cards usually tack on additional charges because they have to go through Bangkok to get approval. These additional charges can be very high—10-20% of the total bill. Ask before you get too emotionally invested in a lovely item. If you are not used to carrying a lot of cash, you'll find your shopping opportunities will be very limited in Myanmar. Our recommendation: Take lots of US$10, $20, $50, and $100 bills with you. The US dollar goes a long way in Myanmar.

3. **Packing and shipping surprises:** Most merchants are either unwilling or unable to pack or ship. If you insist, chances are you will be in trouble when your item arrives.

They generally lack expertise in this area. Packing usually involves disguising an item by covering it with a sheet of newspaper. Our best packing and shipping is through the Green Elephant House. Also check with your hotel for recommendations on shippers. Expect difficulties and don't be surprised if this whole process becomes expensive.

4. **Disappointing designs and quality:** It almost goes without saying, Myanmar is not a design center for jewelry, furniture, or clothes. Everything here has a decidedly Third World or old-fashioned look about it. While jewelry is ostensibly a good buy in Myanmar, the designs leave much to be desired. They are not stylish for most Westerners. You'll find much better quality and designs in Bangkok, Singapore, and Hong Kong. Be very careful about jewelry purchases. Know what you are buying and prices on comparable stones elsewhere. The same holds true for clothes and furniture.

5. **Shopping in residential areas:** Don't expect to do all of your shopping in one location, although the downtown area near the Traders Hotel and the Bogyoke Aung Sun (Scotts) Market is a good starting point. Quality shopping in Yangon is spread throughout the city, but especially in residential neighborhoods where merchants operate from their homes. This is especially true in the case of art and antique shops. Plan to have a car and driver on hand to take you to many of these out-of-the-way places.

Once you've resigned yourself to operating in a quick "cash and carry" economy, and you've brought lots of cash reserves with you, and probably an extra suitcase (if not, head for the local market to get extras), get ready to do some fun shopping. Here are our favorite picks for Yangon:

Antiques and Decorative Items

❑ **Green Elephant House:** *278, U Wi Sara Road, Kamayut Township, Tel. 526-685. Also has a shop at the Inya Lake Hotel, Sin Myanmar Elephant House (Tel. 552-858, ext. 1706). Open 9am-6pm.* If you visited the Elephant House in Bangkok (286/69-71 Soi Pattana, Suriwongse Road), you'll probably instantly recognize this place. It's owned and operated by the same Myanmar designer and entrepreneur, Cheri Aung-Kin, who also operates a large furniture factory on the outskirts of Yangon (Sun Myanmar Elephant House, Sein Kyaw Oil Compound, Sein Kyaw Road, Nwe Aye Quarter, Tawbon Township, Tel. 579-709, e-mail: *smyanmar@datserco.com.mm*). The Green Elephant House has the best collection of antiques and home decorative items in Myanmar. Tastefully designed lacquerware, furniture, and accessories fill this expansive showroom. Be sure to examine the uniquely designed wicker and lacquer furniture which the Green Elephant exports all over the world from its Yangon factory. They also carry some wonderful large glazed pots which are unique to Myanmar and which make wonderful indoor or outdoor decorative pieces. Unlike most other shops in Yangon, this one is well organized to handle shipping and it can take credit cards which must be processed through than Bangkok office (expect an additional fee for this special service). The adjacent Green Elephant Restaurant also is one of the best restaurants in Yangon for local cuisine. Top quality, very reliable, and expensive. Fixed prices but some things may be on sale with a 10-20 percent discount.

❑ **Augustens:** *Thiri Mingalar 2nd Street; 23, A. Attiya Road, Kamayut Township. Open Monday through Friday, 5-8pm and Saturday and Sunday, 1-8pm (may have new hours).* Take lots of cash with you since you are likely to buy several things here, and cash is the only way you can buy. A long-time favorite of embassy personnel who line up at his doors for the 5pm opening, Augusten is a fascinating and very personable character. He offers some excellent quality antiques at very reasonable prices. You'll find everything here, from old bronze rain drums and lacquerware to carved dragons, containers, and opium weights. Since you can easily do all your antique shopping in Myanmar at this shop, make sure it's one of your very first stops in Yangon. Augusten is especially famous for his sourcing capabilities—he seems to be able to always find excellent quality antiques, furniture, accessories, and silver. If he doesn't have something in stock (this is a very tiny and cramped shop), he'll probably find it for you. He's especially noted for his silver boxes and figures, a favorite purchase amongst embassy personnel. Very reliable but sometimes unpredictable. A small-time operator, Augusten is not set up to ship abroad. Take everything with you or see his friend, Sonny, at the Green Elephant House who knows how to both pack and ship. Don't expect to bargain much here since Augusten usually quotes a fair first price, although his pricing can be unpredictable; he's also known to "make mistakes" in pricing. Take things with you if you can.

❑ **Madame Thair Curios Gallery:** *649 Myakantha Street, 5 ½ Miles, Pyay Road, Tel. 526-140. Open daily 9am-6pm.* You have to see this to believe it, a real aberrant Yangon institution! It's good to have an orientation to this place before you arrive. Offers some very good quality antiques and textiles in a rustic bordello-style setting. But shopping here is as much a cultural experience as it is an exercise in shopping. Each room, including Madame Thair's bedroom, yields new and unique treasures. You're in for a real treat here, one which you may not be prepared for as you mistakenly conclude that you have indeed met a crazy lady. Madame Thair is well known for her eclectic tastes and eccentric behavior—she has the flair for the dramatic (she may decide to look at your palm and tell your fortune while you shop or change her clothes in your presence), but she is one very shrewd operator! As soon as you walk through the door of her combination shop and house, she'll size you up for the financial kill. She may distract you with her antics, but rest assured the asking price for any item reflects her assessment of your "ability to pay." She is known to raise the price of an item from US$200 to US$2000 just to make you think it's especially valuable and then dramatically reduce the price so you'll think you're getting a real bargain. At other times, she'll see you get interested in an item and then refuse to sell it to you until "pressured" to do so. Her cleaver pricing and selling strategies work in many cases. Many shoppers who are unfamiliar with Madane Thair find this to be one of the strangest shopping experiences of a lifetime; some are turned off and flee immediately! Never fear. Madame Thair is a great act (her rambling and chaotic shop is her stage), perhaps one of the best shows in town. It's a game here, so bargain hard for everything and be just as dramatic and crazy in your exchange. There's nothing crazy about this lady—just a very shrewd entrepreneur and character who does quite well with such bizarre behavior.

❑ **Creator Craft:** *39, Khattar (Short) Street, Sanchaung Township (Tel. 510-286). Open 9am-5pm.* Offers good quality lacquerware and woodcarvings.

ART

❑ **Orient Art Gallery:** *121(E), Thanlwin Road (Windermere Road), Kamayut Township (Tel. 530-821). Open 9am-6pm.* Operated by owner and artist Thant Zin, this gallery offers some very nice quality paintings at reasonable prices. Represents 30 to 35 artists. Look for some very attractive paintings depicting temple and village scenes.

❑ **New Treasure Art Gallery:** *84/A, Thanlwin Stret, Golden Hill Avenue, Golden Valley, Bahan Township (Tel. 526-776). Open 8am-8pm.* This large and well organized gallery includes lots of interesting watercolors and oils. Represents over 100 artists.

❑ **Zillion Art Gallery:** *10/2, Aung Min Gaung Road (Windermere), Kamayut Township (Tel. 533-935). Open 9am-5pm.* Includes numerous oil paintings with many Buddhist themes. Owned and operated by artist Thet Aung whose paintings are well represented here.

❑ **Golden Valley Art Centre:** *54D, Golden Valley (Tel. 533-830). Open 9am-7pm.* Housed in two building, this is a very nice gallery offering top quality paintings. Many depict Buddhist, floral, and country themes. Changes exhibits every three months. Represents 30 artists.

HANDICRAFTS AND TEXTILES

❑ **Bogyoke Aung San (Scotts) Market:** *In downtown Yangon, across the street from the Traders Hotel.* This is Yangon's main enclosed market for arts, crafts, textiles, jewelry, and household goods. It's a very clean and well organized market with hundreds of small stalls selling similar items. Bargain for everything here. After awhile, everything starts looking the same!

❑ **Shwedagon Pagoda Complex:** You'll find lots of small vendor stalls and shops both outside and along the long covered arcades that lead to the entry ways to this temple complex. Similar to an indoor shopping mall, the shops here sell puppets, lacquer, bronze items, make up, and religious paraphernalia. A very pleasant place to browse after taking in the fascinating sights and sounds of this temple.

❑ **Happy Hearty Souvenir Shop**: *33, Pyay Road, 6½ mile, Hlaing Township (Tel. 530-986). Open 9am-6pm.* Don't let the name of this shop turn you off. Offers a good collection of *kalaga* items, silver, puppets, Shan bags, tapestries, clothes, T-shirts, jewelry, baskets, textiles, silver, carvings, leather goods, lacquerware, books, maps, videos, and postcards. Includes two jewelry shops located at each end of the building. Accepts Visa, American Express, and JCB cards for jewelry purchases only.

❑ **Madame Thair Curios Gallery**: *649 Myakantha Street, 5 ½ Miles, Pyay Road, Tel. 526-140. Open daily 9am-6pm.* See above under "Antiques." Includes a large collection of textiles in her bedroom!

Gems, Jewelry, and Silver

❑ **Gems Emporium and Museum**: *66, Kaba Aye Pagoda Road (Tel. 656-169). Open Tuesday through Sunday, 1oam-5pm.* Here's the one-stop-shop for gems and jewelry! After visiting the top floor, which is a nice museum displaying gems, jewelry, and stones, be sure to browse through the first three floors of the building. Here you'll find the largest collection of jewelry and gem dealers (100+) in Myanmar displaying loose stones and jewelry from small shops. It's all here—diamonds, rubies, jade, silver, and pearls. You may want to focus on purchasing loose stones since the jewelry settings are not great. The best shops are found on the first level. Most shops will offer a 25-35% t discount but you can probably get a 40-50% discount if you bargain hard. Most shops accept major credit cards.

❑ **Golden Land Jewelry and Gems**: *Strand Hotel (Tel. 23333, ext. 1715) and Summit Park View Hotel, 350, Ahlone Road, Dagon Township (Tel. 279-666, ext. 172).* Offers a nice selection of gems and jewelry produced from their own mines and workshop.

❑ **May Bharami**: *Stand Hotel (92, Strand Road, Tel. 281-532) and New World Inya Lake Hotel (37, Kabaaye Pagoda Road, Tel. 662-866).* Small but good quality shop offering jewelry, silver, and lacquerware.

❑ **Bogyoke Aung San (Scotts) Market**: *In downtown Yangon, across the street from the Traders Hotel.* This popular market includes numerous gem and jewelry stalls inside the enclosed market as well as several air-conditioned shops, such as the **Jewels Palace** (Room 21, Front Row, Bogyoke Aung San Market), that face the main street. Lots of gold, rubies, and jade. Jewelry is not particularly stylish. Most shops appear relatively honest—will point out the difference between a real ruby versus a spinel.

❑ **Myanmar VES**: *66 Kaba Aye Pagoda Road (Tel. 661-902). Open Monday through Friday, 9:30am-4:30pm and Saturday, 9:30am-12noon.* A major exporter of jewelry to Europe and North America.

❑ **Myint Mo Oo**: *75 Bo Thu Ra Road (Tel. 530-852). Open 8am-5pm.* A good source for jade carvings.

❑ **Aung Kyaw Oo Silver Shop**: *450 Thein Byu Road (Tel. 243-230. Open Monday through Saturday, 9am-5pm.* Offers a good selection of quality silver.

ACCOMMODATIONS

You'll find lots of good accommodations in Yangon these days for all types of budgets. Two of the very best hotels, which are centrally located in relation to the city shops and main market, are the Strand and Traders:

❑ **The Strand Hotel**: *92 Strand Road, Yangon, Myanmar, Tel. (951) 243-377, Fax (951) 289-880, North America 1-800-447-7462.* The list of guests who have stayed at the Strand over the years would read like a "Who's Who". At its inception it was described as "the finest hostelry east of Suez". The legendary Strand underwent three years of extensive renovations and reopened in 1993 restored to its former pre-eminence as a classic hotel. There are only 32 rooms in the renovated property, plus the Strand Suite. Rooms are spacious with a separate alcove for the sitting area. Rooms feature high ceilings, polished wood floors and are decorated with local Burmese art and crafts. The large bathrooms feature double vanity sinks and a bathtub and separate shower enclosure. The formal Strand Grill is pleasant with its turn-of-the-century ambience while the Strand Café provides local Burmese cuisine and light Western selections in a relaxed atmosphere. There are two small shops with good quality local products within the hotel. Massage; Business Center.

❏ **Traders Hotel:** *223 Sule Pagoda Road, Yangon, Myanmar, Tel. (951) 242-828, Fax (951) 242-800.* Part of the Shangri-La Hotel Group, Traders Hotel is a brand name created to offer accommodation on a value-for-money basis but with the same high level of service as Shangri-La's luxury range of hotels. Our experience at Traders, Yangon is that they have succeeded! Before Traders opened in Yangon, trainees were sent to the Singapore Shangri-La for training and the training shows in the staffs' delivery of service to hotel guests. Walk into the lobby of the new 22-storey Traders Hotel and you immediately notice the cool marble and warm wood tones with traditional lanterns overhead. Guestrooms are generously proportioned, comfortably furnished and tastefully decorated. The bathrooms are spacious and the vanity surrounding the sinks are topped with marble. Amenities are complete with toothbrushes, toothpaste, and razors in addition to expected essentials such as shampoo, conditioner, and body lotion. There is a tea/coffee maker with a selection of beverages and a mini-bar refrigerator which guests may stock themselves at min-mart prices. Suites are very spacious and the Traders Club floors provide extra privileges including fresh fruit in guest rooms, complimentary breakfast, coffee and tea all day, and evening cocktails. Many rooms and suites have a view of the Shwedagon Pagoda which glows gold at night. Summer Palace offers Cantonese cuisine; Tategoto serves Japanese dishes; The Gallery offers Italian selections and seafood; and Traders Café offers Burmese and International menus. Shopping arcade on ground floor. Close to Sule Pagoda and shops. Fitness Center and Rooftop Pool; Business Center; Convention and Banquet Facilities.

ENJOYING YOUR STAY

There's lots to see but little to do in Yangon beyond a three-day stay. Be sure to visit the city's number one attraction both during the day and at night—**Shwedagon Pagoda**. This is one of the most fascinating Buddhist temple complexes in Asia. You can easily spend a couple of hours walking bare foot around the complex as well as shop in the many adjacent shops that line the four main entrances to the pagoda. You can learn a great deal about Buddhism and Myanmar culture by visiting this intriguing religious complex.

THE ROAD TO MANDALAY

One of the best ways to see Myanmar is to join Venice Simplon Orient Expresses' wonderful Road to Mandalay cruise and tour which takes you by a luxury river cruiser along the Ayeyarwady River for three, four, and seven-day visits to Mandalay, Bagan, and Mingon. It doesn't get any better than this for traveling through one of the most fascinating areas of Myanmar and Southeast Asia.

❑ *E&O Services Singapore, (65)227-2068 phone, (65)224-9265 fax; E&O Services UK (171)805-5100 or book through Abercrombie and Kent, 1520 Kensington Road, Oak Brook, IL 60521, Tel. 1-800-524-2420, Fax (630) 954-3324.* The ox-cart driver fills the last of the water jars, places it in the cart alongside two others, climbs up on the cart and standing between two water jars urges the two oxen back up the dirt road. You watch as the ox-cart disappears in a trail of dust. Then you glance across to the opposite side of the river where the white spires of pagodas rise in the distance. The tinkle of temple bells wafts across the placid water where fishermen are casting nets. It seems as if you are in a time warp and time has stood still. But you are lounging comfortably on a deck chair cruising through an exotic landscape little changed in the past century. Of all the lands of the fabled Orient, perhaps none has retained the charm of its past more than Myanmar, until recently known as Burma.

The Road to Mandalay has always been the river. Long before Rudyard Kipling popularized it in literature, the Ayayarwady River (formerly Irrawaddy) was the only way for people or trade goods to move from Yangon to Mandalay. So Road to Mandalay is an apt name for the luxury boat plying the river between Bagan (Pagan) and Mandalay. Approximately US$6 million was spent to refurbish a luxury Rhine riverboat and another million was spent to transport her from Hamburg to Myanmar.

The Road to Mandalay is a luxurious way to see the centuries old sights of Buddhist temples, villages and the people who live along the river. After a shore excursion, it is a welcome respite to come on board The Road to Mandalay and retire to the air conditioned comfort of your suite or cabin or head up to the observation deck for a plunge in the pool or a drink while you watch the sunset over the pagodas on the far bank of the Ayayarwady.

Each suite or cabin has an outside view, en-suite facilities, and are tastefully decorated. In the public areas, Burmese carved wood art, framed prints as well as a bronze rain drum reflect the traditions and handicrafts of Myanmar as well as the luxury which is synonymous with the Orient Express. Television broadcasts are available while the boat is in Mandalay and Bagan; two in-house movie channels are available otherwise. International calls via satellite to anywhere in the world are easily direct dialed. There is a small library on board, a small boutique, a medical doctor, even a complimentary mail service for airmail postcards.

Dinner is served in a comfortable dining room with one seating. Served by polite and efficient waiters, the food is quite good as could be expected from the tradition of the Orient-Express, and our dinner companions were interesting and cosmopolitan. Breakfast and lunch are served buffet style and selections at lunch often center around a theme from a nearby destination with Thai, Chinese or Indian entrees. To get the desired quality of meat and produce, most food items are flown in from Singapore.

Though there are choices of a 3, 4, and 7-night itinerary, essentially the Road to Mandalay program includes time in the capital, Yangon, either prior to or following the river cruise. Another option includes a six- day cruise only. The city tour of Yangon hits the highlights of the city including its centerpiece—the Shwedagon Pagoda. If you are enchanted by its magic, you may chose to return to the Shwedagon on your own for a second visit. After sunset, the Shwedagon platform takes on an ethereal presence.

The Road to Mandalay river cruise between Bagan, site of over 2000 pagodas, and Mandalay, with ruins of its royal palace and Mandalay Hill studded with pagodas, provides rare glimpses of picturesque riverside villages and lush countryside punctuated by ornate pagodas. Major sites visited in both Bagan and Mandalay are part of excursions from the boat. In Bagan we visited several pagodas, then climbed to the top of one to watch the sunset over the Bagan plain. The leisurely time spent traveling on the river is nicely balanced with sightseeing excursions. The staff is constantly providing amenities to make the journey comfortable and programs are conducted onboard to provide information to help passengers better understand the culture they are passing through. In each instance, after we had visited a temple and engaged in the obligatory "footwearing prohibited" as the signage at some temples indicated, (all visitors to temples in Myanmar must remove sock/stockings as well as shoes—only bare feet are clean enough to walk upon the temple floors) a crew member would hand out cooled, moistened towelettes so we could clean our feet before putting on our shoes.

All shore excursions are included in the price of the trip as are all meals and entertainment onboard the boat. In Yangon the hotel, breakfast, and city tour are part of the tour price giving participants freedom to try their choice of restaurants in the capital for lunch and dinner.

The Road to Mandalay operates between September and May. November thru February tend to be the cooler months, though Myanmar is definitely tropical and hence "cool" is a relative term. Book directly with Abercrombie and Kent in the U.S. or call or fax the Orient-Express office in Singapore or the U.K.

SHOPPING MANDALAY AND BAGAN

Both Mandalay and Bagan are well worth visiting on any trip to Myanmar. Mandalay, the last capital before the British colonized Myanmar in the 19th century, is especially well known for its fort, hills, temples, arts, and crafts. You'll find many shops and vendor stalls selling handicrafts and textiles in the **Central (Zeigyo) Market** (two large buildings along 84th Street, between 27th and 28th streets).

Mandalay also is noted for its many art galleries and tapestry shops. One of Myanmar's leading artists and stellar craftsmen, U Sein Myint, who regularly exhibits his works abroad, maintains two galleries that are well worth visiting. **Sein Myint** at 42 Sanga University Road, Nanshei Ywatha Quarter (Tel. 26553) displays his wonderful watercolors which depict traditional Myanmar scenes. Also famous for his work with traditional tapestries, the *kalagas*, this gallery displays his tapestry art. Be sure to visit his other gallery that is primarily devoted to his intricate tapestries: **Sequins House**, 42, 62nd Street (between 16th and 17th streets), Nan Shei (Tel. 26553). Another interesting shop worth visiting for tapestries and other handicrafts is **Mann Swe Gon Handicrafts** (27th Street, between 72nd and 73rd streets).

Bagan is one of the most fascinating destinations in all of Asia—Myanmar's equivalent to Cambodia's Angkor Wat.

Whatever you do, don't miss Bagan. The town is now divided into two sections—Old Bagan with its extensive temple ruins and archeological work and New Bagan with its residential and commercial settlements. Thousands of temple ruins dot the eerie landscape of Old Bagan. You can easily spend several days here touring the temples and enjoying this very quiet, laid back community along the banks of the Ayeyarwady River. Constantly under restoration, some of the temples are off limits to visitors.

While there is not much to do in Bagan other than tour the temple ruins (go by horsecart) and see a puppet show, Bagan does have a few shops worth visiting. They primarily sell lacquerware and puppets which are Bagan's two major products. The best shop in town is **U Ba Nyein and Son Lacquerware Shop** in New Bagan (Tel. 70050). This large factory/shop includes a lacquer demonstration area, where you can see the traditional red lacquerware being made from bamboo or horse hairs, as well as a shop area that offers a wide selection of traditional lacquer bowls, plates, cups, and trays. This shop also supplies several shops in Yangon with lacquerware, but prices there are nearly five times what they are at this factory source. You'll also find several other smaller lacquer factories and shops in Bagan. Also look for an interesting old glass factory, **Na-Gar Glass Factory**, on the outskirts of town. Operating for nearly 50 years, this factory produces attractive colored glass items, from glass elephants and nativity scenes to drinking glasses. You're bound to find something here that would make a great, and inexpensive, gift for family or friends.

One of the great highlights of visiting Bagan is to catch the gorgeous sunsets, which are unlike any we have seen elsewhere in the world. Load up on film and head for the beautiful Ananda Temple in Old Bagan. You won't be disappointed. This place, along with much of Myanmar, seems so unreal. It is indeed a very special place that you will remember for a lifetime. If you are like many others who have ventured here, you'll be glad you decided to be politically incorrect by going to Myanmar to discover its many delightful treasures and pleasures. Myanmar, along with Thailand, may become your favorite travel destination. We're certain you'll really enjoy this very special place with its bountiful treasures and pleasures!

Index

The Authors

WINSTON CHURCHILL PUT IT BEST—*"My needs are very simple—I simply want the best of everything."* Indeed, his attitude on life is well and alive amongst many of today's travelers. With limited time, careful budgeting, and a sense of adventure, many people seek both quality and value as they search for the best of the best.

Ron and Caryl Krannich, Ph.Ds, discovered this fact of travel life 17 years ago when they were living and working in Thailand as consultants with the Office of the Prime Minister. Former university professors and specialists on Southeast Asia, they discovered what they really loved to do—shop for quality arts, antiques, and home decorative items—was not well represented in most travel guides that primarily focused on sightseeing, hotels, and restaurants. While some guidebooks included a small section on shopping, they only listed types of products and names and addresses of shops, many of which were of questionable quality. And budget guides simply avoided quality shopping altogether, as if shopping was a travel sin!

The Krannichs knew there was much more to travel than what was represented in most travel guides. Avid collectors of Thai, Myanmar, Indonesian, and South Pacific arts, antiques, and home decorative items, they learned long ago that one of the best ways to experience another culture and meet its talented artists and craftspeople was by shopping for local products. Not only would they learn a great deal about the culture and society, they also acquired some wonderful products, met many interesting and talented individuals, and helped support the continuing development of local arts and crafts.

But they quickly learned shopping in Asia was very different from shopping in North America and Europe. In the West, merchants nicely display items, identify prices, and periodically run sales. At the same time, shoppers in the West can easily do comparative shopping, watch for sales, and trust quality and delivery; they even have consumer protection! Americans and Europeans in Asia face a shopping culture based on different principles. Like a fish out of water, they make many mistakes: don't know how to bargain, fail to communicate effectively with tailors, avoid purchasing large items because they don't understand shipping, and are frequent victims of scams and rip-offs, especially in the case of gems and jewelry. To shop a country right, travelers need to know how to find quality products, bargain for the best prices, avoid scams, and ship their purchases with ease. What they most need is a combination travel and how-to book that focuses on the best of the best.

In 1987 the Krannichs inaugurated their first shopping guide to Asia—*Shopping in Exotic Places*—a guide to quality shopping in Hong Kong, South Korea, Thailand, Indonesia, and Singapore. Receiving rave reviews from leading travel publications and professionals, the book quickly found an enthusiastic audience amongst other avid travelers and shoppers. It broke new ground as a combination travel and how-to book. No longer would shopping be confined to just naming products and identifying names and addresses of shops. It also included advice on how to pack for a shopping trip (take two suitcases, one filled with bubble-wrap), comparative shopping, bargaining skills, and communicating with tailors. Shopping was serious stuff requiring serious treatment of the subject by individuals who understood what they were doing. The Krannichs subsequently expanded the series to include separate volumes on Hong Kong, Thailand, Indonesia, Singapore and Malaysia, Australia and Papua New Guinea, the South Pacific, and the Caribbean.

Beginning in 1996, the series took on a new look as well as an expanded focus. Known as the Impact Guides and appropriately titled *The Treasures and Pleasures . . . Best of the Best*, new editions covered Hong Kong, Thailand, Indonesia, Singapore, Malaysia, Paris and the French Riviera, and the Caribbean. In 1997 and 1999 new volumes appeared on Italy, Hong

Kong, and China. New volumes for 2000 cover India, Australia, Thailand, Hong Kong, Egypt, Singapore and Bali, Israel and Jordan, and Rio and São Paulo.

Beginning in May 2000, the Impact Guides became the major content for launching the new *i*ShopAroundTheWorld Web site:

www.ishoparoundtheworld.com

While the primary focus remains shopping for quality products, the books and Web site also include useful information on the best hotels, restaurants, and sightseeing. As the authors note, *"Our users are discerning travelers who seek the best of the best. They are looking for a very special travel experience which is not well represented in other travel guides."*

The Krannichs passion for traveling and shopping is well represented in their home which is uniquely designed around their Asian, South Pacific, Middle East, North African, and Latin American art collections. *"We're fortunate in being able to create a living environment which pulls together so many wonderful travel memories and quality products,"* say the Krannichs. *"We learned long ago to seek out quality products and buy the best we could afford at the time. Quality lasts and is appreciated for years to come. Many of our readers share our passion for quality shopping abroad."* Their books also are popular with designers, antique dealers, and importers who use them for sourcing products and suppliers.

While the Impact Guides keep the Krannichs busy traveling to exotic places, their travel series is an avocation rather than a vocation. The Krannichs also are noted authors of more than 30 career books, some of which deal with how to find international and travel jobs. The Krannichs also operate one of the world's largest career resource centers. Their works are available in most bookstores or through the publisher's online bookstore: *www.impactpublications.com*

If you have any questions or comments for the authors, please direct them to the publisher:

Drs. Ron and Caryl Krannich
IMPACT PUBLICATIONS
9104 Manassas Drive, Suite N
Manassas Park, VA 20111-5211
Fax 703-335-9486
E-mail: *krannich@impactpublications.com*

More Treasures
and Pleasures

THE FOLLOWING TRAVEL GUIDES CAN BE ORdered directly from the publisher. Complete the following form (or list the titles), include your name and address, enclose payment, and send your order to:

IMPACT PUBLICATIONS
9104 Manassas Drive, Suite N
Manassas Park, VA 20111-5211 (USA)
Tel. 1-800-361-1055 (orders only)
703/361-7300 (information) Fax 703/335-9486
E-mail: *singapore@impactpublications.com*
Online bookstores: ***www.impactpublications.com*** or
www.ishoparoundtheworld.com

All prices are in U.S. dollars. Orders from individuals should be prepaid by check, moneyorder, or credit card (we accept Visa, MasterCard, American Express, and Discover). We accept credit card orders by telephone, fax, e-mail, and online (visit Impact's two online travel bookstores). If your order must be shipped outside the U.S., please include an additional US$1.50 per title for surface mail or the appropriate air mail rate for books weighting 24 ounces each. Orders usually ship within 48 hours. For more information on the authors, travel resources, and international shopping, visit ***www.impactpublications.com*** and ***www.ishoparoundtheworld.com*** on the World Wide Web.

Qty.	TITLES	Price	TOTAL
___	Travel Planning on the Internet	$19.95	_____
___	Treasures and Pleasures of Australia	$16.95	_____
___	Treasures and Pleasures of the Caribbean	$16.95	_____
___	Treasures and Pleasures of China	$14.95	_____
___	Treasures and Pleasures of Egypt	$16.95	_____
___	Treasures and Pleasures of Hong Kong	$16.95	_____

__ Treasures and Pleasures of India	$16.95	_____
__ Treasures and Pleasures of Indonesia	$14.95	_____
__ Treasures and Pleasures of Israel & Jordan	$16.95	_____
__ Treasures and Pleasures of Italy	$14.95	_____
__ Treasures and Pleasures of Paris and the French Riviera	$14.95	_____
__ Treasures and Pleasures of Rio and São Paulo (Brazil)	$13.95	_____
__ Treasures and Pleasures of Singapore and Bali	$16.95	_____
__ Treasures and Pleasures of Thailand	$16.95	_____

SUBTOTAL ------------- $ _____

■ Virginia residents add 4.5% sales tax $ _____

■ Shipping/handling ($5.00 for the first title and $1.50 for each additional book) $ _____

■ Additional amount if shipping outside U.S. $ _____

TOTAL ENCLOSED ---------- $ _____

SHIP TO:

Name _____

Address _____

_____

_____

Phone Number: _____

PAYMENT METHOD:

❑ I enclose check/moneyorder for $ _____ made payable to IMPACT PUBLICATIONS.

❑ Please charge $ _____ to my credit card:

❑ Visa ❑ MasterCard ❑ American Express ❑ Discover

Card # _____

Expiration date: _____/_____

Signature _____

Experience the "best of the best" in travel Treasures and Pleasures!

Emphasizing the "best of the best" in travel and shopping, the unique Impact Guides take today's discerning travelers into the fascinating worlds of artists, craftspeople, and shopkeepers where they can have a wonderful time discovering quality products and meeting talented, interesting, and friendly people. Each guide is jam-packed with practical travel tips, bargaining strategies, key shopping rules, and recommended shops, hotels, restaurants, and sightseeing. The only guides that show how to have a five-star travel and shopping adventure on a less than stellar budget!

New for 2000!

▶ *The Treasures and Pleasures of Australia: Best of the Best.* April 2000. ISBN 1-57023-060-9

▶ *The Treasures and Pleasures of Hong Kong: Best of the Best.* April 2000. ISBN 1-57023-115-X

▶ *The Treasures and Pleasures of Singapore and Bali: Best of the Best.* April 2000. ISBN 1-57023-133-8

▶ *The Treasures and Pleasures of Thailand: Best of the Best.* April 2000. ISBN 1-57023-076-5

▶ *The Treasures and Pleasures of India: Best of the Best.* January 2000. ISBN 1-57023-056-0

Order Online! www.impactpublications.com

Rave Reviews About The Impact Guides:

Travel and Leisure: *"An excellent, exhaustive and fascinating look at shopping."*

Travel-Holiday: *"Books in the series help travelers recognize quality and gain insight to local customs."*

Washington Post: *"You learn more about a place you are visiting when Impact is pointing the way. The Impact Guides are particularly good in evaluating local arts and handicrafts while providing a historical or cultural context."*

- ▶ *The Treasures and Pleasures of China: Best of the Best.* 1999. 317 pages. ISBN 1-57023-077-3

- ▶ *The Treasures and Pleasures of the Caribbean.* 1996. 371 pages. ISBN 1-57023-046-3

- ▶ *The Treasures and Pleasures of Indonesia.* 1996. 243 pages. ISBN 1-57023-045-5

- ▶ *The Treasures and Pleasures of Italy.* 1997. 271 pages. ISBN 1-57023-058-7

- ▶ *The Treasures and Pleasures of Paris and the French Riviera.* 1996. 263 pages. ISBN 1-57023-057-9

- ▶ *The Treasures and Pleasures of Singapore and Malaysia.* 1996. 282 pages. ISBN 1-57023-044-7

Authors: Drs. Ron and Caryl Krannich are two of America's leading travel and career writers with more than 40 books to their credit. They have authored 10 books in the Impact Guides series, including volumes on Hong Kong, Singapore, Malaysia, Indonesia, Italy, and France.

Order Toll-free! 1-800/361-1055

The Nancy Chandler Shopping Maps!

Be sure you're armed with the latest authoritative and fun maps for discovering the treasures and pleasures of Bangkok and Chiang Mai. For nearly two decades, these annually revised maps have provided invaluable guidance to Thailand's best shops, restaurants, hotels, and sightseeing. Jam-packed with lots of practical information. Don't venture into the streets of Bangkok and Chiang Mai without these fabulous resources to complement your *Treasures and Pleasures of Thailand: Best of the Best*. Prices include First Class shipping within the U.S. and Canada. International orders should add US$3.00 to total.

Qty.	TITLES	Price	TOTAL
__	Map of Bangkok	$9.95	_____
__	Map of Chiang Mai	$9.95	_____
__	Both Maps (Bangkok & Chiang Mai)	$18.95	_____

TOTAL ENCLOSED -------------- $ _____

SEND TO: Impact Publications, 9104 Manassas Drive, Suite N, Manassas Park, VA 20111 U.S.A. Order toll-free with credit cards: 1-800-361-1055. Order online: *www.impactpublications. com* or *www.ishoparoundtheworld.com*. In Thailand, these maps are available in major bookstores and hotel shops or they can be ordered directly from the publisher: Nancy Chandler Graphics (see page 33 for order/contact information).

Plan Your Next Trip On the Internet!

Travel Planning On the Internet: The Click and Easy™ Guide
Ron and Caryl Krannich, Ph.D.s

The Internet has fast become an invaluable resource for savvy travelers. You can now quickly go online for airline tickets, hotel and cruise reservations, restaurants, shopping, visa applications, tours, newspapers, translations, travel gear, tips, and information on your favorite destinations—nearly everything you need to know or want about travel. Here's the book that pulls it all together. Identifying over 1,000 key Web sites dealing with all aspects of travel, the new Click and Easy™ *Travel Planning on the Internet* is your passport to a whole new world of travel planning in cyberspace. Use this invaluable guide to quickly plan your next great trip or explore new travel options. Even use it while traveling to find great restaurants or shops! $19.95 plus $5.00 shipping.

TO ORDER: Use the form on pages 358-359 or order online: *www.impactpublications.com* or *www.ishoparoundtheworld.com*

Travel the World for Treasures!

Welcome to *i*ShopAroundTheWorld, an Internet site that brings together the best of the best in shopping and traveling around the world. If you enjoy shopping, be sure to visit our one-stop-shop for great advice, resources, discussion, and linkages to make your next trip a very special adventure. Discover how to:

- Prepare for a shopping adventure
- Find quality shops and products
- Bargain for the best prices
- Identify local shopping rules
- Order custom-made goods
- Handle touts and tour guides
- Avoid shopping and travel scams
- Pack and ship goods with ease
- Select the best hotels and restaurants
- Use the Internet to travel and shop
- Find inexpensive airfares and cruises
- Travel independently or with tours
- Hire cars, drivers, and guides
- Schedule times and places
- Choose the best sightseeing
- Enjoy terrific entertainment

…and meet talented, interesting, and friendly people in some of the world's most fascinating destinations. Join our community as we travel to the intriguing worlds of artisans, craftspeople, and shopkeepers in search of fine jewelry, clothing, antiques, furniture, arts, handicrafts, textiles, and numerous other treasures to grace your home and enhance your wardrobe. Best of all, shop and travel online before and after your next trip!

www.ishoparoundtheworld.com